VIEW FROM THE RIGHT

VOLUME III: CONTROVERSIES AND VIEWPOINTS

ALAIN DE BENOIST

VIEW *from* THE RIGHT

A Critical Anthology of Contemporary Ideas

VOLUME III

Controversies and Viewpoints

Translated by Roger Adwan

ARKTOS
LONDON 2019

ORIGINAL TITLE	*Vu de droite: Anthologie critique des idées contemporaines* (Paris: Copernic, 1977)
ISBN	978-1-912975-21-1 (Paperback) 978-1-912975-22-8 (Hardback) 978-1-912975-23-5 (Ebook)
TRANSLATOR	Roger Adwan
EDITOR	Roger Adwan and Martin Locker
COVER AND LAYOUT	Tor Westman

Arktos.com fb.com/Arktos @arktosmedia arktosmedia

CONTENTS

CONTROVERSIES

VIEWPOINTS

CONTROVERSIES

OVERTURES

THE ROOTS OF COINCIDENCE

'I DO NOT THINK THAT the universe is a charitable organisation', Arthur Koestler[1] writes.

> Whatever the case, we are still part of it, and we must strive to make the most of things. Although the very limits of our biological equipment may well condemn us to beholding eternity through the keyhole, let us at least attempt to free the latter so as to make use of our eyes, no matter how weak our eyesight may be.

In *The Roots of Coincidence*, seventy-two-year-old Arthur Koestler proceeds to cautiously examine the delicate issue of parapsychology, including extrasensory perception[2] and thought transmission.[3]

In 1932, the first parapsychological experimental laboratory was established at Duke University in North Carolina, USA. Its example was quickly echoed elsewhere and today, the number of university parapsychological departments is already beyond count.

Then, in 1969, the American Parapsychological Association was granted membership in the famous AAAS (American Association for the Advancement of Science), an event that acted as a consecration.

Koestler remarks:

---

1 TN: Arthur Koestler (5th September, 1905–1st March, 1983) was a Hungarian-British author and journalist.

2 TN: Generally shortened to ESP.

3 TN: Otherwise known as telepathy.

> It is an undeniable fact that, during the past ten to twenty years, parapsychological research has been made more rigorous, statistical and computer-based [...]. The study of extrasensory perception has become an empirical sort of science, as austere (and all too often as dull) as the training of lab rats or the patient cutting of planaria.[4]

In the US, it is NASA that has taken matters into its own hands, so much so that 'the public was quite surprised to find out, several months after the Apollo 14 mission of February 1971, that astronaut Mitchell had, while in full flight, attempted to establish telepathic contact with four pre-selected subjects'. Other experiments had previously been conducted on board the Nautilus submarine.

In the USSR, Professor Leonid Vasiliev[5] began publishing the results of his own work on 'tele-hypnosis' in 1960. 'According to his reports, hypnotised subjects had successfully been awoken through a remote transmission of telepathic orders. Using the very same means, one had managed to trigger the fall of subjects that had been hypnotised while standing. Further experiments with a focus on interurban telepathic communication ensued, including some between Leningrad and Moscow, for instance'.

Indeed, we have all, at one time or another, been under the impression that despite having our backs turned, we somehow 'sensed' the presence of a person that we could neither have seen nor heard coming. We have also perhaps experienced situations where we suddenly thought of and expressed the same idea as the one that our own interlocutor was about to share. But how are we to ascertain that what we are dealing with is anything more than mere coincidence?

THE ADVANCEMENT AND SURPRISING DEVELOPMENTS OF MICROPHYSICS

Koestler responds to this objection by introducing the 'roots of coincidence' notion, meaning that of *probability calculation*. He writes:

---

4 TN: A planarian is a kind of flatworm of the Turbellaria class. Planaria can, in fact, be cut into pieces, with each piece retaining the ability to regenerate into a complete organism.

5 TN: Leonid Leonidovich Vasiliev (1891–1966) was a Russian Soviet parapsychologist and physiologist who played a decisive role in establishing the first parapsychological laboratory in Leningrad.

> The cornerstone of both probability theory and modern physics by and large is embodied by the "law of large numbers", which, to put things simply, states that the more trials are carried out, the closer the actual ratios of correct and incorrect answers will converge on the probability of coincidence.

When playing a 'heads or tails' game, for instance, there will always be one chance out of two for the coin to fall on the side that one has bet on. And since this ratio is a constant one, the coin is bound to fall 5000 times on the 'heads' side and 5000 on the 'tails' side whenever one conducts 10,000 trials or attempts. Probability calculation thus comes across as the offspring of paradox and mathematics, since 'it enables us to accurately predict the global result of a process comprising a large number of events, each of which remains, in itself, unpredictable'.

Koestler goes on to add:

> If, on the contrary, one notices persistent deviations in a series involving several thousand trials, the only reasonable and scientific conclusion is that some other factor, beyond the workings of coincidence, must account for the result.

And this is precisely what happens in the case of telepathy. In 1934, psychologist Rhine[6] published his reports on 85,000 card draws conducted in cooperation with a number of select subjects. The cards themselves were simple and of five different types. One of the subjects would draw a card, look at it and 'memorise' it. Another subject, located in an adjoining room (or alternatively in another building), would attempt to 'guess' the card in question. There was therefore one chance out of five, or 20%, for the answer to be correct. 'And yet, the general performance average was of twenty-eight correct answers out of a hundred; never in a million years could coincidence explain such a result'. Further experiments, all of which have been far more complex, have been done since and have yielded the same results.

Could there thus be some 'laws of *seriality*' that differ from the laws of *causality* of the classical type? Such is the opinion adopted by physicist Wolfgang

---

6 TN: Joseph Banks Rhine (29th September, 1895–20th February, 1980) was an American botanist who founded parapsychology as a branch of psychology as well as the parapsychology lab at Duke University.

Pauli[7], the man who discovered the 'exclusion principle' that bears his name; and many other researchers have since followed suit.

In *Sense and Nonsense in Psychology* (Penguin Books, Harmondsworth, 1967), Hans J. Eysenck, one of the greatest contemporary psychologists, writes the following:

> Unless there exists a gigantic conspiracy involving approximately thirty faculties worldwide, in addition to several hundred well-respected scientists within their various disciplines (many of whom were initially hostile to the claims of parapsychologists), the only conclusion that can be drawn by a non-prejudiced observer is that there is indeed a small number of people with the ability to perceive information that is either present in the minds of others or in the surrounding world, using means yet unknown to science. This is not to be interpreted as support granted to such notions as survival after death, philosophical idealism, and so on. And yet it is so.

At this point, Arthur Koestler remarks that 'orthodox' science itself has some surprises in store for us. And it is modern physics in particular that equates to a genuine 'emancipation of the human spirit in relation to the human view of things'.

The latest developments in the field of microphysics have indeed brought to light a number of surprising concepts. Still today, the average layman is reluctant to admit that two plus two can sometimes total five and that 'negative mass', 'anti-particles' and 'holes' in space do actually exist. The average person could hardly fathom a universe where, for instance, *objects* could be of a *temporal* nature while *events* retain a *spatial* one; nor could such a person ever comprehend that an electron can be located in two places at once, pass through two openings simultaneously,[8] jump from one orbit to another without traversing any intermediary space ('as if the Earth suddenly passed into the orbit of Mars, without having to migrate in any way'), etc.

---

7 TN: Wolfgang Ernst Pauli (25th April, 1900–15th December, 1958) was an Austrian-born Swiss and American theoretical physicist and one of the pioneers of quantum physics. In 1945, he was awarded the Nobel Prize in Physics for his 'decisive contribution through his discovery of a new law of Nature, the exclusion principle or Pauli principle'.

8 TN: All of this is a reference to quantum physics and the fascinating and conclusively proven aspects of what is generally termed 'the double slit experiment'.

This 'impossible universe', however, one that has been revealed to us by both the theory of relativity and *quantum* mechanics,[9] is very real indeed. This allows Koestler to affirm that 'the unthinkable phenomena of extrasensory perception (whether telepathy, premonition or clairvoyance) seem less absurd in the light of the equally inconceivable propositions made by modern physics'.

Koestler, in fact, prohibits himself from reaching a conclusion. Belonging to the 'recalcitrant convert' species whose members combine scepticism with certitude, his only request is for ongoing experiments to be pursued on a larger scale and be strictly monitored.

He also allows us to anticipate a certain 'reconsideration of the relations between our body and mind', in the sense of achieving greater *psychosomatic* unity. If the spirit is to be found solely in matter itself, then matter must also *be* spiritual, he states. One could thus draw a comparison between the manner in which '*immaterial* fields' in physics are connected to the substantial aspects of material particles and the manner in which our states of consciousness relate to our brain's own substance. James Jeans[10] would thus have been proven right when stating back in 1937 that 'the universe begins to look more like a great thought than like a great machine'.

Some uncertainties do, of course, persist. No matter how spectacular they are, the results that have thus far been obtained are not yet fully convincing. Furthermore, supposing that it did indeed exist, extrasensory perception would in all likelihood remain purely erratic: 'It is impossible to control its underlying unconscious processes'. And last but not least, one must bear in mind that throughout history, the qualified scientists that have allowed themselves to be mystified by astute charlatans in all good faith are innumerable.

In *Le treizième César,*[11] Henry de Montherlant[12] writes:

---

9 TN: The rules and principles by which relativity and quantum physics respectively abide are in blatant contradiction with each other. Many physicists, including the late Stephen Hawking, have attempted to reconcile the two by striving to establish a so-called 'theory of everything'. All efforts in this direction have, unfortunately, proved entirely fruitless. We do, therefore, inhabit an 'impossible universe'.

10 TN: Sir James Hopwood Jeans (11th September, 1877–16th September, 1946) was an English physicist, astronomer and mathematician.

11 TN: The Thirteenth Caesar.

12 TN: Henry Marie Joseph Frédéric Expedite Millon de Montherlant (20th April, 1895–21st September, 1972) was a French essayist, novelist and dramatist; he was elected to the

> Seldom do I dream, nor do I have any interest in dreams, whose role is providential in the eyes of all those scribblers who hunger for false strangeness; indeed, genuine strangeness is to be found in life itself and cares little for the stuff of dreams. I have occasionally had seemingly premonitory dreams, but save for a single one, what they "announced" never actually took place.

It is said that science has attained *increasing* knowledge in an ever-*decreasing* number of topics; to which Koestler adds: 'Science represents the most glorious exploit of our human spirit, yet it also remains its most cruel source of frustration'.

The Roots of Coincidence, an essay by Arthur Koestler. Calmann-Lévy, 192 pages.

THE HIDDEN ASPECTS OF THE IMPOSSIBLE

VOLTAIRE[13] **WAS ONCE INFORMED BY** 'clairvoyants' that they predicted his demise at the age of thirty-two; yet he was actually eighty-four years old when he passed away. In a display of humour, he remarked that should one ask two astrologists whether a certain child would ever reach adulthood and one gave a positive and the other a negative response, at least one of them would not be mistaken in his claims.

In the Second Epistle to Timothy,[14] Saint Paul mentions the pharaoh's magicians, who used their own miracles in response to Moses'. Shortly afterwards,

Académie française in 1960.

13 TN: François-Marie Arouet (21st November, 1694–30th May, 1778), otherwise known as Voltaire, was a French Enlightenment author, historian and philosopher famous for his wit, his criticism of Christianity and his advocacy of freedom of religion, freedom of speech and the separation of church and state.

14 TN: In the New Testament, the Second Epistle to Timothy is one of the three Pastoral Epistles traditionally attributed to Saint Paul.

the Roman philosopher Celsus[15] wrote a treatise that has since mysteriously vanished but whose title is still known to us: *Against Magicians*.

Nowadays, the number of 'occult sciences' is in excess of twenty, stretching from metagnomy (divination) to spiritism and also including telekinesis (the moving of objects without direct contact), the study of ectoplasms, levitation and haunting phenomena, 'supra-normal' photography, and others.

On the occasion of the referendum that was held on 8th January, 1961, a 'magician' informed Radio Luxemburg that he could confidently guess the results in advance. On the eve of the ballot, with the TV cameras rolling, he thus entrusted a bailiff with a small box. Two days later, the bailiff was provided with the key and proceeded to open the box. What he found inside was a tube containing a piece of paper on which the results were inscribed most accurately. Incited by its own listeners, the radio station expressed its amazement at the 'miracle' that had taken place and turned to a specialist in 'parapsychological' matters, Mr Robert Tocquet. The latter was quick to unveil the deception.

The key to the mystery lay… in the key that unlocked the box:

> This key, one of abnormal size, actually contained the famed "magical" tube, which it automatically released by means of a special mechanism as soon as it was introduced into the lock.

HINDU ROPES AND 'SPIRITUALIST TOUCHES'

A professor at a Civil Engineering School, Mr Tocquet, who also happens to be a magician, has continued to draw attention to himself. Having inspired people to dream (in *Médiums et fantômes,*[16] *Les mystères du surnaturel,*[17] and *Le bilan du surnaturel*[18]), he now exerts himself to demystify such claims. His latest work reveals the very methods employed by the falsifiers of credulity, providing us with an entire inventory of their 'tricks'.

---

15 TN: Celsus was actually a 2nd-century Greek philosopher and an opponent of early Christianity. He is best known for his literary work entitled *On the True Doctrine*.

16 TN: Mediums and Apparitions.

17 TN: The Mysteries of the Supernatural.

18 TN: An Overview of the Supernatural.

He remarks that telepathy is, more often than not, part of 'music hall occultism'. The operator and his assistants make use of a mnemotechnical code (involving gestures or utterances) that allows them to transmit dozens of words, perhaps even entire sentences, with astounding speed.

Another successful ploy:

> The experimenter writes a short phrase or makes a sketch on a square piece of paper. The paper is thereafter placed in an envelope, which is then sealed. Next, the envelope is given to the "metagnome", who touches it with his hands, presses it against his forehead and ultimately specifies its contents.

And here is the explanation:

> While manipulating the envelope, the "medium" has simply imbued it with 95% pure alcohol. This liquid renders the paper temporarily transparent, allowing one to read what is written or see what has been drawn. It takes the alcohol less than a minute to evaporate, while the envelope remains intact.

As for levitation, it can hardly be achieved outside 'space capsules', where the laws of gravity are cancelled. On earth, it appears to be constantly simulated. Psychoanalyst Schrenck-Notzing developed an interest in a certain Karl Krauss, a man who produced some incredible 'levitations'. Here is Mr Tocquet's account of things:

> The experiment always took place in complete obscurity. Participants would hold the subject's hands, while his feet could be located thanks to the presence of luminescent strips of material. The medium would first ask to be covered with a sheet, so that he could "concentrate his powers". A minute later, the sheet would be pushed aside and, suddenly, the assistants would watch as both of the medium's feet left the ground and gradually ascended.

In actual fact,

> once he had been covered with the sheet, Krauss would proceed to remove one of his shoes and fasten it to the other using a large clasp. Having cast the sheet aside, he would slowly lift the foot bearing both shoes and swing it in the air. All these movements were always made silently and without allowing the hands of the testers to detect any abnormal or suspicious contractions.

In India, the 'Hindu rope' once left a lasting impression on the majors of the British army. It is now common knowledge, however, that 'the rope was hollow and its base contained an interlocking metallic tube system whose extension, once the rope had been cast, formed a telescopic tube with sufficient rigidity to allow a trained child to climb all the way to the top'. A similar trick is used when the Ganges channels its muddy waters along and 'fakirs' are seen walking on water:

> Following a speech about his own divine powers, the yogi strips off his clothes and, standing barefooted and wearing nothing but a loincloth, sets out to walk across the water, slowly and majestically.

The night before, of course, a thick rope had been stretched a few centimetres beneath the river's surface:

> The miracle itself is no more than a tightrope walker's performance.

And when spiritualists are heard asking 'Spirit, are you there?', it is the medium who responds. Mr Tocquet explains how this can be achieved.

> Once the middle finger's nail has been coated with colophony, the hand is placed upon the table with the middle finger bent. The fingernail then adheres to the tabletop and the slightest and utterly imperceptible contraction of the finger, even at short distance, produces a pronounced crackling sound, one that is analogous to a blow.

With their hands concealed in darkness, mediums accomplish their 'spiritualistic touches' by means of 'a certain pliant and extremely lightweight ruler that has been placed into their jacket's inner pocket and is then taken into the mouth and unbent at the right moment'. Using calcium sulphide, strontium, and ferrocerium, one produces excellent quality 'mysterious rays' and 'halos'. And as regards 'ectoplasms', what is generally used are balloons or gauzes that are then skilfully rolled out. Mr Tocquet points out:

> Among regurgitating subjects, even the stomach can be used for concealment. Mrs. Duncan[19] was thus able to conceal a prodigious number of objects in her own stomach (several meters of extra-fine gauze, engravings, photographs, rubber

---

19 TN: Victoria Helen McCrae Duncan (25th November, 1897–6th December, 1956) was a Scottish medium and the last person to have been imprisoned under the British Witchcraft

gloves, and other things as well) and then, during her pseudo-trance, regurgitate the lot with extraordinary ease.

The instant materialisation and dematerialisation of a "ghost" can both be achieved by means of a black veil or a petroleum lamp. Such a lamp, of ovoid shape and egg-like size, is concealed beneath the large white sheet covering the medium. When the lamp is turned on, it lights up and the apparition becomes visible; when switched off, the ghost simply vanishes. In addition to this, the lamp itself is held in the palm of the medium's hand, allowing an impressively spectral light to illuminate the face.

FAKIRS AND STIGMATICS

In connection to stigmatics, the author writes that 'the trophic disorders, ulcerations, eschars, and erythema displayed by hysterics are very often self-induced. And yet the differences between such accidents and the common sickly stigmata, as well as most suggestion-generated ones, are sometimes insignificant appearance-wise. Similarly, the very partition that separates the *stigmatised* from the *hysterical* is, at times, quite thin'.

Pierre Janet[20] has studied the case of a stigmatic named Madeleine, which he presents in his book *De l'angoisse à l'extase.*[21] Following extensive meditations on Christ's crucifixion, Madeleine displayed stigmata that consisted in the presence of excoriations on the palms of her hands, her feet, and her left breast. The inquiry showed that 'Madeleine often sank into crises of ecstasy which kept her absolutely motionless for hours on end, with her feet crossed and fists clenched. One thus understands that the great pressure exerted by the limbs could indeed have caused natural excoriations in precisely the right places. And this occurred all the more easily since, generally speaking, the state of ecstasy surfaced on the eve of her period, at a time when circulatory issues were accentuated'.

Act of 1735. She is widely known to have produced fraudulent ectoplasm made from cheesecloth.

20 TN: Pierre Marie Félix Janet (30th May, 1859–24th February, 1947) was a pioneering French psychologist, philosopher and psychotherapist specialising in dissociation and traumatic memory.

21 TN: From Anguish to Ecstasy.

This is where one touches upon the problematic of the pathological manifestations of faith, upon those 'inferior forms of mysticism' to which Philippe de Félice[22] dedicated a first-rate series of books: *Poisons sacrés, ivresses divines*[23] (A. Michel, 1947), and *L'enchantement des danses et la magie du verbe*[24] (A. Michel, 1957).

The procedures resorted to by fakirs are of a simpler nature. Those who climb 'sword ladders' make sure that the previously-sharpened blades are obliquely positioned and bevelled. By contrast, those that lie upon a bed of nails need not even take such precautions:

> It is all too easy to understand that if a man whose actual weight is, say, seventy kilos places his body upon a hundred nails, each nail will only support 700 grams of weight and the resulting force will not suffice to ensure the penetration of what is often a more or less flexible nail with a slightly blunt tip.

The skill displayed by manipulators is immense, but credulity also intervenes in the process. Those that Mr Tocquet calls 'imaginative interpreters' are, at their own expense, the most loyal allies of all 'magi' and 'clairvoyants'. Their good faith never fails, and their enthusiasm makes them fierce propagandists. It was La Fontaine[25] who once remarked: 'Man is of ice when it comes to the truth, but of fire when it comes to lies'. In 1935, a Parisian doctor name Louis Couderc sent a randomly chosen number of correspondents a 'prediction' bulletin (whose contents were identical in all cases). It did not take long for him to receive an entire mass of mail fraught with statements along the following lines: 'You have read my life as if it were a book'.

Such credulity is closely connected to the Coué method[26] and the astounding powers of both suggestion and autosuggestion. It is, for instance, possible to make someone that is allergic to milk sick by making them drink a glass of water but convincing them that it is actually milk that they are drinking. This

22 TN: Philippe de Félice (31st March, 1880–6th March, 1964) was a Reformed clergyman, theologian, religious historian and mass psychologist.

23 TN: Sacred Poisons, Divine Drunkenness.

24 TN: The Enchantment of Dances and the Magic of Words.

25 TN: Jean de La Fontaine (8th July, 1621–13th April, 1695) was a French fabulist and one of the most widely read French poets of the 17th century. His fables are among the most influential ever written.

26 TN: Meaning conscious autosuggestion.

is the vast domain of 'psychological medicine', 'organic neurosis' and placebo effects.[27]

In 1903, René Blondlot, a distinguished professor of physics at the university of Nancy and a correspondent of the French Academy of Sciences, believed himself to have discovered mysterious rays which he baptised 'N rays' (thus named in honour of his own city of birth). These rays, whose actual properties he determined and whose wavelength he even managed to measure, became the focus of numerous scientific communications and hypotheses, each more stupefying than the last. Convinced of the existence of such rays, further scientists took turns contributing and bringing countless clarifications to the topic. It took several years for people to acknowledge the fact that 'N rays' have never existed outside their inventor's own imagination.

In 1958, France was said to be home to an estimated 40,000 healers, compared to 38,000 doctors. Nowadays, the estimates are of about 60,000 astrologists and 'clairvoyants' but barely 44,000 priests. Such 'magical' activities are not subject to legal punishment.

In 1950, a certain Georges Roux, who worked as a deputy inspector at the mail sorting facility of the Avignon railway station, discovered that he was actually 'Christ reincarnate'. Shortly afterwards, he founded the Universal Christian Church and established his identity as the 'Christ of Montfavet'; but the Pope refused to acknowledge him as such. He thus chose to become a healer, banning his disciples from resorting to a doctor's assistance: 'If a sick person dies, it is because the Lord has willed it so'. Over a period of six years, Roux managed to convert a total of 6,000 people but was ultimately condemned following several deaths in his own entourage.

PARANORMAL PHENOMENA

The entire issue lies in ascertaining whether, in the final analysis, *all* events declared 'paranormal' are the result of mistakes, illusions or hoaxes.

[27] TN: A placebo effect is a remarkable phenomenon in which a placebo, meaning a fake treatment, inactive substance or saline solution, can sometimes lead to visible improvement in a patient's condition simply because the person expects it to be helpful.

There are numerous authors that affirm this, beginning with Jean Rostand,[28] who writes:

> Unless proven wrong, I consider all physical phenomena such as the remote moving of objects, levitation, materialisation and so on to be no more than vulgar hoaxes. As for mental phenomena, including the transmission of thoughts or telepathy, premonition, clairvoyance, etc., they all seem to be, depending on the case, either ascribable to pure coincidence or to fraud, regardless of whether the latter is committed consciously or not. (*Science fausse et fausses sciences.*[29] Gallimard, 1958)

According to Mr Robert Imbert-Nergal,[30] 'never in over twenty centuries have occult sciences succeeded in providing us with as little as a handful of phenomena that can be reproduced independently of the observer, the location and the circumstances in which the activity is conducted. This generalised deficiency suffices to ruin, once and for all, the pretension of paranormal phenomena to be classified as scientific facts' (in *Les sciences occultes ne sont pas des sciences.*[31] Ed. Rationalistes, 1959).

And here is what Mr Guy Fau[32] affirms:

> One must never stop repeating that of the thousands of experiments that have been carried out, every single one, beyond any and all exceptions, has allowed us either to demonstrate the presence of trickery or, at the very least, to establish the fact that, whenever serious monitoring took place, nothing occurred at all. (*Les charlatans devant la justice*[33])

Mr Tocquet, who is part of the International Metapsychic Institute (an Institute that was founded in 1919 by physiologist Charles Richet, a Nobel prize winner), begs to differ. An uncompromising adversary of all charlatans,

---

28 TN: Jean Edmond Cyrus Rostand (30th October, 1894–4th September, 1977) was a French biologist and philosopher.

29 TN: Erroneous Science and False Science.

30 TN: Robert Imbert-Nergal seems to be an author who has targeted occultism with sharp criticism, denying it the right to be called a 'science'.

31 TN: Occult Sciences Are No Sciences at All.

32 TN: Guy Fau (23rd June, 1909–1st June, 2000) was a French essayist and author.

33 TN: When Charlatans Are Brought to Justice.

he nonetheless presents himself as an 'ardent defender of metapsychics' and declares that 'authentically paranormal phenomena do indeed exist'.

Such was once the viewpoint espoused by Alexis Carrel,[34] William Crookes (the inventor of cathodic rays), Paul Broca,[35] Richet himself, and Julian Huxley.[36] Today, the same conviction is adhered to by Arthur Koestler, as well as many other American and Soviet scientists.

Very recently, psychologist Hans J. Eysenck (*Planets, Stars and Personality*, in *New Behaviour*, 1975, pages 246 to 249), who based his claims on the works of Michel and Françoise Gauquelin (*Songes ou mensonges de l'astrologie.*[37] Hachette, 1969), allowed himself to assert the following: 'It seems certain that the time of the year which coincides with one's date of birth is intimately connected to each person's personality'. An abnormally high number of sport champions and military figures, for instance, are apparently born 'under Mars', whereas most actors and scientists are allegedly born respectively 'under Jupiter' and 'under Saturn'. If one is to believe Mr Eysenck, who is anything but a credulous man or a mystic, the likelihood that such a phenomenon could be attributed to mere coincidence is less than one in a million.

In an entirely different field, some interesting electrophysiological experiments have been conducted upon certain great mystics when in a state of ecstasy. The EEG (electroencephalogram) revealed an unwavering permanence of Alpha waves in their bodies, which are characteristic of a 'calm state of mind' (unlike Beta waves, which relate to an 'attentive state of mind'): as long as the trance lasted, no *arrest reaction* (a passage from Alpha to Beta waves) took place, regardless of what stimulations were introduced.

---

34 TN: Alexis Carrel (28th June, 1873–5th November, 1944) was a French surgeon and biologist who won the 1912 Nobel Prize in Physiology or Medicine for his pioneering vascular suturing techniques.

35 TN: Pierre Paul Broca (28th June, 1824–9th July, 1880) was a French physician, anatomist and anthropologist. He is most famous for his research into 'Broca's area', a region of the frontal lobe that has been named after him.

36 TN: Sir Julian Sorell Huxley (22nd June, 1887–14th February, 1975) was a British evolutionary biologist, eugenicist, and internationalist. He was also an advocate of natural selection and a prominent figure in mid-20th-century modern synthesis.

37 TN: The Fabric of Dreams or Astrological Fabrications.

This is what Mr Aimé Michel[38] writes on the topic:

> When a yogi (or a zazen) is submitted to various tests which, by mobilising attention, cause an arrest reaction in every normal man, he remains unaffected. The Alpha condition persists as if nothing were wrong. This result is obtained not only in the area of the temples, the occiput and the parietal bones, but through all other electrodes as well — the Alpha mode invades the brain in its entirety, and the latter thus finds itself in a completely idle state. The fact that such a state can persist in spite of all external stimulations, even the most dramatic ones, proves that all the stimulations are *voluntarily* shut down before reaching the cerebral cortex, which acts as the centre of both our consciousness and our intellectual and voluntary operations. The mystic has acquired the ability to tame the nervous system which transmits the sensations that originate from our organs and usually reach the different specialised "areas" of the brain. (*Le mysticisme,*[39] CAL-Retz, 1973; and *Psychologie,*[40] November 1973)

NON-CONTRADICTORY DETERMINISM?

The debate thus seems to have been reduced to a dialogue of the deaf, and one can wonder whether, ultimately, the problematic regarding the truthfulness and untruthfulness of parapsychological phenomena only seems unsolvable as a result of being *inadequately presented.* Whatever the case, such is the hypothesis proposed by Mr Marc Beigbeder[41] in his essay on *A Possible Logic in Paranormal Phenomena* (in *Nouvelle école,*[42] number 30, Winter 1976–77).

Mr Beigbeder begins by reminding his readers that every scientific fact only exists through a *theory*, and vice versa. At present, experimental theory is mainly based on the notion of *statistical determinism*. This determinism, however, is necessarily *contradictory* precisely because it is merely statistical. In our scientific language, the word 'always' only has absolute value for conventional reasons: it would be more accurate to use 'almost always' when highlighting all that is founded on statistics. Yet as soon as one considers (both

38 TN: Aimé Michel (12th May, 1919–28th December, 1992) was a French writer who specialised in the topic of UFOs; he also had a degree in psychology and philosophy.

39 TN: Mysticism.

40 TN: Psychology.

41 TN: Marc Beigbeder (11th August, 1916–2nd March, 1997) was a French author.

42 TN: *Nouvelle école* is a French intellectual magazine run by Alain de Benoist and Michel d'Urance.

monitorable and monitored) facts as a *majority* of events relating a certain theory, one must also acknowledge 'event-driven regulatory exceptions, the *rare structural counter-examples* which, although acting as an exception to the dominant rule that has thus far been more or less exclusively formulated, still express a complementary antagonistic rule representing a minority of rare cases, one that has been "forgotten" or underestimated by the prevailing axiom and the manner in which it is outlined'. In other words, every event-based system rooted in statistical majority necessarily 'bears within itself' a minority of cases which, owing to the very presence of theory, serve as exceptions to the rule.

Paranormal phenomena — among which one should further distinguish para-biological, para-physical and parapsychic phenomena in the strict sense of the word — could, if one believes Mr Beigbeder, correspond to such 'exceptions'.

This could account for one of the traits of paranormal phenomena, which Mr Robert Tocquet reminds us about using the following terms:

> Paranormal phenomena cannot be reproduced at will and are, as a result of this, eminently suspicious whenever presented in a constant and regular manner. (Meaning that they are not *reproducible* due to their actual 'minority' status with respect to theory.)

This would also explain why it is as impossible to *prove* such phenomena using current scientific theories as it is to reject them in the name of *scientific fact*. Mr Beigbeder remarks:

> And yet it is into our current scientific understanding that the advocates of paranormal phenomena attempt to incorporate the latter, and it is above all by means of our contemporary scientific instruments, in application of known scientific calculations, that they strive to establish such phenomena. We must free ourselves of this deadlock. And the best means to achieve this lies undoubtedly in putting forward novel theoretical proposals, proposals that could, with the help of innovative devices whose construction they would foster, either be authenticated or discredited.

Due to its focus on large numbers and averages and its resulting adoption of a global and probability-based shape, statistical determinism lacks the ability to evaluate the truthfulness or untruthfulness of cases that are *necessarily* exceptional. It is, furthermore, founded upon a non-contradictory identity axiom. By definition, the very value of such an axiom is determined by the non-contradictory aspect of the object being studied. This is why it found itself rather mistreated following the emergence of the kinetic theory of gases[43] and, most of all, the development of microphysics. And it is probably because it favours and even sublimates identity non-contradiction that current scientific logic 'has implicitly proceeded to exclude in advance all such "exceptions" from science, on the basis of its own operational and verificatory possibilities; in actual fact, however, such "exceptions" represent the few regulatory and contradictory manifestations of a system which could perhaps incorporate so-called paranormal phenomena'. Consequently, Mr Beigbeder believes it necessary to *reconsider* the notion of statistics and proposes, in harmony with the conceptions of Stéphane Lupasco,[44] the creation of new kinds of calculations characterised by *contradictory axioms* and '*the logic of the included third*';[45] calculations with the capacity to account for and *verify* exceptions as a *minority that contradicts the norm*, thus defining paranormal phenomena as 'a relative minority-based excess'.

It would thus seem that numerous phenomena only appear to be 'paranormal' because they contradict the traditional conception of causality or the usual perspective founded upon the course of time. And yet the essential revolution brought about by quantum mechanics has consisted in the sidelining of the old concept of causality. As highlighted by Mr Rémy Chauvin[46] ('Physique

---

[43] TN: The kinetic theory of gases describes a gas as a large number of small particles (atoms or molecules), all of which are in constant, random motion.

[44] TN: Stéphane Lupasco (11th August, 1900–7th October, 1988) was a Romanian philosopher who developed non-Aristotelian logic.

[45] TN: The theory of the Included Middle, literally 'the logic of the Included Third' (position), is an idea proposed by Stéphane Lupasco in 1951 (in *The Principle of Antagonism and the Logic of Energy*). The notion pertains to physics and quantum mechanics and could also have wider applications in further domains such as information theory and computing, epistemology, and theories of consciousness. The Included Middle is a theory proposing that logic has a three-part structure, namely the position of asserting something, the negation of this assertion, and a third position that is neither or both.

[46] TN: Rémy Chauvin (10th October, 1913–8th December, 2009) was a biologist and entomologist, and a French Honorary Professor Emeritus at the Sorbonne, PhD. He was also known for defending the rights of animals and for displaying great interest in such topics

et Parapsychology',[47] in *Question de*, issue number 13, third trimester 1976), not only does microphysics prove that it is the observer that *creates* science, but that it is in fact man that *creates* the universe; meaning that 'in the absence of observers, there would be no phenomena at all.'[48] This paradoxical remark raises the issue of our universe's organisation 'prior to' the appearance of man. Precisely, however, 'there is nothing truly accurate that can be termed as being "before" or "after" in Relativity or quantum physics; it all depends on one's reference system, on one's position in space-time in relation to the phenomenon itself.' If we thus were, for instance, to define *precognition* as a 'memory of the future' (a situation where the brain perceives events that will only impact it in the future), we would have a better understanding of the words of Olivier Costa de Beauregard, the head of research at the CNRS[49] and the author *of Deuxième principe de la science et du temps*:[50]

> I wholeheartedly wish for parapsychology to become a genuine science so that light can be shed upon the results obtained in quantum physics.

Only by breaking with traditional logic and the linear conception of time will we stand some *chance* of *grasping* paranormal phenomena.

Les dessous de l'impossible,[51] an essay by Robert Tocquet. Ed. Spéciales, 280 pages.

---

as parapsychology, life after death, psychics, clairvoyance and the UFO phenomenon, sometimes writing under the pseudonym Pierre Duval.

47 TN: Physics and Parapsychology.

48 TN: One of the principles of quantum physics is that reality does not exist until it is experienced. Prior to this 'experiencing', there are only 'potentialities'.

49 TN: The National Centre for Scientific Research.

50 TN: The Second Principle of Science and Time.

51 TN: The Hidden Aspects of the Impossible.

PRINCETON GNOSIS

THEY LONG TO RESEMBLE THE sages that once belonged to the schools of the waning Antiquity, to be akin to the Epicureans[52] and the Stoics,[53] while simultaneously mistrusting both Marx[54] and Freud[55] and abhorring Wilhelm Reich[56] and Marcuse[57]. What they seek is a new kind of deism and perceive 'ideologists in the same manner as monks once viewed Church priests: as being lost in the world'.

These bizarre individuals are all American academics and scientists. In a book bearing the enigmatic title *La gnose de Princeton*,[58] Mr Raymond Ruyer, a professor at Nancy University, labels them 'neo-Gnostic'.

During the first century of our era, Gnostics affirmed that the world was dominated by the Spirit; that the Spirit faced (or rather created) its own resistance and opposition, namely Matter; and that it was through *knowledge* that man could attain salvation.[59] (By contrast, the Church Fathers put the *libido sciendi* on the same footing as other forms of concupiscence.)

---

52 TN: Founded around 307 BC, Epicureanism is a philosophical system based upon the teachings of the ancient Greek philosopher Epicurus, who was an atomic materialist, thus following in the footsteps of Democritus.

53 TN: Stoicism is, above all, a philosophy of personal ethics rooted in its own system of logic and views on the natural world. It states that from a social perspective, the path to happiness is found in the acceptance of the moment as it presents itself; this is achieved by not allowing ourselves to be controlled by our desire for pleasure or our fear of pain, by using our minds to understand the surrounding world and to play our role in nature's plan, and by working together and treating others fairly and justly.

54 TN: Karl Marx (5th May, 1818–14th March, 1883) was a German philosopher, economist, historian, political theorist, sociologist, journalist and revolutionary socialist.

55 TN: Born Sigismund Schlomo Freud, Sigmund Freud (6th May, 1856–23rd September, 1939) was an Austrian neurologist and the founder of psychoanalysis, a clinical method for treating psychopathology through dialogue between a patient and a psychoanalyst.

56 TN: Wilhelm Reich (24th March, 1897–3rd November, 1957) was an Austrian doctor of medicine and second-generation psychoanalyst.

57 TN: Herbert Marcuse (19th July, 1898–29th July, 1979) was a German-American philosopher, sociologist, and political theorist associated with the Frankfurt School of Critical Theory.

58 TN: Princeton Gnosis.

59 TN: In actual fact, many Gnostics believed the Spirit to be trapped in the material world, a world which had been created by a lesser deity, the *demiurge*, and acted as a veil preventing the return of the confined spiritual spark to the realm of the Unknown/Alien/True

The new gnosis adopts the affirmations of the old one but attempts to conform them to positive science. It states that the Spirit *forms* Matter, 'representing its sole and unique fabric'; that no material reality could precede consciousness; and that consciousness is both the 'place' and the envelope that constitutes material reality.

THE WORLD IS INTELLIGENT

Although this reference to gnosis dates back to 1969, the movement itself is older than that. It actually surfaced around 1963–64, among both Princeton University Researchers and those of the Pasadena Astronomical Centre, and asked 'anti-paradoxical questions' such as: 'When breathing, do we still take in air molecules inhaled by Julius Caesar at the time of his assassination?' (The answer is: 'Yes, probably dozens of them whenever we inhale'.)

In the eyes of the Gnostics, there is both a 'place' and an 'underside' to the universe: through observation, all that we can perceive is the outer part of the universe, which is embodied by its *underside*, and not its 'internal consciousness', which is its *location*. Vulgar materialism consists in thinking that 'everything is *external*', that 'everything is an object'; in short, in considering the universe to be the actual place. We cannot, however, truly get to know a universe to which we ourselves actually belong. Man can no more be reduced to a mere *description* of himself than a flower ever could; or even the world, for that matter.

On the other hand, the neo-Gnostics assert that the universe constitutes one whole; that all the phenomena taking place within it are solidary. The organisation of the world is the very *condition* of its existence: a 'purely chaotic' universe could never exist. In this regard, the new gnosis is connected to the philosophical tradition which has, since the days of Leibniz,[60] claimed that life can only be interpreted and conceived of as part of the relations that tie it to

---

God. Only 'Gnosis', meaning a special kind of knowledge that is acquired through spiritual awakening and direct communion with the Unknown God, can thus release the Spirit of man from its material prison.

60 TN: In philosophy, Gottfried Wilhelm von Leibniz (1st July, 1646–14th November, 1716) is most famous for his optimism, i.e. his conclusion that our Universe is, in a restricted sense, the best possible one that God could have created, an idea that earned him a great deal of derision, especially at the hands of Voltaire.

our universe's entirety. It is a sentiment that is also encountered with Giordano Bruno,[61] as well as Shaftesbury, Herder, Goethe, Schelling and Schleiermacher.

Goethe[62] writes:

> If there was no solar aspect to the eye itself, how could it ever perceive the sun?

The Gnostics explain:

> If I strike the table with my fist, a determinable event simultaneously occurs in Sirius or the Andromeda nebula.

Descartes[63] used to say: 'I think, therefore I am'. For their part, the Gnostics declare: 'I think, therefore *there is* thought in the universe'; just as the weather forecast says 'it is raining on Paris'. And they specify that every thought, meaning every self-presence, is noticed at the time when it is expressed: it is a 'here-and-now'.

Next, they proceed to endow the universe with *mental* qualities that stem from the organisation that it displays. The world is *intelligent*; but here, 'intelligent' means 'functional'. In this respect, everything that 'functions' is intelligent: 'A dog is as intelligent as a human, an infusorian as intelligent as a dog, and a molecule as intelligent as an infusorian'.

In some way, the universe's ingenuity *precedes* our own: Biologists Crick and Watson would never have existed if our genetic code had not presided over the constitution of their genes in accordance with the scheme that they themselves *afterwards* established.

Mr Ruyer writes:

> Molecules and atoms understand their own functioning better than physicists do. Who else could thus know what physicists are still ignorant about with regard to atoms if not atoms themselves?

---

61 TN: Giordano Bruno (1548–17th February, 1600) was an Italian Dominican friar, philosopher, mathematician, poet, and cosmological theorist who believed in an infinite universe with no centre. He was eventually tried for heresy and burned at the stake.

62 TN: Johann Wolfgang von Goethe (28th August, 1749–22nd March, 1832) is a renowned German writer who also acted as a statesman.

63 TN: René Descartes (31st March, 1596–11th February, 1650) was a French philosopher, mathematician, and scientist. He has been dubbed the father of modern Western philosophy, and a major part of subsequent Western philosophy is a response to his writings.

Another mistake made by the proponents of scientism consists in picturing individual life as a space of time between two voids: the void preceding life and the one that follows the latter. To the neo-Gnostics, this parallel is devoid of any and all meaning. Only death itself, *and none other*, is an unprecedented event. They explain: 'We have been alive since the beginning of the world'. Indeed, the cells which we are made of derive from the division or fusion of other living cells, which in turn stem from pre-vital molecules. In other words, life is all that they have *ever* known. Death, on the other hand, is a radical novelty and absolute rupture. There is no survival beyond it; there is, however, a 'pre-life', one that is as old as life itself.

Consequently, the past of every man reaches as far as the past of his own lineage, that of his species, and that of all the living cells whose 'continuation' he represents. Every man is the 'twin' of his own ancestors: not within space itself, but within *time* — 'None of the currently living beings has ever died. Just like myself, they all date back to the beginning of the world'.

In addition, all deaths are merely individual. Life, for its part, goes on: it is akin to an immensely long sentence, one that is punctuated with commas:

> There are billions of human hands and eyes that turn into dust in the cemeteries; but the hand, as a type of living organ, has subsisted and been *evolving* since the dawn of the primates.

Man's superiority over the rest of the living world stems precisely from the fact that he has inherited 'the longest message of all'. Man is a 'temporal giant', Mr Ruyer writes.

Whenever it describes anti-coincidence (necessity) through coincidence, order through disorder, and the message through background noise, materialistic science is, according to a further gnostic postulate, once again proceeding *in reverse within the underside*. By doing so, it comes up against the issue of 'emergent properties': how could what is more come out of what is less? The new gnosis reverses this perspective. It states that it is disorder that accompanies and marks the limits of order, not the other way around.

'In order to get things back on their feet, it is every morphogenesis that must be interpreted as a psychogenesis', Mr Ruyer notes.

THE 'OBSERVABLES' AND 'PARTICIPABLES'

In the beginning, there was absolute Blindness, materialists claim. To which the Gnostics respond by saying: in the beginning was anti-coincidence. They thus strive to establish a new sort of deism.

In contrast with the current tendency, which rejects the Father in the name of the Son, the new gnosis resuscitates the notion of God and 'abandons Jesus-Christ and his apostles in the hands of the hippies'.

God is thus defined as the cosmos in its entirety, this cosmos which was perhaps *one* some ten to fifteen billion years ago, is incarnated in each and every one of us and whose *becoming* continues in every present moment. This cuts Saint Augustine's[64] question short when he asks: 'What was the Lord doing before he created the heavens and the earth?'

This universe-God does not, of course, correspond to the usual conception of the divine. Mr Ruyer writes:

> The God whose apparent body is constituted by the Tree of Life is neither infinitely powerful nor infinitely wise; neither infinitely good nor just. He errs, fails in many of his branches, which then wither away. He often contradicts himself and devours himself.

He is *thought* yet lacks a *brain*; the latter is embodied by the trees that have been formed. He never *utters a word* but allows us all to *speak*. He does not represent an order that is given, yet he enables ordering. He is not a *text* to be read but a *language* to be spoken. Better yet: He does not demand nor ask for anything. One only serves him by living one's life.

'When the wheat grows, the demons are struck with terror', Nietzsche[65] once wrote.

The Gnostics contrast what is *participable* (whatever gives time its meaning) with materialistic science, which only recognises the *observable* (meaning

---

64 TN: A Roman African, Saint Augustine of Hippo (13th November, 354–28th August, 430) was an early Christian theologian and philosopher from Numidia whose writings exerted great influence upon the development of Western Christianity and philosophy.

65 TN: Friedrich Wilhelm Nietzsche (15th October, 1844–25th August, 1900) was a German philosopher, cultural critic, composer, poet, philologist, and Latin and Greek scholar whose work has exerted a profound influence on Western philosophy and modern intellectual history.

all objects upon which observations can be made). The new gnosis consists in granting the 'participable' access to the scientific domain.

In the second part of his book, Mr Raymond Ruyer presents the *praxis* that stems from the scientific 'theology' espoused by the Gnostics. It is essentially a kind of *wisdom*, one that is completely at odds with the 'ideological nuisances' that he himself described so well in a previous book.

This *praxis* might surprise some people with its 'isolationism'. Indeed, the Gnostics do not struggle for any cause and reject any and all doctrine. Displaying cynicism with regard to both Church and state, they dismiss all crusades, proselytism, rites and conversions. Never secretive, they still remain discrete. As the very heirs of those Puritans who once chose to emigrate across the Atlantic, they declare: 'We now emigrate once again, heading towards a spiritual continent'.

All ceremonials are banned in their eyes. Wisdom consists in ridding oneself of all 'cerebral intoxications', and the 'game' in discovering the game's rules. According to Mr Ruyer, 'the gnostic movement is an attempt to constitute a philosophical — and secondarily social — aristocracy by means of discrete and silent co-option'.

This attempt manifests itself through a whole series of 'assemblages', a term popularised by Eric Berne[66] in *Des jeux et des hommes*[67] (Stock, 1966), meaning through a sequence of more or less systematised mental attitudes which, on the basis of a single event or more, enables one to redirect spirits in a direction deemed compatible with the set objectives. The new gnosis thus displays a tendency towards a type of 'intimateness with the universe', one that is as reminiscent of the vitalism of Nietzsche and D. H. Lawrence[68] as of Stoic ethics. It also — or above all, perhaps — brings to mind the views advocated by writer

---

[66] TN: Eric Berne (10th May, 1910–15th July, 1970) was a Canadian-born psychiatrist who, in the middle of the 20th century, created the theory of *transactional analysis* as a way of explaining human behaviour.

[67] TN: Games and Men.

[68] TN: David Herbert Lawrence (11th September, 1885–2nd March, 1930) was an English writer and poet. His collected works represent, among other things, an extended reflection upon the dehumanising effects of modernity and industrialisation. Some of the issues Lawrence explores are sexuality, emotional health, vitality, spontaneity, and instinct.

and philosopher Samuel Butler (1835–1902), whose ideal of *good breeding* is embodied rather successfully by Tom Jones.[69]

Does this movement have a founder? Does it have any masters? Mr Ruyer chooses not to mention any names. The bibliography, however, suggests those of astronomers Fred Hoyle and Gustav Stromberg, biologists William S. Beck and Walter M. Elsasser, cosmologists Dennis W. Sciama and Gerald J. Whitrow, and physicists Walter A. Weisskopf, Edmund T. Whittaker and David Bohm. It also refers to the works of a certain group of scientists whose conclusions were popularised by Arthur Koestler, particularly in *The Ghost in the Machine* and *Drinkers of Infinity*.

AN UNCONSCIOUS MEMORY IN THE MAKING

What should one make of this Princeton gnosis, then? Its necessarily speculative character remains quite ambiguous. With regard to certain aspects, the God that the neo-Gnostics define as the 'place' of the universe, this God that represents 'the Thought whose brain is embodied by the created world', is rather similar to the God of the Bible, the universal *Logos*. But whereas the latter is a static God whose creation has been *provided* once and for all, the Princetonian God is an immense *becoming*, one that undergoes ceaseless self-transformation, makes 'mistakes', is heading *in a certain direction* but does not, in principle, actually *know* where He is heading to.

It is Samuel Butler, who authored *Erewhon* (1872) and *Life and Habit* (1877), that exerts particular influence on this level. A friend of both Charles and Francis Darwin, Butler developed the notion that evolution is not the result of natural selection but is triggered by a constantly *growing* 'unconscious memory' passed down from generation to generation. He thus believed himself to have reinstated finality into science (albeit a reverse one).

The neo-Gnostics take a stand against 'social' anthropology, Zen Buddhism and vulgar psychoanalysis, yet their doctrine may well end up awakening a new sort of universalism, as remarked by Mr Ruyer himself, in fact:

> Given cosmology's totalising aspect regarding both space and time, it must totalise both observers and the observed, the points of view and the points viewed, *egos*

69 TN: Despite his philandering, singer Tom Jones has remained profoundly religious throughout his career.

> as a "here-and-now" and *egos* as an "elsewhere", all pasts and all futures, all movements as a deforming factor and all movements of deformation.

And then there is this statement:

> God is present in the cosmos, in every being, in the unity of all beings and in their biological progress; in no way could he be found in the history of peoples. (See also the article written by Abbé Jean Milet in *Le Monde moderne*,[70], issue number 11, winter 1975–76.)

Last but not least, the main reproach with which one can target this school (provided that it is indeed a school that we are referring to) is that it falls prey to a kind of reverse reductionism. Reductionistic theoreticians generally reduce culture to nature, consciousness to life, and life to lifeless matter. As for the neo-Gnostics, they proceed to reduce the entire universe to a 'consciousness' they call 'God'. ('The universe is in its entirety culture, not nature'.) To be honest, such a formula could institute a great diversity of *perspectives*, depending on the actual manner in which it is conceived of. From the neo-Gnostic point of view, however, it does seem to be the case that it ends up eliminating the *qualitative* differences that do exist between the various levels of reality, thus simultaneously restricting the *autonomy* that is ever so specifically human. It would therefore be desirable to have the neo-Gnostics explain themselves in this regard.

La gnose de Princeton, an essay by Raymond Ruyer. Fayard, 303 pages.

In *Les cent prochains siècles*[71] (Fayard, 1977), Mr Ruyer attempts to outline 'man's historical destiny according to the new American Gnosis'. Declaring himself convinced that the 'God of long-term history' is even less subject to dethronement than the 'God of the cosmos', he uses the following words to explicitly detail the 'gnostic' conception of the human phenomenon:

'Men are only human because they last both biologically and historically. Just as an authentic organism is a reproduction-capable organism, "to be a people" is to last as a people, to reproduce as a people in cultural continuity. An "instantaneous people" would only be an amassment or a crowd. And it is because it is meant to last that a nation gradually creates all its institutions. This "creation" is instinctive in the sense that it reaches beyond rational

70 TN: A French magazine.

71 TN: The Next Hundred Centuries.

technology and the geometrical analysis of current situations. Duration in a "meaningful" world is not synonymous with inertia but with continuous creation. [...] Men are happiest in a "durable", disciplined and conservative society. Even if their material lives are hard, their mental and psychological nourishment is superior. They remain without anguish and are endowed with greater genuine intelligence. A people's victory over death is the one, true consolation in the face of individual perishing'.

Mr Ruyer adds that in the eyes of the new Gnostics, 'man's great task is to render culture biologically healthy. They are convinced that this task is not insurmountable, but also believe that it grows so much more difficult when culture transforms into civilisation that it will require trials and errors lasting hundreds of centuries. It is their conviction that the archetypal error that prevents man from reaching a solution lies in simplifying the issue either through biologism or through cocksure educationism'.

FIGURES

ALFRED FABRE-LUCE

IN *LES CENT PREMIERS JOURS DE GISCARD*,[1] Mr Alfred Fabre-Luce[2] has chosen to sing the praise of an 'enlightened and tolerant government' and its 'exceptionally intelligent and open' leaders. Not only is Mr Giscard-d'Estaing his own master but also 'the master of time'. With the following nuance: 'He hopes to achieve grand political ambitions thanks to an ever-growing authority, an authority that events may not end up bestowing upon him'. As for Mr François Mitterrand, he 'has already returned to the ease of opposition, to the delight of criticism, to the raging purity of all those who need not worry about responsibility'.

The author is clearly under a spell and expresses the following reservation: 'We are under threat of intelligence'. It is, however, a concern that is quickly warded off: 'France has already experienced worse perils'. Such a tone is surprising; in the past, readers were accustomed to more acerbic ferocity.

Some time ago, Mr Alfred Fabre-Luce proceeded to assess himself:

> At times, I turned towards the Right, at others towards the Left, so as to face what seemed the gravest danger to me.

So as to publish his 'Memoirs' in *J'ai vécu plusieurs siècles*,[3] he chose to give his work a dialogue-based form. He thus responded to the questions asked

1 TN: Giscard's First Hundred Days.

2 TN: Alfred Fabre-Luce (May 16th, 1899–May 17th, 1983) was a French journalist.

3 TN: I Have Lived Through Several Centuries.

by a couple named Henriette and Philippe Levillain,[4] both of whom held an 'agrégé'.[5] Additionally, he proceeded to answer a large number of questions that he himself had asked. But it is not necessarily the 'interviewee' that played the part of the accomplice.

Mr Fabre-Luce lived through three centuries, meaning three *eras* whose very span seemed a hundred years long to him and during which he fought on two distinct fronts. The first century came to an end around the 1930s. The second, characterised by excessive syncopation ('One witnessed a simultaneous acceleration in the pace of events and the accentuation of contrasts'), did not end in 1945, lasting instead until about 1960 ('Seen from the 1960s, existentialism is an outdated notion'). The third one, which we are still experiencing, might last even less.

Following a brief career as an embassy attaché, Alfred Fabre-Luce shifted his gaze towards journalism and literature and has not ceased to write since the onset of the 1920s.

His memories of what came before that include a bourgeois family, a Piedmontese nanny, lessons at Jeanson-de-Sailly and then attending the *Collège de France*. With a simple formula, he justifies his own nostalgia:

> To be young is to be in love with oneself.

His first bouts of admiration belonged to Léon Blum[6] and Joseph Caillaux.[7] Even at that time, however, his personal sentiments were at odds with the

---

4 TN: It is all too clear that Henriette and Philippe are entirely fictitious characters, since their surname literally means 'the evil or villainous one'.

5 TN: The 'agrégé' is the highest teaching diploma in France.

6 TN: André Léon Blum (9th April, 1872–30th March, 1950) was a French politician. He was widely considered to belong to the moderate Left and became Prime Minister of France on three different occasions. When Germany defeated France in 1940, he became a staunch opponent of Vichy France. Tried by Vichy on trumped-up charges, he was imprisoned in the Buchenwald concentration camp. After the war, he resumed a transitional leadership role in French politics, helping to bring about the French Fourth Republic.

7 TN: Joseph-Marie-Auguste Caillaux (30th March, 1863–22nd November, 1944) was a French politician of the Third Republic. He was among the leaders of the French Radical party and became Minister of Finance, but his progressive views led him to oppose the military and thus alienated him from his conservative counterparts.

prevailing catchwords. In *Le secret de la République*[8] (Grasset, 1938), he mentions his first campaigns: 'Against Poincaré's[9] "Germany will pay" and against Herriot's[10] "universal peace". Against the Ruhr war[11] and the false conciliation of the jurists. Against the Ethiopian sanctions of 1935[12] and the Rhineland abstention of 1936,[13] against the latent rise of Fascism on the 6th of February[14] and against the mismanagement of the *Front populaire*'.[15]

---

8 TN: The Secret of the Republic.

9 TN: Raymond Nicolas Landry Poincaré (20th August, 1860–15th October, 1934) was a French statesman who served three times as Prime Minister of France. He also became the President of France from 1913 to 1920 and was famous for his openly anti-German attitudes. At the Paris Peace Conference, he favoured the re-occupation of the Rhineland, which he was able to carry out in 1923 as Prime Minister.

10 TN: Édouard Marie Herriot (5th July, 1872–26th March, 1957) was a French Radical politician of the Third Republic who became Prime Minister on three occasions, in addition to spending many years as president of the Chamber of Deputies. He was also the leader of the first *Cartel des Gauches* (meaning leftist Cartel), a governmental alliance between the Radical-Socialist Party and the socialist French Section of the Workers' International (SFIO) which lasted until the end of the Popular Front (1936–38).

11 TN: The Occupation of the Ruhr (German: *Ruhrbesetzung*) was a period of military occupation of the German Ruhr valley by France and Belgium in response to the Weimar Republic's failure to make its second reparation payment of the £6.6 billion dictated by the *Triple Entente* in the aftermath of World War I.

12 TN: The 'Abyssinia Crisis' was a 1935 crisis that began with what was called the Walwal incident in the conflict between the Kingdom of Italy and the Empire of Ethiopia (then commonly known as "Abyssinia" in Europe). Although the League of Nations voted for sanctions against Italy, the latter simply ignored them and signed special agreements with both France and Britain, ultimately establishing control of Ethiopia.

13 TN: This is a reference to the marching of German troops into the Rhineland on March 7th, 1936. The action was directed against the Treaty of Versailles, which had laid out the terms subsequently accepted by the defeated Germany. Surprisingly, the Allies simply abstained from any adequate response.

14 TN: The 6th February crisis (1934) was an anti-parliamentarist street demonstration in Paris organised by several 'far-Right' leagues and culminating in a riot on the *Place de la Concorde*, near the seat of the French National Assembly. In reaction, the police shot and killed fifteen demonstrators. The events are considered to have been a very real attempt to overthrow the *Cartel des gauches* government elected in 1932.

15 TN: The Popular Front or *Front populaire* was an interwar alliance of Left-wing movements that included the French Communist Party (PCF), the French Section of the Workers' International (SFIO) and the Radical and Socialist Party.

He specifies: 'This position-taking of mine has classified me alternately as a leftist and a rightist, yet always as an opposer'. Throughout his existence, he has manifested the same repugnance for Manicheanism. As for systematic minds, they have reproached him for wanting to be a partisan of ideal truth instead of a plain partisan. No matter what subject he has approached, however, what he has stated has always been both new and sound. He writes: 'A manifestation of mental independence arouses the hostility of all fanaticisms'; which is precisely what oafish hearts cannot bear.

Already in *Le secret de la République*, he deplored the fact that 'the French showed no interest in what was causing their demise'.

In 1924, he releases *La Victoire.*[16] Raymond Poincaré proceeds to ask newspapers not to mention this book. In 1936, he is hounded for an article on the devaluation of the French franc. Under the Occupation, his *Journal de la France*[17] results in great success for him, as well as in two arrests: first at the hands of German services in July 1943, then in September 1944 at the hands of those who conducted the purge. 'The Lorraine cross cannot serve as an emblem for our entire country', he would write.

In 1942, in his *Anthologie de la nouvelle Europe*[18] (Plon), he presents a list of thinkers for whom 'man is an heir', to use the expression coined by Maurras[19] and then adopted by Moeller van den Bruck;[20] a list that associated the names of Pascal, Proudhon, Valéry, Stefan George, Drieu la Rochelle, Paul Nizan, Kolbenheyer, Hans Grimm, Renan, Machiavelli, H. S. Chamberlain, Péguy, Friedrich Sieburg, Nietzsche, Michelet, Wagner and Napoleon. In it, he declares: 'Realism: such is the foremost virtue of those who shall reconstruct the

16 TN: The Victory.

17 TN: The Journal of France.

18 TN: Anthology of the New Europe.

19 TN: Charles-Marie-Photius Maurras (20th April, 1868–16th November, 1952) was a French writer, politician, poet, and critic. He contributed to organising the *Action française*, a political movement that was monarchist, anti-Semitic, anti-parliamentarist, and counter-revolutionary, also acting as its principal philosopher.

20 TN: Arthur Moeller van den Bruck (23rd April, 1876–30th May, 1925) was a German cultural historian and author. He is most famous for his controversial book entitled *Das Dritte Reich* (The Third Reich, 1923), which advocated German nationalism and had a major impact on the Conservative Revolutionary movement and, at a later point, on the Nazi Party itself (which he did not, however, support).

national, aristocratic and revolutionary Europe'. The book arouses indignation within the extreme Left but is also banned in Germany: it highlights 'the existing contradiction between the national aspect of the German revolution and its pretension to exporting it'.

Shortly after the Liberation, *Au nom des silencieux*[21] is published, a book that denounces the excesses committed by the Resistance. The book is seized, as is another one bearing the title *Double prison*:[22] what memories! Next in line is *Haute Cour*[23] (1962), a pamphlet targeting General de Gaulle that would have to be printed in Switzerland.

It is thus very knowingly that Mr Fabre-Luce criticises all 'censorships', whether conducted by the Resistance, 'historical' Gaullism or the extreme Left. Here is an example:

> In the wake of World War I, one was prohibited from saying that responsibility for the conflict did not rest upon a single country. For greater safety, the ones that drafted the treaty of Versailles[24] proceeded to turn Germany's unique responsibility into the very foundation of the resulting damage reparations. One thus thought it necessary to nurture this myth to ensure the payments.

Fifty years later, 'Communist censorship strived to conceal the fact that our interwar history had not been a mere historical clash of good guys and bad guys separated by an ideological line. And above all, it forbade us to reveal that Stalin, sheltered by an official policy of support of democracies, had always sought an agreement with Hitler. On its part, Gaullist censorship banned people from saying that the armistice had been justified in some regards and that the Vichy government[25] had initially been a legitimate one'.

---

21 TN: In the Name of the Silent Ones.

22 TN: A Double Prison.

23 TN: High Court.

24 TN: The Treaty of Versailles (French: *Traité de Versailles*) was the most significant of the peace treaties that brought an end to World War I. It included the so-called 'War Guilt Clause', one of the most important and controversial stipulations requiring Germany and its allies to accept full responsibility for causing all the loss and damage resulting from the war.

25 TN: The Vichy government was the official government of France after Germany defeated and occupied it at the start of World War II. It was essentially a puppet government controlled by the Germans.

In 1966, Alfred Fabre-Luce publishes *L'Histoire démaquillée*,[26] in which he states that 'such disguising still continues today'.

Mr Fabre-Luce has declared himself an impassioned anti-Gaullist. An over-passionate one, perhaps. He has devoted several books to de Gaulle: *Gaulle deux*[27] (1958), *Le plus illustre des français*[28] (1960), *Haute Cour* (1962), *Le couronnement du prince*[29] (1964), and *L'anniversaire*[30] (1971). De Gaulle's character is still an obsession for him: 'He is still present or, at least, only vanishing bit by bit. On television, only legendary programmes are dedicated to General de Gaulle, broadcasts that lack any and all serious discussion. We shall pay dearly for this hagiography'. He does remind us, however, that he was in favour of de Gaulle's return in 1958 and that the 18th of June Appeal was, in his eyes, a 'noble gesture'.

A SEXUAL POLICY

He has travelled a lot; whether over distances, through time or across the realm of ideas. Hence his 'cosmopolitan' labelling, one that he does not hesitate to bestow upon himself:

> It is above all Europe which embodies the very cosmos that I inhabit. This is not due to an arbitrary choice, but to the fact that it represents the domain of our most profound affinities and our greatest possibilities for action.

A pioneering European, Alfred Fabre-Luce has always refrained from 'confusing patriotism and propaganda'. Prior to the war, he fought against 'petty' nationalism, which was but 'a popular passion aroused and exploited by the bourgeoisie within the scope of what it considered to be its own interest: that is precisely what Poincaré represented'.

---

26 TN: Undisguised History.

27 TN: Gaulle Two.

28 TN: The Most Illustrious Frenchman.

29 TN: The Crowning of the Prince.

30 TN: The Anniversary.

Nowadays, he believes that the 'Franco-German couple' which Jules Romains[31] spoke of may yet become the dominant element in the European whole.

The word 'couple' is quite appropriate. Having been feminine during the Romantic period, Germany reclaimed its virility with Bismarck.[32] Robert Brasillach[33] once said: 'We have slept with Germany'. To which Mr Fabre-Luce adds: 'One could extend this history to include our time and say, for instance, that placing the burden of guilt upon Germany has been an attempt to feminise the latter and that Brandt had evaded the attempt by combining his kneeling before a Jewish memorial[34] (in an attitude of humility) with a domination of the German mark that restored Germany's virile strength'.

From page to page, figures emerge as if drawn with a quill: André Malraux,[35] Mussolini, Oppenheimer, and also Ben-Gurion:[36]

> He recited to me the long list of peoples mentioned in the Bible. Save for the Jews, all of them had long since vanished. This fact aroused a legitimate sort of pride in Ben-Gurion. This atheistic man had ensured that the Bible was taught in schools so that all small Israelites could hear the following words uttered by a God that he himself did not believe in: "I shall make the Jews into a great nation".

---

31 TN: Jules Romains, born Louis Henri Jean Farigoule (26th August, 1885–14th August, 1972), was a French poet and author and the founder of the literary movement known as 'Unanimism'.

32 TN: Otto Eduard Leopold, Prince of Bismarck, Duke of Lauenburg (1st April, 1815–30th July, 1898) was a conservative Prussian statesman who dominated German and European affairs from the 1860s until 1890 and was the first Chancellor of the German Empire between 1871 and 1890.

33 TN: Robert Brasillach (31st March, 1909–6th February, 1945) was a French author and journalist and the editor of *Je suis partout*, a nationalist newspaper. He was executed for advocating collaborationism, denunciation and incitement to murder. The execution remains the focus of controversy, because Brasillach was executed for his 'intellectual crimes' and not his military or political actions.

34 TN: The term *Kniefall von Warschau*, also known as *Warschauer Kniefall* (both meaning 'Warsaw genuflection' in German), refers to a gesture of humility and penance by German Chancellor Willy Brandt towards the victims of the Warsaw Ghetto Uprising.

35 TN: André Malraux (3rd November, 1901–23rd November, 1976) was a French novelist and art theorist who was also involved in politics, acting as France's Minister of Information and Minister of Cultural Affairs under de Gaulle.

36 TN: Born David Grün, David Ben-Gurion (16th October, 1886–1st December, 1973) was the primary national founder of the State of Israel and the first Prime Minister of Israel.

Already in 1929, following a trauma in his youth (namely the death of his brother), Alfred Fabre-Luce took position 'in favour of a sexual policy', particularly when declaring his support for the use of contraceptives.

And this is what he wrote in 1933 in *Pamphlet* magazine (which he himself had founded):

> A tendency has manifested itself to acknowledge the limitation of births as an ineluctable fact and to humanise it by gradually replacing clandestine abortion with its legal counterpart and legal abortion with contraception. Let us hope that France is not sidelined in this movement, a movement that represents civilisational progress.

To which he then added that 'none of the prohibitions based on an absolute respect of life could ever be maintained'. At the time, such audacity was scandalous.

Thirty years later, in *Six milliards d'insectes*[37] (Arthaud), he mentioned the limits of demographic expansion ('the Black Friday when every man will only have one square metre at his disposal'). Published in 1962, the book shocked its readers. Indeed, ecology had not yet become fashionable.

Rejecting both hypernatalists and Malthusians,[38] Mr Fabre-Luce attempts, in matters of familial planning and abortions, to remain faithful to the 'divine measure' advocated by the Greeks. Both in China and Latin America, he was struck by the following remark: 'All women long to have children, but there are none who want to have a child on a yearly basis'. He views reproduction as 'a tragedy involving four characters: a man, a woman, a child, and the state'.

He simultaneously denounces both the pan-sexualism pervading modern times ('A mother grows concerned and seeks counsel because her thirteen-year-old daughter is still a virgin') and the trend of 'psychoanalytical and guilt-inducing eroticism'.

He puts scientism and spiritualism on equal footing for being mere 'unilateralisms'.

This, however, does not prevent him from appreciating the perspectives unveiled by science. This is what he states in *Six milliards d'insectes*:

---

37 TN: Six Billion Insects.

38 TN: Meaning both those who would increase natality and those who would curb it.

> We underestimate hereditariness these days. As background differences are reduced through class levelling and communicational progress, we will be driven to recognise its importance. Both in agriculture and animal breeding, eugenics has triumphed around us. The vegetables, fruit, eggs and meat that we consume are all the result of genetical perfecting. To claim that man is forever incapable of such progress is to confine him to a prideful solitude within nature and thus to rise up against the modern scientific movement in its entirety.

THE POWER OF CONFUSION AND THE VOLUPTUOUSNESS OF WORDS

In 1966, he publishes *La mort a changé*[39] (Gallimard), in which he quotes Valéry's[40] words: 'Death is basically the impossible: our notion of it is comprised of its *certainty* and its *impossibility*'.

Today, he remarks: 'I chose to tackle the most taboo subject of all. In this era, death seems more obscene than sex itself'. Whereas during the 19th century, one proceeded to cover up their genitals, the 20th century has led people to exhibit theirs. Hearses, by contrast, are to remain hidden.

Approaching the issue of voluntary euthanasia, Alfred Fabre-Luce has expressed his wish for mankind to become sufficiently civilised to 'temper the unavoidable disaster embodied by death'. He writes:

> To shorten someone's agony is to show respect for an existence that is nearing its end by sparing it an ultimate humiliation that would spoil it. To prolong a state of human degradation and oppose an imminent and ineluctable death by abusing our scientific resources — that is what constitutes an act of impiety, rather.

On the religious level, Mr Fabre-Luce wrote an *Open Letter to the Christians* in 1969 (Albin Michel). In it, he explains that his studies of the ancient sources of Christianity have driven him towards a kind of 'modernism' and that he is in favour of stripping the Church of all dogma. This standpoint is reminiscent

---

39 TN: Death Is Not What It Used to Be.

40 TN: Ambroise Paul Toussaint Jules Valéry (30th October, 1871–20th July, 1945) was a French poet, author, and philosopher.

of Julian Huxley's *Religion without Revelation* or perhaps even J. M. Guyau's[41] *Morale sans obligation ni sanction.*[42]

He believes that Christianity has been undergoing an irreversible transformation:

> Owing to the sole rarefication of priests, we are heading towards a profound transformation of Catholicism.

There are four traits which, from his perspective, seem characteristic of this 'third century' of ours: the importance of the media, the influence of the United States, the haunting presence of the Third World, and the new sexual morality.

The month of May 1968 saw Alfred Fabre-Luce in the streets of the Latin Quarter. The budding leftist movement aroused contradictory feelings in him, which he expressed in *Le général en Sorbonne*[43] (Table Ronde):

> Those who have not experienced the events of May 1968 in Paris have not felt a genuine passion for life.

It was also an opportunity to break with 'the bourgeois milieus that feign to despise an intellectual movement to which they have otherwise yielded by using its vocabulary and imagery on a daily basis'.

Simultaneously, in *Les mots qui bougent*[44] (Fayard), he denounced the power of confusion and the voluptuousness of words which intellectuals indulge in:

> One imposes one's own vocabulary so as to take hold of people's minds, proceeding from one ostentation to another in order to captivate people. One attracts adolescents with slogans, just as one would attract larks using mirror reflections…

He remarks that 'an unequal society (moderately unequal and rather mobile) is more dynamic than a rigidly caste-based economy or one that has been levelled at the very bottom'.

---

41 TN: Jean-Marie Guyau (28th October, 1854–31st March, 1888) was a French philosopher and poet.

42 TN: A Morality Devoid of Obligations and Sanctions.

43 TN: The General at the Sorbonne.

44 TN: Moving Words.

To be successively liked and disliked by everyone — such seems to have been the fate of this bourgeois liberal, who wanted to act as a witness to his own age. As an introverted person, he has never lost his taste for navigating across still waters; yet he has never ceased to launch 'fiery attacks that were never meant to last'. And there he is now, having already lived through three quarters of a 'chronological' century. Is he too young? Or too old, perhaps? Here is his answer:

> A certain tension between the young and the old is desirable. It helps young people desist infantilisms, while enabling the elderly to maintain their combativeness.

J'ai vécu plusieurs siècles, an essay by Alfred Fabre-Luce. Fayard, 405 pages.
Les cent premiers jours de Giscard, an essay by Alfred Fabre-Luce. Laffont, 275 pages.

ROGER CAILLOIS

THE *ACADÉMIE FRANÇAISE* INCLUDES AT least one stone and insect lover among its ranks: sixty-three-year-old Roger Caillois, who was elected in 1971 to replace Jérôme Carcopino.

Displaying a strong neckline akin to that of a Spanish *feria* bull, thick eyebrows and black, straight hair, Roger Caillois was born in Reims, yet his appearance is more suggestive of the South of France. His vocation ripened in Latin America. A translator of both Jorge Luis Borges'[45] and Pablo Neruda's[46] works, he runs the *Croix du Sud*[47] collection at Gallimard publishing.

---

45 TN: Jorge Francisco Isidoro Luis Borges Acevedo (24th August, 1899–14th June, 1986) was an Argentine short-story writer, essayist, poet and translator. He is considered an important figure in Spanish-language literature. His best-known books, *Ficciones* (Fictions) and *El Aleph* (The Aleph), published in the 1940s, are compilations of short stories interconnected by common themes, including dreams, labyrinths, philosophy, libraries, mirrors, fictional writers, and mythology.

46 TN: Ricardo Eliécer Neftalí Reyes Basoalto (12th July, 1904–23rd September, 1973), better known as Pablo Neruda, was a Chilean poet-diplomat and politician. He managed to get himself noticed as a poet when he was only thirteen years old and wrote in a variety of styles. In 1971, he was awarded the Nobel Prize for Literature.

47 TN: Southern Cross.

'Ibero-American authors will become the great literatures of tomorrow', he says.

As a shy nineteen-year-old adolescent, he participated in the 'surrealist insurrection' and adhered to André Breton's[48] group. Three years later, he reacted to the bewilderment triggered by the 'jumping beans' affair.

Someone had brought Breton some 'jumping beans' from Mexico. At the sight of the 'hazardous movements that these objects spontaneously made', Breton was ecstatic. Caillois, whose surrealism had not affected his common sense, took it upon himself to open the beans up, discovering the tiny worms that made them swirl. This manifestation of 'vulgar rationalism' caused him to be 'excommunicated'.

A MASTERED WORLD

Caillois' whole career alternated between two different levels: that of an instinctive attraction to anything marvellous and that of his wilful reaction against irrationalism. We are indebted to him for establishing the logical and perhaps even scientific analysis of the great categories of imaginative life: the poetic, the fantastical, and the sacred.

In 1938, while working as a professor in Beauvais, he contributed to the founding of the *Collège de sociologie*, in cooperation with Georges Bataille and Michel Leiris. A year later, he left France for Argentina, where he ended up trapped following the onset of hostilities. Soon, he proceeded to establish the French Institute of Higher Studies in Buenos Aires and began publishing the *Lettres françaises*[49] magazine, before initiating his traveling and meeting with Pablo Neruda and Georges Bernanos.[50] In 1944, he returned to France with the *Pasteur Vallery-Radot* mission.

---

48 TN: André Breton (18th February, 1896–28th September, 1966) was a French author, poet, and anti-fascist. He is renowned for having been the founder of Surrealism. His writings include the first Surrealist Manifesto (*Manifeste du surréalisme*) of 1924, in which he defined surrealism as 'pure psychic automatism'.

49 TN: French Letters.

50 TN: Louis Émile Clément Georges Bernanos (20th February, 1888–5th July, 1948) was a French writer who fought as a soldier in World War I. A Roman Catholic with monarchist tendencies, he condemned what he considered to be French defeatism in World War II. Many of his books have been translated into English and published in the USA and Great Britain.

Then, in 1952, he launched a magazine called *Diogène*, which focused on 'diagonal sciences' (meaning philosophy and human sciences) and whose editor-in-chief he remains. He is also the head of the cultural development division at the UNESCO, having previously been in charge of literature. His main works include *Les impostures de la poésie*[51], *L'homme et le sacré*,[52] *Babel, Le rocher de Sisyphe*,[53] *Poétique de Saint-John Perse*,[54] *Au coeur du fantastique*,[55] and *L'écriture des pierres*[56] (1970).

His work on Saint-John Perse[57] is proof of his great interest in the kind of poetry that is fraught with order, splendour and hierarchy and that acts as a perfect response to Julien Gracq's[58] definition: 'The poetry of a mastered world, arranged in a noble fashion; the poetry of Achilles' shield and the enumeration of ships'.

Keeping his distance from any symbolism defined as an 'attempt to achieve absolute unrealism, an obstinate propensity for reducing things to a more or less flawed representation of some transcending entity' (Jacques Delort, *L'étique européenne à travers l'oeuvre de Saint-John Perse*,[59] in *Etudes et recherches*[60] number 2, May 1975), Perse had always preferred to embrace and glorify 'the tragic ruins of what is real'. In his work, in which he simultaneously proclaims the nobleness of the flesh and the 'innocence of the senses', he never ceases to underline the twofold power of heroism and nostalgia.

'Neither the situation of the dead nor that of the weak is any of our concern', he declares (*Vents*,[61] I, 6).

---

51 TN: The Deceptions of Poetry.

52 TN: Man and the Sacred.

53 TN: The Sisyphean Boulder.

54 TN: The Poetics of Saint-John Perse.

55 TN: At the Heart of the Fantastical.

56 TN: Stone Writings.

57 TN: 'Saint-John Perse' was one of the pseudonyms used by Alexis Leger (31st May, 1887–20th September, 1975). Leger was a French poet-diplomat who won the 1960 Nobel Prize of Literature 'for the soaring flight and evocative imagery of his poetry.'

58 TN: Born Louis Poirier, Julien Gracq (27th July, 1910–22nd December, 2007) was a French writer.

59 TN: European Ethics, as Seen Through the Work of Saint-John Perse.

60 TN: Studies and Research.

61 TN: Winds.

In a letter to Roger Caillois, Saint-John Perse wrote: 'It seems to me that the very philosophy of the poet could perhaps be essentially reduced to the old, elementary "rheism" of ancient thought; just like that of our pre-Socratics in the West'. Poetry must embody 'a powerful chanting for men, like a shivering that spreads through an ironwood' (*Anabase*,[62] VI).

Alain Bosquet[63] writes: 'At the start of the book that he dedicated to it, the relationship between Roger Caillois and poetry is that of a man falling prey to a demon'. The demon is, however, quickly tamed. Caillois is the enemy of disorder, so much so that he longs to extend the empire of reason to the heights where imagination had hitherto been alone to roam, and a little too comfortably at that. For it is up to poetry to prove itself so as to justify its own existence.

'Yes indeed, I was so intolerant that I felt that it was not enough for a thing to exist to have the right to be present', Roger Caillois once wrote.

POETRY = EQUILIBRIUM + EFFORT

In contrast to the poet-prophets who 'attempt to dazzle people', he mentions the example of Saint-John Perse, the poet of grandeur and reality. He declares: 'Poetry is not merely a matter of words but, above all, a question of things'. What things, then? Rocks, insects, nature; life, basically.

A crucial stage: Caillois discovers the 'periodic table of elements' developed by Russian scientist Mendeleev. It serves as evidence of the fact that if the world is indeed infinite, the number of elements it comprises is not. And just like in the theory of sets, these elements only acquire their respective meaning in relation to each other: they only *exist* through interaction. Genuine *novelties* are simply new *combinations*. Using simple series-based logical deduction, Mendeleev incidentally succeeded in designating the elements that were already known, as well as those that remained to be discovered (which, indeed, they were). Mr Caillois writes:

---

62 TN: Anabasis.

63 TN: Born Anatoliy Bisk, Alain Bosquet (28th March, 1919–8th March, 1998) was a French poet.

> Lifting the psychedelic veil of the goddess of Sais[64], Mendeleev was able to show that it concealed neither disorder nor a swarm of larvae, nor the rising of saps, yeast and delirium; it was, instead, a network of quantifiable relations, a more severe sort of drunkenness. (*Cases d'un échiquier,*[65] Gallimard, 1970)

Roger Caillois then defines poetry using a single formula: equilibrium and effort, meaning the opposite of verbal 'gesticulation'. He targets those who confuse the avantgarde with the breaching of syntactic rules:

> Poetry is both the art of verses and the art of image. It could be either one of the two, or both at the same time. Through the use of verse, it strives to be unalterable, while using images in an attempt to be inexhaustible. When the two virtues coincide, the grandest poetry is attained. (*L'art poétique*[66])

Having taken it upon himself to clarify poetic discourse, Roger Caillois 'purges' another key domain: that of the fantastical. Paradoxically, he demonstrates that the latter cannot be felt as such by a strictly rational mentality. 'In a world of miracles, the extraordinary loses its potency'. What the domain of fantasy requires is the presence of Dionysus and Apollo, side by side. In the preface to the first edition of his beautiful *Anthologie du fantastique*[67] (Club français du livre, 1958), Mr Caillois remarks:

> The fantasy of terror comes across as an absolute and relatively late invention of scholarly literature. [...] Fantastical literature is, above all, synonymous with *playing* with fear. Any certitude displayed by the adepts only serves to exacerbate the readers' *critical* mindset.

---

64 TN: Neith (alternatively Nit, Net, or Neit) was an ancient Egyptian deity who was said to be the first and prime creator. She was the tutelary goddess of Sais and is sometimes equated with the goddess Isis. The 'veil of Isis' is a metaphor and allegorical artistic motif in which nature is personified as the goddess Isis covered by a veil or mantle, representing the inaccessibility of nature's secrets.

65 TN: The Squares of a Chessboard.

66 TN: Poetic Art.

67 TN: Anthology of the Fantastical.

Roger Caillois has never forgotten about the 'jumping beans'. His entire work is a justification of the following statement by Mme du Deffand:[68] 'Do you believe in ghosts? — No, but I dread them'.

Roger Caillois, an essay by Alain Bosquet. Seghers, 182 pages.

RAYMOND ABELLIO

> A life only allows one to genuinely self-reflect once its meaning has become clear to one, when the veils of naïveté, ignorance and activism have fallen and it has thus experienced its second birth, in the same way that Buddha is said to have been born twice.
>
> RAYMOND ABELLIO

NIETZSCHE ONCE SAID: 'THE MAN of the future is the one that shall be endowed with the longest memory'. With his bald temples and rough accent, seventy-year-old Raymond Abellio believes that he has experienced two births. His darkly framed and thick glasses give him the look of a debonair mutant.

FROM THE ARIÈGE TO PARIS

In 1966, he declared to Marie-Thérèse de Brosses:[69] 'Were I to recount the story of my life, I would divide it into three parts which I would title in the following order: submission, rebellion, and liberty' (*Entretiens avec Raymond Abellio*,[70] Belfond).

He has since begun to keep his own journals. The first volume gives a presentation of the milieu he originated from: his family came from Toulouse and his ancestors were either carters or journeymen carpenters — a peasant

[68] TN: Marie Anne de Vichy-Chamrond, marquise du Deffand (1697–23rd September, 1780) was a French hostess and patron of the arts.

[69] TN: Marie-Thérèse de Brosses is a journalist, writer and reporter.

[70] TN: Interviews with Raymond Abellio.

autarchy that characterised his forefathers. As a schoolboy, Georges Soulès (by his real name) was always the first in everything save for catechism:

> For us, the real priests of this waning society were the secular teachers, men that shared the modest destiny of clergymen but whose vocation was quite stronger; they were those for whom God had become the end and the ideal accomplishment of our humanity in motion.

Although never a prophet in his own region, it is to Occitania that Soulès belongs above all. His mother was 'some kind of Albigensian or Cathar[71] that had descended from the uplands of the Ariège'. This is an important fact, because what the Cathars denounced as capital sin was 'the scandal of an impersonal God that burdened with incomprehensible wrath a world that He himself had created in its actual shape and form'. The Pope was the father that they denied. 'The martyrdom of Albi was, from the West's perspective, nothing but the repetition of the Son's martyrdom'.

Having turned twenty, the young Occitan goes north to Paris. He is accepted at the local polytechnic school, 'a place characterised by the subtlest and the greatest of social transmutations'. He then convinces himself to participate in the destruction of the old order. His taste for rigorousness guides him towards socialism. Whenever on an outing, Soulès the polytechnician purchases *Le Quotidien*[72] and *L'Humanité*.[73]

1931 marks the advent of the 'X-crise' group.[74] In 1932, the Polytechnic Centre of Collectivist Studies is born, with Jules Moch and Louis Vallon. Georges Soulès becomes its first secretary, before joining the Socialist Youth

---

71 TN: The Cathars were a Gnostic group that dominated the South of France well into our era. They were simply slaughtered in what is known as the 'Albigensian crusade', which is considered by many scholars and historians to have been plain and simple genocide.

72 TN: There are several newspapers called 'Le Quotidien', but the author is clearly referring to a daily newspaper published in France by *Cartel des Gauches* between the World Wars.

73 TN: *L'Humanité* is a French daily newspaper. It was formerly an organ of the French Communist Party and still maintains links to it.

74 TN: The *Groupe X-Crise* was a French technocratic movement created in 1931 in response to the 1929 Wall Street stock market crash and the Great Depression. Founded by former students of the Polytechnic School (nicknamed 'X'), it advocated economic planification as opposed to the then dominant ideology of classical liberalism, which was considered to have failed.

movement. Inside the SFIO,[75] he struggles for the revolutionary Left (whose Trotskyite and pacifistic members were hostile towards Blum) and for the *Redressement socialiste*[76] tendency. Meetings, activism, and the first plots. In 1936, Soulès becomes a member of Jules Moch's[77] cabinet. Between 1937 and 1939, he is part of the steering committee of the French Socialist Party.

Then comes the rise of Fascism. This turn of events unravels all analyses. Soulès thus evolves and breaks with Marxism. In 1946, he publishes, in cooperation with André Mahé, a work entitled *La fin du nihilisme*[78] (Sorlot), a collection of conferences held in 1940–41 at the Oflag IV D in Germany, where he was imprisoned. In it, he criticises the numbing of instincts and the mistakes made by finalistic ideologies. He heralds the age of the revolutionary combatant, the perfect harmony between man and history. As written by André Mahé and Georges Soulès, 'there has always been some sort of dualism expressed in the West's history. And even in Europe's own behaviour has this twofold attraction been affirmed, this temptation to which it has alternately been subjected by virile and feminine values, by the values of strength and charity'.

They thus conclude:

> It is no longer Happiness that we seek; what we seek instead is the triumph of Will and Life.

Having returned to Paris, Georges Soulès becomes the auxiliary of the blood and soil 'egregores' and, soon enough, along with Mahé, the Joint Secretary of the 'second' Social Revolutionary Movement (MSR), the movement which outlived Eugène Deloncle[79] and was gradually drained of its former 'balaclava-disguised' activism.

---

75 TN: The previously-mentioned French Section of the Workers' International, a French socialist political party that has since vanished.

76 TN: Socialist Recovery.

77 TN: Jules Salvador Moch (15h March, 1893–1st August, 1985) was a French politician who also fought for France in World War II.

78 TN: The End of Nihilism.

79 TN: Eugène Deloncle (20th June, 1890–17th January, 1944) was a French engineer and Fascist leader.

Following the Liberation, Georges Soulès disappears. In 1946, however, a novel entitled *Heureux les pacifiques*[80] is published. Its hero, Robert Saveilhac, bears a strong resemblance to the vanished man. As for the author, his name is Raymond Abellio.

MEN OF KNOWLEDGE AND POWER

'It was in the 1930s, upon reading *The Crusade Against the Grail* by German writer Otto Rahn, that I first thought of choosing Abellio as a pseudonym. Rahn reminded his readers that Abellio had been the name of a Celtic god, or rather a Celtiberian deity, Apollo's Phoenician avatar'. With the surname 'Soulès' originating from the word *sol*, meaning 'sun', 'the forgotten presence of a solar god in a region entirely impregnated with magical blood raised the enigma to a level of almost religious mystery'.

Not only has Mr Abellio changed his name, but he has also met a spiritual master. Former teacher Pierre de Combas (represented by Pujolhac in *Heureux les pacifiques*) had, as always, come at the right moment:

> He proceeded to explain to me that the world would change without my involvement and that the best means to trigger real change in it actually lay in my ability to understand myself.

The man of *knowledge* thus contrasts with the man of *power*. And what is knowledge? 'The thought according to which everything that exists has *meaning*, paired with the latter's conquest'. Nowadays, however, wisdom must once again be steeped in secrecy. 'Our era is too passionate to handle the presence of wise men at the head of the state'.

Politics leads to the making of choices, and Raymond Abellio has availed himself of the freedom that allows one not to choose anymore. He states:

> Life, and particularly political existence, has taught me that no one ever "sacrifices" anything: this is true of the most devoted militant, who follows the path of *destiny* that seems most exhilarating for him.

'I have not voted a single time since the war; for as long as thirty years. Politics is no longer any of my business, you see: I am no longer able to choose', he now

80 TN: Blessed Are the Peacemakers.

adds. (He does remark, however, that 'Europe is currently being colonised by the US-Russian sphere of influence through the presence of international companies. The same process is being conducted by Russian Marxism on the level of intellectual research' — as stated in an interview with *Question de*, issue number 4, third trimester 1974)

Raymond Abellio's own *destiny* is henceforth influenced by the Hebraic Bible, the Bhagavad-Gita,[81] Keyserling,[82] Berdyaev[83] and phenomenology.[84] The stages that his thoughts have gone through are epitomised by significant works bearing highly revelatory titles: *Vers un nouveau prophétisme*[85] (1948), *Les yeux d'Ezéchiel sont ouverts*[86] (1950), *Assomption de l'Europe*[87] (1954), *La fosse de Babel*[88] (1962), *La structure absolue*[89] (1965), and *La fin de l'ésotérisme*[90] (1973).

In *Assomption de l'Europe*, he reaffirms his conviction:

> It is not into this world that one must nowadays put some order, but into our own thoughts. We have conducted a sufficient number of experiments in our world, and it is not in vain that we have borne the weight to such heights. The world is *here*, not elsewhere. [...] At the most sensitive core of Europe, in the very place that it believes itself most absent from, one witnesses the accumulation of the ultimate refusal and attention which, through the mysterious reversibility of redemption, actually embody its genuine presence. [...] I have been attempting to visualise what those hours of transfiguration might be like on the day when

81 TN: The Bhagavad Gita, often referred to simply as the Gita, is a 700-verse Hindu scripture written in Sanskrit and belonging to the Hindu epic Mahabharata.

82 TN: Count Hermann Alexander von Keyserling (20th July, 1880–26th April, 1946) was a Baltic German philosopher.

83 TN: Nikolai Alexandrovich Berdyaev (18th March, 1874–24th March, 1948) was a Russian political and Christian religious philosopher who placed great emphasis on the existential spiritual significance of human freedom and the human person.

84 TN: Phenomenology is the philosophical (or possibly psychological) study of the structures of (subjective) experience and consciousness. It was established by Edmund Husserl in the early years of the 20th century.

85 TN: Towards a New Prophetism.

86 TN: Ezekiel's Eyes Are Open.

87 TN: The Assumption of Europe.

88 TN: The Pit of Babel.

89 TN: The Absolute Structure.

90 TN: The End of Esotericism.

warriors shall turn into priests and, no longer having anything to defend that has not been left in ruins, discover themselves to be the wealthiest men in the world.

WITHIN A SOUL AND A BODY

At the threshold of 1971, Mr Abellio asked himself two questions: 'Is it in my power to seize the apparent disorder afflicting my daily physical and mental life, to master it by means of the sole clarity of my spirit and to bring to light the order that it conceals? And would I always be able to clearly justify this new order, to account for it both verbally and in writing so that, enlightened through speech, actions may be even more readily mastered?'.

It is these questions that the compendium entitled *Dans une âme et un corps*[91] strives to answer. In it, Raymond Abellio has chronicled these past years. It is a chronicle in which daily reflections, meetings and literary reviews act as props in the building of a mind that exerts itself to encompass it all.

Many figures surface in it, including Marie-Thérèse de Brosses; Dominique de Roux;[92] Doctor Hubert Larcher, the head of *Revue métapsychique;*[93] Elisabeth Antébi, who authored a rather fanciful (and highly partial) inquiry into contemporary esotericism; Maryse Choisy, who was Teilhard de Chardin's[94] friend and wrote *Un mois chez les filles*,[95] before launching the Global Alliance of Religions; in addition to some rather picturesque individuals such as the mysterious Mrs A., the tenacious propagandist of the *Panharmonie*[96] monthly bulletin, an organ of the 'Association for Full-Scale Individual and Collective Harmony and Complete Oecumenism, i.e. the French section of the World Spiritual Council'. Mrs A. bears a striking resemblance to baroness Cramouillard, the president of the Universal Mystical Union depicted by

---

91 TN: Within a Soul and a Body.

92 TN: Dominique de Roux (17th September, 1935–29th March, 1977) was a French author and publisher.

93 TN: Parapsychological Magazine.

94 TN: Pierre Teilhard de Chardin (1st May, 1881–10th April, 1955) was a French idealist philosopher and Jesuit priest who trained as a paleontologist and geologist, contributing to the discovery of the 'Peking Man'.

95 TN: A Month Among the Girls.

96 TN: Pan-Harmony.

Mr Gabriel Matzneff[97] in his novel *Nous n'irons plus au Luxembourg*[98] (Table ronde, 1972).

In a disorderly fashion, Raymond Abellio mentions all that he sets his heart on: Saint Augustine and the Tao, the debate between Husserl and Heidegger,[99] Xavier Sallantin's[100] work on Chinese epistemology, Wittgenstein's[101] logic ('A man who knew how to be quiet'), and the madness of Antonin Artaud.[102]

He has attempted to write an essay on *The Foundations of Cosmology*, in cooperation with Charles Hirsch, a polytechnician of Hungarian descent and a disappointed communist. It was initially a matter of 'systematising the use of quaternity'. Mr Abellio had already proposed replacing the ancient tripartite distinction between sovereign priests, warriors and growers with a four-caste social division: men of knowledge, men of power, managers and implementers. This time, however, the purpose is to go further. 'We are in the process of demonstrating the identity[103] of both *Yijing* logic and the dialectic of absolute structure, which reconcile and even unify structure and genesis'. There is an alleged connection between the sixty-four codons of the genetic code and the sixty-four hexagrams found in the *Yijing*, the traditional manual of Chinese divination. The *quarks* of nuclear physics are also to be taken into account. It would all act as a confirmation of the 'universal combinatorial mathematics' that Leibniz dreamt of.[104]

---

97 TN: A French Writer.

98 TN: No Longer Shall We Go to Luxemburg.

99 TN: Both of whom contributed to the field of phenomenology.

100 TN: A French Philosopher.

101 TN: Ludwig Josef Johann Wittgenstein (26th April, 1889–29th April, 1951) was an Austrian-British philosopher who focused mainly on logic, the philosophy of mathematics, the philosophy of mind, and the philosophy of language.

102 TN: Antoine Marie Joseph Artaud, otherwise known as Antonin Artaud (4th September, 1896–4th March, 1948), was a French dramatist, poet, essayist, actor, and theatre director and is considered one of the major figures of both 20th-century theatre and the European avant-garde.

103 TN: In mathematics, the term 'identity' is synonymous with 'equation'.

104 TN: The Latin term *characteristica universalis*, meaning 'universal characteristic', is a universal and formal language imagined by German polymathic genius, mathematician, scientist and philosopher Gottfried Leibniz, a language with the ability to express mathematical, scientific, and metaphysical concepts.

Pursuing his approach, Abellio targets every conceivable form of triad and trinity. 'The Christian Trinity of the Father, the Son and the Holy Spirit has now been sterilising Western theology for twenty centuries: what is missing from it is the Mother and the Daughter' (Abellio may have made this remark under the influence of the Kabbalah). He reproaches Nietzsche for his 'lack of inner femininity' and quotes the following statement made by Jesus in the Gnostic gospel of Thomas: 'Every woman that makes herself male shall enter the kingdom of heaven'.

The quotes abound, many of which are truly beautiful; including the words of Goethe when targeting pure ideas: 'Planting a concept as if it were a picket'. Or this precept of the Bhagavad-Gita: 'Perform the action that is to be performed without attaching yourself to it and while renouncing its fruit'.

Abellio also quotes this reflection made by Meister Eckhart[105] on the topic of the harmful effects of 'negative criticism': 'I am often asked about what burns in hell. Authorities usually reply: "It is free individual will and self-interest"; but I say unto you: it is the "not" that is burnt out in hell'.

THE PHYSICS OF SOCIAL ENTROPY

The tragedy pervading Christianity is summarised in one sentence: 'Although *democratic* in its mysticism, it remains *aristocratic* in its gnosis and cannot manage to hold the two aspects together'.

In *La fin du nihilisme*, one already encountered the following words:

> Priests have ceased to be men that live through God and have, instead, become men who live off God.

Regarding the Church crisis, Mr Abellio writes:

> I have read that in Rome, a certain clergyman once declared, with the approval of the hierarchy, that it was necessary to strip the gesture of benediction of all magical content in the minds of the faithful. But what would then be left of it? A gentle wind? A small movement that comes and goes through the air? I say that those people's hollowness can only arouse wrath.

105 TN: Eckhart von Hochheim (c. 1260–c. 1328), commonly known as Meister Eckhart, was a German theologian, philosopher and mystic.

Marxism is equally contested. It is not a *philosophy* of history — and much less *the* philosophy of history — but a sort of *physics*. Raymond Abellio specifies:

> I call "evil" anything that encourages levelling and *uniformisation* both within nature and within man. There is natural entropy but also social entropy. As a science, Marxism embodies the physics of social entropy.

Incidentally, Marxists are but men of power, a power that lacks any and all *depth*:

> Although born of the ingenious brain of a Jew, Marxism ceases to tolerate Jewish subtleness, the *separating* power of the Jews or their perpetual openness the moment it becomes the ruling dogma. I have spied upon the stubborn faces of all the Brezhnevs[106] and the Kosygins[107] a look akin to the one found in the eyes of obstinate mules, especially when they find themselves in a group, each making sure that he avoids looking at the others. Just as we have had the blue line of the Vosges[108], they have their own red one — the Party's.

By definition, the fundamental issues of artistic creation, sexuality and metaphysics evade all social instrumentalisation. Just like his Cathar ancestors, Mr Abellio expresses his interest in them by means of esotericism. And yet he rejects facility, impersonal mysticism, and the example of 'holy women whose "I" is abolished all too quickly and whose own ecstasies seem but a copy of an ideal ecstatic state that they have supposedly heard of'. Among esoteric 'occultists', what he denounces is the 'incomprehensible' scorn that they hold for 'the West's scientific endeavours' (interview with *Question de*, op. cit.).

> I do not use the word "event" in the plural anymore, for there is but one event, one that explains them all and clarifies them retrospectively — man's departure from the sphere of time.

---

106 TN: Leonid Ilyich Brezhnev (19th December, 1906–10th November, 1982) was a Soviet politician who led the Soviet Union from 1964 to 1982 as the General Secretary of the Central Committee (CC) of the Communist Party of the Soviet Union (CPSU), presiding over the country until his passing in 1982.

107 Alexei Nikolayevich Kosygin (21st February, 1904–18th December, 1980) was a Soviet-Russian statesman during the Cold War.

108 TN: The expression 'blue line of the Vosges' is attributed to Jules Ferry (late-19th century) in the context of post-war 1870, when it served as a reminder to the French that Alsace, located on the other side of the mountains, was under German rule.

There is a *vision* connected to this affirmation — that of Asia, the receptacle of genuine intellectual Marxism, now rushing into Europe once again and thus closing the circle of the East-West dialectic that has characterised the past twenty centuries:

> That is when the extremes shall conjoin in the symbiosis of the Occitan spirit and the social physics of the East. This passion and assumption of the West shall, from our era's perspective, mark the end of the dialectic in which God became man and lead towards the adventure in which man becomes God.

As for Raymond Abellio, he believes that he already is *above* time. There is a certain self-detachment that constitutes a sort of fullness. And it is in this manner that man shall ultimately take his revenge:

> One must allow neither beings nor things to take their leave of absence. For it is up to us, when the time comes, to do so ourselves. That is when death shall have less power than us, and there shall not even be a death: for we will have internally assembled and carried off all that we have loved.

> Ever since I was born, my life has been a source of profound feelings to me, like a state of *agony* reaching towards an unknown *rebirth*, a faithful reflection of Europe's life over the past sixty years.

A SPIRIT IN THE DARKEST NIGHT

In the space of half a century, Raymond Abellio has successively overcome all the doctrines that he has turned to; or, to be more precise, what he has done is 'digested' them, for one does indeed not overcome an idea unless one ventures *to its very limit*, starting within. Hence the reason why every self-conscious ideology can only seek to eliminate the heretic whose mind is both vast and brilliant and who only became a disciple in order to better *abolish* his masters. Such is at least the logic which men of power abide by, as described by Mr Abellio himself.

This journal was bound to end with a question that betrays dissatisfaction: 'And here we are; the show is over and the night dark. What is left? If only one could respond and say: the truth within a soul and a body. But the body and the soul sink into slumber and only the spirit is wakeful. What is left, then? The answer is: no one'.

One obviously only a*vows* what one cannot pledge through *vows*.

Ma dernière mémoire,[109] recounted by Raymond Abellio. Gallimard, 226 pages.
Dans une âme et un corps, the journal of Raymond Abellio. Gallimard, 273 pages.

JULIUS EVOLA

'WHAT I AM ABOUT TO state does not concern the ordinary man of today. On the contrary, I have in mind the man who finds himself involved in today's world, even at its most problematic and paroxysmal points; yet he does not inwardly belong to such a world, nor will he give in to it. He feels, in essence, that he belongs to a different race from that of the overwhelming majority of his contemporaries' (*Ride the Tiger*).

With his barely visible aristocratic beard, emaciated face and tall stature, philosopher Julius Evola wrote for a minority of people; for the men who had remained 'standing among the ruins'. He passed away in his Corso Vittorio Emanuele home in Rome, on 11th June, 1974; he was seventy-six years old.

'It was around 15:15, just as had been predicted to him and he himself avidly desired', declared Mr Pierre Pascal, a friend of Evola's and a writer who has translated several of his books into French.

Julius Evola was, in Italy, the most eminent representative of a 'traditional' thought that he himself traced back to Joseph de Maistre,[110] Taparelli d'Azeglio[111]

---

109 TN: My Last Memory.

110 TN: Joseph-Marie, Comte de Maistre (1st April, 1753–26th February, 1821) was a French-speaking Savoyard philosopher, author, lawyer, and diplomat. He was also an advocate of social hierarchy and monarchy in the aftermath of the French Revolution.

111 TN: Born Prospero Taparelli d'Azeglio, Luigi Taparelli (1793–1862) was an Italian Catholic scholar of the Society of Jesus who was particularly concerned with the issues arising from the industrial revolution.

and Solaro della Margherita.[112] He had sometimes been compared to German Ernst Jünger[113] and, more rightfully, to French esotericist René Guénon.[114]

In the old conflict that opposed the Guelphs (i.e. the exclusive partisans of the Papacy) to the Ghibellines, for whom the Roman-Germanic Empire was, just as much as the Church itself, an institution with a supernatural character, Evola's heart led him to side with the latter.

AGAINST THE MODERN WORLD

Born in Rome on 19th May, 1898, Julius Evola experiences his first literary encounters with the works of Nietzsche, Michelstädter[115] and Otto Weininger[116] (*Sex and Character*). During World War I, he serves as an artillery officer on the battle front. Next, he participates in the avant-garde cultural movements that were, at the time, developing in Italy: Dadaism with Tristan Tzara and Futurism with Marinetti. Several poems and paintings thus see the light of day. In 1920, he publishes a brochure on *Abstract Art*, as part of the Dada collection of Zürich. The event is a consecration.

His scientific education, however, drives him to look beyond such endeavours. A first series of essays expresses his interest in philosophy (*The Theory of the Absolute Individual*, 1920), esotericism (*The Hermetic Tradition*, 1931), and the movement of ideas (*The Mask and Face of Contemporary Spiritualism*, 1932).

---

[112] TN: Clemente Solaro, Count della Margherita (21st November, 1792–12th November, 1869) was a Piedmontese statesman who was strongly attached to the principles of autocracy. He openly opposed every attempt at political innovation, which resulted in his being bitterly hated by the liberals.

[113] TN: Ernst Jünger (29th March, 1895–17th February, 1998) was a highly decorated German soldier, writer, and entomologist. Towards the end of the Cold War, his unorthodox writings about the impact of materialism on modern society were already widely regarded as conservative rather than radical nationalist.

[114] TN: René-Jean-Marie-Joseph Guénon (15th November, 1886–7th January, 1951) was a French writer and intellectual. He remains a highly influential figure in the field of metaphysics and is considered an important author of the Traditionalist School.

[115] TN: Carlo Michelstaedter or Michelstädter (3rd June, 1887–17th October, 1910) was an Italian author, philosopher, and man of letters.

[116] TN: Otto Weininger (3rd April, 1880–4th October, 1903) was an Austrian philosopher who published the posthumously acclaimed *Geschlecht und Charakter* (Sex and Character). He committed suicide at the age of twenty-three.

From 1927 to 1929, he runs the *Ur* magazine and, a year later, takes charge of *La Torre*. He explains:

> The term *ur* is an ancient denomination of "fire", but it also relates to what is "primordial" and "original" (a meaning that has been preserved in German).

The year of 1934 is marked by the publication of a crucial work: *Revolt Against the Modern World*. The book is a sort of manifesto in which Evola describes, in an effort to contrast them, 'two universal types, two a priori categories of civilisation': the *modern* world and the world of *tradition*, a tradition that associates Western esotericism (the Templar adventure and the mystery of the Grail) with a return to the sources of pre-Christian antiquity and a 'hyperborean' past.

The notion of progress is rejected from the very outset:

> Nothing seems more absurd than this idea of progress which, alongside its corollary of modern civilisational superiority, has created "positive" alibis for itself by falsifying history, injecting minds with pernicious myths and proclaiming its own superiority within the crossroads of the plebeian ideology from which it, in fact, stems.

In Evola's eyes, the modern world is 'a petrified forest with chaos at its very centre'. The history of the past two millennia has therefore not been one of progress, but one of *involution*.

Evola compares the West to a body:

> Having previously been alive and endowed with mobility, the organisms are overcome by rigidity, transforming the body into a cadaver. Then commences the terminal phase of decomposition.

He then adds:

> We have entered the final state of a cycle. The reign of the machine, the thriving of materialism and invasive egalitarianism are its clear signs. The noose of Bolshevism and Americanism, both of which are founded upon an *economistic* conception of life, tightens around European culture. We are living in the dark age of the ancient Indians (the *Kali-Yuga*), the iron age of the classical tradition, and the age of the wolf of the Nordic world. Tradition lies forgotten.

Having thus inverted the historical perspective, Evola makes no effort to conceal this methodological bias:

> The questions with which we concern ourselves most are those in which all materials of "historical" and "scientific" value matter least; those in which all that is devoid of *historical* truth and *demonstrative* power, whether myth, legend or saga, acquires, for this very reason, superior validity and thus becomes the source of a more genuine and more certain knowledge. [...] It is in this way that the Rome of legends shall speak to us in a clearer language than the worldly Rome, and the legends of Charlemagne shall enable us to gain a better understanding of what it meant to be king among the Franks than the period's chronicles and positive documents ever could. One shall thus not concern themselves much with discussions and "demonstrations". The truths which enable us to comprehend the traditional world are not those that are "taught" and "discussed". They either are or are not: one can only *remember* them.

He concludes:

> Only a return to tradition within a new, unitary European consciousness will be able to save the West.

Immediately upon its release, the book causes a great deal of commotion. Having read it, poet Gottfried Benn declares himself 'transformed'. In Evola's Italian homeland, however, the reactions are mixed. Despite his connection to Mussolini, Julius Evola has a large number of adversaries among the ranks of the Fascist Party. Philosopher Giovanni Gentile also adopts a hostile attitude. The aristocratic pessimism that emanates from Evola's work does not suit an era that practices make-to-order triumphalism, and his *Pagan Imperialism*, published in 1928, still causes severe teeth-grinding in concordatarian[117] milieus.

Evola continues to show his interest in esotericism. Following *The Hermetic Tradition*, he publishes *The Doctrine of Awakening*, which focuses on the asceticism of Buddhism, and *The Yoga of Power*. In his *Mystery of the Grail* (1937), he proceeds to study the foundations of 'the Empire's Ghibelline tradition'. He also paves the way for 'spiritual anthropology' and, abiding by

117 TN: A concordat is an agreement or treaty, particularly one between the Vatican and a secular government in matters of mutual interest.

the example of Ludwig Ferdinand Clauss (*Rasse une Seele*,[118] 1933), undertakes to define race in accordance with criteria that are not strictly biological (*The Myth of Blood*, 1937; *Synthesis of the Doctrine of Race*, 1941).

In 1945, Evola finds himself in Vienna at a time when the city suffers a violent bombardment. With his spinal column injured, he is hospitalised for several months; his legs would remain paralysed.

He returns to Italy in 1948. Two years later, in an essay entitled *Orientations*, he presents novel ideas that would later be developed in *Men Among the Ruins* (1953). Next in line are *The Metaphysics of Sex* (1958), *Ride the Tiger* (1961), *The Path of Cinnabar* (1963), *The Bow and the Club* (1968), and others.

THE ORGANIC STATE

In *Men Among the Ruins*, Evola touches upon the political question in a most straightforward manner. Addressing himself to rightist Italian youths, he proposes that they embrace 'a general vision of life and a rigorous doctrine of the state'. He contrasts the modern state with the ideal of the organic state previously praised by both Vico[119] and Fustel de Coulanges:[120] it is a state in which each has his own place, just as, in an organism, every organ has its own. He says that the state represents a *whole* that is as spiritual as it is 'physical' and is not the 'reflection' of society. What it is, instead, is the agent that *transforms* and *structures* society and, by assigning a certain destiny to it, turns a cohesionless aggregate into a genuine ensemble that has been raised to the level of political dignity.

---

118 TN: Ludwig Ferdinand Clauss (8th February, 1892–13th January, 1974) was a German anthropologist, psychologist, and influential race theorist in the Third Reich. His most renowned work is entitled *Rasse und Seele*, meaning 'The Race and the Soul'.

119 TN: Born Giovan Battista Vico, Giambattista Vico (23rd June, 1668–23rd January, 1744) was an Italian political philosopher, rhetorician, historian and jurist of the Age of Enlightenment. He criticised the expansion and development of modern rationalism and was an apologist of Classical Antiquity, a precursor of systematic and complex thought (in contrast with Cartesian analysis and other types of reductionism) and the first expositor of the fundamentals of social science and semiotics.

120 TN: Numa Denis Fustel de Coulanges (18th March, 1830–12th September, 1889) was a French historian whose first great book, *The Antique City* (1864), mirrored his in-depth knowledge of the primary Greek and Latin texts.

> The *foundation* of every genuine state lies in the transcendence of its principle, meaning of the principle of sovereignty, authority and legitimacy. It is thus to the sphere of the sacred that the ancient Roman notion of *Imperium* essentially belongs, which, in its specific sense preceding the expression of a system of supra-national territorial hegemony, designates the pure power of command, the almost mystical force and *auctoritas* assumed by whoever exercises leadership functions and possesses the quality of a leader, whether in the religious and military sphere or that of the patrician family (the *gens*) and, pre-eminently, that of the State (the *res publica*).

The state thus comes across as an essentially masculine notion. Its relations with the people (the fatherland, the nation) are analogous to those of a man with a woman or of a *pater familias* with his own family, and, within Indo-European beliefs, even those between heaven and the earth:

> In ancient Rome, the notion of state and *imperium*, of sacred power, was thus closely connected to the symbolic worship of virile heavenly divinities, of the light and of the superior world, which embodied the opposite of the obscure region of Mothers and chthonic divinities.

It was only when the *imperium*'s resources had been depleted, when the population was no longer in a state to perceive its *meaning*, that, unable to draw their legitimacy 'from above', heads of state took it upon themselves to claim it 'from below'. Such was democracy, Caesarism, dictatorship and tyranny — different systems whose power was, however, drawn from a single source (the *demos*) and which all lead to communism, whose openly declared objective is the very *suppression of the state*.

In the process, Julius Evola denounces the egalitarian illusion as mere logical absurdity:

> Several equal beings would no longer be "several" but *one*. To desire "the equality of many" thus implies a contradiction in the very terms used.

In a hierarchised society, by contrast, one could easily envision different 'levels of equality':

> With the hierarchic idea enjoying recognition, the notion of "peer" and "equal" was, in the past, oftentimes aristocratic. In Sparta, the title of *omoioi*, of equals, was exclusively applied to the elite that held the reins of power and was subject to

revocation in the event of indignity. Likewise, in ancient England, the "peer" title was, as we all know, the exclusive prerogative of lords.

Giambattista Vico, who inspired Montesquieu, had already stated:

> Initially, what men desire is bodily liberty, then the liberty of their souls, meaning freedom of thought, and equality with others; thereafter, they long to surpass their equals; finally, they strive to place their superiors beneath themselves. (*Scienza nuova*, II, 23)

Simultaneously, Julius Evola displayed great care in distinguishing between the elitism of Bonapartism and that of Machiavellianism. He viewed Bonaparte as the successor of the *condottieri* of the Renaissance, of the tribunes of the Roman plebeians and the 'popular tyrants' that emerged in ancient Greece following the decline of aristocracies. One is faced with Bonapartism whenever the leader derives his authority from *someone other than himself*, whenever he presents himself as a 'son of the people' and not as the 'representative of a more accomplished humanity that affirms a *superior principle*'.

Evola writes:

> Whereas the traditional concept of sovereignty and authority implies *distance* and it is this feeling of distance which, among the inferior, awakens veneration, natural respect and an instinctive disposition to obedience and loyalty towards the leader, what takes place here is the very opposite: on one side of power, one witnesses the abolition of distance, and on the other, an aversion for it. The Bonapartist leader [...] disregards the principle according to which the wider the foundation becomes, the higher the summit must be located. A succubus of the "popularity" complex, he is fond of all manifestations that could bestow upon him the feeling, however illusory, of being granted popular support and approval. In this case, it is the superior that is actually in need of the inferior to experience a feeling of worthiness, and not the other way around, as would be the norm.

Evola thus comes down in favour of *ascetic power*:

> It is right for superiority to be associated with power, but only under the condition that power is founded upon superiority and not superiority upon power.

He then quotes Plato:

> Genuine leaders are those that only assume power out of *necessity*, since they know no equals or superiors who could be entrusted with such a task. (*Republic*, 347 c)

THE RIGHT TO BEAR ARMS AND MILITARY DUTY

Likewise, 'military style' (which is but one of the aspects of heroic values) must not be confused with militarism or war:

> The notion of war cannot be reduced to materialism, nor is it synonymous with an exaltation of the brutal use of force and destructive violence. The calm, conscious and controlled shaping of one's inner being and behaviour, one's love of distance, hierarchy, order, and the faculty to subordinate one's own passionate and individual element to higher principles and ends, especially under the sign of honour and duty, are among this idea's essential elements and constitute the foundation of a precise *style* that was bound to substantially vanish whenever *nationalistic* democracies, in which the *duty* to do one's military service superseded the *right* to bear arms, replaced states where all those elements corresponded to a long, strict and caste-like *tradition*.

Julius Evola reminds us that, nowadays, wars have by no means disappeared. On the contrary, they have become *total* wars. In addition to impacting all civilians, they now affect the entire population which, by virtue of the egalitarian principle, finds itself compelled to wear the military uniform.

In Evola's eyes, the elite man is thus not an exceptional man, a brilliant leader or even a genius, but 'the one that bears within himself the expression of a tradition and "spiritual race" that owes its grandeur not to man himself but to a *principle*, an idea — as part of a certain sovereign impersonality'. Here, the decisive criteria are character and spiritual *type*, far more so than intelligence itself. For 'the worldview (*Weltanschauung*) of an uneducated man can indeed be more accurate than that of a writer, and that of a soldier, a member of the aristocratic class or a peasant who remains faithful to his land more resolute than a bourgeois intellectual's, a professor's or a journalist's'.

One's 'worldview' is not an individual matter either but, instead, the result of a *tradition*. It is the 'organic resultant of the forces to which a given type of civilisation owes its own *form*'.

Evola adds:

> Culture only ceases to be a source of danger to the one who *already* possesses a worldview, specifically because he is endowed with an inner configuration that serves as a reliable guide to him and allows him to discern, as is the case with all organic assimilation processes, what can be assimilated from what is to be rejected. [...] One of the worst consequences of the "free culture" that has been made accessible to all is that the minds which are incapable of discriminating in accordance with sound judgement, those that do not yet have a shape of their own, find themselves fundamentally disarmed on the spiritual level when faced with all kinds of influences.

Once again, Julius Evola reaffirms the fact that it is not the masses that he is addressing but the *Egregoroi*: the ones who bear within themselves the *idea* of regeneration; those who, having 'crystalised' themselves in history, remain forever standing ('All that is left is for us to see how many men shall indeed manage to remain standing among so many ruins; in order to understand'). Evola tells these well-born men that it is pointless to strive to *directly* resist the surrounding chaos, for the current is far too strong to be contained. A better option is for them to endeavour to take control of a *process* deemed inevitable. This is what he writes:

> One must determine to what extent one can take advantage of destructive upheavals; to what extent, thanks to inner resoluteness and orientation towards transcendence, the non-human aspect of the modern world could foster the experiences of a superior life and superior liberty instead of leading towards the subhuman (as is the case with most of its current forms).

A Far Eastern formula summarises his advice: 'Ride the tiger', so that you can avoid being bitten and perhaps also direct its course.

TO SUCCESSFULLY TRANSCEND FROM ABOVE

What Evola thus proposes is indeed a radical opposition to bourgeois society, yet one that *reverses* the contestation whose expression we are witnessing today (and which only embodies its relative antithesis). Moreover, it is not the bourgeoisie as a social class that he targets but the bourgeoisie as a *spiritual type*, meaning 'all that relates to bourgeois *mentality*, with its conformism, its psychological and romantic extensions, its moralism and its concern to lead a petty, safe life in which fundamental materialism is counterbalanced by humanitarian and democratic sentimentalism and grandiloquence'.

He then goes on to specify that just 'as in traditional civilisations the bourgeoisie occupied an intermediary social position between the military-political aristocracy and the people, so are there *two ways*, a positive and a negative one, to transcend it as a category, to take position against the bourgeois type, civilisation, values and mindset. The first possibility consists in following a direction that leads *lower still*, meaning towards Marxist social values that contrast with what is termed "bourgeois decandentism". [...] The result could only be a *new regression*: one heads towards something that is located beneath one's person, not above it'.

> There is, however, another possibility, namely that of a struggle and requirement to fight against the bourgeois spirit, against an individualism and false idealism that are even more determined than those of leftist movements, but with a direction which, in this case, *leads upwards*. This second possibility is connected to a revival of heroic and aristocratic values that are assumed in a *natural* and clear manner, without any rhetoric or grandiloquence. For one can keep their distance from all that is merely human and especially subjective; despise bourgeois conformism with its petty egoism and moralism; espouse a style of active impersonality; love all that is both essential and real in the superior sense, unhindered by the mists of sentimentality and intellectualistic structures; and dedicate oneself to radical "demystification". One can do all of that while still standing on one's own two feet, being affected by the obviousness of all which, in life, reaches beyond the latter and drawing specific rules of action and behaviour from it.

A MEMBER OF THE 'POLAR STAR' PARTY

At the time of his passing, Julius Evola had been living reclusively for a period of thirty years, unable to move his legs and surrounded by his paintings, his books and the friends that still dropped by to visit him. Having become the thought leader of a certain part of the Italian Right, and particularly that of a growing number of youths, he never ceased to be attacked by an extreme Left that claimed to see in him the 'occult' ideologist of a new 'Holy Vehm' Order.[121]

---

121 TN: The Vehmic courts, *Vehmgericht*, 'Holy Vehme', or simply Vehm are names given to a 'proto-vigilante' tribunal system of Westphalia, Germany, which was active during the later Middle Ages and whose proceedings were often secret. Following the execution of a death

Evola remained impassive, however, having decided once and for all not to allow himself to be dragged into the field of polemics.

Quoting Lao Tzu, he says: 'A man of virtue does not argue'.[122]

Testimonianzie su Evola,[123] a tribute book published in 1973 and edited by Mr Gianfranco de Turris, is evidence of the great influence Evola exerted.

Mr Pierre Pascal likens Evola's grave and haughty personality to that of Montherlant: each was a solitary giant. He says: 'They were both members of the "Polar Star" party'.

❦

Men Among the Ruins, an essay by Julius Evola. Sept couleurs, 252 pages.

Testimonianze su Evola, a collection of essays published and edited by Gianfranco de Turris. Ed. Mediteranee, Rome, 235 pages.

❦

One of Evola's last books to be published in Italy is a collection of articles entitled *Ricognizioni*[124] (Mediteranee, Rome, 1974). In France, in addition to *Men Among the Ruins*, there are translations of *The Doctrine of Awakening* (Adyar, 1956; second edition by Archè, Milan, 1976), *The Metaphysics of Sex* (Payot, 1959 and 1976), *The Hermetic Tradition* (Ed. Traditionnelles, 1961 and 1968), *Ride the Tiger* (La Colombe, 1964), *The Mystery of the Grail* (Ed. Traditionnelles, 1967), *The Yoga of Power* (Fayard, 1971), *Revolt Against the Modern World* (Ed. de l'"Homme, Brussels, 1972), and *Mask and Face of Contemporary Spiritualism* (Ed. de l'Homme, Brussels, 1972).

Headed by Mr Paolo Andriani, the Julius Evola Foundation has expressed its intention to preserve the books and manuscripts left behind by Evola and to 'defend the values of a culture that is consistent with Tradition', establishing its headquarters in the writer's former home (Corso Vittorio Emanuele 197, Rome).

A collective work on *Julius Evola, the Man and the Work* was published in 1977 by Copernic Editions. It includes texts by Jean Varenne, Michel Angebert, Pierre Pascal, Renato Del Ponte, Robert de Herte[125] and Vintila Horia.

❦

---

sentence, the corpse was typically hung on a tree for people to see, simultaneously serving as a deterrent to others.

122 TN: I have found no evidence of such exact words ever being spoken by Lao Tzu, the renowned Chinese philosopher and writer considered the founder of philosophical Taoism.

123 TN: Testimonials to Evola.

124 TN: *Recognitions* (Arktos, 2017).

125 TN: Robert de Herte is Alain de Benoist's alias and pseudonym.

JEAN CAU

> Let none count on me when it comes to subsidising, at tax payer's expense, so-called artistic expressions whose only purpose is to destroy the foundations of our society. Those who knock at this Ministry's door with a begging bowl in one hand and a Molotov cocktail in the other will have to make a choice!

UPON UTTERING THESE WORDS IN Paris in early May 1973, Mr Maurice Druon, then Minister for Cultural Affairs, triggered a huge wave of hues and cries. The *intelligentsia* spoke of a 'scandal', as people marched in the streets and published petitions.

That is when a voice was heard, putting things right. By referring to matters using the past tense and resorting to a great deal of irony, 'Mr Maurice Druon proceeded to put his foot down in 1973 and basically declared that the democratic state was sick and tired of playing the role of the silver fox supporting a tart that spends her time insulting him, threatening him with an untimely death and swooning with love, on the other side of the partition, in the arms of a gigolo whose red scarf possesses the strange virtue of seducing all the ladies. From his armchair, Mr Druon screamed that he was fed up with producing a play in which he relentlessly played the part of a cuckold'.

The voice was that of Jean Cau, in *Paris-Match*.[126] Readopting a serious tone, he then added:

> Let us open our eyes and stop dreaming. We are truly in 1973, and I have been woken by people shouting "Death to Druon!". The Landerneau intellectual is in a state of madness and no matter how much one showers him with self-evident facts, the jet only manages to increase his wiggling. We are, then, in 1973 and are experiencing, under the impact of the most incredible deceptions, the crumbling of an entire world. Therein lies the question; the entire question. In a daze, this society witnesses its own waning and massification in a 20th century that has now become demographically, industrially and urbanistically uncontrollable. Petrified, its eyes widened in horror, it beholds the colossal phenomenon embodied by the end of Christianity, stuttering as it wonders whether it is even possible to experience human liberty when the latter is devoid of all transcendence. That is when its artists wince and suffer convulsions, its comedians disrobe, and its intellectuals hasten to orbit around planet Utopia in swarms.

126 TN: *Paris Match* is a French-language weekly news magazine.

Wearing a jacket and displaying short hair, fifty-two-year-old Jean Cau has the eyes of a man that has seen enough to know what he is talking about. Although he has followed the same classic path as many of today's intellectuals, he has, for a change, done so in reverse.

AN 'ENFANT TERRIBLE'[127]

Back in the 1960s, Jean Cau embodied one of the 'progressive intelligentsia's' greatest hopes. Collaborating closely with Jean-Paul Sartre, he wrote for both *Les Temps modernes*[128] and *France-Observateur*.[129] In *L'Express*,[130] he published sensational interviews that were both appreciated and dreaded. Robert Lazurick,[131] Alain de Lacoste-Lareymondie,[132] and young paratroopers: under the weight of his questions, interviewees brayed as if they were horses being whipped and readers shivered. It was a time when his talent enjoyed recognition without any reluctance. He was thus awarded the *prix Goncourt*[133] in 1961 for his book entitled *La pitié de Dieu*.[134]

People readily recognised him around 1963, on the terrace of the *Café de Flore*. He wore his hair long and a shawl around the neck. The Left's 'false audacities' already annoyed him and he often attacked 'living-room revolutionism'. Back then, there was a lot of talk about 'modern socialism' and 'neo-capitalism', and Jean Cau used to reproach his friends for their lack of adjustment:

---

127 TN: 'Enfant terrible' is an original French expression denoting someone who behaves in an unconventional or controversial way.

128 TN: *Les Temps modernes* (Modern Times) is a French journal whose first issue appeared in October 1945. It was once considered Jean-Paul Sartre's own journal.

129 TN: *L'Obs*, previously known as *France Observateur* and *Le Nouvel Observateur* (1964–2014), is a weekly French news magazine and the most prominent French general information magazine in terms of audience and circulation.

130 TN: *L'Express* is a French weekly news magazine whose headquarters are in Paris.

131 TN: Robert Lazurick (1896–1968) was a French politician and a member of the Chamber of Deputies from 1936 to 1941, representing the department of Cher.

132 TN: Alain de Lacoste-Lareymondie was a controversial French politician who strongly opposed the 'Gaullist treason' of Algeria.

133 TN: The *Prix Goncourt* is an award in French literature given by the *Académie Goncourt* to the author of 'the best and most imaginative prose work of the year'.

134 TN: God's Mercy.

> Formerly, capitalism was a matter of having children work in mines. Nowadays, it is defined as compulsory school attendance until the age of 16. Capitalism was once synonymous with the presence of slums, of a sixty-hour week without a single day off; nowadays, it is Club Med. It's time the Left understood this.

The Left, however, clearly failed to understand, and Jean Cau left. His trip to Algeria awakened profound doubts in his mind and his news report, in which he described what he had seen, earned him bitter criticism.

Two years later, he publishes *Le meurtre d'un enfant*,[135] a narrative in biographical form in which he begins to organise his ideas. It also constitutes a source of inner purification for him. 'What is an adult if not one who inherits a childhood? What is an adult if not the betrayer and murderer of a child?'.

The book is fraught with imagery. An egg and a pebble. The pebble is tough and accurate. It is also faithful, characterised by the loyalty of stone. The egg, on the other hand, 'is akin to love: if rotten, it only stinks when broken'. And it is Jean Cau who begins to break the eggs of his own past — the war, the Liberation. He feels equally Jewish and 'Nazi', meaning different. He asks:

> What teenager of my generation never dreamt, both briefly and shamefully, of being the twenty-year-old SS youth who, having taken out his dagger, spread butter on a slice of bread, his back propped against his tank?

He passes judgement upon a certain type of intellectual:

> Allow me to propose an infallible recipe to anyone that longs to succeed in today's literary or cinematographic field — let them write a book or shoot a film in which men have been reduced to a wreck, to zombies, to spineless and mushy invertebrate creatures, and where women, by contrast, have gained absolute power over these tattered virilities. Their success is guaranteed.

Leftist milieus greeted the book with a slightly awkward smile. The 'enfant terrible' had a taste for paradox and was, furthermore, becoming a source of weariness and concern.

He has since acknowledged the impact which politics in general and, above all, General de Gaulle's *style* have had on him:

---

135 TN: The Murder of a Child.

> I must admit that he contributed to my awakening. At last, the *great man* was among us, a man alongside whose pantaloons the egalitarian and breathless parties of democracy barked. At long last, the admirable master stood at the head of the horde!

In his eyes, de Gaulle seemed like one of the survivors of a generation in which heads of state still retained a certain significance: Stalin, Mussolini, Churchill, Hitler, and Mao Zedong. Jean Cau contrasts their immense shadows with the dull reality of 'petty administrators':

> Look at them! Look at them, will you? Behold our politicians' horrible languid maws (*keep smiling!*); the courtier-like faces of department managers. They are indeed *salesmen*, for the very power of nations is measured in relation to their own mercantile activity. The moist glow of submission to the crowd, the mass, and the majority is what flickers in their eyes. Where has the exemplary face gone to? Where is the severe and exemplary voice? Where are the harsh words that drive the best people to gather among the crowd as the latter, now tamed, finds itself possessed by a sense of will, instead of being agitated by a gloomy sort of fever?

Le meurtre d'un enfant ends with a challenge:

> I used to be a member of the assault platoon and part of the leftist *intelligentsia*, but the years of service that I dedicated to them had me in a state of permanent scepticism, of often derisive contemplation. One reproached me for having such an attitude and unjustly equated it with a crime… Well, let it be my crime, then!

THREE BOOKS, ONE LONG CRY AGAINST DECLINE

When asked today about his former friendships, Jean Cau remains silent. Nietzsche once gave the example of Mirabeau,[136] who had no recollection of the insults or infamies he had been subjected to — for one only remembers what one takes seriously. And for Nietzsche, the most 'earnest seriousness' is that of 'a child at play'.

Jean Cau plays and forgets, and thus writes with a hammer. He proceeds to align his ideas as they occur to him, in a series of pamphlets: the result is an occasionally baroque sort of disorder from which various aphorisms emerge.

---

136 TN: Honoré Gabriel Riqueti, Count of Mirabeau (9th March, 1749–2nd April, 1791) was a leader of the early stages of the French Revolution. A noble, he was involved in numerous scandals before the start of the Revolution in 1789, leaving his reputation in ruins.

In 1967, in his *Open Letter to Western Dog Heads*,[137] he expresses his opinion on the notion of 'difference' between men and women, Whites and Blacks, etc. In 1968, in *Le pape est mort*,[138] he undertakes to analyse the authority-liberty binomial:

> To this very day, socialism and liberty have failed to prove that they can be united in matrimony without having one of them — eek! — strangle the other.

In the wake of the May riots, when, at the Sorbonne, anarchists smeared inscriptions such as 'the more one makes love, the more one conducts a revolution', Jean Cau writes, perplexed: 'And what do you think of that, oh Robespierre[139], Lenin[140] and Mao Zedong'?[141] He is overcome with indignation as a result of hearing Daniel Cohn-Bendit's[142] friends shout: 'We are all German Jews' and 'CRS[143] = SS'. He expands on things further:

---

137 TN: In French, the term *tête de chien*, meaning 'dog head', has been used to describe Parisian people as being both fierce and cantankerous. Jean Cau seems to have chosen to grant the expression a broader application.

138 TN: The Pope is Dead.

139 TN: Maximilien François Marie Isidore de Robespierre (6th May, 1758–28th July, 1794) was a French lawyer and politician, as well as one of the best known and most influential figures associated with the French Revolution and the Reign of Terror. He campaigned for universal male suffrage in France, price controls on basic food commodities and the abolition of slavery in the French colonies. He was an ardent opponent of the death penalty but played a crucial role in arranging the execution of many political opponents, and of King Louis XVI, which led to the establishment of a French Republic.

140 TN: Vladimir Ilyich Ulyanov (22nd April, 1870–21st January, 1924), better known as Lenin, was a Russian communist revolutionary, politician and political theorist. He served as head of government of Soviet Russia from 1917 to 1924 and of the Soviet Union from 1922 to 1924. Under his administration, Russia and the wider Soviet Union became a one-party communist state governed by the Russian Communist Party. Ideologically a Marxist, he developed political theories known as Leninism.

141 TN: Mao Zedong (26th December, 1893–9th September, 1976) was a Chinese communist revolutionary who became the founding father of the People's Republic of China, which he ruled as the Chairman of the Communist Party of China from its establishment in 1949 until his death in 1976.

142 TN: Daniel Marc Cohn-Bendit is a French-German politician. He was a student leader during the unrest of May 1968 in France and also co-president of the European Greens–European Free Alliance in the European Parliament.

143 TN: The *Compagnies Républicaines de Sécurité* (Republican Security Companies), abbreviated to CRS, are the general reserve of the French National Police. They are primarily

> If, in future, the gates of genuine concentration camps were shut, detaining swarms of genuine Jews, none of you would go out and "demonstrate" with a black flag fluttering in front of you, demanding that the gates be opened. It scares me, dear students, to hear you play with slogans of such gravity. CRS = SS, really? Or is it perhaps your sincerest wish for the CRS to *genuinely* become the SS? What you had better do, rather, is ask yourselves whether by defining Others as something they are not, you will not end up, sooner or later, forcing them to become what you have been claiming all along.

In *L'agonie de la vieille*[144] (1969), Jean Cau takes a seat at the bedside of democracy and composes a funeral dirge:

> I can hardly imagine (as is said of ketchup when it starts to go off) how one could still manage to "catch up" on democracy. Every day, in this Western park of ours, I watch as its tiny flame wanes, as if it were a lamp running out of oil and smouldering [...]. There are three forms of Catholicism currently collapsing: that of Rome, that of Washington and that of Moscow; and upon their ruins, the ryegrass of nationalism silently grows. And herein lies the supreme derision: should an international sentiment surface tomorrow, it will draw both its impulses and cementation from the threat embodied by a billion xenophobic Chinese nationalists, all of whom are armed to their very teeth.

One last step is taken with *Le temps des esclaves*[145] (1971):

> It will have taken me years of reflection and lucidity before I finally dared to question — and express in the form of questions — the sacrosanct *egalitarianism* which had, up until recent years, been my milk and honey.

Jean Cau says that men are not equal and targets the weakness of the masses:

> Let us state the facts both harshly and clearly. It takes more than a thousand tendencies to create a will. With a thousand currents, what you have before you is not a river but a maze of streams that follow the craziest directions. And I say to you: a thousand heresies do not equal a Church, nor do a thousand desires result in love. What would you do with a thousand soldiers that lack the leadership of a captain? Or of children that have neither father nor master? And what would a

---

involved in general security missions, but the task that they are most famous for is crowd and riot control.

144 TN: The Old One's Agony.

145 TN: The Era of Slaves.

> million words be worth without stylistic organisation, or millions of men that do not constitute a people? One might as well call it all a magma.

Although *Le temps des esclaves* is an important book, little has been said about it:

> The book's lack of success did not arouse any bitterness in me, as I had chosen to rid my reflection of all contemporary grime and of all kinds of trends and courtyard conformism. One cannot rage against the wolves and be part of the pack. I have made my choice and am willing to pay the price for the silence or hostility that surrounds some of my writings.

So as to allow people to gain a better understanding of the significance he attaches to this text, Jean Cau published *Les écuries de l'Occident*[146] in 1973. To the first part, which picks up where *Le temps des esclaves* left off, the author added a second and entirely new part. The style is a sparkling one. Formulas follow one another in quick succession, each as accurate and sharp as a blade. The book has a subheading: *Traité de morale I.*[147] There would also be another: *La grande prostituée.*[148] Together, the three books form one single long cry against decline.

Jean Cau specifies his diagnosis:

> This century has gone mad, losing its mind to all the cowardice, resignations, lies, deceptions and ugliness; and what one has labelled its "civilisational crisis" is, in fact, nothing but the fearful rejection of all grandeur.

He then adds:

> Going against the grain or, idea-wise, against all that the prevailing intellectual utopianism whispers or shouts in our ears, I state, in all tranquillity, that decadence is perfectly combinable with scientific progress and that our societies are not necessarily experiencing ascension and good health just because they conduct heart transplants, land on the moon, break the wall of sound and align Nobel prizes in onion rows: Euclid, Archimedes, Theophrastus, Hipparchus, Herophilus, and a hundred others rose to the very firmament of science at a time when both Athens and Greek power sank into the depths.

---

146 TN: The Stables of the West.

147 TN: Treatise on Morals I.

148 TN: The Great Prostitute.

All one can do is witness and take stock of the situation:

> For when the day comes for people to be astounded by our failures, our grand-nephews must, after all, be made aware of the fact that there were at least a few soldiers who refused to put down their weapons and raise their hands in surrender.

Les écuries de l'Occident and *Le temps des esclaves* are both dedicated to Japanese writer Yukio Mishima, the lieutenant of the Imperial Army who, on 25th November, 1970, took his own life in public because he could not bear living in a country where the notion of fatherland no longer meant anything.

> With his black visor rendering his eyes invisible, the lieutenant unsheathes his Samurai sword, whose blade casts a still and brilliant reflection, before proceeding to wrap it in a layer of white silk paper. Protruding out of this sheathe, only the tip of the blade remains visible, approximately four fingers long. Using both hands along the silk paper, he clasps the sword and plunges its uncovered extremity into his own belly, at the level of his left groin, and slowly eviscerates himself.

The 'great prostitute' is, in fact, none other than the *ugliness* that egalitarianism secretes. With its warm and unsavoury tongue, it licks at our contemporaries. Jean Cau defines it with a single formula, one that simultaneously defines egalitarian thought: 'Whatever breeds hatred of life'.

Never has anyone, in recent times, reaffirmed the rights of life over verbal constructions and 'justifications' with such strength. Time leads to the dispersion of words and history to the oblivion of masses; cities, sands and empires are submerged in water; yet life remains. 'Life is in the right. It never discusses things; it arises, that's all'. Alexis Carrel once said that 'the quality of life is more important than life itself' (in *Man, the Unknown*), which Jean Cau clarifies further:

> What is valuable is not life itself, but what one does with it. […] There are a few *destinies*, and the rest are just lives that lack any and all interest: nothing but the stuff of women's novels, idle rumours, the crackling of bubbles rising from the sludge of a pond when stirred, and cinematographic tales.

DEATH AND THE DEVIL

In answer to the plebes that ask for 'reasons to live', Jean Cau responds that there are none:

> All that there is are *passions* for life. There are certain strengths, momentums, loves and instincts. As regards reasons, however, there are none.

The author resorts to images rather than explanations. He mentions Albrecht Dürer's[149] *Ritter, Tod und Teufel*, which depicts a Knight riding his horse through life, flanked by Death and the Devil:

> He is invincible and victorious. It is of no concern to him whether one follows him or not. For valour has no need of recompense.

History, however, only bestows a destiny when 'life flows in torrents within the veins of a *people*'. And if the present no longer has a future, it is because it has severed its ties to its own past. Jean Cau writes:

> Any people that longs for a future must grant and ordain upon itself a simple past and, if at all possible, one that is completely organised and distorted through *myth*.

To which he adds:

> The deeper into the distant and virtually immemorial past the roots of a myth delve, the more sap will inundate its trunk and the vaster and higher its foliage will reach. Is there thus anyone who would fail to notice that the most obscure, profound and distant of all myths is that of race? It is henceforth the latter that the Blacks of America resort to and through which Israel has experienced its rebirth. "The Jewish people" is the term used by Ben-Gurion, and once awareness of it has been stirred up within the people, race awakens upon demand…

Just as a sportsman must remain 'in good shape', 'the same is true of a people and a civilisation: they must, likewise, stay *in shape* and believe in their own fitness' (the expression is a reworking of Spengler's[150]). When lacking courage, man, whose origins are an *enigma*, always strives to come up with *justifications*

---

149 TN: Albrecht Dürer (21st May, 1471–6th April, 1528) was a painter, printmaker, and theorist of the German Renaissance. His most famous engravings, paintings and etchings include *Ritter, Tod und Teufel* (*The Knight, Death, and the Devil*, created in 1513), *Saint Jerome in his Study* (1514) and *Melencolia I* (1514).

150 TN: Oswald Arnold Gottfried Spengler (29th May, 1880–8th May, 1936) was a German historian and philosopher of history with a pronounced interest in mathematics, science, and art. He is most famous for his book entitled *The Decline of the West* (*Der Untergang des Abendlandes*). Spengler's model of history postulates that any culture is a superorganism with a limited and predictable lifespan.

that make his situation seem *normal*. The same applies to peoples. When their past is obscure or disparate, they adopt a *naturally* internationalist attitude; this marks the beginning of a reversal of values.

Faced with life, Jean Cau has discovered the *anti-life* — an ebullition of moods, doctrines and trends. A type of human that is in a state of perpetual agitation, fuelling his own febrility with utopias:

> Our decadence is nothing but the sharp and prying, slimy and slippery, subtle and ironic, powerless and wordy, jealous and critical triumph of the *ever-denying mindset*.

Whenever life, defined as strength and health, sinks into abatement, the ill person, sitting in an armchair, suddenly acquires great intelligence. They reflect and discover 'valid reasons' for their current state, wondering whether health is not basically something rather detestable. After a while, they convince themselves that this is indeed the case; and soon enough, they make others ill as well, persuading them that it is in such a state that supreme good actually lies.

Jean Cau states: 'Ideas hate life, and so does intelligence'. It is his book's *leitmotiv*. He thus advocates an aesthetical conception of life and not a moral one. The Beautiful, he says, matters more than the Good. All things considered, is great vice not preferable to small virtue? 'To be worth in evil what one would be worth in good — why not, if there is *value* in it? What is irremediable, however, is when one is not worth anything at all'. This is why one must wish 'to die in *a state of beauty*, just as an absolved Christian does in a state of grace'.

Hence the fundamental idea according to which art and history are but one and the same thing. The only difference between a genius and a great man lies in the material that they work with. Just like life itself, masterpieces 'are, indeed, *causeless*. They do not persuade; they strike'. A man and a people are masterpieces to be sculpted and, likewise, seek to tear themselves away from matter. When artists are too numerous, however, the work is necessarily formless.

Jean Cau contrasts what is 'true', in which he detects nothing but illusion, with what is *real*. Hence his response to his contradictors:

> Your invincible dialectics, quibbler's discourse, massive treatises and computers stand helpless in the face of all that, within me, burns your words to ashes.

Jean Cau perceives two tendencies that clash in our world: a tendency of life, which leads towards *difference*, and a tendency of death, which leads towards *equality*:

> Let us make love, not war, but where exactly shall we do so? In the Sargasso Sea. And how shall we make love? Through a sorry mixture of psychedelic orgies. To do so is to forget that love and war have not always been in a state of enmity.

In a world devoid of enemies, there are no friends either: one only *loves* insofar as one is also able *not to love*. And when everything is of equal value, everything is worthless:

> War used to result in young people's deaths. True enough. Sustained peace, however, kills and drains youth. Furthermore, war singles out the Others. The enemy. I am only an individual to the extent that Others exist and my very being is exasperated all the more strongly and intensely when this Other chooses to object and espouse self-denial. Enemies are a necessity: they hold me to my own definitions, force me to embrace myself, and compel me to draw the line that demarcates me from the rest and within which my difference is very much alive.

In a further essay entitled *Ma Misogynie*,[151] Jean Cau mentions the specific characteristics of both men and women. He praises love and motherhood:

> Every mother who brings a child into this world believes herself to be giving birth to a king. Looking at his own child, every father considers it to be the Lord of the Earth. All of this is very well and good, very powerful and very sweet, and very un-democratic. An ever-indignant and masochistic mother, democracy demands equality for all her children, even at the cost of their resulting worthlessness. Should any one of them break free and raise himself above the latter, the wicked mother proceeds to scold him and says: "Be like your brothers! Be their equal!"

The Church, which once served as a last recourse for some, is also in a pitiful state because of its current self-reflection phase. Jean Cau scoffs at Christianity, which he perceives as a 'religion of slaves, one that shall forever be impacted by its own origins'.

---

151 TN: My Misogyny.

> A Maoist clergyman? What can be more natural than that? The recipe is a very simple one: take a priest, remove his faith, and you're left with... what exactly? One hell of an egalitarian democrat! The staunchest of them all. It should come as no surprise that so many communist leaders, beginning with Stalin, were once seminarians themselves. [...] Christianity's egalitarian message is in the process of coming true and it is for this very reason that the Church is dying.

The West is thus facing a 'breakdown of faith':

> We are men of faith that have been left faithless, men that can be approached and beseeched: "Give us some faith, we beg of you!" We so long to say "yes", but to whom? To what? For we do not ask the priest, the leader, the master to "discuss" matters with us, to understand us and to play what is basically the role of a social assistant; all we want is for them to be there, to stand there in an attitude of great severity or goodness.

MARX WAS A FRUSTRATED BOURGEOIS

What Jean Cau reproaches the Judeo-Christian conception of morality for is the fact of 'preaching the guilt of the strong and the innocence of the weak'. In *Le meurtre d'un enfant*, he already wrote:

> Yes indeed, whenever the victim cries "Go on, strike, I care not!", the tormentor is bound to find himself quite annoyed, all the more so when he is entirely in the right and the victim is guilty of absolute misbehaviour.

In *Les écuries de l'Occident*, the parable of the Master and the Slave is extensively developed. The Slave has managed to persuade his Master that his domination, meaning the very fact of being the Master, is a source of misery to him as well. The Master eventually believes him and acquires the conviction that 'all *great* existence is one of *guilt*'. And ever since then, 'the brotherly Slave has been driving a nose-ring through the Master's nostrils'.[152]

Jean Cau writes:

> It is impossible, by definition, to equal others from above, which accounts for the fact that egalitarian societies are necessarily pervaded by tedium or despair. Love supposes the presence of a Master. Once there are no longer any genuine Masters,

[152] TN: This is a metaphor that expresses the Slave's ability to *control* his former Master's behaviour, just as one would control a bull's actions by piercing one of the most sensitive parts of its body, namely its nose, with a large metal ring.

> *the entire society is one of slaves.* Those slaves, however, are all sad and hollow. In this kind of society, the bourgeois is nothing but a promoted and shameful slave.

From Spengler's perspective, 'Marx was a frustrated bourgeois; hence his hatred of the bourgeoisie'. In Jean Cau's eyes, the *bourgeois* is a 'promoted slave' longing to forget his own origins and convinced that the sole fact of owning property bestows nobility, when, in actual fact, what he presents us with is nothing but the latter's *detestable caricature* (which is all the more serious since this caricature is not always perceived as such and the dissenter himself ends up believing in this equivalence of aristocratic and bourgeois values, albeit in an effort to contest).

> The bourgeoisie sells everything; its members are genuine mercantile scoundrels. And democracy itself is embodied by the bourgeoisie. On its part, a people may, even when aspiring to baseness, still be able to recognise grandeur. Bourgeois democracy? Never.

The morality of the bourgeoisie is that 'it is better to be a live dog than a dead lion', which is the equivalent of forgetting that the dog will eventually die *as well* and that 'before his death, the lion was indeed alive; and lion-like'. In ancient times, 'both aristocrats and peasants were willing to come to terms with having their sons led to their deaths. The bourgeois, on the other hand, "harbours" his children because neither courage nor heroic obedience are part of his legacy. The aristocrat says: "If my son is a coward, he sullies my good name"; as for the peasant, he states: "If I fail to defend my land, my enemy will claim it". By contrast, this is what the bourgeois says: "If my son is killed, who will be my heir and succeed me in running the business?"'.

The transition of an aristocracy rooted in the people (for whom politics stems from the sovereign function) to a mercantile bourgeoisie (for whom politics belongs to the economic sphere of influence) also corresponds to a passage from 'great politics' to 'petty politics':

> How does one define *politics*? Is it the fact of governing people? I, for one, say that this is not the real issue and that it is a matter of providing them with reasons to live and to die, of bestowing self-forgetfulness upon them. And people's reasons to live have always been *identical* to their reasons to die. To remove either lot is to collapse the other.

In yet another essay entitled *Pourquoi la France*,[153] Jean Cau condemns America, the archetypal bourgeois land and mother of 'the young leftist bourgeoisie which, through its utopian internationalism and absolute lack of responsibility', plays the same role in relation to Europe on the level of nations as the bourgeoisie does on the class level in relation to aristocracy.

Jean Cau has never forgotten that he was born in the Aude department in 1925 and that he comes from a long line of peasants. This is what he writes in *Les écuries de l'Occident*:

> My very origin has determined my belonging to the people. My ancestors have been peasants since the dawn of time, and the very nobility of my lineage and race is epitomised by the fact that we have never bought nor sold anything. Our hard work, yes indeed — for what we give is our own blood.

The age that we now live in, however, is one of weakness: this is what all the insufficient self-manifestation has come down to:

> Any show of power leads to finger-pointing and is soiled with spittle. Children, women, delinquents, criminals and madmen loudly protest their own "oppression" and disarm the hand that either beat them or *protected them*. And the more one's head is gnawed at by the termites of weakness, the more one's body is disintegrated by violence. Echoing the pace at which our laws grow ever weaker, the criminality in our walls gains in strength, manifesting its presence with the loud sound of solicitor-like chattering. Such is also decadence: the death of laws, the proliferation of jurisprudences and the confusion of thoughts.

Firmness is, instead, *doubly* strong:

> Just imagine a President of the Republic who would declare: "Should France be attacked, either by conventional means or using an atomic bomb, I solemnly swear that it would rather choose death than submission!". Such a president would render our country invulnerable. "Let us abstain from attacking these madmen", the enemy would say, "they are capable of sacrificing their lives to the very last man *in the name of honour*". I invite the one who would seek this supreme office to ask himself: will he, or will he not, pick liberty over life and death over slavery? His response to this single question should decide which direction our votes take. My own voting slip would bear the name of anyone who would say: "I promise

153 TN: Why France?

> you death over dishonour". Admittedly, of course, my candidate might end up only securing two votes: his own and mine.

OUR FUTURE'S SECRET

There is a key philosophical thread that runs all the way through Jean Cau's books, one that is easily identifiable. He remarks:

> Nietzsche and Marx have inaugurated the formidable debate of our new age.

At the end of 1968, André Malraux confided in *Encounter* magazine:

> During the 19th century, the prevailing prediction was that the 20th century would be an internationalist one. The facts, however, have shown that it was not Marx, but Nietzsche that had been right all along.

Nietzsche chose to add a subheading to *Thus Spake Zarathustra — A Book for All and None*. In reference to *Les écuries de l'Occident*, Jean Cau has stated that the book 'targets anyone who, upon reading it, finds himself feeling concerned'. As for Nietzsche, he once wrote: 'The atmosphere rare and pure, danger lurking near, and the spirit filled with joyous wickedness. 'Tis all of a piece'. Jean Cau expands on things:

> Where am I? I am where I choose to be, in the place where I feel free and unclad, in the crisp air that immerses me and strengthens me with the knowledge of harsh and therefore perfectly untimely blatancies.

Crisp and light air and untimely considerations: Nietzsche's presence is implicit in this statement. In this book punctuated with aphorisms, he dances to the point of breathlessness.

In the space of ten years, Jean Cau has become the intelligentsia's bad conscience. His former admirers feel that he has 'lost some of his talent' ever since he ceased to align himself with them. In *L'Express*, a certain author made the following melancholic observation:

> This is not the first time that the Left has, along the way, lost one of its brilliant worker's sons who society has exceptionally allowed to get too close to the banquet.

Cruelly alone (or almost), Jean Cau laughs it off. He writes:

> In France, the leftist adventure through our cultural regions is an absolutely hilarious one. The Mandarin culture has approached the people with a facial expression akin to that of a modern clergyman on his way to a brothel, and the result was almost instantaneous: only the middle and petty bourgeoisie proceeded to treat itself to the cultural revolution one celebrated in some temples. On their part, the people simply went to the *Châtelet*,[154] on a fishing trip or calmly turned on their TV sets.

Les écuries de l'Occident is marked by a certain kind of despair. However, Bernanos is quoted in it as well:

> The highest form of hope is despair, overcome.

One even prophesies in it:

> In the name of God, it is all too late. In the name of man, it was and still is mere utopia. For both these reasons, let us approximate and declare that it is the irrational that awaits us next, just around history's corner.

And here is Jean Cau's conclusion:

> The throats of millions of men are filled with the chant that they long to intonate. One, however, wonders what words should be included to coincide with the rhythm and what exact Jerusalem one should be walking towards. Therein lies our future's secret.

Prior to the cleaning of his stables, Augeas[155] spent thirty years living in the most unpleasant conditions. And it is now the 'stables of the West' that await… Hercules' coming.

Les écuries de l'Occident, an essay by Jean Cau. Table Ronde, 255 pages.
La grande prostituée, an essay by Jean Cau. Table Ronde, 164 pages.
Le temps des esclaves, an essay by Jean Cau. Table Ronde, 200 pages.
Pourquoi la France, an essay by Jean Cau. Table Ronde, 158 pages.

154 TN: This is, in all likelihood, a reference to the *Place du Châtelet*, a public square in Paris where the *Grand Châtelet* stronghold once stood.

155 TN: In Greek mythology, Augeas was the king of Elis and the father of Epicaste. His stables, which housed the single greatest number of cattle in the country, had never been cleaned until the arrival of the great hero Heracles (Hercules).

RAYMOND RUYER

THE TWO MAIN TOPICS THAT characterise Raymond Ruyer's books are, on the one hand, the intricate connections between the *consciousness* and the *body* and, on the other, the philosophy of biology, to which he adds further essays with a focus on the philosophy of values, cybernetics, utopia, and other subjects as well. Nevertheless, the very subtleness of his thought, his concern to avoid fashionable trends (which come across as 'unilateralisms' in his eyes), and his broader rejection of ideological systems can, at times, render his works disconcerting, perhaps even difficult to access when read by those that lack sufficient awareness.

In 1963, he would state: 'Reading Kierkegaard[156] aroused an intense sort of repulsion in me'. Raymond Ruyer, who was born in 1902, admits having already been 'shocked' by existentialism in his youth. The scandal, in his eyes, does not lie in the 'world's absurdity', nor in the fleetingness of our existences; it is, instead, embodied by the fact that at the very instant of his passing, man is still unable to pierce the veil of the basic enigma:

> If what God is offering us is a voyage through existence, he has not given us the slightest instructions on how to proceed.

In his *Esquisse d'une philosophie de la structure*[157] (Alcan, 1930), which follows a first essay on Cournot,[158] he distances himself from dogmatic spiritualism:

> Man can never exit the sphere of the universe of forms through faith or the impulses of his own heart; nor, for that matter, through metaphysics.

At the same time, however, he accuses materialism of dissolving the originality and perhaps reality of 'human feelings, pleasure and pain, which paganism once actually deified, rendering them realities in the full sense of the word'.

His approach is therefore a purely *phenomenal* one. Behind the systems, what he seeks are simple and objective truths:

---

156 TN: Søren Aabye Kierkegaard (5th May, 1813–11th November, 1855) was a Danish philosopher, theologian, poet, social critic and religious author who is widely considered to have been the first existentialist philosopher.

157 TN: An Outline of the Philosophy of Structure.

158 TN: Antoine Augustin Cournot (28th August, 1801–31st March, 1877) was a French philosopher and mathematician.

> It is of little importance whether a tree is an idea, a material machine, a system of monads, a perception or an essence: what does matter is the description of its roots, its *liber*, its leaves and its flowers; the fact that by looking at it, what I receive is a mere image of it and not the tree itself. Nothing matters much as long as all the structural details agree.

In his eyes, the universe is but an ensemble of *ordered forms*. One's knowledge of these forms exhausts *all* of reality: 'There is no mysterious residue whatsoever'. He writes:

> The universe and all forms arise by proving their presence; nothing exterior could ever justify them.

In parallel to this, he attempts to demonstrate both the convenience and sufficiency of *structural* descriptions:

> A tree is merely a system of curves and torsions affecting space-time. And thanks to the sensorial modulations of my cerebral cortex, the conscious representation that I have of the tree is, likewise, nothing but a *structural* system.

There is thus a *correspondence* between the structures. To travel and to prepare an itinerary on a planning scheme are, for instance, two different things; yet there is *structural analogy* between the two actions:

> Casting a look upon the map is equivalent to looking at the landscape: it guides our behaviour in the same manner.

THE PHILOSOPHY OF STRUCTURE

Soon enough, however, Mr Ruyer realises that there is a fundamental difference between the *mechanic* and the *organic*. One is not reducible to the other since, in the organic sphere, there is interaction between all present elements, so much so that the whole in itself is more than the mere sum of its parts. Consequently, consciousness is not mere 'knowledge of something' but, indeed, a global reality that not only joins together all the knowledge one has acquired in the very nature of their being but also adds something further to it.

Espousing Leibniz's intuitions, as well as those of Schopenhauer[159] and German Romantic psychologists, Mr Ruyer apprehends the fact that, all things

---

159 TN: Arthur Schopenhauer (22nd February, 1788–21st September, 1860) was a German philosopher. He is most renowned for his 1818 work entitled *The World as Will and Representation*

considered, every *structural domain* is, in some way, a 'field of consciousness'; or, as he himself has termed it, a 'consciousness-of-being'.

Heredity, for example, determines certain *potentials*, which are then modulated by one's environment. Simultaneously, however, certain *actions* are institutionalised as *functions*. Some *psychological forms* are improvised and anchor themselves in the brain, just as *organic forms* undergo improvisation and imbed themselves in living protoplasm or *physicochemical forms* in space-time. By means of repetition, some actions create a certain *irreversibility* in one's mental functions, through some kind of mental *self-coaching*. What results from this are habits—and *circuits* of habit—that contribute to the shaping of individual existence and destiny (such is also the view advocated by the proponents of 'philosophical anthropology'). The brain, in other words, does not initially contain, in any microstructural form whatsoever, the preformation of what it will become (just as a fertilised egg could never be a 'homunculus', i.e. a being in a state of reduction); what it does comprise, instead, is the potential faculty to *undergo self-construction* within the limits of its own constitution and to *re-create* itself over time.

The strict structuralism of *Esquisse d'une philosophie de la structure* thus turns out to be highly insufficient: 'The dimensions of space-time do not contain all of reality'.

Beginning in 1934, Raymond Ruyer envisages the possibility of laying the foundations of a genuine philosophy of life, one that would remain separate from both mechanism[160] and vitalism,[161] as well as from pure biologism and empty-headed spiritualism. He thus dismisses both the explanation that asserts organic specificity through a separate principle (the soul in the traditional sense) and the materialistic one, which reduces the organism to physicochemical phenomena and the psychological memory to 'material cerebral remnants'.

(expanded in 1844), in which he characterises the phenomenal world as the product of a blind and insatiable metaphysical will.

160 TN: Mechanism is the belief that natural wholes (principally living things) are like complicated machines or artefacts, composed of parts lacking any intrinsic relationship to each other. Thus, the source of a thing's activities is not the whole itself, but its parts or an external influence on the parts.

161 TN: Vitalism is the belief that 'living organisms are fundamentally different from non-living entities because they contain some non-physical element or are governed by different principles than inanimate things'.

Last but not least, he rejects the empiricist view which turns the spirit, at the time of one's birth, into a clean slate that is identical for each one of us.

In *La conscience et le corps*[162] (PUF, 1937), he writes the following:

> The key to the values created by man is undoubtedly found in his organic life. A spirit that would, by some sort of miracle, represent pure knowledge would not produce any values and would consequently not feel any emotion. And yet these values — and, as a result, our emotional states — are elaborated and specified by our evaluating consciousness. They derive from the interaction between our organic requirements and our consciousness level.

During the last war, Raymond Ruyer found himself interned in an *Oflag*. Accompanied by biologist Etienne Wolf, he studied teratology and also worked on the analysis of dreams in cooperation with F. Ellenberger, a young geologist.

ALLUDING TO THE 'THEOLOGICAL SPHERE'

In 1946, Raymond Ruyer publishes his *Eléments de psychologie* (PUF), a book in which he delves deeper into the idea that the structure of an organic domain depends simultaneously on formative instincts and what he himself has labelled 'trans-spatial matters'. He affirms that man is in a state of temporal continuity not only in relation to his human and animal ancestors but also with respect to the entire universe, whose every element can, from a space-time perspective, be considered an avatar of a common primordial being. This conception leads to a neo-finalism, one that refers, through restoration, to a 'theological sphere' that acts as the source of all individualised activities, all forms and all laws.

It is to the study of this 'theology' that Raymond Ruyer has primarily been dedicating himself since 1946, which enables us to consider his seemingly very different works such as *Le monde des valeurs*[163] (Aubier, 1948), *Philosophie de la valeur*[164] (Armand Colin, 1952), *Néo-finalisme*[165] (PUF, 1952), *La cybernétique et l'origine de l'information*[166] (Flammarion, 1954; reedited in 1968), and *La genèse*

---

[162] TN: Consciousness and the Body.

[163] TN: The World of Values.

[164] TN: The Philosophy of Value.

[165] TN: Neo-Finalism.

[166] TN: Cybernetics and the Origin of Information.

des formes vivantes[167] (Flammarion, 1957) to be fragments of a single *Summa Theologica.*

Since life is a *becoming*, Mr Ruyer stipulates that the process cannot be reduced to its *topicality*—which brings ruin upon any and all philosophies with a focus on the latter.

> What a man does and says right here, right now, can only be comprehended through a psychological intention which, by means of its ubiquity, dominates the different stages of his action. This intention is, on its part, only comprehensible through a subconscious or instinctive intent that is even more difficult to localise; and the latter, in turn, only makes sense through an uncommunicable sort of Sense.

The real antagonism is therefore not between matter and consciousness, which constitute one single whole within every active individuality, but between matter and the '*here-now*' consciousness, as well as the trans-individual and trans-spatial spirit that is the source of all topicalities, bestowing *meaning* upon them.

Mr Ruyer soon notices that striving to identify the 'theological sphere' is an unachievable task:

> It is impossible for one to conceive of the original Source. All one can do is allude to it.

Even on its own, however, this 'allusion' is a capital one. Indeed, it is by outlining the limits of the unknowable, by delimiting as accurately as possible what we cannot know, that we can contribute to giving the knowable its *meaning*:

> If the Framing is unknowable, the obviousness of its reality can only increase.

The result is a superior definition of the notion of God, a definition that evades the traps of any and all dualism. If we are 'the heirs of the entire universe', it is because the universe might be, or might have been, 'one single being'. It is this *continuous* being that can be called God.

Already in 1930, Raymond Ruyer had written:

> The universe is not a God, but every form is an absolute akin to a God; it has its own being, within itself, and it is unnecessary to duplicate it by separating

167 TN: The Genesis of Lifeforms.

> the absoluteness of its being from it so as to render it an idea. (*Esquisse d'une philosophie de structure*)

Then, in 1952, having refuted the notion of coincidence, he specified:

> If X has never commenced to exist and cannot conceive of themselves as an object, then they are God.

In 1968, in *Dieu des religions, Dieu de la science*[168] (Flammarion), he declares atheism an 'impossibility'. Insofar as the entire universe is already *there* and we are *caught* in it, the question of knowing whether God exists or not is indeed devoid of meaning. Longing to 'identify' God is as puerile as having a geographer expect to see an ideal axis coming out of the earth to designate the North Pole. Inversely, if atheism is excluded, then so is theism:

> If none can lack God, none can find him either.

God is therefore not merely this 'more' that is responsible for the fact that, when taken as a whole, the world is *more* than the sum of its parts; he is also the universe to the extent in which it manifests itself within us. This means that we, too, exist as God. As a being, the individual is not free; yet his activities are. And it is in the sense that his activities are free that he is indeed a continuing creation and not a created being (a *creature*). Basically, this is man's sole freedom: that of continuing the creation, of playing the role of the creator in his own actions and choices. That is how he fashions a soul for himself:

> Our soul forges itself by forging our body and the bodily extensions represented by our tools. (*Néo-finalisme*)

THE PARADOXES OF CONSCIOUSNESS

In his most recent works, Raymond Ruyer has deepened various aspects of this philosophy. It was particularly in 1966 that he examined the *Paradoxes of Consciousness and the Limits of Automatism* (Albin Michel). Hence this statement, which we owe to Marcel Achard:[169]

---

168 TN: God of religions, God of Science.

169 TN: Marcel Achard (5th July, 1899–4th September, 1974) was a French playwright and screenwriter whose popular sentimental comedies allowed him to maintain his position as

> If I cared enough for someone to want to keep them, I would, in fact, love them too much to desire to keep them under such conditions.

Such paradoxes originate from the fact that each domain of consciousness masters itself as part of a kind of self-flyover, an 'auto-vision without vision', allowing it to evade our common space-time's 'step-by-step' properties, as is the case with the microphysical domains that it relates to (which coincides with Mr Stéphane Lupasco's opinion on the issue of the 'third matter').

In *La cybernétique et l'origine de l'information* (1954 and 1968), Mr Ruyer strives to demonstrate that the mechanic will never replace the organic, even though it may still enlighten it on numerous levels:

> One will never be able to explain life and consciousness through a mechanistic sort of cybernetics.

This process leads to the outlining of 'a new deism, one that closely unites faith and technology, one's ability to *exist* and one's *savoir vivre*' (*Dieu des religions, Dieu de la science*). Raymond Ruyer replaces the humanism of Feuerbach, Marx, the existentialists and all Leftism, which are but 'sub-products of a dated mechanical science and an archaic conception of matter', with a 'reality-based' humanistic philosophy:

> If one proceeds to reposition man in his line of individuality, to relocate his domain of environment-organising consciousness to the organic domain responsible for the organisation of chemical structures, to re-place the domain of chemical structures upon the field of primary curvatures and torsions of space-time, one realises that man is not a stranger to the universe but rather a manifestation of the very essence of reality.

The philosophy of Raymond Ruyer is a philosophy of science in the sense that it dismisses any philosophy that would dismiss science ('Knowledge is either scientific or false'). Simultaneously, however, it relies on scientific knowledge to answer the enigma of the Sphinx and get as close to the nameless unknowable as possible. If there is such a thing as *philosophical science*, then there is also, by extension, a *wisdom-technology*. One thus readily perceives all the factors that placed the author of *Ideological Nuisances* in a position to be seduced by the

---

a highly recognisable name in his country's theatrical and literary circles for five decades.

'Gnostics' of Princeton; beginning with the essential theory of a 'redemption through knowledge'.

Dieu des religions, Dieu de la science, an essay by Raymond Ruyer. Flammarion, 247 pages.
La cybernétique et l'origine de l'information, an essay by Raymond Ruyer. Flammarion, 255 pages.
Paradoxes de la conscience et limites de l'automatisme, an essay by Raymond Ruyer. Albin Michel, 287 pages.

ARTHUR KOESTLER

WITH HIS HAIR SLICKED ACROSS the skull, his eyes wrinkled along the corners, and his feline gaze, Arthur Koestler is as unsettling as he is charming.

Who is Arthur Koestler, then? 'An odd individual', asserts Mrs Danielle Hunebelle.[170]

'One of the foremost writers of his time', explains professor Pierre Debray-Ritzen,[171] the creator of two television shows dedicated to Koestler in January 1971, in a lively, well-documented and accurate essay that comprises the major part of a recent *Booklet* published by *éditions de l'Herne*.

Arthur 'Köstler' was born into a Jewish family in Budapest in 1905: it is the year of the Kishinev[172] and Baku pogroms,[173] which acted as the early warning signs of the Revolution.

Upon turning fifteen, he is stricken with 'political neurosis'. During Béla Kun's[174] dictatorship, which he experiences most intensely, he feels himself

[170] TN: Danielle Hunebelle (10th May, 1922–28th March, 2013) was a French actress, journalist, filmmaker and writer.

[171] TN: Pierre Debray-Ritzen (27th February, 1922–7th July, 1993) was a French psychiatrist.

[172] TN: The Kishinev pogrom was an anti-Jewish riot that took place in Kishinev, then the capital of the Bessarabia Governorate in the Russian Empire, on 19th and 20th April, 1903. Further rioting erupted in October 1905.

[173] TN: The growing tension between Armenians and Azeris (often instigated by the Russian officials who feared nationalist movements among their ethnically non-Russian subjects) resulted in mutual pogroms in 1905–1906.

[174] TN: Born Béla Kohn, Béla Kun (20th February, 1886–29th August, 1938) was a Hungarian Communist revolutionary and politician who was also the de facto leader of the Hungarian

become a 'Romantic Communist'. Following the fall of the 'Commune', he departs and settles in Vienna with his mother.

It is there, in the Austrian capital, that he gets to know his first 'shaman': Wladimir Jabotinsky. Hailing from Odessa, just like Trotsky, this Jewish nationalist now comes across as a genuine paradigm of the Zionist idea. In 1919, he establishes the Jewish Legion. At the time of the Arab uprising of 1920, he organises the defence of the Israeli communities of Jaffa and Jerusalem. In 1924, he founds the 'Zionist revisionist' movement, a movement that would give birth to the *Irgun Zvai Leumi* (IZL) and *Stern* terrorist groups before inspiring the Likud, the Israeli rightist party.

He exerts considerable influence upon Koestler. Feeling committed to Zionism 'rather by chance', the latter devotes himself entirely to the cause between 1922 and 1929. Having given up his studies, he travels to Palestine in order to work in a kibbutz. What ensues is his first disillusionment.

He declares:

> I realised that in order to be a peasant, one required a vocation that I myself lacked. The experience and disappointment were bitter. I had attempted to embrace the absolute; the result was failure.

After the kibbutz, he does a bit of everything. He wanders about, sleeping on beaches and selling lemonade in the streets of Haifa. It is now April, 1926. In Tel-Aviv, Koestler becomes a lobbyist in the advertisement field, a nightclub host, and an editor of Hebraic fairy tales. He travels across several countries of the Near-East and then returns to Europe — to Berlin, specifically.

In yet another article of *Herne's Notebook*, Mr Olivier Bourdet-Pléville[175] analyses with great intelligence and finesse the ambiguity pervading Koestler's 'Zionism'. He writes:

> For Koestler, Zionism represented one of many occasions to impassion himself for a cause, for a crusade, to surrender himself entirely to it and then distance himself from it, before ultimately burning the ships, to use an expression that he himself coined and that often surfaced in his books.

Soviet Republic in 1919. After the failure of the Hungarian revolution, Kun emigrated to the Soviet Union, where he worked as the head of the Crimean Revolutionary Committee. He also contributed to the organisation of the Red Terror in Crimea (1920–1921), in which he himself participated.

[175] TN: A French author and poet.

Indeed, Koestler was animated by a burning desire to devote himself to an idea. Zionism was, in his eyes, an adventure; Judaism, by contrast, was of no interest to him: he even denounced its 'essentially racial and national character'.

FROM RUSSIA TO THE SPANISH WAR

In Germany, Arthur Koestler turns to journalism, working for *Ullstein Verlag*. In July 1931, his participation in the overflight of the Arctic by zeppelin earns him celebrity status. A few months later, he secretly joins the German Communist Party (DKP); he is twenty-six years old. He explains:

> I was drawn to the communists because, first of all, they constituted a response to the Nazi threat and, secondly, because I had been seduced by the Soviet utopia, just like other authors of my generation.

Once again, his commitment is profound. As early as 1932, he asks to be allowed to emigrate to the USSR. In *Hiéroglyphes*,[176] he gives a faithful account of his stay there, during which he successively resided in Kharkov (with his friend Alex Weissberg), in the Caucasus, and finally in Moscow.

When Hitler seizes power, Koestler is immersed in the drafting of a book on the first five-year plan.[177] Very soon, however, his enthusiasm collapses.

> No matter how communistic I was, I found life in the USSR terribly depressing.

In 1934, he sets off for France, where he is gripped by a hollow sort of anxiety. The dream of 'warm comradery' vanishes in the face of the realities characterising the struggle against 'factionalism'. In 1935, Koestler catches wind of the first purges, Kirov's[178] assassination, and the Moscow trials.[179] The result is his

---

[176] TN: Hieroglyphs.

[177] TN: The first five-year plan of the Union of Soviet Socialist Republics (USSR) was a list of economic goals created by General Secretary Joseph Stalin and based on his policy of Socialism in One Country. Its implementation lasted from 1928 to 1932.

[178] TN: Sergei Mironovich Kirov (27th March, 1886–1st December, 1934) was a prominent early Bolshevik leader in the Soviet Union who rose through the Communist Party to become head of the party organisation in Leningrad. He was shot dead by a gunman at his offices in the *Smolny* Institute.

[179] TN: The Moscow Trials were a series of trials organised in the Soviet Union between 1936 and 1938, at the instigation of Joseph Stalin. They targeted so-called Trotskyists and the members of the 'Right Opposition' of the Communist Party of the Soviet Union.

first suicide attempt (two more would be added at a later point). That is when he undertakes to write, in German, a novel entitled *Spartacus*.

The novel covers the history of a denatured revolution. In it, Spartacus, the leader of the slave revolt against Rome, is advised by a member of the Jewish sect of the Essenes, a man who practices an egalitarian and messianic sort of communism. It is a transparent message. The book would only be completed in the summer of 1938.

Meanwhile, the Spanish war breaks out, like a lightning bolt out of the blue. Shortly after the onset of hostilities, Koestler sets off to report. The articles he publishes in the *News Chronicle* are met with great acclaim. In February 1937, he is in Malaga when the city falls into the hands of nationalist troops. Despite having the opportunity to run, he chooses not to; so as to witness things.

Placed under arrest, he is transferred to the prison of Seville, where he is interned in a cell reserved for those condemned to death. One of the great masterpieces of prison literature is born out of the notes he then accumulates: *Spanish Testament*. 'A reluctant waltz with death', Mr Debray-Ritzen writes.

Just like Koestler himself, the book's protagonist is locked in a capital punishment cell. One day, he hears one of his companions in misfortune chant *The Internationale*. Alone.

> He sang and sang further. It was inhuman. Oh, how we loved him! Yet none dared sing along with him; for fear of the consequences.

After three months of incommunicado detention, Koestler is exchanged for the wife of a Francoist officer. A worldwide protest had arisen in his favour and the Pope himself had become involved.

Upon his return to France, he is still a republican but no longer a communist: 'Inside, it was over'. He sends the Party a resignation letter and begins to pen *Darkness at Noon*.[180]

Written in English and published in England in 1941 (and five years later in France), the novel would enjoy considerable success: the French version would result in the sale of more than half a million copies. Its main character, Bolshevik commissary Kubarov,[181] is the very prototype of the fanatical

180 TN: *Sonnenfinsternis*.

181 TN: Rubashov, actually.

communist militant, a sort of composite of Bukharin,[182] Radek[183] and Trotsky[184] that falls prey to one of the purges. Accused of being a 'counter-revolutionary', just like Artur London,[185] he is compelled to embrace self-denial and ends up espousing self-criticism.

Through this isolated case, Koestler indicts a regime in which the individual has no place. He demonstrates that such a regime collapses the instant one introduces respect for the human person, just as an equation necessarily 'collapses' once a zero, or the infinite, is added to it. (The historical testimonies published thereafter would confirm every single aspect presented by this depiction of the Soviet purges, a depiction which, in its description of Stalinism, had at least had the merit of antecedence.)

TO INTEGRATE INTO THE ENVIRONMENT

In 1940, having spent two years in Paris in charge of *Die Zukunft*, a weekly aimed at German emigrants, Arthur Koestler travels to England.

From 1942 to 1948, Palestine finds itself once again at the very centre of his concerns, resulting in a new novel: *Thieves in the Night*.

In 1948, Koestler witnesses first-hand the birth of the state of Israel. There is, in his eyes, no doubt that the latter has conquered its right to exist. Simultaneously, however, he feels that Zionism has lost its *raison d'être*: he advises the Jews who do not wish to live in Eretz-Israel to renounce Judaism and

---

182 TN: Nikolai Ivanovich Bukharin (9th October, 1888–15th March, 1938) was a Russian Bolshevik revolutionary, Soviet politician and prolific author on revolutionary theory. Arrested in February 1937, he was charged with conspiring to overthrow the Soviet state and executed in March 1938, after a show trial that alienated many Western communist sympathisers.

183 TN: A Marxist, Karl Berngardovich Radek (31st October, 1885–19th May, 1939) played an active role in the Polish and German social democratic movements before World War I; he was also an international Communist leader in the Soviet Union after the Russian Revolution.

184 TN: Born Lev Davidovich Bronstein, Leon Trotsky (7th November, 1879–21st August, 1940) was a Russian revolutionary, Marxist theorist, and Soviet politician whose particular strain of Marxist thought is known as Trotskyism. He was assassinated in Mexico City.

185 TN: Artur London (1st February, 1915–8th November, 1986) was a Czechoslovakian communist politician and co-defendant in the Slánský Trial. He was sentenced to life imprisonment but released after Stalin's death in 1953.

integrate into their surrounding environment. He also deems it detrimental for one to harbour a sentiment of double allegiance within the Diaspora, for fear of its susceptibility to foster or trigger a rebirth of antisemitism.

He declares:

> To speak more bluntly, I consider it a crime on the part of parents who neither believe in the Jewish doctrine nor abide by its commandments to impose the stigmata of difference upon a defenceless child that never asked for them.

In his *Trail of the Dinosaur*, he writes the following:

> I consider myself above all a member of the European community and, in second place, a naturalised British citizen of uncertain or mixed racial origin who, while accepting the ethical values our Helleno-Judeo-Christian tradition, chooses to reject its dogmas. How others categorise me is their own business.

Since then, Koestler has never returned to Israel.

THE ISSUES OF REVOLUTIONARY ETHICS

During that same period (1946), the publication of *Darkness at Noon* in France unleashes the fury of local communists, who immediately proceed to classify the author among renegades and 'Hitlero-Trotskyites'.

Droit et Libérté magazine writes that, 'being a Trotskyite, Arthur Koestler serves the interests of reactionism and fascism'. In *L'Action*, Pierre Courtade explains that Koestler had actually been appointed by the Intelligence Service, the Anglo-Iranian Petroleum Co. and the *Comité des forges*.[186] *L'Humanité-Dimanche* described the house which Koestler owned at Fontaine-le-Port as the headquarters of the 'Cold War military staff'. *Les Cahiers du communisme* denounced him as 'the archetypal adventurer and provocateur'. As for Roger Garaudy,[187] he asserted that 'Arthur Koestler's articles are an unvarnished admission of his ultimate ends, namely the destruction of the USSR, Communism, general democracy and France in particular'.

---

186 TN: The *Comité des forges* (Foundry Committee) was an organization of leaders of the French iron and steel industry from 1846 to 1940.

187 TN: Roger Garaudy (17th July, 1913–13th June, 2012) was a French philosopher, French resistance fighter and a prominent communist author who converted to Islam in 1982 and changed his name to Ragaa Garaudy.

In 1950, Mr Jean Kanapa, one of the French Communist Party's own theoreticians, publishes a lampoon entitled *Le traître et le prolétaire, ou l'entreprise Koestler & Co. Ltd.*[188] In it, he points out that Koestler is a pervert who scorns women, is only geared towards financial gain and has put himself at the disposal of American trusts!

In a speech delivered in the spring of 1947 (*The Dilemma of Our Time*), Arthur Koestler addresses the issue that weighs most heavily upon his heart, the one around which most of his work has never ceased to revolve, namely the clash between efficacy and morality.

Should one accept, as maintained by Thomas Aquinas,[189] a lesser evil so as to avoid a greater one? Does a leader being pursued by his enemy have the right to jeopardise the lives of all his men in an attempt to salvage one man that has been left behind? By launching an atomic bomb upon Hiroshima in the hope of hastening the end of the conflict, can a government accept, without demeaning itself, the very principle of 'total war' that it previously condemned with such great firmness? Is it preferable to hold oneself to one's principles or rely on the laws of success? At what point does the surgeon's necessary lancet become the butcher's cleaver?

Spartacus, *Darkness at Noon* and *Arrival and Departure*[190] are three books whose very *leitmotiv* is embodied by the issue of revolutionary and, more broadly, political ethics.

Spartacus sets the example of a leader whose pursuit of his own ideal compels him to act 'mercilessly in the name of mercy'. And yet, when he is on the point of establishing a genuine sort of tyranny, he hesitates; and it is this hesitation that causes his downfall. In *Darkness at Noon*, Rubashov adopts the very opposite attitude but discovers that 'when left to its own devices, reason is a crooked compass, so much so that the goal ends up vanishing in the mist'. Both approaches lead to a dead-end.

---

188 TN: The Traitor and the Proletarian, or the Koestler & Co. Ltd Enterprise.

189 TN: Saint Thomas Aquinas (1225–7th March, 1274) was a Dominican friar, Catholic priest, and Doctor of the Church. He was a hugely influential philosopher, theologian, and jurist in the tradition of scholasticism, within which he is also known as the *Doctor Angelicus* and the *Doctor Communis*.

190 TN: The French title is *Croisade sans Croix*, meaning 'Crusade Without a Cross'.

In the absence of a better option, Koestler proposes that one abide by two principles whose fragility he acknowledges:

> To admit that a certain share of harshness is inseparable from human progress and that the end only justifies the means within very narrow boundaries.

It is only in 1952 that Koestler decides to settle in London once and for all and remain in the Kensington flat which he occupies to this very day. He then feels the need to draw up an assessment of the first part of his life. Two volumes of his memoirs would successively be published: *Arrow in the Blue* (1953) and *Hieroglyphs* (1955).

Beyond that point, the author puts the past behind him and vows never to write anything on politics again.

> I had the feeling that my job was done. I did not want to repeat the same things over and over.

He thus begins to tread a new path from that time on. Behind the political, he has discovered the sphere of psychology. This discovery leads him to the field of neurophysiology, then that of biology, and ultimately towards all of modern science. Already as a child, he was driven by a passion for mathematics. He expresses his intention to henceforth dedicate himself 'to history and the current state of science, as well as to its impact upon our worldview' — the fact of attending American universities allows him to 'recycle' himself.

The first book of this 'new series' is published in 1959 and entitled *The Sleepwalkers*. In it, Koestler pays homage to several great visionaries: Kepler, Copernicus, Galileo, and the ancient Greeks. Having studied their respective works, he draws the lesson that the progress of science is an uncertain process, for what has been acquired remains under threat at all times. He also deplores the separation of faith and reason and attempts to reconcile the two.

REDUCTIONISM

Other more ambitious books would follow in quick succession: *The Act of Creation* (1964), *The Ghost in the Machine* (1967), *Drinkers of Infinity* (1968), *The Case of the Midwife Toad* (1971), and *The Roots of Coincidence* (1972). In all these books, Koestler rises up against a scourge of modern times: 'reductionist' ideology, defined by Mr Quentin Debray[191] as the 'mental attitude which consists in thinking that complex phenomena can be understood and explained by *cutting them up* into simpler elements, naively perceiving the simple as a mere *part* of the complex' (*Arthur Koestler face à la connaissance*[192]).

Reductionism thus reduces every epistemological process to *analysis*. Koestler remarks: 'Analysis is an essential part in any scientific process. It is, however, insufficient'. Only synthesis allows one to appraise the 'more' that sets a whole apart from the mere addition of its parts.

Hence the criticism of behaviouralism, structuralism, Marxism and Freudism, all under a common denominator. ('Psychoanalysis is a verbal system of jugglery, a mixture of metaphors and conclusions', Koestler declares).

In August 1968, in a chalet located in Alpbach, in the Tyrolian part of Austria, Arthur Koestler organises a sort of anti-reductionist 'council'. It is attended by psychologists David McNeill and Jean Piaget, neurophysiologists and geneticists Paul MacLean, W. H. Thorpe and C. H. Waddington, epistemologist Ludwig von Bertalanffy (who is considered the father of the 'general theory of systems'), economist F. A. von Hayek, professors Seymour Kety, Jerome Bruner and Holger Hyden, and others. The symposium proceedings are then published in London under the title *Beyond Reductionism* (Hutchinson, 1971). Unfortunately, they have not yet been translated into French.

This improvised conference also provided Koestler with the necessary content for another novel entitled *The Call-Girls*, a kind of key-based pamphlet targeting the 'princes of knowledge' in which Koestler humorously mocks the scientists that cross the world back and forth, offering not their bodies but their knowledge and minds to the highest bidder.

The reductionist position is built around three fundamental principles.

1) **Man cannot be put into equations.** The 'reality' of the universe can be apprehended on four different levels: that of microphysics (energy), that of macrophysics (matter), that of biology (life) and, last but not least, a specifically human level, one that is particularly characterised by *culture* and *historical consciousness*. Man's belonging to the first three levels is shared with increasingly limited 'parts' of the universe that are, so to speak, concentric.

---

[191] TN: Born in 1944, Quentin Debray is a psychiatrist. His father was Pierre Debray-Ritzen.

[192] TN: Arthur Koestler in the Face of Knowledge.

Only the fourth level is exclusive to humans and can neither be *reduced* to the former levels nor *grasped* through analysis alone.

From one level to the next, i.e. from the quantum level to that of the human psyche, one notices a growing *complexity* and *differentiation*. As a result, a purely quantitative analysis is bound to mirror reality less and less as one rises from one level to another. In other words, the more *complex* an ensemble is, the less one can distinguish and 'reduce' its variables (known as *heteromorphisms*) in order to conduct an analysis.

'A *holon*[193] located on a higher level in the hierarchy enjoys more "degrees of liberty" than a holon located on a lower level', Arthur Koestler writes.

In the course of the 1930s, *physicalist* doctrines already confirmed the *inexistence* of anything that could not be *quantified*, beginning with our states of consciousness. As for behaviourism, which has experienced great development since World War II, it has adopted the essential part of this suggestion by promulgating the simplistic idea 'that one can study *psychology* using the methods and concepts of traditional *physics*' (Koestler). Already in 1953, B. F. Skinner[194] had thus written:

> Since mental or psychological events cannot be measured using the instruments of physics, there is all the more reason to reject them. (*Science and Human Behaviour*)

There is a certain American futurology that is founded upon the same implicit belief. When asked about the work conducted by Mr Hermann Kahn[195] at the Rand Corporation, Mr Georg Picht, the scientific adviser of the West German government, declared in 1971:

> Kahn believes himself able to *quantify* everything. He thinks he can maximise his hold on things through a maximum of mathematisation. He proceeds to

---

193 TN: A *holon* (derived from 'holos', meaning 'whole' in Greek) is something that is simultaneously a whole and a part. The word was coined by Arthur Koestler in his book *The Ghost in the Machine* (1967)

194 TN: Burrhus Frederic Skinner (20th March, 1904–18th August, 1990), commonly known as B. F. Skinner, was an American psychologist, behaviourist, writer, inventor, and social philosopher.

195 TN: Herman Kahn (15th February, 1922–7th July, 1983) was a founder of the Hudson Institute and one of the preeminent futurists of the latter part of the 20th century. He initially reached prominent status as a military strategist and systems theorist at the RAND Corporation, an American nonprofit global policy think tank partly financed by the US government.

> extrapolate current scientific data and technologies into the future, without troubling himself in any way with the social, political and moral forces that might come into play. In short, he abides by a recent trend and places his blind faith in the quantitative information that a computer can process, never asking himself any questions with regard to all the human preconditions that ceaselessly upset our predictions. Indeed, our analyses seem to demonstrate that the great political and economic mutations of the future evade all mathematisation and cannot be stored on punched cards.[196]

This statement coincides with Koestler's own affirmation that 'man cannot be reduced to mathematical equations'.

IS MAN VANISHING?

Consequently, the 'mechanistic' approach considers *insignificant* all the radical innovations that *exceptional* individuals may well introduce into our historical becoming, individuals whose intervention has not, a priori, been subject to any sort of necessity. It is thus in line with the excesses of a certain 'quantitative' historiography, as well as with Marxist theory, according to which only the masses shape history, those very same *masses* that are comprised of equal individuals and that can, as such, be 'managed' by both computers and the *media*.

2) **A whole is more than the mere sum of its parts.** Being purely analytical, the reductionist approach evades, by the same token, all the attributes that define systems as systematic. Simultaneously, it thus neglects all *emergent properties* as well, those that result from the manner in which the different parts are *laid out* in relation to one another and that characterise *the whole as such.*

It is enough, for example, to reflect upon structuralist doctrines one tiny bit to realise that, far from contributing to a better understanding of a given subject, their principle effect, and perhaps even their *objective*, is to make the latter *disappear*. The same is true of numerous 'human sciences' whose only scientific aspect, as stated by Roger Caillois, lies in their conceited pretension to actually become a science and which constitute the genuinely unique case

---

196 TN: A punched card is a card perforated according to a code, formerly used to program computers.

of a discipline that essentially strives to proclaim the inexistence of its own object.

Structuralist theoreticians are indeed the very first to proclaim 'man's death'. 'Man is vanishing', Michel Foucault[197] writes in *Les mots et les choses.*[198] In his *Writings*, Jacques Lacan[199] describes the subject as 'a thirty-six-legged calf', with Lévi-Strauss[200] declaring it 'an unbearable and spoilt child'. On his part, Althusser[201] declares that 'the absolute condition to finding something out about men is to reduce the philosophical myth of man to ashes' (*Pour Marx*[202]). Mr Claude Lévi-Strauss, who does not conceal the fact that he has undertaken 'to transform the human into the non-human', summarises the project as follows: 'We believe that the ultimate goal of human sciences is not to construct man but, instead, to *dissolve* him. [...] Once all specific humanities have been absorbed into a general humanity, it shall be necessary to reintegrate culture into nature and ultimately life into the very ensemble of its physicochemical conditions' (*La pensée sauvage*[203]). It does not get any clearer than this.

3) **The major theoretical alternatives are to be overcome.** The anti-reductionist position implies an intention to grasp not a *decomposed* man or one that has been *reduced* to one of his elements or another, but man *as a whole.* All types of *unilateralism* must therefore be rejected. From such a perspective, the terms 'materialism' and 'spiritualism' become obsolete. Metaphysicians fantasise about the possibility of a soul that remains separate from the body, while behaviourists imagine the existence of a soulless body that has been freed of the 'illusions' of consciousness. In the eyes of the former, God has

---

197 TN: Paul-Michel Foucault (15th October, 1926–25th June, 1984) was a French philosopher, historian of ideas, social theorist and literary critic.

198 TN: Words and Things.

199 TN: Jacques Marie Émile Lacan (13th April, 1901–9th September, 1981) was a French psychoanalyst and psychiatrist. Some have called him 'the most controversial psychoanalyst since Freud'.

200 TN: Claude Lévi-Strauss (28th November, 1908–30th October, 2009) was a French anthropologist and ethnologist who played a decisive role in the development of the theory of structuralism and structural anthropology.

201 TN: Louis Pierre Althusser (16th October, 1918–22nd October, 1990) was a French Marxist philosopher.

202 TN: For Marx.

203 TN: The Savage Mind.

created man in his own image. For the latter, the best means to familiarise oneself with human nature is to study the behaviour of rats. On the one hand, we are faced with theomorphism and, on the other, with 'ratomorphism'. The time has thus come for man to be likened to man.

These three principles allow one to gain an entirely new conception of both the universe and life.

One usually accounts for all consciousness phenomena, particularly in the case of men, through a simple complexification of the cerebral structure. Beyond a certain evolutionary threshold, the complexification impacting the size and arrangement of our cortical neurones is said to have resulted in the presence of the human cortex, allegedly at the same time as hominisation itself occurred.

Such an explanation seems to be well-founded: consciousness thus become an attribute of the cerebral *system* as such. However, the fact of having 'reduced' the phenomena of consciousness to their physiological support is not necessarily a source of complete information to us. Although we are familiar with the *origin* of consciousness, we remain ignorant of its *nature*. We still need to determine in what ways consciousness, which stems from the very arrangement of the cortex, *differs* from the latter. And this, of course, applies to all domains. A child *comes* from its parents yet *does not embody* its parents; a child is, in fact, the embodiment of *all* its ancestors (at different levels) but also something more, something that originates from a new 'order' within its own genetic stock. For man is a living *being* and not *merely a lifeform*. Life itself stems from the physicochemical but is not *only* physicochemical in essence. What would be problematic about it, otherwise?

Physical and chemical elements never ask themselves questions; we, on the other hand, ask ourselves the eternal ones: What are we? Where do we come from? And where are we heading? Thus far, we have contented ourselves with two types of response: the one offered by metaphysicians, which, in most cases, implies a recourse to a creative deity, and the one presented by reductionist ideologies, all of which are reducible to some form of *mechanism*, in the event, of course, that they do not collapse into a simplifying unilateralism (i.e. Marxism, Freudianism).

These so-called explanations are nothing of the sort. Apart from being rigorously unverifiable, the first ones pose more problems than they resolve.

Furthermore, they imply the presence of an entire dogmatic theology whose postulates are indemonstrable. The second ones purely and simply evade the problem. They proceed to show us the ways in which man is an animal, how this animal 'originates from' elementary cells, how the latter 'derive' from physicochemical processes and how these processes relate to the waves and corpuscles of microphysics. What they do not tell us, by contrast, is *in what ways* the physiochemical can be *distinguished* from the elementary atom, life from matter, the superior primate from micro-bacteria and man from other animals. They emphasise the resemblances and not the differences. It is these differences, however, that establish *identity*.

TRANSCENDING THE ALTERNATIVES

Reductionism commences and already triumphs in what Sir Julian Huxley has termed *nothing-else-butism*. In an interview with *Nouvelle école* magazine (Winter 1974–75), Konrad Lorenz[204] highlighted the following:

> If one says that all of life's processes are, in the final analysis, physicochemical ones, one states the truth. But the moment one states that they are *nothing but* physicochemical processes, one falls into reductionism.

What reductionist theoreticians are reluctant to admit (generally because they are prisoners of both traditional logic and the mechanistic conceptions of the previous century[205]) is that the continuity of causal order could go hand in hand with a 'natural' rupture; meaning that the universe is the theatre of sudden *qualitative* leaps that result in a given level 'transcending' the one from which it stems, in such a way that the laws that had previously applied become, henceforth, invalid. In parallel, they refuse to comprehend that *identical* parts that have been arranged differently can actually lead to *different* results as well, owing to a change in their respective *positions* and not to a transformation of their very *nature*.

What we are facing here is a fundamental incomprehension of what a system implies due to the very fact of being a system, meaning an ensemble where

---

204 TN: Konrad Zacharias Lorenz (7th November, 1903–27th February, 1989) was an Austrian zoologist, ethologist, and ornithologist who shared the 1973 Nobel Prize in Physiology or Medicine with Nikolaas Tinbergen and Karl von Frisch.

205 TN: The 19th century.

effects can take place both retroactively (the *feedback* of cybernetics) and in the traditional direction; where 'the environment's retroaction only serves to guide, correct or stabilise a pre-existing behavioural system' (Koestler); and where all elements interact with one another in such a way that, just like in a chess game, the moving of a 'pawn' does not merely alter the latter's position but also impacts the arrangement and significance of the entire system.

In short, as stated earlier, reductionism implies one's refusal to acknowledge the fact that within a system, the whole can actually be *more than the sum of all its parts* and that the whole as such could have certain properties that cannot be found in any of its components when taken separately.

Let us consider an electrophone. No matter how an amateur dismantles it, he will never manage to identify the part where the sound is 'to be found'. This is because the sound is an *emergent property*, one that surfaces when the different parts are arranged in *this very manner*. The same is true of sweet taste, which cannot be separately found in carbon, oxygen or hydrogen but is present in sugar, although the latter is only composed of these three elements. Likewise, the attributes of the H_2O composite (water) are neither found in oxygen nor in hydrogen. And the list goes on.

Unlike what the advocates of reductionism claim, emergent properties are not due to mere coincidence (In Koestler's eyes, evolution cannot be explained solely through fortuitous mutations: 'Evolution plays out in accordance with rules that limit its possibilities while leaving sufficient space for an infinite number of mutations'). So as to explain these properties, one does not need to resort to the arsenal of old scholasticisms either. They are not 'underlying' aspects of the very nature of the 'previous' elements, like those microscopic homunculi that one believed to be 'hidden' within germinal cells during the Middle Ages. Indeed, they only surface when the different parts of a system are arranged or amended in one way or another and are not only the result of the presence of the elements in question but also of the manner in which the latter are organised. Consequently, what is *more* can relatively emerge from what is *less*.

Arthur Koestler's great merit has therefore been his ability to avoid falling into the double trap of the two conventional solutions. He has thus transcended all the alternatives connected to the old logic of the excluded middle (materialism-spiritualism, mechanism-vitalism, etc.), while simultaneously extracting a *third position*, one that constitutes, almost invariably, a synthesis of its two counterparts and, as a result, outreaches them both.

One could, however, criticise some of his assertions, especially the notion that the human brain suffers from a 'defect', a defect that consists in an incomplete capacity to control our primal impulses through reason and that allegedly acts as the source of an aggressiveness endangering the future of humanity.

This idea is presented in the third part of *Ghost in the Machine*. In it, Koestler reaffirms his view that man has fallen victim to a sort of 'error' or 'accident' in the course of his own evolution. This 'accident', which is responsible for a coordination deficiency between the brain's old and recent structures, is said to turn man into a kind of 'paranoiac', gravely jeopardising his future. Koestler writes:

> Man's original equipment comprises some innate error or defectiveness that predisposes him to self-destruction.

He adds:

> The appearance of the human neocortex is the only case where evolution has granted a species an organ which the latter does not know how to use.

This twofold affirmation seems debatable.

A MULTI-STOREY BRAIN

Paul MacLean and Papez[206] have demonstrated that the differences one notices between our emotional conduct and our intellectual behaviour are founded upon a physiological factor, namely a dichotomy in the functioning and relation between the paleocortex and the neocortex. Just like all scientific discoveries, however, this finding is an absolutely neutral one from a moral point of view. It reveals to us *how* the human brain functions but does not tell us that this very functioning is 'bad', nor that we should regret the manner in which it occurs. Koestler is the one who introduces such a *regret* by presenting us with

206 TN: In 1937, James Papez suggested that the circuit connecting the hypothalamus to the limbic lobe was the basis for emotional experiences. Later on, Paul D. MacLean reconceptualised Papez's idea and coined the term 'limbic system'. Recent studies have however shown that the circuit plays a more significant role in memory functions than in emotions.

an entirely subjective opinion rooted in his own personal sentiment, in the values that he focuses on and, in all likelihood, in the experiences that he has had. One cannot therefore agree with him when he suggests that this *opinion* is but the necessary result of the stated facts.

The assertion according to which the human species is a 'failed' one is nothing new. Innumerable thinkers have dreamt of both an *ideal* man and 'the best of all possible worlds', and their doctrines have, generally speaking, only served as a basis for various utopianisms.

Each one of us, of course, wishes that man behaved in a thoughtful and reasoned manner. While telling us that man is indeed *reasonable*, however, it is precisely *reason* itself that shows us that he is not entirely *rational* and that it is because of this fact that he cannot be quantified.

MacLean has shown that the human brain comprises several 'storeys', with only one being exclusive to man: the neocortex. The remaining two storeys have been bestowed upon him by his animal heritage. The human brain is, therefore, a *compound whole*, and one fails to see why one would ever be expected to think that a specific part of this whole is more 'detestable' than another. If man were just another animal, he would have *no* neocortex. If he were entirely rational, he would *only* have a neocortex. His mind constitutes an *ensemble* in which a dialectical relation between reasoning and emotion, as well as between reasoned decisions and impulses, is developed on a permanent basis. The logic of anti-reductionism requires us to avoid reducing this whole to one of its parts alone and to accept man as he is, in his *entirety*.

It is a fact that the 'old brain', ever dominated by impulses, neither verbalises nor conceptualises and *thinks* — to use Arthur Koestler's own words — through 'preverbal, prerational and prelogical thought'. It does not follow, however, that it is always in the *wrong*. Another fact is that, thanks to his 'new brain', man gains access to the domain of abstract ideas and conceptual thought and that he can, for instance, apply reasonable thinking to experiences that he himself has never had or learn the kind of motor coordination that he has never actually performed. And yet this does not mean that the neocortex is always *right*. Koestler himself acknowledges all that artistic and even non-artistic creation owes to our ancient brain (see Anthony Storr's *Dynamics of Creation*). There are also instances where the first impulse, the most 'unreasoned' one, turns out to be the best. Inversely, it often happens that our reasoning goes astray. Is reductionism not, after all, also a 'product' of the neocortex? And whenever the spirit loses itself in the voluptuous contemplation of pure ideas, is it not a fundamental impulse stemming from the paleocortex that enables it to revert to the path of non-deceptive realities? Under such conditions, prudence is a necessity. To recognise the primacy of the neocortex is one thing, but to place our blind trust in it another. Even if we were to suppose that all truths are perceived thanks to its presence, *all* that it expresses would not necessarily be true.

Maclean has incidentally highlighted the great difficulty in rendering unto every 'brain' its own due. The neocortex seeks out 'alibis' for the paleocortex. A thousand times over, our reasoning only aims to bestow a veneer of reason upon our most unreasoned instincts. And when Koestler states that the human species is the victim of 'error', how can one be certain that it is his neocortex expressing itself at that very moment? Indeed, was he not the one who declared that 'at the end of the day, all our declarations are based upon beliefs'? (In an interview with *L'Express*, 13th July, 1970.)

One is, likewise, only left in doubt when Koestler declares that man's forehead has been branded with a 'dimension of *madness*', a madness that is said to manifest itself through an exaggerated tendency towards conflict due to the paleocortex.

The affirmation that humanity in its entirety should be considered stricken with mental disease coincides, paradoxically, with the position of antipsychiatry (Koestler writes: 'What we seek is a remedy to the paranoid dispositions of the people we call normal'). What it reveals as well is a certain *rejection* of the human condition, since Koestler views this 'madness' as a *defining* feature of mankind, while simultaneously denouncing it: 'Man has always been insane. Since the dawn of civilisation, human sacrifice has existed in all cultures' (as stated in the above-mentioned interview).

All the pages dedicated to language in *The Ghost in the Machine* are just as astounding. Indeed, Koestler perceives language as an 'illness that is specific to man' and writes:

> Language is man's greatest glory. But it is also one of his greatest servitudes, since it erects barriers between the different groups.

Owing to its very *structure*, language is allegedly a source of conflict:

Without language, there would be no war. Wars are waged because of words.

Even independently of the fact that the most 'silent' species are far from being the most pacifistic, such an accusation cannot be upheld. If what we are dealing with here is, yet again, a specific trait characterising mankind, it is one that makes us a species capable of using syntactic and abstract language; and what constitutes our superiority are specifically the 'linguistic barriers' and the 'separatist forces of language' denounced by Koestler. It is because language manifests a 'segregating' disposition allowing man to apply customised definitions to heteromorphisms that we can mentally adapt to the greatest variety of situations. In the absence of syntactic language, there would be no hominisation and no human beings.

A KEY TO OPEN ALL DOORS

One thus witnesses Koestler, on the one hand, 'regretting' the power retained by the emotions and impulses that emanate from the paleocortex over the human spirit and emphasising the presence of the neocortex (which is indeed the specifically 'human' part of our brain), while, on the other, acknowledging the fact that some of the traits he deplores and condemns are, likewise, *constitutive* elements of the human phenomenon, thus making it very unlikely for anyone to erase them without having man vanish by the same token. What we are facing here, it seems, is a fundamental contradiction.

Indeed, in order to 'correct' nature, Koestler proposes that we resort to some 'drug' or 'miracle-cure' — 'chemical harmonisers', for instance — which would inhibit our 'wicked penchants'. One wonders, however, in what way our human nature would be 'normalised' through a chemotherapeutical intervention that would deprive it of some of its specific traits. And having received such treatment, would man not plummet to an infrahuman level? These are all questions which Koestler does not seem to ask himself.

In the end, one notices that Koestler would like to preserve, within our human nature, all that he personally considers advantageous, while eliminating all that he regards as 'harmful'. With man 'condemned if he remains what he is', one must, he states, 'stabilise and harmonise people without genuinely castrating them nor sterilising them mentally'. His proposal is a squaring of the circle in the true sense of the word: how is one to remove one side of the coin while preserving the other?

During the same interview, a journalist observed: 'One encounters in your writings the same desire to seek a global explanation, a key that opens everything... You once sought it in Communism, but did not find it, and now you seek it in your work on the two brains'. To which Koestler responded:

> I agree. A key to open all doors. It's naïve, but that's basically it.

Unfortunately, the search for such a key, one to which everything could be reduced, is already a sign of reductionism. There is no 'key to open all doors', no universal explicative key. There are only plural realities, relative and contingent ones that establish both man and the universe in their diversity; realities that must be accepted and *desired* not as one wishes they were but as they genuinely are.

Within the rigorous mind that Arthur Koestler possesses, the thirst for the absolute has therefore never been completely quenched. Being too honest and too intelligent to make a fool of himself, he fails to break free of a certain kind of messianism.

At the same time, however, his perpetual fear of being 'trapped' by a system and obsession with present and future dangers—an obsession that was fuelled by his experience of totalitarianisms—has brought about an inner *malaise* which, on several occasions, almost cost him his life and has constantly compelled him to burn all that he believed he could adore. Hence this cantilever-like situation, which acts as a source of 'defiant' inspiration and continuous challenge, one that places him, as he himself has stated, on a 'tightrope' between two worlds or two momentums.

This 'crusader without a cross' has actually carried them all. An inner fire burns within him, consuming him yet never exhausting him. Which direction is he going to opt for next? With this 'odd individual', anything remains possible.

'Koestler', a special issue of *Cahiers de l'Herne* (42, Verneuil street, 75007 Paris, France), 468 pages.

Except for *Spanish Testament*, which has been published by Albin Michel, all of Arthur Koestler's books have come out (in their first editions, that is) through Calmann-Lévy.[207] The most recent one, *The Thirteenth Tribe* (1976), is a study of the Khazar people who, during the early-9th century, converted massively to Judaism and are said to be the source of a major part of our contemporary Jewish people.

In his *Ce que je crois*[208] (Grasset, 1976), Mr René Huyghe[209] tackles quite extensively the issue of reductionism. He vigorously denounces this doctrine, which has been 'introduced into numerous knowledge domains: just as the psychological has been "reduced" to the physical, so shall the unconscious be to the libidinal — under Freud's authority — and, just as arbitrarily, the social to the economic'.

The Alpbach symposium proceedings, known as *Beyond Reductionism*, have been published and edited in English by Arthur Koestler and J. R. Smythies and are currently being translated.

---

207 TN: Alain De Benoist is referring to French publications and editions.

208 TN: What I believe.

209 TN: René Huyghe (3rd May, 1906–5th February, 1997) was a French writer on the history, psychology and philosophy of art.

COUNTER-FIGURES

ANTONIO GRAMSCI

THERE WAS ONCE A TIME when Marx was simply read; nowadays, he is imposed. He is not merely a trend: the vast majority of all that is published in the ideological domain today is located *inside* the scope of Marxism, and fashion no longer focuses on anyone but those authors who, in relation to Marx, introduce a number of personal variations. Sometimes it is Lukács,[1] at others Rosa Luxemburg,[2] then again Wilhelm Reich.

Recently, it was Gramsci's turn, and Gallimard published a first collection of his *Political Writings* covering the 1914–1920 period.

Antonio Gramsci is, alongside Lukács, the most renowned 'independent Marxist-Leninist' of the Stalinian period. He is, above all else, the theoretician of 'cultural power'.

Gramsci was born in Sardinia in 1891. A Don Bosco-like legend has turned him into a shepherd's son. In actual fact, his father was an official. At the age of three, following a fall in a stairwell, he suffers spinal column deformation, leaving him hunchbacked for the rest of his days. At the age of seventeen, a scholarship allows him to enter university. He arrives in Torino in 1911. Two years later, he joins the Italian Socialist Party (PSI), immediately becoming a militant in the 'Left wing'. He also contributes to the writings of the *Avanti!* daily and the *Grido del popolo* weekly.

---

1 TN: Born György Bernát Löwinger, György or Georg Lukács (13th April, 1885–4th June, 1971) was a Hungarian Marxist philosopher, aesthetician, literary historian, and critic.

2 TN: Rosa Luxemburg (5th March, 1871–15th January, 1919) was a Polish Marxist theorist, philosopher, economist, anti-war activist, and revolutionary socialist.

On 1st May, 1911, he launches the *Ordine nuovo* weekly, in collaboration with Terracini[3] and Palmiro Togliatti.[4]

At the time, the communist world was in a state of complete turmoil. Beginning in 1918, certain currents declared themselves in favour of a 'critical support' of Russian Bolshevism. These currents refused to accept the hegemony of the *Komintern* (the Communist International) without questioning. In Germany, this was the case of the groups which would go on to form the KAPD (Communist Workers' Party of Germany) in 1920, together with Rosa Luxemburg and Karl Korsch.[5] The same applied to Pannekoek's[6] 'councilists' in the Netherlands. Their opposition particularly impacted parliamentary action, which they considered inadequate for the purpose of socialist struggle, and the role of syndicates, whose revolutionary virtues they questioned.

This position, which would thereafter be adopted by numerous leftist movements, is denounced by Lenin in *'Left-Wing' Communism: An Infantile Disorder*.

In Italy, within the PSI, two 'Left-wing' groups clash: one is led by Amadeo Bordiga,[7] the other by Gramsci.

Gathered around the *Il Soviet* journal, in Naples, the 'Bordiguists' call for the creation of an ultra-hierarchised and ultra-centralised revolutionary party. Unlike their counterparts, the authors of the *Ordine nuovo* contrasted the 'council communists' with 'party communists', denouncing 'organisational fetishism', meaning the idea that everything had to be subordinate to the party's interests.

The syndicate's purpose, Gramsci writes, 'is one that could be labelled commercial': it consists in 'enhancing the work of a certain category of workers within the bourgeois market', which bears no connection to revolution. As

---

3 TN: An anti-fascistic politician.

4 TN: Togliatti was the leader of the Italian Communist Party.

5 TN: Karl Korsch (15th August, 1886–21st October, 1961) was a German Marxist theoretician.

6 TN: Antonie (Anton) Pannekoek (2nd January, 1873–28th April, 1960) was a Dutch astronomer, Marxist theorist, and social revolutionary. He was one of the main theorists of council communism (councilism).

7 TN: Amadeo Bordiga (13th June, 1889–23rd July, 1970) was an Italian Marxist, a contributor to Communist theory, the founder of the Communist Party of Italy, a leader of the Communist International and, at a later point, a leading figure of the International Communist Party.

for the 'party's religion', which is connected to bureaucratism and elitism, it is expressed through the 'desire to cultivate the apparatus for the latter's own sake' (*Notes on Machiavelli*). The conclusion? Both the party and the syndicate could act as the *agents* of the revolution but could never be its privileged *forms*, which would then come to merge with it.

With his pronounced features, large nose, black hair and lorgnette, Gramsci participates in all congresses. That is when he enunciates his famous watchword: 'Only the truth is revolutionary'.

In parallel, he elaborates a theory of 'factory councilism', whose central idea states that the proletariat must establish its dictatorship by means of organisms that are spontaneously created within it. The crucial word here is 'spontaneously', implying a return to square one.

BORDIGUISTS AND 'SOCIAL TRAITORS'

Gramsci thus turns his attention to the 'factory councils' in which a synthesis is supposed to take place between the economic infrastructure and the political superstructure: during the first phase of the communist society, the global proletarian state will be born of the coalition of factory and countryside councils, giving rise to 'direct democracy'. He writes:

> Factory commissioners are the sole true social (economic and political) representatives of the working class, since they are elected through universal suffrage by all the workers, on the very working premises.

In April and September 1920, an immense strike action shakes the North of Italy. It is quite an event:

> For the first time in history, the proletariat is initiating a struggle for the control of production without having been driven to action by either hunger or unemployment. (*Ordine nuovo*, 14th March, 1921)

In Torino, Gramsci is in charge of all corporate soviets. He says:

> Every factory is an illegal state, a proletarian republic that lives from day to day!

Very soon, however, the enthusiasm decreases. The PSI's right wing 'breaks' the movement and social democracy loses ground. Furthermore, the decision made by Lenin to accelerate the communist scissions within socialist parties hastens things further. On 21st January, 1921, in Livorno, the PSI's 'communist faction' becomes the Italian Communist Party. Although both Gramsci and Togliatti participate in its creation, it is ultimately Bordiga that takes control of it thanks to his superior organisation.

Shortly afterwards, a new crisis makes its presence felt in the International. Concerned about the 'reaction's' headway, Lenin advocates a Popular Front policy. In Italy, Bordiga refuses to collaborate with 'social traitors'. He claims that Fascism, 'an instrument of the bourgeoisie', will vanish automatically with it. This sectarian attitude of his robs him of mass support. On 30th October, 1922, Mussolini seizes power.

A few months earlier, in Moscow, Gramsci had been appointed as a member of the Komintern's executive committee. Aware of the importance and gravity of the disagreement between the PSI and the Kremlin, he chooses to take the 'Bordiguists' head on and reclaim the party 'from within'; but the support he expects fails to materialise. In Germany, an attempt to ally the socialists with the communists in October 1923 ends in failure. Fearing the birth of a 'leftist' International led by Bordiga with the support of Trotsky (who is already part of the opposition), Moscow takes advantage of the opportunity to conduct a new offensive against the 'Right'. Gramsci thus finds himself alone.

In 1924, he still manages to get elected as an MP in the region of Veneto and launches the *Unità* journal on the 12th of February. In January 1926, the Italian Communist party holds a congress in Lyons, France. Gramsci succeeds in imposing his theories and becomes its Secretary General. By then, however, it is already too late: cut off from its voters and exhausted by internecine conflicts, the party is prohibited on the 8th of November and goes into hiding. Gramsci is arrested, transferred to the island of Utica, and sentenced to twenty years' imprisonment.

It is there, in his cell, that he writes his most important texts: *The Prison Notebooks*, divided into thirty-three leaflets and 3000 handwritten pages.

Free from the contingences of action, Gramsci rethinks the entire praxis of Marxism-Leninism. He particularly reflects on the great socialist setback of the 1920s: How is it possible that the awareness of men is 'late' compared to what their class situation is expected to dictate upon them? How do dominant castes 'naturally' ensure the obedience of the dominated classes? Gramsci answers all these questions by having a closer look at the notion of *ideology* and making a decisive distinction between 'political society' and 'civil society'.

THE THEORY OF CULTURAL POWER

Gramsci uses the expression 'civil society' (a term used by Hegel[8] yet criticised by Marx) to designate the whole of the 'private' sector, meaning its system of needs, jurisdiction, administration, and corporations, but also the intellectual, religious and moral domains.

The mistake that had been made by the communists lay in their belief that the state was no more than a simple political apparatus. However, the state 'also organises consent', which means that it manages things by means of an *implicit ideology*, one that is founded upon values espoused by most members of society. This 'civil' apparatus comprises culture, ideas, habits and traditions, stretching all the way to 'common sense'.

In other words, the state is not a mere apparatus of *coercion*. Alongside direct domination and the authority it exercises by means of *political power*, it also benefits from ideological 'hegemony' and people's *mental adherence* to a worldview that consolidates it and justifies it, both of which stem from its activities of *cultural power* (see also the distinction made by Althusser between 'the state's repressive apparatus' and 'the state's ideological apparatuses').

Distancing himself from Marx, who reduced 'civil society' to its economic infrastructure alone, Gramsci realises perfectly that it is within this very civil society that worldviews, philosophies, religions and all implicit or explicit intellectual and spiritual activities are elaborated and disseminated, thus enabling the creation and perpetuation of social consensus (he failed to see, however, that ideology is also connected to mentalities, that is to the mental *structure* of each given people). Reintegrating civil society into the level of superstructure and associating it with ideology, upon which it indeed depends, he henceforth differentiates two forms of superstructure in the Western world: on the one hand, civil society and, on the other, the political society or the state per se.

Whereas in the East the state is everything and the civil society is both 'primitive and gelatinous', the communists of the West must remain aware of the fact that the 'civil' aspect is an addition to the 'political'. If Lenin, who did

---

8 TN: Georg Wilhelm Friedrich Hegel (27th August, 1770–14th November, 1831) was a German philosopher and a significant figure of German idealism.

not realise this, succeeded in seizing power, it is because in Russia, the civil society was inexistent. In developed societies, no claiming of *political* power is possible without a prior seizure of *cultural* power:

> A seizure of power does not solely occur through a political insurrection that takes charge of the state but also through *a long ideological activity within the civil society* that allows one to lay the necessary foundations. (Hélène Védrine,[9] *Les philosophies de l'histoire.*[10] Payot, 1975)

The 'shift to socialism' is channelled neither through a putsch nor through direct confrontation but, instead, through the *subversion* of minds.

The central issue in this war of position is *culture*, which acts as the command post of values and ideas.

Gramsci thus simultaneously rejects traditional Leninism (the theory of revolutionary confrontation), Stalinist revisionism (the strategy of the Popular Front) and Kautsky's[11] theories (the establishment of a vast workers' assembly). Both instead of 'party work' and in parallel to it, he suggests replacing 'bourgeois hegemony' with 'cultural proletarian hegemony', right under the noses of the established authorities. Overcome with *values* that are no longer its own, the existing society will thus be shaken at its very foundations and all that one will have to do is exploit the situation in the political field.

Hence the role assigned to intellectuals: 'to win the cultural war'. Here, the intellectual is defined by the function he exercises in relation to a given type of society or production. Gramsci writes:

> Every social group born on the primary field of an essential function within the world of economic production *organically* creates, at the same time, one or several layers of intellectuals that bestow upon it *homogeneity* and *awareness* of its own function not only in the economic domain, but also in the social and political one. (*Intellectuals and Cultural Organisation*)

Using this (highly expanded) definition, Gramsci distinguishes between organic intellectuals, who ensure the ideological cohesion of a certain system,

---

9 TN: Born on 5th June, 1926, Hélène Védrine is a French philosopher.

10 TN: The Philosophies of History.

11 TN: Karl Johann Kautsky (16th October, 1854–17th October, 1938) was a Czech-Austrian philosopher, journalist, and Marxist theoretician.

and traditional intellectuals, i.e. the ones representing the old social classes that persist through the disruption of production relations.

It is at the level of 'organic intellectuals' that Gramsci recreates the *subject* of history and politics — 'the organising *Nous* of other social groups', to use the expression coined by Mr Henri Lefebvre[12] (*La fin de l'histoire.*[13] Minuit, 1970). The subject is no longer the Prince nor the state, nor even the party, but the intellectual avant-garde connected to the working class. It is this avant-garde which, through 'termite-like work', fulfils a 'class function' by becoming the spokesperson of the groups represented in the forces of production.

It is also responsible for granting the proletariat the necessary 'ideological homogeneity' and *awareness* to ensure its *hegemony* — a concept which, with Gramsci, replaces and transcends that of 'proletarian dictatorship' (insofar as it stretches beyond the political and encompasses ideology).

PLURALISM AND EVANESCENT CONSENSUS

In the process, Gramsci expands upon the means he deems appropriate for 'permanent persuasion': appealing to popular sensibility, a reversal of values at power level, the creation of 'socialist heroes', and the promotion of theatre performances, folklore and songs (when defining these objectives, what he draws inspiration from is the initial fascist experience and its first successes). Communism, he says, must resolve its own issues by taking the Soviet experience into account, but without attempting to passively follow this model. This leads him to highlight the specificity of national problematics. In his eyes, political action and strategy can neither afford to neglect the complexity of societies nor their temperament, mentalities, historical heritages, cultures, traditions, class relations (including their ideological aspects), etc.

Gramsci was very well aware of the fact that the post-fascist period would not be a socialist one. He did, however, think that the latter, once again dominated by liberalism, would represent an excellent opportunity to practice

---

12 TN: Henri Lefebvre (16th June, 1901–29th June, 1991) was a French Marxist philosopher and sociologist, best known for his pioneering of the critique of everyday life, his concepts of the 'right to the city' and the production of social space, and his work on dialectics and alienation. He targeted Stalinism, existentialism, and structuralism with rather sharp criticism.

13 TN: The End of History.

cultural subversion, because the proponents of socialism would, *morally* speaking, be in a position of power.

From this 'democratic detour' shall rise a new *historical bloc* managed by the working class, with traditional intellectuals either won over or destroyed. (When using the term 'historical bloc', a notion that was particularly based on a study of the situation pervading the Mezzogiorno, what Gramsci is actually referring to is a system of political alliances associating infrastructure and superstructure, centred around the proletariat and founded upon 'history', meaning upon classes and their structure within society.)

This vision of his has proved prophetic, not only because it is specifically in liberal regimes that subversion enjoys the greatest freedom of action but also because, being pluralistic, these regimes are characterised by a weak consensus that fosters the interference of intellectuals into political struggles. Mr Jean Baechler[14] writes:

> An evanescent consensus is what typifies the pluralistic type of order. Indeed, political pluralism, meaning the institutional acknowledgement of the legitimacy of divergent and competitive projects, is intrinsically a consensus corruptor. Under the sole impact of the mechanism of competition, the plurality of parties leads one to perceive ever more clearly the multiplicity and variability of the apportionments, institutions and values. If the worst comes to the worst, there is nothing that the members of such a society could unanimously agree on. (*Qu'est-ce que l'idéologie?*[15] Gallimard, 1976)

We thus find ourselves in a vicious circle. The activities of the intellectuals contribute to the destruction of the general consensus, with the dissemination of subversive ideologies adding to the intrinsic flaws of pluralist regimes. Yet the more one reduces the consensus, the stronger the ideological demand (which the activities of intellectuals must then meet). The *ideological majority* thus finds itself inverted.

Antonio Gramsci dies of tuberculosis on 25th April, 1937. His sister-in-law collects his *Notebooks* and ensures their circulation.

In the spring of 1944, the Italian Communist Party comes out into the open again under the leadership of Palmiro Togliatti (1893–1964). Appropriating a

---

14 TN: Born on 28th March, 1937, Jean Baechler is a French sociologist.

15 TN: What Is Ideology?

part of Gramsci's theories, he turns himself into an advocate of 'polycentrism', of the plural orthodoxy of the different communist parties. At the start of the 1960s, this theory would exert great influence upon dissident communist youths. (Having been won over by 'avant-gardism', the 'Italians' of the Communist Student Union would end up inside the leftist movement in 1968.)

In Italy, Gramsci's work was published from 1948 to 1950 and his 'official' biography in 1951. In France, the extreme Left has been passionate about him since 1968. To this day, approximately fifteen books have been dedicated to him. At Gallimard, a total of seven volumes are expected to come out, four of which will be devoted to his *Prison Notebooks.*

This small disabled Sardinian man thus posthumously benefits from the results of a strategy that he himself once elaborated.

Indeed, although it is only now that French Leftism is discovering Gramsci, it has long understood his essential lesson, namely that an *ideological* majority is more important that a *parliamentary* one and that the former always heralds the latter; a parliamentary majority is, on the other hand, destined to collapse in the absence of its ideological counterpart.

Political Writings I, 1914–1920, an essay by Antonio Gramsci. Gallimard, 461 pages.
Lire Gramsci,[16] an essay by Dominique Grisoni and Robert Maggiore. Ed. Universitaires, 186 pages.
Gramsci et la théorie de l'Etat,[17] an essay by Christine Buci-Glucksman. Fayard, 234 pages.
Pour Gramsci,[18] an essay by Maria-Antonietta Macciocchi. Seuil, 432 pages.
La pensée politique de Gramsci,[19] an essay by Jean-Marc Piotte. Anthropos, 302 pages.
Notes sur Gramsci,[20] an essay by Alfonso Leonetti. Etudes et documentation internationales, 230 pages.
Gramsci et la question religieuse,[21] an essay by Hugues Portelli. Anthropos, 321 pages.

From Arturo Labriola, who introduced Marxism into Italy, to Palmiro Togliatti, who was among the founders of the Italian Communist Party and, after 1944, the president of the

16 TN: Reading Gramsci.

17 TN: Gramsci and the Theory of State.

18 TN: For Gramsci.

19 TN: Gramsci's Political Thought.

20 TN: Notes on Gramsci.

21 TN: Gramsci and the Religious Question.

Italian parliamentary communist group, 'Italo-Marxism' has always exerted a certain appeal on French extreme Left currents. At the beginning of the 1960s, it was under the influence of Togliatti's 'polycentrist' theories that several leaders of the Communist Students' Union initiated an evolution that would lead them towards Trotskyism and Maoism. More recently, in the aftermath of the May 1968 events, numerous small groupings willingly entered into the Italian leftist organisations' sphere of influence (PSIUP, 'Il Manifesto', Brigades Rouges, Lotta continua, Servire il popolo, and others).

Some Trotskyists such as Mr Pierre Broué believe that a certain convergence took place towards the end of Gramsci's life between the latter's views and those advocated by Trotsky. Alfonso Leonetti, one of his former companions-in-arms, even claims that, while in prison, Gramsci joined the 'Trotskyist' opposition. M. A. Macciocchi, by contrast, likens 'Gramscism' to the spirit of the Chinese cultural revolution. In fact, however, Gramsci differs from both Mao Zedong (through his actual anti-Leninism) and Trotsky (through the important role he bestows upon the working-class' grass roots). What such comparisons mirror are, above all, affinities resulting from one's own personal commitments.

To gain some insight into the Anglo-Saxon approach to 'Gramscism', see John M. Cammet's book entitled 'Antonio Gramsci and the Origins of Italian Communism' (Stanford University Press, Stanford, 1967).

THE FRANKFURT SCHOOL

'IT IS NO COINCIDENCE THAT in the interwar period, a period marked by the crisis of liberal capitalism and the rise of fascism, a group of Jewish bourgeois liberals established an institute whose purpose lay in the critical analysis of society', writes philosopher Jürgen Habermas. Indeed, during that time, the Jews perceived 'society as an obstacle to such an extent that a sociological perspective became, so to speak, natural for them' (*Der deutsche Idealismus der jüdischen Philosophen*[22]).

By discovering the philosophy of the Frankfurt School or 'critical theory' with a forty-year delay, France has once again plunged itself into the atmosphere of the Weimar Republic.[23]

22 TN: The German Idealism of Jewish Philosophers.

23 TN: The Weimar Republic is an unofficial, historical designation for the German state during the years of 1919 to 1933.

OTHER MAVERICKS

In the aftermath of World War I, an intense philosophical fermentation manifests itself in Germany. One proceeds to translate Kierkegaard and publish Marx, as Nietzsche exerts decisive influence upon people's minds. Heidegger,[24] Husserl[25] and Jaspers[26] publish their most important works. And while Neovitalism and Neoromanticism (Hans Driesch, Wilhelm Dilthey, Ludwig Klages, Hermann von Keyserling, and Oswald Spengler) maintain the tradition of the philosophies of life in a state of flourishment, a new school surfaces, one that intends to 'rethink Marxism'.

In contrast with the 'national' philosophy inspired by Schelling,[27] Schopenhauer and Nietzsche, it proposes a cosmopolitan doctrine, a doctrine that acts as the heir of the *Aufklärung* (the philosophy of the 'Enlightenment'), the Hegelian Left (Bruno Bauer, Feuerbach) and Ludwig Börne's[28] radical Jacobinism.

We are now in February 1923. At the University of Frankfurt, Max Horkheimer[29] and Friedrich Pollock[30] found the *Institut für Sozialforschung* (the Institute for Social Research). In his *History and Class Consciousness*,

---

24 TN: Martin Heidegger (26th September, 1889–26th May, 1976) was a German philosopher and a seminal thinker in the Continental tradition and philosophical hermeneutics. He is widely regarded as one of the most original and crucial philosophers of the 20th century.

25 TN: Edmund Gustav Albrecht Husserl (8th April, 1859–27th April, 1938) was a German philosopher who established the school of phenomenology.

26 TN: Karl Theodor Jaspers (23rd February, 1883–26th February, 1969) was a German-Swiss psychiatrist and philosopher whose ideas greatly influenced modern theology, psychiatry, and philosophy.

27 TN: Friedrich Wilhelm Joseph Schelling (27th January, 1775–20th August, 1854) was a German philosopher. He is generally considered to represent the midpoint in the development of German idealism.

28 TN: Born Loeb Baruch, Karl Ludwig Börne (6th May, 1786–12th February, 1837) was a German-Jewish political author and satirist and is considered part of the Young Germany movement, although many rather stress his adherence to Jacobinism, the most renowned political movement of the French Revolution (1979–1989).

29 TN: Max Horkheimer (14th February, 1895–7th July, 1973) was a German philosopher and sociologist famous for his contribution to 'critical theory' and classified as a Western Marxist.

30 TN: Friedrich Pollock (22nd May, 1894–16th December, 1970) was a German social scientist and philosopher. He was one of the founders of the Institute for Social Research in Frankfurt and a member of the Frankfurt School of neo-Marxist theory.

Georg Lukács announces, during that same year, 'the reign of the category of totality' and renders the proletariat sacred.

In January 1931, Horkheimer takes charge of the Institute. The following year, the first issues of *Archives for the History of socialism and the Workers' Movement* (the future *Journal of Social Science*[31]) see the light of day. They include articles by Herbert Marcuse,[32] Walter Benjamin,[33] Max Horkheimer, Theodor Adorno,[34] Erich Fromm,[35] Friedrich Pollock, Leo Löwenthal,[36] and Henryk Grossmann,[37] all of whom come from the Jewish-German middle or great bourgeoisie. Hermann Weil, a German-Argentine trader, provides the necessary funding.

The school is thus launched. Other Marxist mavericks gravitate towards it: Lukács, Wilhelm Reich, Karl Korsch, and Wolfgang Abendroth.[38]

The year is 1933. Hitler rises to power: the journal is prohibited and the Institute shut down. The members of the Frankfurt School take the path of exile.

---

[31] TN: Alain de Benoist is clearly referring to the Institute's *Zeitschrift für Sozialforschung* (Journal for Social Research), which was renamed *Studies in Philosophy and Social Science* when the Institute became affiliated with Columbia University.

[32] TN: Herbert Marcuse (19th July, 1898–29th July, 1979) was a German-American philosopher, sociologist, and political theorist who criticised capitalism, modern technology, historical materialism and entertainment culture, arguing that they represent new forms of social control.

[33] TN: Walter Bendix Schönflies Benjamin (15th July, 1892–26th September, 1940) was a German Jewish philosopher, cultural critic and essayist whose thoughts were a combination of German idealism, Romanticism, Western Marxism, and Jewish mysticism.

[34] TN: Born Theodor Ludwig Wiesengrund, Theodor W. Adorno (11th September, 1903–6th August, 1969) was a German philosopher, sociologist, and composer known for his critical theory of society.

[35] TN: Erich Seligmann Fromm (23rd March, 1900–18th March, 1980) was a German-born American social psychologist, psychoanalyst, sociologist, humanistic philosopher, and democratic socialist.

[36] TN: Leo Löwenthal (3rd November, 1900–21st January, 1993) was a German sociologist usually associated with the Frankfurt School.

[37] TN: Henryk Grossmann (14th April, 1881–24th November, 1950) was a Marxian economist, historian, and revolutionary from Galicia.

[38] TN: Wolfgang Abendroth (2nd May, 1906–15th September, 1985) was a socialist German jurist and political scientist.

Having become an international society, the Institute initially moves to Geneva and then to the *Ecole normale supérieure*[39] of Paris. Its journal is taken over by Félix-Alcan editions, but events soon escalate. From 1934 onwards, the School emigrates to the US, where the foundations are already laid for its arrival. The Institute spends the war at the University of Columbia.

The victory of the Allies puts an end to this diaspora. Horkheimer (1895–1973) and Adorno (1903–1969), the group's most prominent representatives, return to Germany in 1949. As for Marcuse and Fromm, they remain in the US, where they follow a path of their own. Born in 1898, Walter Benjamin takes his own life in 1940, somewhere along the Spanish border, after trying some hashish in 1938 (while in Marseille).

That is when the School's influence peaks. In post-1945 Germany, it is in relation to the Frankfurt School that most thought currents define themselves.

1975 is upon us. Horkheimer passed away two years earlier and Marcuse is the only founding member of the Institute still alive. Born in 1929, Jürgen Habermas, Adorno's former assistant, has succeeded him. In France, several books are translated in quick succession. At Payot, Mr Miguel Abensour, the head of the 'Political Critique' collection, announces the publication of essays by Horkheimer (*Beginnings of the Bourgeois Philosophy of History*), Adorno (*Negative Dialectics*), Ernst Bloch (*Natural Law and Human Dignity*), and Habermas (*Theory and Practice — The Problem of Legitimation in Advanced Capitalism*).

The works of the Frankfurt School are concerned with the most diverse domains, but what one encounters in them is, above all, a reflection on reason.

For Horkheimer (*The Dialectic of Enlightenment*, 1944; *Eclipse of Reason*, 1947), the entire history of human thought can be summarised as a struggle between 'vital myths' and reason, with the latter striving to organise the world in accordance with the principles of liberty and progress (as propagated by the *Aufklärung*): totalitarianism sprouts up whenever myths take precedence over reason. And yet Horkheimer states that even reason itself can become totalitarian; it can 'fall ill'.

---

39 TN: The main teacher-training college.

THE SCIENTIFIC-TECHNOLOGICAL COMPLEX

Connected under current circumstances to calculating thought and 'self-preservation', reason can become an instrument in the service of domination. The reason of state and scientific reason are both 'paranoid' forms of reason. When implemented, the positive is transformed into the negative, meaning that reason 'betrays' and serves the purposes of the irrational, which, in clear terms, means the purposes of nature and life.

If Nazism turned out to be possible and if, as written by Wilhelm Reich in one of his famous texts, 'the masses *desired* fascism', it is because it managed to 'restrain' reason and subjugated it to vital instinct. Habermas writes:

> What makes fascism totalitarian is the fact that it seeks to put at the service of domination the rebellion of a nature oppressed by this very domination.

Having thus been 'instrumentalised', reason plays an opposite role to the one assigned to it by the 'Enlightenment' and 'turns into mythology'.

Based on this, the School's theoreticians believe that they can identify new forms of totalitarianism. Their criticism of scientific reason in particular leads them to denounce the consumerist society and (to use Marcuse's phrase) 'the identification of the reality principle with the performance principle'.

Marx had only perceived social and economic exploitation as a source of alienation; the Frankfurt School ventures further than that. Taking an opposite stance to the opinion that a totalitarian society is necessarily 'dictatorial', it strives to demonstrate that liberal society exudes a form of alienation that is even more fearsome. The criticism of alienation is thus extended to include all anthropological sectors, in the hope of obtaining a more satisfactory theory of historical movement.

Horkheimer states that the rationalised world 'eliminates' the individual through the very fact of proposing material opulence to him. Indeed, the latter fosters inner alienations. It is 'repressive', perhaps even 'over-repressive', because it is not only accepted but also desired (at a level where traditional repression generates a resistance leading towards revolt).

After 1945, the School begins to target the power of the *Kulturindustrie* more specifically, accusing the *media* of being responsible for the conditioning of minds. Adorno declares that the radio and the cinema are essentially 'fascistic' (they bestow upon fascism its form, 'just as the printing press did for the Reformation'). He specifies that if the worst comes to the worst, an all-penetrating speech does not need to have any content: its 'content' is entirely embodied by the fact that it reaches the heart of every home (such a theory is also advocated by Marshall McLuhan[40] in *The Medium is the Massage*, Pauvert, 1968). Marcuse goes on to add that the very fact of giving everyone their own voice is totalitarian, because any indiscriminately afforded freedom is unjust and, additionally, a source of indifference.

Denouncing the 'scientific-technological complex', Jürgen Habermas writes:

> It is science and technology that have now assumed the function of granting domination its *legitimations*.

On his part, Adorno affirms that the language of 'authenticity' is the last 'asylum of the Nazi ideology'. As for Horkheimer, he emphasises the fact that the activities conducted by ideologists, just like those of researchers, relate directly to the interests of the ruling class. Thomism,[41] for instance, helped the Church incorporate the period's scientific progress and thus perpetuate its power by seizing the opportunity to replace Platonic speculation with Aristotelian categories better suited to contemporary science. This theory (which heralds the contemporary criticism of science) will be developed by Jürgen Habermas in *Knowledge and Human Interests*, a book which focuses on the existing ties between the state of societies and the shape and content of epistemology.

Reinforcing the accusation of 'potential fascism', Adorno widens its scope to encompass virtually all institutions: every hierarchy is founded upon 'arrogance' and 'submission'; the family is a 'factory of reactionary ideology', a father a 'superior being that a child is masochistically compelled to identify

---

40 TN: Herbert Marshall McLuhan (21st July, 1911–31st December, 1980) was a Canadian professor, philosopher, and public intellectual. His work is widely considered one of the cornerstones of the study of media theory.

41 TN: Thomism is the theology of Thomas Aquinas or his followers. Aquinas was an Italian Dominican friar, Catholic priest, and Doctor of the Church. He was an immensely influential philosopher, theologian, and jurist in the tradition of scholasticism, within which he is also known as the *Doctor Angelicus* and the *Doctor Communis*. The name 'Aquinas' identifies his ancestral origins in the county of Aquino, in present-day Lazio.

with', etc. Erich Fromm also condemns patriarchy and praises the sense of 'liberty and equality characterising the matriarchal structure'.

A 'JUST CONSCIENCE'

During the 1960s, Habermas finds himself at the centre of an epistemological polemic in which he would stand particularly against Arnold Gehlen[42] and Popper's[43] German disciples. Countering Gehlen, according to whom institutions are rigorously necessary for man to be able to *construct* himself in his own specificity, Habermas advocates the *necessarily* 'repressive' and 'alienating' character of *any and every* institution.

From this perspective, the proletariat no longer constitutes a privileged class but is alienated — just as 'bosses' and technocrats are — by the belief that social problems will be resolved through an overabundance of goods. Horkheimer writes:

> Its revolutionary will has invested itself into an activity in which one accommodates to the reality of things!

By the same token, social criticism reverts to what it was like during the 'Enlightenment' period: a bourgeois theory, as acknowledged by Habermas in *Theory and Practice*.

To be honest, the 'Frankfurtists' do not reject Marx's teachings; they only reproach him for allowing his teachings to degenerate into vulgar economism. The theory of growing pauperisation, observes Horkheimer, has become 'obsolete'. One must therefore graft a 'science of just conscience' onto orthodox Marxism. This is precisely what Ernst Bloch[44] strives to do when reproaching Marxist bureaucracy for having forgotten that socialism was a *theology* before becoming political economy.

In three of his books, namely *The Spirit of Utopia* (1918); *Thomas Münzer as a Theologian of Revolution* (1921: Julliard, 1964 and UGE/10–18, 1975), in

---

42 TN: Arnold Gehlen (29th January, 1904–30th January, 1976) was an influential conservative German philosopher, sociologist, and anthropologist.

43 TN: Sir Karl Raimund Popper (28th July, 1902–17th September, 1994) was an Austrian-British philosopher and professor. He is generally regarded as one of the 20th century's greatest philosophers of science.

44 TN: Ernst Bloch (8th July, 1885–4th August, 1977) was a German Marxist philosopher.

which he praises the 14th-century leader of the Anabaptist sect that preached the advent of a strictly communistic egalitarian millennium; and *The Principle of Hope* (1954–57, three volumes), Bloch lists the messianic myths that could revive Marxism's 'theological foundation'. Resorting to 'utopian energy', he even envisages a new sort of prophetism and writes:

> One must contemplate the path of socialism as stretching not only from utopia to science but also from science to utopia.

Having become the head of the Karl Marx Institute of Leipzig after the war, Ernst Bloch would be excluded from the Communist Party in 1961 before taking up a post at the University of Tübingen.

Since their return from exile, the members of the School have been haunted by one single obsession: how does one define a system that could never become complicit in the established order?

Horkheimer and Adorno respond: by rendering speech so 'mobile' that it becomes intangible. This is what they label '*negative* thought'. According to Adorno, the latter consists in seeking in every aspect of things its implied limits and self-negation. This negative aspect is as important as the positive one: its comprehension reinstates the possibility of a genuine dialectic.

NON-WORK

Adorno's criticism of Wagner (*Essay on Wagner*, Gallimard, 1966) thus erects the negative viewpoint of *the critic* into an absolute principle (a principle of *utter* truthfulness), by contrasting it ideologically with the *artist's* 'affirmative' point of view. The latter is declared to be founded *upon* and *by* trickery as a result of its false claim to be the product of the spirit itself. Following the discovery of the realities of class struggle, art can no longer, and *should* no longer, according to Adorno, have a clear conscience. Aware of itself being no more than a 'sham', it must deny itself as part of a *non-work* that reveals, in an immediate fashion, that it is but a 'fabricated product' born of human alienation, while continuing to denounce itself and awaiting the day when the abolishment of class struggle shall trigger the abolition of the very conditions in which the existence of that work of art was rendered possible.

One thus realises that the 'dialectical reason' advocated by the Frankfurt School is one that never ceases to *deny*. It seeks the contrary, then the contrary's contrary, then the contrary of all: what it secretes is an 'eternal no'. Within this system, awareness itself becomes negation — the negation of all the mediations that intervene between the individual and the 'whole'. Such thought, whose sole aim is to 'critically' dissect the real using an incessant kind of pilpul, could never be constructive. It does, however, possess an immense power of subversion.

It also goes hand in hand with a complete sort of *pessimism* marked by the twofold imprint of Freud and Kafka[45] and rooted in the conviction that the entire world is in the hands of the 'enemy'; that *every* society is inevitably repressive (Walter Benjamin writes that 'there is not a *single* cultural document that does not simultaneously document barbarism'); and that *negativism* is indeed the only means available to man that could allow him to play his cards right.

Hence their staging of the non-tragic, which, on the level of praxis, suddenly inverts itself either into sheer messianism or an evasion of reality, depending on the case.

Being at the very heart of institutions, the state finds itself particularly targeted. 'The state is the devil' — these are the exact words written by Ernst Bloch, who denounces its 'harsh and impious materiality', so much so that Mr Jean-Marie Vincent[46] perceives the Frankfurt School as 'the announcement of a new phase of Marxism, of a new settling of accounts with the old reason of state'.

Logically, this doctrine leads to a desperate aspiration for the end of history, for our species' reintegration into *nature*, for a time when all tensions shall subside, all alienations vanish and man reclaim the fullness of his metaphysical being. In a striking passage taken from his essay on Thomas Münzer,[47] Ernst Bloch writes:

---

45 TN: Franz Kafka (3rd July, 1883–3rd June, 1924) was a German-speaking Bohemian Jewish novelist and short story author and is widely considered one of the prominent figures of 20th-century literature. His concepts can generally be described as absurd and negative.

46 TN: Jean-Marie Vincent (6th March, 1934–6th April, 2004) was a French philosopher.

47 TN: Thomas Müntzer (c. 1489–1525) was a German preacher and radical theologian of the early Reformation whose opposition to both Martin Luther and the Roman Catholic

> We have sufficiently experienced the world's history and witnessed a sufficient and even excessive number of forms, cities, works, phantasmagorias, and *obstacles born of culture*. At present, it turns out to be impossible for the Kingdom not to come.

This kingdom is one where 'Marxism and the dream of the unconditional shall ultimately' unite, 'advancing at the same pace and incorporated into the very same plan of action'.

In 1968, Horkheimer condemned the violent character of the students' protests (whose aspirations he otherwise approved of), fearing that it would result in a new kind of totalitarianism. As explained by Adorno, the students were stricken with the same 'weakness of the self' that the masses had fallen prey to when surrendering to fascism: their anti-authoritarianism could, at any moment, be overwhelmed by an infatuation with authority.

Such an attitude is very revealing indeed.

PROGRESS, AN IDEOLOGY OF REACTION

In response to Marx's affirmation that critical analysis must, as stated in his *Theses on Feuerbach*, be followed by a specific action of transformation, the Frankfurt School proposes that theory 'emancipate itself' from practice. Remaining logical throughout, its representatives have always stayed warily away from action, all to the great discontentment of a certain part of the extreme Left, whose members reproached the Frankfurt school for its 'contempt for involvement'.

This last trait suffices to demonstrate both the strength and the weakness of the School. Dissolving all thought in a social sort of relation and reducing all sociology to 'ideology', it represents a much more efficient type of criticism of the modern world than orthodox Marxism. However, owing to its excessive fear of being 'taken over', its hypercriticism, and its mental febrility, it condemns itself to powerlessness: to assert that *all* power is a source of corruption is to forever renounce the exercise of power. Destined to remain in 'perpetual motion' and embrace constant criticism without ever proposing anything, it automatically leads to failure.

Church led to his open defiance of late-feudal authority in central Germany.

As remarked by Mr Jean-Michel Palmier,[48] this fact has been acknowledged by Horkheimer himself (who, at a later point in life, freed himself of his obsessions by practically returning to Judaism) when he wrote that 'democracy does not exist anywhere' and that progress has become the 'ideology of reaction'.

From the perspective of dialectical thought, the dialectic itself is to be overcome. Only then will one witness the end of contradictions. Yet if the world is only comprised of contradictions, how could a 'just' state of affairs ever be real? That is the very core of the issue.

'Critical theory' offers one of the most accomplished examples of a doctrine exclusively focused on the negative. It demonstrates the sterilising power (and, ultimately, the power of death) that pervades an intellect which is only driven towards criticism and gradually reaches a point where it targets everything with denial and dissolution.

L'Ecole de Francfort,[49] an essay by Pierre V. Zima. Ed. Universitaires, 193 pages.

La théorie critique de l'Ecole de Francfort,[50] an essay by Jean-Marie Vincent. Galilée, 154 pages.

Traditional and Critical Theory, an essay by Max Horkheimer. Gallimard, 315 pages.

Eclipse of Reason, an essay by Max Horkheimer and Theodor Adorno. Gallimard, 282 pages.

Technology and Science as Ideology, an essay by Jürgen Habermas. Gallimard, 212 pages.

Knowledge and Human Interests, an essay by Jürgen Habermas. Gallimard, 386 pages.

Adorno: art, idéologie et théorie de l'art,[51] an essay by Marc Jimenez. UGE/10–18, 192 pages.

Ernst Bloch, utopie et espérance,[52] an essay by Laënnec Hurbon. Cerf, 148 pages.

48 TN: Jean-Michel Palmier (19th November, 1944–20th July, 1998) was a French philosopher and art historian.

49 TN: The Frankfurt School.

50 TN: The Critical Theory of the Frankfurt School.

51 TN: Adorno's Art, Ideology and Theory of Art.

52 TN: Ernst Bloch — Utopia and Expectancy.

HERBERT MARCUSE

BETWEEN 1963 AND THE EVENTS of May 1968, *édition de Minuit* sold 300 copies of *Eros and Civilisation*. With his white hair, thin lips and cigar, the author, seventy-eight-year-old Herbert Marcuse, was virtually unknown at the time. Along with *Soviet Marxism*, *Eros and Civilisation* was his only book to have been published in French. Since then, dissenters have turned him into one of their thought leaders. From 1868 to 1973, nine of his books were translated, some of which had actually been written thirty or forty years earlier.

Herbert Marcuse deserved, in all honesty, neither such excessive indifference nor such excessive fame.

According to his biographers — Alasdair MacIntyre, a forty-seven-year-old professor at the University of Brandeis, as well as André Nicolas, André Vergez and Jean-Michel Palmier — 'Marcuse, who was born into an old Jewish family in 1898, found his way into our global consciousness in May 1968'. In actual fact, he found his way into the German Social-Democratic Party in 1917 and then Karl Liebknecht's[53] and Rosa Luxemburg's revolutionary movement in 1919. Being a former student of Husserl and Heidegger, he then published a thesis on Hegel.

In 1933, the advent of National Socialism compels him to escape to Paris. There, he meets the members of the Frankfurt School, to whom he has very close ties. For several months, he collaborates with them on the *Journal of Social Science* before departing to the United States.

A few years later, in 1936, he publishes a series of *Studies on Authority and the Family* in cooperation with Adorno. In the end, he takes up a teaching position at Columbia, Harvard, Brandeis and San Diego University. Towards the end of the 1950s, he publishes *Eros and Civilisation* (1955) and *Soviet Marxism* (1958), followed by *One-Dimensional Man* (1964) and *A Critique of Pure Tolerance* (1965).

A neo-Marxist and even Freudo-Marxist theoretician, Herbert Marcuse develops a critique of society similar to that of the Frankfurt School, but adds numerous personal viewpoints to it.

---

53 TN: Karl Liebknecht (13th August, 1871–15th January, 1919) was a German socialist and, alongside Rosa Luxemburg, a co-founder of the Spartacist League and the Communist Party of Germany.

NEUROSIS AND SOCIETY

In the past, he explains, human life was characterised by two dimensions: the *social* one and the *individual* one. By means of the former, man integrated into society; thanks to the latter, he retained his faculty to question this society. Today, this distinction has vanished. Culture, the *mass media* and leisure have reduced man to a single dimension.

This theory, a fundamental one with Marcuse, is judged to be at the very least simplistic by Jérôme Deshusses,[54] who wrote the following in *La gauche réactionnaire*[55] (Laffont, 1969):

> *One-Dimensional Man* is, to a large extent, a conformism worthy of ignoration. The Marcusian way of seeing things is characterised by a wager *against* man which, at times, borders on naiveté. He does not grant man any power of dissuasion, setback distance or possibility to criticise.

It is nonetheless on such a basis that Marcuse targets symbols of authority, the 'protagonists of domination': family fathers, political leaders, employers and the state. Preaching a 'fatherless society', he adopts the argumentation used by the 'Frankfurtists' and the 'Freudo-Marxists' (Wilhelm Reich, Erich Fromm): there is no social liberation without a sexual one. It is no longer social injustice that is the focus of his resentment but constraint itself, meaning *alienation* — an alienation that has become the common law of all human beings.

Eros and Civilisation develops a line of thought founded upon one of Freud's famous works: *Civilisation and Its Discontents.* Unlike orthodox Freudians, Marcuse states that Freud's very essence is to be found in the following sentence: 'The repression and inhibition of impulses is indispensable for the maintaining of civilisation and its institutions'. Indeed, according to Freud, there is a direct connection between social organisation and *neurosis*: man is allegedly the sole animal that 'inhibits' itself, creating civilisation so as to achieve better inhibition. The result is that every *constructed* society rests upon alienation:

'The notion according to which a non-repressive civilisation is impossible is the very cornerstone of the Freudian theory', Marcuse observes.

---

54 TN: Born in 1941, Jérôme Deshusses is a French author.

55 TN: The Reactionary Left.

It is this Freudian pessimism that Marcuse adopts. He, too, asserts that, since they 'repress' our impulses, all societies are a source of constraint and all progress comprises — and, if the worst comes to the worst, actually *represents* — a regression. Yet he ventures even further when considering impracticable Freud's proposal in which the latter strives to sublimate the instinct of death 'so as to allow the self to satisfy its vital needs'. He writes:

> The systematic sacrifice of the *libido*, i.e. its rigorously imposed rerouting through socially useful activities and manifestations, *is the very definition* of civilisation.

Simultaneously, however, Marcuse seems to reproach Freud for having enrooted every possible society in this law of 'repression'; he declares that since the renouncement level demanded by society in the name of its implicit ideals has now become 'unbearable', man must abolish most of these demands in order to reclaim some possibilities of happiness.

What we are facing here is a bizarre contradiction, an analytical mistake that has not evaded Mr Jean-Marie Benoist's[56] attention:

> While acknowledging the spectral, meaning *fantastical*, character of any non-repressive society, whose advent Freudian analysis tends to demonstrate as unattainable by confining it to the realm the imaginary, Marcuse suddenly shifts his reasoning and, within the same sentence, undertakes a revolutionary process affecting civilisation: the advent of a non-repressive society thus becomes a dogmatic stipulation. (*Marx est mort*,[57] Gallimard, 1970)

Hence the following conclusion:

> With Marcuse, the discourse presented in May 1968 did not, as was assumed, access the pathways of criticism but sank, in fact, into the metaphysical antithesis of unacknowledged dogmatism.

THE ROLE OF FRINGE GROUPS

This discourse is combined with the argument of 'repressive tolerance'. Generally speaking, tolerance arouses sympathy. Due to this very fact, says

---

56 TN: Jean-Marie Benoist (4th April, 1942–1st August, 1990) was a French philosopher.

57 TN: Marx Is Dead.

Marcuse, it *alienates* and 'represses'. It is a paradoxical theory that leads to the following affirmation:

> Civilisation has to defend itself against the spectre of a world that could be free. (*Eros and Civilisation*)

From this perspective, Soviet Marxism and Western capitalism are judged to be equally 'repressive'. The two systems, for that matter, tend to converge through technology, thanks to the very rationality which Marcuse drowns in sarcasm in the name of *pure reason*.

> The type of rationality that triumphs nowadays is that of Greece. It is the one that defines itself as a succession of power relations and views nature as an object to dominate. In a world where technological rationality is the only dimension, the happy consciousness harbours the belief that reality is rational. (*Eros and Civilisation*)

For Marcuse, what is real is not, in fact, rational. The 'happy consciousness' is a disaster, for it has defused the 'proletarian bomb'.

This is because workers are the first to be 'trapped' by the illusions of 'repressive tolerance'. When 'slumlords' are not taking advantage of their work, 'holiday merchants' are taking advantage of their free-time. Unlike what Marx had hoped for, the time of 'freedom' thus remains that of 'necessity'. Yet it is rather a false freedom that we are dealing with, since the current definition of 'leisure' still belongs to the interstices of the yield principle. The truth is that the proletariat has been *gently* disarmed and its qualities not only neutralised, but 'reversed for the benefit of the prevailing ideology'. By connecting the fulfilment of general interests to the realisation of one's private interests, advanced capitalism has taken control of the revolutionary potential of the masses. The working class has become the 'objective' *accomplice* of the existing order:

> Repression is interiorised. Modern society is capable of digesting class struggle.

Under these conditions, Marcuse recommends relying on 'fringe groups' — on those small groupings which neither society nor reformism have yet taken over because they are sheltered within the 'contradictions of the established order': immigrant workers, eternal rebels, those that have lost their social status, asylum residents, youths that have broken with socialisation (the

Jugend-Proletariat which Thierry Maulnier[58] spoke of), proletarian-like intellectuals, and so on.

A place of choice is reserved for students, who are 'on the fringes' and remain *aware* of their own condition. Marcuse perceives them as the sole *potential revolutionaries*. They are the ones, he says, who can bring the machine to a halt and the institutions to a standstill by organising a 'long march' through them. It is within them that the 'Great Refusal', the power of negation regarded as the necessary counterpoint to the 'repression' of the structures, is now concentrated in the form of a refusal to play along.

Mr Jean Baechler details this strategy:

> One can neither bet on a frontal attack, nor on spontaneous decomposition or the proletariat. The bearers of revolution can thus only be embodied by elements that are *outside* the economic and social system. Due to the fact that these forces do not occupy any strategic position, they cannot hope to access power directly by controlling the shift levers. One therefore falls back on local actions whose purpose is to *paralyse* the system. Wherever the power relations are favourable, be it in universities, cultural centres, or factories that have been taken over, the revolutionaries will take the necessary steps to paralyse the institutions. Attacks will be perpetrated against key establishments or symbols so as to sabotage and alert the public opinion. There will come a point when the system finds itself blocked and the revolutionary forces can break through the defences. (*Qu'est-ce que l'idéologie*? Gallimard, 1976)

Unlike the more traditional representatives of the Frankfurt School, Marcuse does not hesitate to justify one's recourse to violence, declaring:

> When slaves are unaware of their own enslavement, one must make use of violence and sensitise them to happiness *against their will*.

For the purpose of achieving this 'sensitisation to happiness', revolutionary minorities will thus resort to violence, reserving themselves the right to 'eliminate both rivals and pernicious opinions'. At the same time, they shall eradicate freedom of expression, since the latter contributes to the 'propagation of error'.

Strangely enough, Marcuse adopts some of Marx's illusions. The author of *Capital* was convinced that the tensions he had been noticing within the

---

58 TN: Born Jacques Talagrand, Thierry Maulnier (1st October, 1909–9th January, 1988) was a French journalist, essayist, dramatist, and literary critic.

apparatuses of production would worsen until reaching a maximal number of 'contradictions' from which the communist revolution would then arise. Marcuse declares:

> My most serious doubt regarding the success of the great American affluent society rests upon its neofascistic character. Repression will get worse. Both the internal and international contradictions of American capitalism will be exacerbated. The opposition will have to mobilise all of its strength to avoid having the working class fall into the hands of fascism, etc. (Declarations made to Hans Magnus Enzensberger, in *C'est demain la veille.*[59] Seuil, 1973)

Jean Marabini[60] remarks:

> In the end, Marcuse realises Marx's dream of having his revolution first establish itself in America.

Not everything is wrong with Marcuse's latest criticism of the cost efficiency principle, which has become the absolute principle of modern societies. Far from it, actually. Unfortunately, his analysis is entirely spoilt by his systematism and utopian negativism. Marcuse believes that a return to the principle of quality goes hand in hand with the advent of a 'liberated' — and more egalitarian — society, whereas historical experience offers a contrary demonstration: it is because egalitarianism triumphs that the individual has ceased to be a person, becoming, instead, a pawn that has been robbed of his own autonomy by a soulless society; it is because ancient societies were inegalitarian and hierarchised and neither 'morals' nor abstract rationality represented their basic foundations that it was possible to maintain the prevalence of quality over yield. On this level, Marcuse has missed the mark completely.

His alienation theory is not any more convincing either. Not only is it obvious that every society is alienating, but the very same is true of any sort of existence and presence in the world. Life is but a series of constraints, and pleasure, i.e. the *libido*, is equally a source of alienation, since it embodies attachment, perhaps even submission, to a not-self. The (dreamlike) rejection of *all* alienation is therefore synonymous with the rejection of life itself.

---

59 TN: Tomorrow's Vigil.

60 TN: A French historian and author.

Last but not least, the theory of 'repressive tolerance', combined with that of a utopian 'happiness' that should be *imposed* upon those that do not desire it using force if necessary, can, in actual fact, only lead to the most sombre of dictatorships.

'There could never be such a thing as tolerant repression. Any and all repression is necessarily driven by intolerance', says Mr Jean-François Revel.[61]

Alasdair MacIntyre[62] has no difficulty in demonstrating that the Marcusian doctrine of 'total liberation' acts as the trigger of a novel sort of despotism:

> People no longer have a say, and the choices are not between genuine democracy and the authority of an elite but, instead, between rival elites — the present's repressive elite and the liberating elite of the Marcusian future.

In short, not only is Marcuse's doctrine wrong, 'but if it were widely followed, it would become an actual obstacle to all rational progress and all liberation'.

Eros and Civilisation, an essay by Herbert Marcuse. Minuit, 236 pages (256 pages in Seuil's second edition).

One-Dimensional Man, an essay by Herbert Marcuse. Minuit, 284 pages (320 pages in Seuil's second edition).

Hegel's Ontology and the Theory of Historicity, an essay by Herbert Marcuse. Minuit, 324 pages.

Marcuse, an essay by Alasdair MacIntyre. Seghers, 153 pages.

Sur Marcuse,[63] an essay by Jean-Michel Palmier. UGE/10–18, 276 pages.

Marcuse & McLuhan et la nouvelle révolution mondiale,[64] an essay by Jean Marabini. Mame, 132 pages.

61 TN: Born Jean-François Ricard, Jean-François Revel (19th January, 1924–30th April, 2006) was a French journalist, philosopher, and a member of the *Académie française* from June 1998 onwards. A socialist in his youth, Revel desisted his former convictions and became a prominent European proponent of classical liberalism and free market economics.

62 TN: Born on 12th January, 1929, Alasdair Chalmers MacIntyre is a Scottish philosopher primarily known for his contribution to moral and political philosophy, but also for his work in two further fields: the history of philosophy and theology.

63 TN: On Marcuse.

64 TN: Marcuse & MacLuhan — The New Global Revolution.

LOUIS ALTHUSSER

THE 'CAIMAN' TEACHES PEOPLE HOW to read… No, this is not a secret message. Fifty-six-year-old Louis Althusser, a professor of philosophy and a member of the French Communist Party since 1948, is a 'caiman' (meaning a tutor or teacher entrusted with preparing candidates for the *agrégation*[65] exam) at the *École normale supérieure* and someone whose chosen vocation is to help communists (re)read Marx's writings.

In 1973, after four years of silence (and oblivion too, perhaps), his *Réponse à John Lewis*[66] — a reaction to the views of an English communist where no deference is to be found — allowed the most dogmatic of all French neo-Marxist theoreticians to reclaim a trendy status.

In 1965, Mr Althusser had already published *Pour Marx*. This essay was followed by two further volumes: *Lire 'Le capital'*[67] (1965–66) and a book by P. Macherey[68] entitled *Pour une théorie de la production littéraire*.[69]

What serves as a basis for the 'Althusserian' doctrine is the conviction that Marx's philosophy has remained unfinished and that a 'genuine Marxist philosophy must still be constructed'. Mr Althusser does not hesitate to write:

> While alive, Marx did not possess, and could not enable himself to possess, an adequate concept that would allow him to *think out* what he produced, namely the concept of a structure's efficacy in relation to its elements, which represents the invisible and present-absent keystone of his entire work. (*Lire 'Le capital'*)

The essential part of Marx's writings is said to be embodied by its 'buried' implicit aspect, whether in his books, his 'silences', his slips of the pen or his characteristic lacks.

Using Freud's theories, which revealed to him the true meaning of concealment (and which he propagated at a time when, among communists,

65 TN: The *Agrégation* is a high-level competitive examination for teachers that allows them to enjoy, should they succeed, not only a higher salary but also a less onerous timetable.

66 TN: Response to John Lewis.

67 TN: Reading Marx's 'Capital'.

68 TN: Born on 17th February, 1938, Belfort Pierre Macherey is a French Marxist literary critic at the University of *Lille Nord de France* and a former student of Louis Althusser.

69 TN: For a Theory of Literary Production.

psychoanalysis was mainly perceived through 'the ideological layer of its reactionary exploitation', as stated in *Freud et Lacan*,[70] published in *La Nouvelle critique*[71] in December 1964–January 1965), Mr Althusser undertakes to track down what lies hidden between the lines and within 'the blank spaces in the tightly-knit text', as if he were the Pythia sitting on her tripod.

Reading his writings is not a usual experience, as it consists in seeking out the *unexpressed* in places where others have failed to see anything. There is thus allegedly 'an innocent' and naïve 'sort of reading', as well as a 'knowing kind of reading'—that of the initiates. Communist militants, who were all illiterate until Althusser's advent, had better 'learn to read'.

DETECTING A DISCONTINUATION IN KARL MARX'S WRITINGS

'In actual fact', remarks Mr Raymond Aron[72] in his *Marxismes imaginaires*[73] (Gallimard, 1970), 'when making use of carefully chosen quotes, Althusser attributes to Marx what he himself wants to say, just as several generations of Marxists did before him. The method is that of the theologians'.

If Marxism is genuinely the Good News of our new age, it must be *one of a kind*. This, at least, is how Althusserians think. What is it then which, in this case, characterises Marx's thinking and thus renders it *specific*?

What is unique about Marx, Mr Althusser responds, are the implications of his *Capital*'s 'scientific philosophy'.

Differentiating between 'science' and 'ideology' in Marxism, Mr Althusser asserts that this distinction corresponds to two *periods* in Marx's life. There is thus allegedly not one Marx, but two of them. On the one hand, there is the 'young Marx', the theoretician of an *ideological* historical philosophy still influenced by Kant, Hegel, Fichte and Feuerbach, and, on the other, the 'true Marx', i.e. the man who authored *Capital* (1867) and other mature works. There is a supposed 'epistemological discontinuation' between the two (a

---

70 TN: Freud and Lacan.

71 TN: *La Nouvelle critique* (New Criticism) is the title of a magazine published by the French Communist Party.

72 TN: Raymond Claude Ferdinand Aron (14th March, 1905–17th October, 1983) was a French philosopher, sociologist, political scientist, and journalist.

73 TN: Imaginary Marxisms.

notion borrowed from Gaston Bachelard[74]), one that is said to have taken place around the 1845–1850 period.

Finally, in 1857, Karl Marx purportedly reached complete 'scientificity'. Following a 'fertile loop', his thoughts, which had been shaped by *German ideology* before flourishing in his *Capital*, allegedly allowed him to read into the 'silences' of his time, just like Althusser has done. He is said to have then discovered the rational nucleus (*Kern*) of Hegel's philosophy, which he thereafter freed from its 'mystical shell' (*mystische Hülle*) by 'putting it back on its own feet'. By replacing his ideological focus with an economic one, he supposedly transformed the very foundations of his own philosophy (dialectical materialism or the German *Diamat*), while simultaneously defining it in its specificity.

Mr Althusser says that this 'second Marx' is the one that opened up the 'continent of history' to scientific research (and created the '*science* of history'), relinquishing the old mechanistic conception of materialism to espouse a dialectical one. It is this Marx that dominated idealism in philosophy and reversed the relation of theoretical forces to the advantage of the working class.

Mr Althusser writes:

> Marx established a novel kind of science, meaning that he elaborated a system of new scientific concepts where only an arrangement of ideological notions had previously reigned. He founded the science of history where only the philosophies of history had hitherto existed. (*Lénine et la philosophie*,[75] Maspéro, 1968)

The upheaval he introduced into the Hegelian system is so great that even 'the fundamental structures of the Hegelian dialectic enjoy a different *construction* through him (insofar as he adopts them, which is not always the case) when compared to what they are like with Hegel' (*Pour Marx*).

The union between the Marxist theory and the workers' movement can hence take place, a union which Mr Althusser boldly perceives as 'the greatest event in human history'. Having ceased to act as a tool to *interpret* the world, philosophy turns into a weapon that allows one to *transform* it. No longer is philosophy the mere reflection of class struggle; instead, it *embodies* the latter to the extent that it is expressed in a theory — thanks to it, the working class

---

74 TN: Gaston Bachelard (27th June, 1884–16th October, 1962) was a French philosopher who contributed to the fields of poetics and the philosophy of science.

75 TN: Lenin and Philosophy.

can draw what Lenin called a 'dividing line' between right and wrong ideas (and as such, it no longer has to justify nor *prove* itself, for it is *within itself* that it finds its own justification).

It is therefore exclusively in Marx's 'economic' works that Althusser intends to detect the 'specificity of Marxist discourse', a specificity whose 'unheard-of' novelty he, in turn, longs to develop and 'theorise'.

The objective of this undertaking is to avoid reducing Marx to his critique of capitalism (for if Marx were only someone who criticises capitalism and its mistakes, he would ultimately be nothing more than a theoretician of capitalism, but without the latter's mistakes).

Since no type of capitalism has ever led to socialist or Marxist revolution as a result of the sole interaction of its inner contradictions, it was obviously necessary for neo-Marxist thinkers to introduce some correctives into their doctrine. Indeed, there are only two options: either Marx was mistaken or he has been misinterpreted. In Mr Althusser's eyes, it is out of the question for one to dispute the Holy Scriptures, which form a certain 'totality'. This leaves us with the second position, which Mr Althusser embraces while emphasising a notion which is as central for the 'second Marx' as 'alienation' is for the 'first' — that of *surplus-value*.

'IN THE LAST INSTANCE'

This notion, however, which is founded upon an 'essentialist' and moralising conception of economy, implies that one can reduce various kinds of work whose *qualification* is different to a *single norm*, which is utterly absurd. Furthermore, it is neither quantifiable nor operational. This is why no Marxist economist has ever dared to attempt and calculate its actual rate. Last but not least, surplus-value is directly connected to the *salary* theory and the theory of labour value, both of which are founded upon a law that prices, ever determined by production costs, have never successfully confirmed. And all three notions, embodying the very core of the structure followed by Marx's *Capital*, cannot be dissociated from the criticism of capitalism.

Mr Raymond Aron remarks:

> Grounded in historical materialism, the theory of the capitalistic means of production represents *the essential part* of Marxism, which applies to Marx's own

> version of the latter as well as to that of his epigones, regardless of whether they are revolutionaries or reformists. Marxism, in fact, only aspires to scientific dignity as a theory of capitalism. (Op. cit.)

Mr Althusser bestows extraordinary importance upon the fact that Marx and Engels[76] both supported the hypothesis of the last instance determination of history by the economy. This clarification seems sufficient for him to simultaneously reject idealism and 'economism'. For to state that the economy acts as the determining factor 'in the last instance' is to define it as the *basic structure*, while also acknowledging the existence of other instances (politics, ideology) whose intervention prevents the economic dialectic from exerting exclusive influence and compels one to view society as 'a differentiated and therefore complex and articulated whole'.

It is not enough, however, to believe that the economy is the determining basis of history 'in the last instance' to avoid being accused of idealism.

Questioning the validity of the Althusserian model, Mr Jean-Marie Benoist has correctly demonstrated the speciousness of a 'discontinuation' which, above all, leads to the *inhibition* of the most visibly metaphysical aspects of Marx's doctrine, with these aspects attributed to a 'pre-Marxist' Marx, a proponent of the 'real theoretical revolution' accomplished by Feuerbach.[77]

Indeed, an attentive examination of things shows that far from being able to contrast the 'ideology' of the young Marx with the 'science' of the mature one, one must, instead, consider the second to be the continuation of the first.

One does, of course, notice an evolution between *The Manuscripts of 1844* and *Capital*. Gradually, the 'second' Marx broke free from an excessively unreal conception of 'alienation'. Not only did he reject the concepts of the Hegelian sphere, but simultaneously also the immediate ontology of

---

76 TN: Friedrich Engels (28th November, 1820–5th August, 1895) was a German philosopher, social scientist, journalist and businessman who co-founded Marxist theory together with Karl Marx.

77 TN: Ludwig Andreas von Feuerbach (28th July, 1804–13th September, 1872) was a German philosopher and anthropologist famous for his book entitled 'The Essence of Christianity', whose criticism of Christendom had an enormous impact on generations of later thinkers including Karl Marx, Friedrich Engels, and Friedrich Nietzsche.

the perceptible (meaning the primacy of the *Dasein*[78]), all to the benefit of more radical concepts. He also moved on from a simplistic theory of work alienation (See the Master-Slave topic in *The Manuscripts of 1844*) to a more intricate theory of work understood as *production*, which would henceforth dominate his system. Yet he only did so in order to adhere to *another* ontology of presence, to another immediacy.

Mr Jean-Marie Benoist writes:

> Even if it were true that the history of Western philosophy is indistinguishable from the history of the reign of idealism at the expense of materialism, one would still have to wonder whether the possibility of a symmetric or asymmetric reversal of this hierarchy to the benefit of materialism does not, in fact, borrow all of its resources from metaphysics itself.

Indeed, he adds, 'the reversal which consists in inverting the idea-matter hierarchy into a matter-idea ranking occurs in the "beyond" of an original division that constitutes the very foundation of metaphysics, a division in which the two concepts of "idea" and "matter" act as essences, as *ousiai*,[79] and ultimately as an ontology of presence'. It is '*the division* between "idea" and "matter" *itself* that is *embodied by metaphysics*, independently of the kind of relation maintained by the two terms'. 'To reverse the domination is' thus 'merely to construct, in a manner that remains *internal to metaphysics*, a symmetrical relation from the previous'.

A METAPHYSICAL RELATION

When believing himself to be putting dialectics back on its feet, Marx did not thus tear himself away from the 'venture of the ontology of presence'. Remaining within Parmenides'[80] filiation, he even accentuated the fundamen-

---

78 TN: The term *Dasein* ('being there') is a German word that has been used by several philosophers, most notably by Georg Wilhelm Friedrich Hegel in the meaning of 'existence', 'presence' or 'determinate being'.

79 TN: *Ousia* (Greek: οὐσία) is analogous to the English concepts of 'being' and 'ontic' used in contemporary philosophy. The term *ousia* is translated into Latin as *substantia* and *essentia*, and hence into English as 'substance' and 'essence'.

80 TN: Parmenides of Elea (late-6th or early-5th century BC) was a pre-Socratic Greek philosopher. He is considered one of the founders of ontology (alongside Heraclitus).

tally metaphysical character of the soil into which the discourse of his own disciples would take root once he was gone.

What serves as evidence of this fact is that one encounters the Aristotelian concept of a generic man, of man's own essence, both beyond and beneath the famous 'epistemological discontinuation'. In what are, according to Mr Althusser's assertions, the most 'scientific' texts, Marx persists in defining the revolution as the (re)generation of man's essence, as the (re)coinciding of man with his own peculiarity, as the (re)production of a dis-alienated man-object in which man's own self reclaims its being beyond the alienating constraints of real life. It is actually this 'teleological expectancy of peculiarity', this return of the Other to the Self, this reconciliation between the *genos* and the *ousia*, that defines the 'second' Marx best, the very same Marx who, in his *German Ideology*, goes as far as to state that 'a non-objective being is a non-being'!

The same inspiration underlies the entire analysis of surplus-value: in Marx's *Capital*, the terms 'capitalism', 'proletariat', 'worker', etc. have a constant and transhistorical value ('Ideology has no history') and play a role which can be equated to that of the 'universals' of Scholasticism, within a *unitary* conception of time connected to the logico-metaphysical principle of identity.

The relation between proletariat and social class thus enjoys a metaphysical connection analogous to the relation between Spinoza's substance/attribute and mode. The very notion of class consecrates the resurfacing of the identity principle in conjugation with that of substance. The idea of revolution is a chiasmus through which the relation between proletariat and class finds itself reversed, with the substance-subject-substratum becoming the hidden support for a kind of interspace caught between the categories of essence and accident, etc.

Mr Benoist expands on things further:

> This concept of surplus-value, which acts as the key notion governing all alienation and constitutes the cornerstone of this criticism of political economy, ultimately turns out to be an absence, a never-presence. What this theory of surplus-value produces are *universals*, generics, meaning entities that owe the persistency of their substance to Aristotelian metaphysics. Most analyses in Marx's *Capital* are therefore doubly encumbered: on the one hand, by their inconspicuous borrowing from metaphysical universals and, on the other, by their evasive denial which, as part of a desire to strip away the rags of philosophy, leads one to resort to such

> empirical data as industry, commerce, trade and *production*. An unavowed sort of metaphysics contaminated by *techne*[81]-based thoughts: that is what we end up with.

And here is Mr Benoist's conclusion: the notion of surplus-value, in which Mr Althusser claims to perceive the very essence of Marx's 'scientificity', actually relates to the worst kind of *ideology*. Its presence alone allows us to inscribe Marx's work into the *sphere of metaphysics*.

> What Althusser's reading of Marx actually constitutes is the opaquest blind denial of Marx's non-scientificity.

The very same observation is made by Mr Raymond Aron:

> What the Althusserians have adopted as the scientific core of Marxist economy is, in the eyes of the modern economist, its metaphysical or ideological part. (op. cit.)

Althusser's systematics is entirely founded upon this. With dialectical materialism defined as the 'science pertaining to the evolution of social formations', the existence of societies is, 'in the last instance', reduced to *economic* life as perceived at the level of mere 'social formation', meaning that of *class*. As for history, it lacks a subject, since man is to be re-placed into a 'global' economic perspective, which is governed by structures that are simultaneously causes and effects. At most, it is regarded as driven by an engine, namely class struggle. Man only exists through his integration into a class, which means that he is entirely an *object*: 'in the last instance', he does not act but *is acted upon*. And since the subject category is a constituent element of all ideology and 'ideology addresses individuals as subjects' (*Positions*), the rejection of ideology automatically results in the dismissal of the subject.

On this level, the 'structuralising' Marxism of the Althusserians contrasts with a 'historicising' sort of Marxism that is said to present the laws of history as being equivalent to those of natural sciences (for Hegel, history embodies the accomplishment of the truth). To be more specific, it contrasts with any definition of historicity as an archetypically human reality.

---

81 TN: 'Techne' is a term etymologically derived from the Greek word τέχνη, which is often translated as 'craftsmanship', 'craft', or 'art'. In philosophy, it resembles *epistēmē* in the implication of knowledge of principles but differs in the fact that its intent is to make or to do as opposed to disinterested understanding.

For these same reasons, Mr Althusser and his friends declare themselves hostile to the 'humanism' represented in particular by Mr John Lewis and Roger Garaudy, meaning, to use their jargon, to any 'discourse in which the notion of man fulfils a theoretical function'. Such a discourse is, in their eyes, a variant of moral idealism (one that is often connected to 'primary economism'), a 'leftist' deviation that only takes the 'first' Marx into account and whose theory is founded on the sole concept of individual *alienation*. And yet Mr Althusser asserts that 'one can only find something out about men under the absolute condition of reducing the philosophical myth of man to ashes'.

This statement is in agreement with the major hypotheses of structuralism (whose vocabulary Mr Althusser often borrows): absolute priority is given to the *synchronic* over the *diachronic* (to the spatial over the temporal), as structures replace individuals and culture is resorbed into nature, etc. One must also draw a parallel between these words and Lévi-Strauss's famous formula: 'The ultimate goal of human sciences is not to construct man but to dissolve him'.

Whatever its proponents may claim, Althusserian dogmatic intransigence thus leads to a fanatic sort of idealism. Their 'theoretical practice' is a pure philosophy of concepts. Mr Raymond Aron declares:

> To the great pleasure of those accustomed to philosophical dissertation, their intellectual ratiocinations replace with school-level problematics the perhaps tedious yet still authentic problems that relate to *facts* instead of "structural reality".

Having allowed Mr Althusser to 'theorise' beyond its control for many years, the French Communist Party eventually resigned itself, however timidly, to publishing his *Positions* in 1976 (Indeed, most of his other writings have been released through Maspéro). Whether it all constitutes an 'innocent' reading or not, he is undoubtedly under no illusions when it comes to the influence of a handful of philosophy professors on the masses.

Mr Althusser does not enjoy any unanimity among leftists either. For a while, the manner in which he stressed the importance of 'practice' and the necessity to turn philosophy into a tool of class struggle earned him a decent amount of popularity among the ultra-leftist students and graduates of the *École normale supérieure*.[82] He was, above all, considered a key figure among

82 TN: These students and graduates are commonly known as *normaliens*.

independent Maoists within the so-called 'For Communism' tendency (Alain Badiou and Emmanuel Terray). This, however, was not the case among French Trotskyites. Mr Daniel Bensaïd, a member of the Revolutionary Communist League (LCR), has written the following in *Rouge*:[83]

> Althusser has mastered all the skills of a charlatan.

Mr Emile Bottigelli, an assistant professor in Nanterre, states:

> The Marx that Althusser presents us with is not the real Marx, but an imagined one. (*Structuralisme et marxisme*,[84] UGE/10–18, 1970)

Interviewed in 1968 by the communist Italian daily *L'Unità*, Mr Althusser made the following confession:

> To become a Marxist-Leninist philosopher is not an easy endeavour. Just like any other intellectual, a professor of philosophy is a petty bourgeois. Whenever he opens his mouth, it is the voice of petty-bourgeois ideology that one hears; indeed, its resources and ruses are infinite.

Réponse à John Lewis, an essay by Louis Althusser. Maspéro, 102 pages.
Pour Marx, an essay by Louis Althusser. Maspéro, 264 pages.
Lire 'Le capital', a collection of texts edited by Louis Althusser and Etienne Balibar. Maspéro, 240 and 192 pages.
Positions, an essay by Louis Althusser. Ed. Sociales, 173 pages.
Théorie et politique: Louis Althusser,[85] an essay by Saül Karsz. Fayard, 340 pages.
Marx est mort, an essay by Jean-Marie Benoist. Gallimard, 252 pages.

Note that Mr Althusser, whose theories have often been criticised within the French Communist Party, seems to have nowadays returned to the bosom of communist orthodoxy. In connection to this, one should read his *Eléments d'autocritique*[86] (Hachette, 1973), as well as the text of his 'Soutenance d'Amiens',[87] dated June 1975, which was included in his first (and only) book published by the Party, *Positions* (Ed. Sociales, 1976). In it, Louis Althusser accuses himself of having cultivated paradox and even provocation by declaring, for instance,

83 TN: A Communist Journal.

84 TN: Structuralism and Marxism.

85 TN: Louis Althusser's Theory and Politics.

86 TN: Elements of Self-Criticism.

87 TN: Defence of Amiens.

that 'theory is a practice' and thus putting forward the 'theoretical practice' theory (in contrast with the idealism of pure theory). He also admits having inflated Marx's theoretical 'anti-humanism' and ventured a little too far in his struggle against pragmatism and empiricism, particularly when supporting the internal aspect of 'theoretical practice' relating to the latter's validation criteria, which was synonymous with declaring that a theory is not actually correct simply because it is so, but is proven as such as a result of its correctness ('Here again, what was at stake was the theory's relative autonomy', he writes). Last but not least, he acknowledges his excessive 'flirtation with structuralist terminology'.

The French Marxist magazine *Dialectiques*, which was established in 1973 by 'normaliens' defining themselves as 'leftist communists', published a special issue dedicated to Louis Althusser (numbers 15–16, 1976). The issue focuses primarily on a critique of Stalinism and all socialisms involving a 'bourgeois activity' on the part of the state.

In early 1977, Mr Pierre Fougeyrollas[88] published a violent pamphlet targeting 'leftist idealism' entitled 'Trois essais sur l'obscurantisme contemporain. Contre MM. Lévi-Strauss, Lacan et Althusser'[89] (Savelli). In Mr Althusser's work (which 'is ultimately but a work of exegesis and perhaps even hermeneutics'), the author of 'Contradiction et totalité'[90] (Minuit, 1964) detects a 'perfect example of regression towards Christian idealism'. Here again, he writes, 'we regress, in a hypocritical manner, towards the world of speech, meaning towards words that have been erected into a world at the expense of the very objectivity of historical processes'. He then adds:

'Through his reference to the spirit, Lévi-Strauss ebbs towards Christianity. On his part, Lacan never exits this very same Christianity when going around in circles in his phallic speech. And as for the pseudo-Marxist Althusser, he accomplishes his own Christian regression by adding to dialectical and historical materialism a kind of scholasticism compared to which the medieval one may indeed seem innovative'.

ROGER GARAUDY

'MY HUMAN LIFE STARTED WHEN I became a revolutionary militant in order to satisfy the demands of my Christian faith'.

With his tortoise shell glasses, white hair and turtleneck jumper, sixty-three-year-old Roger Garaudy once desisted Christianity to embrace Communism. He has now relinquished Communism in order to return to Christianity. A very smooth process indeed.

88 TN: Pierre Fougeyrollas (22nd December, 1922–29th May, 2008) was a French philosopher, sociologist and anthropologist.

89 TN: Three Essays on Contemporary Obscurantism — Against Mr Lévi-Strauss, Mr Lacan and Mr Althusser.

90 TN: Contradiction and Totality.

During the thirty years that he has spent on the look-out for the transcendence 'emerging from our era's revolutionary requirements', never has he ceased to assign to Marxism its 'true mission': the *earthly* realisation of the message which traditional Christianity ascribes to the beyond. In other words: the secularisation of evangelical morals, all under the authority bestowed upon him by Engels' theories on primitive ('subjectively revolutionary') Christianity and the words added by Marx merely a few lines after his famous formula stating that 'religion is the opium of the people':

> Religious distress is, at one and the same time, the *expression* of real distress and a *protest* against real distress.

This amounts to saying that despite its lack of originality, this Christianity is, at least, of a very personal nature. It is a religion devoid of original sin, Immaculate Conception ('A dogma that acts as an insult to all mothers'), and 'dualist perversion', one that longs to represent a return to 'sound biblical totality' while relying on the theologies of revolution.

From Christianity itself, what Mr Garaudy has essentially retained is the primacy of charity, the 'revolutionary' content of the Beatitudes and the replacement of aesthetics with morality.

It is this account of a conversion which, in fact, is not quite one that Mr Garaudy has published in *Parole d'homme*,[91] a book which, incidentally, begins with an autobiographical 'overview' and includes numerous passages taken from a previous book: *Peut-on être communiste aujourd'hui?*[92] (Grasset, 1968).

Roger Garaudy was born in Marseille in 1913. In 1936–37, while in Strasbourg, he learnt the basics of theology alongside Karl Barth.[93] At that time, he had already made up his mind. On the religious level, he had converted to Protestantism; on the political one, he had chosen to become a member of the French Communist Party in 1933, at the age of twenty, following a formal and necessary detour at the JOC.[94] He would later state:

---

91 TN: A Man's Word.

92 TN: Can One Be a Communist Today?

93 TN: Karl Barth (10th May, 1886–10th December, 1968) was a Swiss Reformed theologian who is often considered the greatest Protestant theologian of the 20th century.

94 TN: The *Jeunesse ouvrière chrétienne* or Young Christian Workers' association is an organisation originally founded in Belgium.

> I was still a Christian militant and intended to remain so.

Shortly afterwards, having (temporarily) lost his faith, he remained convinced that 'Communism must integrate the very best of Christian values'. He adds:

> For as long as I have lived, this concern with "holding both ends of the chain" has never left me.

In 1937, having been appointed as a professor of philosophy at the school of Albi, he joined the Tarn Office of the Communist Federation. There, he met Maurice Thorez,[95] whose friendship and support he assuredly states he had always had.

He has been a 'permanent' member of the Party since 1944. Elected as a representative of the Tarn department in 1945, he would retain a parliamentary role until 1962 and would most notably act as the president of the National Educational Commission and the Vice-President of the French National Assembly.

AN 'OUTSTRETCHED HAND'

In 1949, while preparing a book on *The Church, Communism and the Christians*, he travels to Rome, where he is received by Jacques Maritain, then ambassador to the Vatican, with 'a great deal of comprehension'. Upon his return, he would declare:

> Marxism would find itself impoverished if Saint Augustine, Saint Theresa of Avila[96] and Pascal[97] became foreign to it.

To which Maurice Thorez responded by writing:

> It had to be said, because it is the truth.

---

95 TN: Maurice Thorez (28th April, 1900–11th July, 1964) was a French politician and longtime leader of the French Communist Party (PCF) from 1930 until his death.

96 TN: Saint Teresa of Ávila (28th March, 1515–4th October, 1582) was a prominent Spanish mystic, Roman Catholic saint, Carmelite nun, author, and theologian of contemplative life through mental prayer. Active during the Counter-Reformation, she was a reformer in the Carmelite Order of her time.

97 TN: Blaise Pascal (19th June, 1623–19th August, 1662) was a brilliant 17th-century French mathematician and physicist who had a dramatic Christian conversion experience and thereafter devoted much of his thought to Christianity and philosophy.

In 1953, in *La théorie matérialiste de la connaissance*[98] (PUF), a book where he defends, in passing, 'the fundamental theory of the heredity of acquired characteristics', he asserts that Stalin 'opens uncharted historical paths and drafts unlimited perspectives of grandeur and happiness with regard to human practice'. He goes on to say:

> Never has philosophy, taken in its noblest possible sense, had such great significance as with Stalin.

A year later, in the Soviet Union, he obtains a Professor of Sciences degree thanks to a thesis on *The Issue of Liberty and Necessity in the Light of Marxism*.

In this book, which would be published in 1955 by éd. Sociales and include a preface written by Thorez, he strives to demonstrate, using a considerable number of Stalin's statements in support, that liberty only flourishes on the other side of the Iron Curtain.

'In no place could the study of the issue of freedom have been conducted better than in the land where genuine liberty now prospers for the first time in our world's history', he assures us.

Twenty years later, Mr Garaudy explains: 'Just like all of my comrades, my knowledge of Stalin was restricted to that which, within him, personified Socialism' ('We did not know about it': that is what the accused of Nuremberg also stated. In connection to the latter, however, this is what Mr Garaudy writes: 'Anyone who executes a criminal order is himself a criminal').

At the CERM (Centre of Marxist Studies and Research), which he would run for a period of ten years (alongside Gabriel Mury, who, having subsequently embraced Maoism, has since passed away), and on the occasion of the Weeks of Marxist Thought, he lays the doctrinal foundations of the policy of the 'outstretched hand'.

Following Vatican II, his efforts in favour of 'dialogue' garner cardinal Koenig's support. In 1962, the Archbishop of Recife, Dom Helder Camara, declares to him in Brazil:

> The next step for you to accomplish, Roger, is to demonstrate that revolution is consubstantial with Christianity.

---

98 TN: The Materialistic Theory of Knowledge.

And that is what he sets out to achieve. In March 1964, he takes a public stand against Ilichev, one of the leaders of ideological work in the USSR, who had stated that religion 'turns man into a layabout, God's slave, someone who is only capable of remaining on his knees and begging for divine grace'. This constituted the very first case where a French Communist Party leader openly criticised a 'theological mistake' on the part of the Soviet Communist Party. This declaration caused quite an uproar.

Soon, May 1968 was upon us — a great red sun arose, dazzling everyone. Tormented by a sort of ideological andropause, Roger Garaudy discovers, albeit late, that some analyses presented by his own party had become 'outdated'. He reproaches the central committee for not venturing far enough in its dialogue with Christian believers. Alongside Aragon,[99] he comes down in favour of free artistic expression.

On 6th February, 1970, during the sixteenth congress of the French Communist Party, he conducts one final intervention, amidst a deathlike silence. All his former friends had cautiously desisted him, along with 'evangelical Leftism' and the 'Third World'.

A FACTOR OF DISORDER

In 1972, after a two-year reflection period, he affirms: 'The issue we face today is that of extending the movement inaugurated by Marx by restarting the dialectic blocked by dogmatism' (*Karl Marx*, Seghers).

This project leads to his *Parole d'homme*, an exalted hymn dedicated to Love, Man and Others. All of which are necessarily capitalised.

Mr Garaudy explains:

> Love is the *opposite of justice*, since the latter consists in treating everyone according to what they actually are, meaning in harmony with what they have done in the past. Love breaks this rule of the game, this law of order. It represents a factor of *disorder*. It is a wager upon man's future. An entire life can be *subverted* by this wager, by this act of love that grants it the necessary space for otherness.

---

[99] TN: Louis Aragon (3rd October, 1897–24th December, 1982) was a French poet and one of the leading voices of the surrealist movement in France. He was also a novelist and editor, a long-time member of the Communist Party and a member of the *Académie Goncourt*.

The great word has henceforth been set loose. There is no longer any need for a definition: all is love and vice-versa. 'Any authentic socialist revolution will be embodied by the triumph of love'; 'Happiness is, above all, love'; 'Your person is shaped by your responses to love's interpellations'; 'Death is but an even greater love'; etc.

A love of whom, then? A love of others; of *all* others. The fact of loving a specific being, a certain individual is already something scandalous in the eyes of Roger Garaudy, who only dreams of universal fusion and of the dissolution of the individual into the 'Great All', seizing every single opportunity to manifest his loathing for the differences, distinctions and inequalities that form the very frame of life.

'Hell is the absence of others',[100] he writes, before adding: 'Happiness begins with the dispossession of the self and one's communion with the all'.

Hence a complete inversion of values: universalism represents the 'good', self-affirmation the 'bad'. Oblivious to the time when he celebrated 'Promethean morality', Mr Garaudy condemns the 'reign of Faust'. He claims that the West, the source of all ailments, has 'impoverished itself miserably' during two decisive periods: the Greek miracle (with its 'sad-faced horsemen') and the Renaissance, which he perceives as the originator of scientism, technicism and colonialism. It is a thought that obsesses him and which he reiterates in all the chapters of his book.

From a general perspective, all that is specifically European, Promethean or simply *masculine* repels him. He sees a clear link between these three kinds of notion. The core of his thought is epitomised by intellectual matriarchy and gynocracy. He declares himself opposed to any relation with nature that would put man in the position of a 'conqueror', preferring to *be conquered* instead. Quoting the words of Aragon ('Woman is the future of man'), he praises the 'feminine dimension denied by our Western and masculine civilisation'.

> The African mask, which renders the invisible visible, is closer and more fraternal to us than the possessive reconstruction of our world in classical art; and the *musique concrète* which helps us unite or merge with the surrounding universe exerts more appeal on us, at times, than the great harmonies through which the monopolising domination of the human spirit once expressed itself.

[100] TN: With these words, Garaudy contradicts Jean-Paul Sartre, who considered others to be the embodiment of hell.

Step by step, he denounces all the structures that act as an obstacle to his dream: traditional education, which renders pupils 'as foolish and talkative as Cicero'; the family, since 'the love of our children becomes specifically human when evading the guardianship of the family'; and ownership: 'The major characteristic of our era lies in the objective reality of the necessary *disintegration* of private company ownership, on society's pain of death'.

Already in 1963, he alleged that the establishment of socialism could allow us to 'extend the lives of men, on average, to the age of 150 or 200'. By observing the 'grandiose construction plan of communism in the USSR', he had gained the conviction that 'only such a regime could ever manage to create a democracy devoid of lies'.

Today still, he has yet to renounce utopianism:

> The ultimate goal of our historical struggle is to conquer this unity of man, allowing each man to simultaneously be a technician and a philosopher, the master of his own destiny and the inventor of his own future.

These topics lack any kind of originality. One might even wonder whether the sterile repetition of the words 'man' and 'human', which contemporary discourse has turned into a sort of rite, does not actually denote the exhaustion of the classic 'human perspective', in a manner that would leave us with merely two means of escape: either from above or from below; either through the progressive or through the regressive; either through the superhuman or through the infra-human.

In unison with contemporary trends, Mr Garaudy bets on the option of regression.

In the end, what strikes readers most when reading *Parole d'homme* is the surprising decrease in standards that seems to have accompanied Mr Garaudy on his career path. *La liberté*[101] (éd. Sociales, 1955), *La théorie matérialiste de la connaissance* (PUF, 1953), and *Qu'est-ce que la morale marxiste?*[102] (éd. Sociales, 1963) were among the books in which some things could indeed have been retold. Yet they were all books that had been well-thought out and structured, books that testified to a certain mental prowess, one that was supported by an occasionally remarkable ability to present arguments.

---

101 TN: Liberty.

102 TN: The Definition of Marxist Morality.

No such thing can be found in *Parole d'homme*, which is but a confused collection of egalitarian ideas and falsely selfless banalities in which the author, having plummeted to the level of a Christian-Teilhardian communist invertebrate, sets out to repeat, page after page, his invocations to 'humanity', using the sniffling tones of a suburban vicar.

Parole d'homme, an essay by Roger Garaudy. Laffont, 256 pages.

Mr Garaudy is currently in charge of an Institute for the interaction and interpenetration of cultures. In his last book, *Le projet espérance*[103] (Laffont, 1976), he once again manifests his contempt for European culture. He has, likewise, returned to his diatribes against the Renaissance, through which he incidentally draws closer to 'classical' Leftism and continues drifting away from the Communist Party. In the 15th issue of *Cahiers d'histoire de l'Institut Maurice Thorez*[104] (first trimester, 1976), a series of notebooks whose main editor is Mr Georges Gogniot, what was actually stated about Thorez is that he 'particularly dignified the Renaissance [...], a period which he, just like Engels, believed to have required and ultimately produced giants'.

On the topic of the excessive use of the word 'love' at the hands of Mr Garaudy and his emulators, see Mr Louis Pauwels' chronicle entitled 'L'amour, ce mot à désinfecter'[105] (in *Le Journal du dimanche*,[106] 24th October, 1976).

IVAN ILLICH

GREEK ANTIQUITY HAS PASSED DOWN to us the myth of Prometheus and his brother, Epimetheus. The former chose to take up the gods' challenge and brought fire to mankind. He would thus become the symbol of a civilisation dedicated to ever overcoming itself. The latter, whose name means 'he who looks back', is entirely different. He married Pandora, who burdened humanity with all conceivable evils and only granted man hope in consolation.

103 TN: Project Hope.

104 TN: The Maurice Thorez Institute's Historical Notebooks.

105 TN: Love, a Disinfection-Worthy Word.

106 TN: *Le Journal du Dimanche* (Sunday's newspaper) is a French weekly newspaper published on Sundays.

'We are pinning our hope on *nature's* generosity', specifies Ivan Illich, a supporter of Epimetheus, who the Greeks considered to be both an oaf and a fool.

Illich is very vocal in his criticism of the Greeks, who 'constructed a society founded upon reason and authority'. The man of today is their heir and 'lives immoderately, as part of a Promethean ideal that has been taken to the extreme', he writes.

Here is an example of 'immoderation': the efforts of medicine to combat disease.

In June 1974, Illich published an article in *Esprit* magazine entitled *The Expropriation of Health*, which began with the following words: 'Medical acts are one of the principal sources of morbidity'. It was followed by a campaign that saw an increase in the number of works sponsored by the 'humanistic' extreme Left and whose culmination came with the publication of a book written by Ivan Illich and entitled *Medical Nemesis*.

An American citizen, Ivan Illich was born in 1926 in Vienna, into a Jewish family of Russian emigrants. He studied at the Gregorian University of Rome. Having obtained a bachelor's degree in theology, he is ordained to the priesthood. In 1951, he heads off to New York, where he would exercise his ministry in the Puerto Rican neighbourhood of Manhattan and attract Cardinal Spellmann's attention.

From then on, his promotion follows a swift pace. In 1956, he is appointed vice-rector at the Catholic University of Puerto Rico. Committed to progressive ideas, it is Latin America that fascinates him: in 2000, 65% of all Christians are expected to inhabit the Third World.

In 1960, he departs for Mexico. In Cuernavaca, sixty kilometres from the capital city, Illich founds what *Chrétiens d'aujourd'hui*[107] magazine calls a 'faith-action laboratory': the *Centro Intercultural de Documentación*[108] (CIDOC). Placed under the chairmanship of a strong Monsignor named Arceo Mendez, the centre would soon attain global recognition. Benedictine Grégoire Lemercier would then launch an experiment of 'convent psychoanalysis' there. Illich himself turns the Centre into a war machine against both

[107] TN: Today's Christians.

[108] TN: Intercultural Centre of Documentation.

'ecclesiastic bureaucracy' ('The largest in the world: 180,000 lifetime officials') and developed countries.

With his dangling hair, high cheekbones, and a smile that reveals his rodent-like teeth, Illich is a man that longs to blow up the structures of the 'bourgeois' world. And from within the Church at that.

TARGETING SCHOOL WITH DESTRUCTION

His strategy is a simple one: we are to break with capitalism, support the 'just struggle' of terrorists and combine the socialist idea with the evangelical Beatitudes. His position statements, founded upon psychoanalysis (Freud), sociology (Durkheim) and political economics (Marx), are remarkably radical. Illich openly declares himself 'subversive'. Besides, the theories that he develops often coincide with the hierarchy's revolutionary orientations.

In 1968, Latin American bishops gathered in Medellin (Colombia) proclaimed themselves in favour of a revolutionary theology. In October 1974, Dom Helder Camara, the archbishop of Recife, stated the following: 'We have, in a certain way, proved Marx right'.

On the religious level, Illich is a supporter of sacerdotal secularisation, as he himself leads the life of 'secular priest'. Yet he does celebrate Mass, and Rome has never disavowed him.

In 1971, two of his books were translated into French: *Deschooling Society* and *Celebration of Awareness*. The first is an anti-teaching pamphlet that will find a supporter in the person of Mr Pierre Emmanuel of the *Académie française*. In it, Illich denounces the mystifying and even 'harmful' character of school institutions. Far from being democratic, he says, schools *perpetuate* inequalities. It is thanks to them that the self-worshiping bourgeoisie endows itself with youths that remain in line with the 'official model'. Schools are therefore of a 'demobilising' nature and are not to be reformed but *destroyed.*

To replace schools, Illich proposes the implementation of 'exchanges among equals'. Here is an example:

'To create a team whose members are willing to help each other in order to understand an article written by Mao, Marcuse, Freud or Goodman.'[109]

---

[109] TN: This seems to be a reference to Paul Goodman (9th September, 1911–2nd August, 1972), an American novelist, playwright, poet, literary critic, and psychotherapist who gained

In *Celebration of Awareness*, it is not only schools that Illich targets, but all *institutions*: the army (whose absurdity is 'obvious'), the police, transport, medicine, the industry and the state.

His doctrine is, once again, a simple transposition of the story of original sin. Before his fall, man was naturally good and knew nothing of the injustices and wars that are consubstantial with history. However, he acquired a belief in the power of 'professionals': from the specialisation of roles emerged the division of labour. Society thus underwent a differentiation process and gave birth to hierarchies. Following the example set by Prometheus, its members sought to take up the challenges of existence. That is precisely how we arrived at the 'Industrial Mode of Production' (IMP): the reign of the 'mega-machine' has gone hand in hand with the advent of the Malign.

ANTI-DEVELOPMENT

In Illich's eyes, the sin of Marxism lies rather in its moderation than elsewhere. In his *Tools for Conviviality*, he writes:

> What interests me is not the opposition between a class of exploited men and a class of tool owners but the opposition involving, above all, man and the very structure of tools.

Man is thus said to have sinned by submitting to the demands of social life, as allegedly confirmed by the 'inhumanity' of *institutions*, which Illich considers to be the embodiment of absolute evil.

In agreement with Marcuse's views on this, Illich asserts that institutions are subject to criticism because inasmuch as they ensure a better relation between men and the world that surrounds them, they objectively reinforce the latter in its current reality. In other words, it would be preferable to have genuinely intolerable institutions, since their presence would facilitate the advent of the revolution. Society is bad — to the very same extent that it is good.

In passing, Illich displays his admiration for primitive societies, those where (*historically* speaking) nothing ever comes to pass:

---

notoriety as a social critic and anarchist philosopher. Goodman was also an activist of the pacifist Left in the 1960s.

> In certain tribes characterised by their small size and great cohesion, knowledge is divided very equitably: each person knows most of what everyone else does.

The solution? To return to a 'convivial' — meaning more *egalitarian* — society, to 'simpler' social relations, to 'poor tools' and social homogeneity. To create 'convivial centres' verging on Fourierist phalansteries and renovated convents.

To underdeveloped countries, anti-development is what Ivan Illich preaches:

> Poor countries will begin their reconstruction with greater ease if they are able to define some tooling limitation criteria.

This is where we plummet into a completely messianic sort of vision. With things going from bad to worse, the world marches towards the Apocalypse. A Great Crisis shall soon come, one that shall strike down the modern Babylon of indecency by abolishing several millennia of exploitation. At that moment, light shall emerge from the chaos. Humanity, rendered angel-like, shall gain access to the heavenly kingdom of socialism. As for history, it shall be resorbed into the 'Great All', marking the end of Cain's children and the return of good old Adam. And in this 'convivial' paradise, we shall witness the virtual renewal of the bread loaf multiplication miracle: 'People will do more and more with less and less', Illich writes.

In Bukharin's utopian communism, everyone is supposed to practice all available trades one by one: there are no more dentists, so go right ahead and pull each other's teeth out. The same regressive doctrine is encountered with Illich, only this time, it is founded upon the myth of a 'good nature'.

Alain[110] once said:

> To dream that ignorant and naïve populations were truly happy before the advent of policemen is still that: a dream.

Indeed, Illich himself is dreaming. His conviction according to which 'natural' man was more in control of his environment than *constructed* man through his institutions betrays his complete ignorance of human societies. Illich longs to disregard the cruelty of primitive societies, the depressing fixity of 'savage

110 Born Émile-Auguste Chartier, Alain (3rd March, 1868–2nd June, 1951) was a French philosopher, journalist, essayist, and professor of philosophy.

thought' and the carnivore's struggle for daily survival. Under the apparent generosity of Rousseau-like idealism, it is a return to the *pre-human* that he proposes. For the institutions that he denounces contribute to the very *definition* of man (including his prehistorical form). Illich's convivial society is not even that of large primates. It would, at best, be an amoebic society.

The excesses pervading Illich's antimedical campaign have also earned him the most severe criticisms. *Le Quotidien du médecin*[111] responded to his claims with a 'counter-investigation'. A *White Book of Pro-Medical Testimonies* has additionally been published, and the French Order of Physicians has reacted as well. Mr Henri Laborit, a specialist in behavioural biology, declares:

> Just like everyone else, I, too, wish to discover this ideal society from which all human disease would be excluded. In the meantime, however, I would rather have myself and not just my sociocultural and professional environment looked at if, for instance, my stomach or bladder were punctured or I found myself stricken with meningitis.

Stripped of all borrowings, banalities, hasty generalisations and truncated statistics, Illich's work essentially comes across as highly superficial and extremely mediocre. Compared to those of Althusser, Marcuse and Lévi-Strauss, his writings (written in collaboration with the students of the CIDOC) strike us as nothing more than an add-on piece. What they express in a radical (and imaged) fashion is, at most, the rejection of challenges and one's anguish in the face of the very realities that our age's various apocalypses feed on. Mr Max Gallo[112] writes:

> What Illich's admirers seek in his words are not argument-based demonstrations. They believe in the battle between Good and Evil and are driven by a nostalgia for a perfect world whose return they hope to experience. And that is all a matter of *faith*. But why is it that Illich feels compelled to disguise this faith as social science?

Tools for Conviviality, an essay by Ivan Illich. Seuil, 160 pages.
Deschooling Society, an essay by Ivan Illich. Seuil, 192 pages.
Celebration of Awareness, an essay by Ivan Illich. Seuil, 129 pages.

---

111 TN: The Physician's Daily.

112 TN: Max Gallo (7th January, 1932–18th July, 2017) was a French author, historian and politician who joined the French Socialist Party in 1974.

Energy and Equity, an essay by Ivan Illich. Seuil, 64 pages.

EDGAR MORIN

'MAN CAN NEITHER BE REDUCED to his *Homo faber* technician aspect nor to his *Homo sapiens* rationalistic side', Edgar Morin writes. 'When contemplating the true face of man, one must consider the myths, celebrations, dances, singing, ecstasy and love... One must not reject his affectivity, neurosis, disorder, and vagaries as being "noise", residue and waste. The real essence of man is to be found in the *Sapiens-Demens* dialectic'.

Displaying long but thinning hair, a domed skull, a pair of glasses and a thick-lipped rictus, Mr Morin, a researcher at the CNRS, belongs to the concerned leftist theoretician species.

The book he published in 1973 is entitled *Le paradigme perdu: la nature humaine.*[113] In contrast with a 'syntagm', linguists define a 'paradigm' as an *element class* (Saussure's[114] 'associative groups') allowing one to assemble a unit. This does not, however, render the book's purpose any clearer.

In order to grasp Mr Morin's discourse, one must, in fact, situate it in the context of currently ongoing discussions regarding the very *status* of human beings.

For centuries on end, a purely metaphysical perception of nature seemed to justify a 'divide' not only between men and animals, but also between life and the inanimate. Countering this conception of things, contemporary scientists have applied themselves to demonstrating that man is equally part of the animal world, that living systems are all related and that life, which emerged from lifelessness, is nothing but 'organised matter'.

Owing to this, some have been very quick to fall into a new illusion which consists in stating that since one can equate the different levels of reality to one

---

113 TN: The Lost Paradigm: Human Nature.

114 TN: Ferdinand de Saussure (26th November, 1857–22nd February, 1913) was a Swiss linguist and semiotician. He is widely considered to have been one of the most influential thinkers in the field.

another, there is 'no fundamental difference' between them. Such is the view of *reductionism*, which emphasises the *similarities* and neglects the *differences*.

By means of a debate on 'emergent properties' and 'sudden qualitative leaps', it is also the question of *limits* that finds itself posed. There is an entire current of trendy ideas that would like to use the fact that nothing is absolute as a pretext to say that 'nothing exists' or that 'everything is of equal worth': since every definition is based on *consensus*, one should allegedly renounce definitions and ban consensuses. The specious aspect of such argumentation is immediately obvious.

There is no 'D day' that would mark a child's entry into adulthood, yet there are still both children and adults. Likewise, both Europe and Asia exist, as do Whites and Blacks and the Antiquity and the Middle Ages. The absence of 'boundary markers' in space-time does nothing to alter a *plural* reality which, indeed, is founded upon the relative and the contingent.

HOMO DEMENS

There are diverging viewpoints among ideologists when it comes to identifying the *specific* traits of the human phenomenon.

Mr Morin's 'paradigm' represents an attempt to take stock of the lessons that can be drawn from the most recent scientific findings in the fields of biology, ethnology, etc. With this intention in mind, he has spent several months in the United States. The results of his efforts are, unfortunately, rather disappointing.

Admittedly, his observations are not all questionable — far from it. Unlike Mr Lévi-Strauss, Mr Morin has the merit of not restricting his research on man to sociocultural archaisms. Furthermore, he demonstrates the sophisms pervading reductionism rather well. In the first part of his book, which is in all likelihood the best one, he reminds his readers that 'we ourselves are primates as well'; that, among our 'inferior' brothers, hierarchy, classes, families and natural selection are the law; and that society, far from being an 'alienating' privilege characterising mankind, is a very widespread form of self-organisation in living systems.

He also quotes the words of Serge Moscovici,[115] who views the hominisation process as 'the human becoming of hunters and not as a future manhunt'.

Last but not least, what he highlights — and with good reason, I might add — is that the development of the brain goes hand in hand with 'rejuvenation', meaning the extension of the prepubescent period during which a child needs to be 'supervised' (which explains the reason why man is an 'animal that can be trained').

None of this is, however, anything new. On this level, Edgar Morin contents himself with intersecting, albeit with a certain delay, the works of Huxley, Tinbergen, Lorenz, Eibl-Eibesfeldt, etc. This is what he writes:

> Ever since Darwin, we have only acknowledged the fact that we are the sons of primates, but not that we are primates *ourselves*.

Moreover, when demonstrating that 'life is a system of permanent reorganisation founded on a logic of complexity', he omits to mention the fact that increasing *complexity* goes hand in hand with *differentiation* and, therefore, *inequality*.

The truth is that despite his declared intentions, his point of view is still distorted by an egalitarian, universalistic and *one-dimensional* conception of the cosmos. It is as if he feared that, by drawing the logical conclusions from the facts he imparts, he would discover truths that he would be unable to bear.

He thus only envisions free will, a characteristic of man, from the perspective of the latter's impulses.

This specificity, he writes, lies in the fact that man is an 'animal endowed with foolishness'. *Homo sapiens* thus becomes *Homo demens*, whose originality is found in a 'dimension of folly'. This results in several naïve statements, including the following one:

> Despite the ethnocultural diaspora, all human beings express themselves essentially through smiles, laughter and tears.

Indeed, tackling the issue of the differences between men, Mr Morin declares them to be 'epiphenomenal'. They are all cases of 'efflorescence'. In his eyes, the

---

115 TN: Serge Moscovici (14th June, 1925–15th November, 2014) was a Romanian-born French social psychologist.

only thing that matters is the fact that they all 'stem from the same anthropo-sociological foundations'. He adds:

> It is the very same *Homo sapiens* that underwent a worldwide diaspora by infinitely diversifying himself on the cultural level.

What he fails to realise is that these cases of 'efflorescence' are precisely what enriches mankind. And he remains unaware (or feigns ignorance) of the fact that, when it comes to man's origin, it is the polycentric theory that is gaining ground on a daily basis, and it seems ever more likely (as shown by Weidenreich's work, which was subsequently expanded by Coon and Thoma) that man's raciation took place *prior to* the *sapiens* stage.

In point of fact, Mr Morin does declare that 'our love of other races must be manifested physically'.

Elsewhere, his admittedly highly abstract rigour gives way to sheer flights of fancy, for instance when highlighting the fact that the ancestors of the *Homo sapiens* species simply 'seceded' from their own species one day, desisting the forests so as to settle in the savannah. He writes:

> It thus seems that the abnormal, the rejected, the *heimatlos*,[116] the adventuresome and the rebellious are the initiators of the hominian revolution.

META-MICRO-MEGA

This rather pithy turn of phrase brings to mind the books which Mr Morin dedicated to the neo-communards (*Mai 1968: la brèche*[117]), to the hippies (*Journal de Californie*[118]) and to other 'abnormal, rejected and *heimatlos*' people. His book thus takes on the shape of a *self-serving persuasion* plea.

What Mr Edgar Morin wants, in fact, is to reconcile the science of today with his lifelong instincts. He writes:

> The purpose is to simultaneously change life, transform the world, revolutionise the individual and unite mankind, and attain a meta-micro-mega society whose expression stretches from inter-personal relations to world order.

---

116 TN: Those without a homeland.

117 TN: May 1968: The Breach.

118 TN: California Journal.

This programme can be summarised with one single heartfelt appeal: 'Praised be the bastards, the genuine representatives of the *Anthropos*!'.

Science, you say? I think not.

Le paradigme perdu: la nature humaine, an essay by Edgar Morin. Seuil, 251 pages.

Mr Morin's 'civilisational project' is rather consistent with the perspectives mentioned (in a satisfied sort of manner) by Mr Jacques Ruffié[119] in his essay entitled *De la biologie à la culture*[120] (Flammarion, 1977):

'Inexorably, mankind is heading towards generalised "milk-chocolatisation", a vast inter-communicating gene pool, and planetary panmixia. This possibility was recently envisioned as part of a certain futuristic novel in which the earth, now largely panmictic and intermixed, is inhabited by a more or less uniform population comprising individuals of average height, swarthy skin and inconspicuously slanting eyes. White characteristics are virtually unrecognisable in this new global man'.

Mr Ruffié, according to whom 'patriotism represents a serious obstacle to the integration of mankind, and thus also to its progress', adds:

'If prehistoric man was part of a horde or tribe and historical man a member of a nation, post-historical men will, on their part, become citizens of the world. Having raised the anchor that bound him to animality, post-historical man will undoubtedly reach a new frontier. By crossing the latter, he shall be rid of the last traces of animal behaviour and shall only display humanised behaviour (sic). Wisdom should then triumph over folly, reason over passion, altruism over egoism, justice over exploitation and modesty over pride'.

Talk about a dream!

119 TN: Jacques Ruffié (22nd November, 1921–1st July, 2004) was a French haematologist, geneticist and anthropologist. He is famous for having founded a discipline called 'blood typing', allowing for the study of blood characteristics to determine the history of the people, their migration and their successive interbreeding.

120 TN: From Biology to Culture.

VIEWPOINTS

ON FRANCE

GARGANTUA'S FRANCE

FOLKLORIST PAUL SÉBILLOT ONCE STATED that 'there is no popular character whose name is as universally known in France as his. It is encountered in both the *langue d'oc* and the *langue d'oïl* regions.[1] Some of his adventures are thus recounted everywhere, so to speak'.

The character in question is Gargantua.

Considering the great diversity of the peoples represented in mainland France, one has often wondered if it is even possible to speak of 'French folklore'. Mrs Nicole Belmont[2] observes:

> It would appear that France, whose geographical boundaries and history border on the respective domains of Germanic-Scandinavian, Roman and Celtic mythology, lacks a mythological system of its own. It is even impossible to detect any remains of what may once have embodied such a system. And when France did eventually take shape as a nation, Christianity had long since established itself upon its territory.

The myth of the 'wild hunt', which is very widespread in both France and Belgium (and is referred to as '*chasse Arthur* or *Artus*', '*chasse* or *Mesnie Hellequin*', and '*chasse Gayère* or *Gallery*', depending in the region), is an example of this. Some of its motifs are encountered in the legends of Saint

1 TN: *Langue d'oc* and *langue d'oïl* are the two principal groups of medieval French dialects. It is the latter that has evolved into today's 'official French'.

2 TN: Nicole Belmont is a French anthropologist specialising in Europeanism.

Hubert[3] and Saint Eustace.[4] The tale depicts a character who, accompanied by his hounds and retinue, is condemned to forever pursue game that always manages to escape. Under the bright moon of a stormy night, he traverses the sky amidst great turmoil. Behind the 'wild hunter' (*Wilder Jäger*) figure, there are some who have identified the traits of the Germanic god Odin or Wotan.

The *Colline inspirée* or 'Sacred Hill' of Sion-Vaudémont in the Lorraine region was, likewise, documented in 1150 AD as *Wodanis Mons*, meaning 'Wotan's Mount'.

As for the myth of the 'werewolf', experts — including Stig Wikander, Mary R. Gernstein, and Przyluski — have shown that it relates directly to, by means of the social vestiges of ancient 'warrior brotherhoods', the conception of the outlaw espoused by Indo-Europeans.

The French domain of legends is nonetheless of an astounding richness, with its rondes of fairies and elves, its ogres, its leprechauns, its conjurers and goblins, its wyverns and dragons, its sliding rocks that reveal hidden treasures, its men that shapeshift into beasts, its pagan heirlooms, its enchanted forests and its sunken cities.

THE SHAPES AND CONSEQUENCES OF CHRISTIANISATION

Following Charles Perrault,[5] whose *Tales* (published in 1697) are almost exclusively of popular origin, contemporary folklorists and ethnographers have exerted themselves to compile, classify and analyse our legends, customs and sayings.

---

3 TN: Saint Hubertus or Hubert (c. 656–30th May, 727) is a Christian saint who is regarded as the patron saint of hunters, mathematicians, opticians, and metalworkers. The iconography of his legend is entangled with that of Saint Eustace.

4 TN: Saint Eustace, who, according to legend, lived in the 2nd century AD, is a revered Christian martyr and soldier saint. While hunting a stag in Tivoli, in the vicinity of Rome, Placidus (as he was originally called) is alleged to have had a vision of a crucifix lodged between the stag's antlers. He immediately converted to Christianity, had both himself and his family baptised and changed his name to Eustace.

5 TN: Charles Perrault (12th January, 1628–16th May, 1703) was a French author who laid the foundations for a new literary genre, the fairy tale, deriving his works from earlier folk tales.

Among them, those that are particularly worthy of mention are Pierre Saintyves (Emile Nourry); Paul Sébillot, who founded the *Revue des traditions populaires*;[6] André Varagnac; and, above all, Arnold Van Gennep (1873–1957), whose monumental work entitled *Manuel de folklore français contemporain*[7] (Picard) remains, however, unfinished.

They all affirm that it is a *pre-Christian* France that looms and survives behind this framework of diffuse beliefs.

Mrs Belmont notes:

> The Church has adopted two attitudes towards such practices. There are some which it considered to be superstitions and which, as a result, it obstinately fought against for centuries on end, albeit often unsuccessfully. There are, however, others that it attempted to Christianise either by replacing "heathen" practices with a Christian content or by intervening directly and imposing Christian rites instead.

In 452, for instance, the Arles Council condemned all those who worshipped fountains, stones and woods. In 658, the Council of Nantes ordained their excommunication.

And yet in the 20th century, the belief that sterile women can acquire the ability to bear children by rubbing themselves against certain menhirs still subsists.

Faced with excessively fierce resistance, the Church preferred to compromise: cathedrals and monasteries were simply erected in places where ancient sanctuaries had previously stood.

This fact is particularly striking when it comes to 'calendar' customs (which are classified as part of a season-based system): we have the Carnival and Lent cycles, as well as those of Easter and May, Saint-John's Eve on the solstice of June, and the twelve days of Christmas-Epiphany that mark the winter solstice.

All Hallows' Day is set on the 1st of November, on the very day when the Celts celebrated Samhain, meaning 'All Souls Day'. Christmas, which is commemorated at the height of the winter solstice, adopted the function previously assumed by the winter celebration of the Sun's rebirth. With its blessing of the palms, Easter took over from the spring feast which celebrated the death and resurrection of the gods of vegetation (commemorated among

---

6 TN: Journal of Popular Traditions.

7 TN: Manual of Contemporary French Folklore.

Indo-Europeans in honour of *Ostara*[8]). The bonfires of the summer solstice have been replaced by those of Saint-John's Eve, the ancient festival of Diana by the Feast of the Assumption, the rites of Dionysus' rebirth by the Feast of the Epiphany, the forty nights of lamentation of Proserpine's mysteries by the Lenten fast, the Roman *Ambarvalia* by the Rogation Days, *Saturnalia* by Carnival, the *Parilia* or celebration of Rome's rebirth by Saint-George's Day, etc.

In Latin countries, few marriages were, until recently, celebrated during the month of May, since the latter is consecrated to the Virgin Mary. Strangely enough, it is this very same month that the Romans considered 'harmful to matrimonial union'.

In Rome, during Saturnalias, masters and slaves would swap roles for a few hours. In the Middle Ages, Carnival fulfilled the same function of 'compensating liberation': everything was allowed, including the fact of passing oneself off for another by means of disguise; one proceeded to crown someone the 'king of fools'; and the list goes on. According to Van Gennep, this period is characterised 'by a temporary suspension of the rules of normal life, by a right to personal or collective insults, and by the emergence of sexual and even erotic acts or, more often, symbols'.

Whereas in Ireland, Saint Brigitte has supplanted the Celtic goddess Birgit, whose functions she partly assumed, there are numerous local saints in France who have, likewise, adopted the virtues of ancient pagan divinities, beginning with healer saints — not to mention the 'Phallic' ones (*Foutin*, *Phallier*, *Génitour* and *Jacut*).

Starting in the late medieval period, at a time when Christianity peaked, one witnessed, on the fringes of Christian rites in their strictest sense, a large number of new 'superstitious' practices relating to what Van Gennep termed 'the fringe folklorisation of Christian worship'. This is evidenced by the presence of Easter eggs, Saint John's herbs and firebrands, the 'Queen of May' rites, the Yule log, christening favours, etc. These are the 'Christian marvels' that have enchanted entire generations of faithful believers, exerting, at times, a greater appeal than dogma itself.

---

[8] TN: *Ēostre* or *Ostara* is a Germanic goddess who, by way of the Germanic month bearing her name, is the namesake of the festival of Easter in some languages.

Among the beliefs connected to the archetypal rite of *passage* which christening undoubtedly is, Nicole Belmont mentions the example of the *chrémeau*:[9] 'It is an "under-hat" that is worn underneath the actual Christening hat and that comes into contact with the Holy Chrism which the child's head is anointed with; hence its name. It is kept most painstakingly by the parents and is often used by all the family's children successively. There is a link of sympathetic magic that ties the child to the hat: should the latter ever be misplaced or damaged, the child's very life would find itself threatened'.

A FAMOUS CHARACTER

Displaying greater optimism than Mrs Belmont, Mr Henri Dontenville[10] does not believe that Christianisation and the diversity of regional traditions have done much in terms of preventing the development of French national folklore.

In several recent books, he enumerates the principal characters of our folklore: *Mélusine* the fairy, *Aymon*'s sons, and especially *Gargantua* the giant.

He views the character of *Mélusine* as one whose name is an altered form of the ancient 'Mère Lusine'[11] (which, on the toponymical level, is to be likened to Lusignan, Lézignan, Lusigny, Lésigneux, etc.) and refers to a 'luminous mother' (as in *lux* or Lucy).

As for Gargantua, the mere popularity of Rabelais's[12] books, however great it may have been, does not obviously suffice to explain the multitude of traditions and legends which focus on him, nor is it sufficient to account for the fact that his presence can be encountered in all French regions, especially in the domain of topographical folklore.

---

9 TN: Translated interpretatively, *chrémeau* means 'chrismal hat'.

10 TN: Born in 1888 in Charenton-le-Pont, Henri Dontenville was a French mythographer and the creator of the *Société de mythologie française* (Society of French Mythology). He passed away in 1981.

11 TN: Literally 'Mother Lusine'.

12 TN: François Rabelais (1483 to 1494–9th April, 1553) was a French author, physician, Renaissance humanist, monk and Greek scholar. Historically, he has been regarded as a writer of fantasy, satire, the grotesque, bawdy jokes and songs. His best-known work is *Gargantua and Pantagruel.*

His gigantic height, strength, enormousness, gluttony, and role as a topographical and hydrographical modeller have turned him into a most famous character. As specified by Mrs Belmont, 'he is given credit for the birth of numerous mountains, hills, mounds, knolls, hillocks, upright stones, lakes, swamps, etc. Gargantua creates mountains and hills either by scraping off the earth that has remained stuck to the sole of his shoes or by dropping the contents of the sack he carries on his back'. The pieces of gravel found in his shoes are huge blocks that he scatters here and there. He leaves entire rivers dry by drinking them up, creates other ones by urinating, jumps over valleys, and so on.

In 1883, in an essay on *Gargantua in Popular Traditions* (which was reedited in 1967 at G.P. Maisonneuve et Larose), Paul Sébillot had already highlighted the giant's extraordinary popularity.

On his part, Mr Dontenville enumerates an astonishing number of *Gargan* mountains, *Gargonne*, *Garganne* or *Gorgeonne* rivers, and 'quoits', 'gravel', 'impressions', 'chairs' and 'hammers' belonging to Gargantua.

Philologists have established the equivalence of 'Gargan(t)' and Gargantua, with the suffix *-tua (-atis, -ates)* expressing the notion of belonging. The initial form was thus *Gargantua-atis*. This suffix was also that of Nantua, a city of the Ain department, whose name derives from *Nantua-atis* (meaning 'from the vale'). As for the form 'gargant', it expresses the giant's ferocious appetite and is found in the Latin term *gurgitis*,[13] as well as in the Provençal term *gargantuan* ('gluttonous man') and the Spanish word *garganton* (meaning 'glutton').

Yet Mr Dontenville ventures even further. He pierces the mystery of this 'national' giant's genuine identity by making use of both the 'gargantuan chronicles' and chapbooks, in addition to the Welsh chronicles, in which a legendary hero called Gurgunt (*Gurgantius* with Gerald of Wales[14] and *Gurgiunt Babtruc* with Geoffrey of Monmouth[15]) is mentioned as early as the 12th century.

The most famous texts recount the manner in which Gargantua's parents, the giants Grandgousier and his wife Gargamelle, were created by Merlin the

13 TN: *Gurgitis* is Latin for 'throat'.

14 TN: Gerald of Wales (c. 1146–c. 1223) was a Cambro-Norman archdeacon of Brecon and a historian.

15 TN: Geoffrey of Monmouth (c. 1095–c. 1155) was a British cleric and one of the major figures in the development of British historiography and the popularity of King Arthur's tales.

enchanter (who belongs to the Arthurian cycle) and how, having undertaken a voyage from east to west (a reference to the solar trajectory), this exceptional family finally arrived in the Mont Saint-Michel bay, where two enormous rocks transported by Gargantua's parents and then cast into the sea ended up forming the Mont Saint-Michel and the neighbouring islet of Tombelaine.

In the Welsh chronicles, Gurgunt is the son of king Belinus and his companion Belisama. Mr Dontenville demonstrates, however, that this very same Belinus is but a 'transposition' of the Celtic god Belenos (also known as Bélen and Belin), a solar divinity that is sometimes likened to Apollo and commemorated by numerous Gallic inscriptions.

THE CULT OF SAINT-MICHEL

One thus gains a better understanding of the fact that Gargantua's name is associated with that of the archangel Saint Michael, the great slayer of dragons and 'pagans'. Originally, Mont Saint-Michel was actually known as Mont Tombe,[16] where the Celts honoured Bélen, the god of light. And it is for this very reason that the Romans referred to it Mons Tumba Beleni.

In 1283, local chronicles bestowed upon it the name of 'Mont-Gargan' or 'Mont-de-Gargan'. As for Tombelaine, 'one cannot perceive it as being anything but the tomb of Belisama', as specified by Mr Henri Dontenville himself.

And here is a complementary detail: there is also a 'Saint Michael's Mount' in Cornwall, a mount whose first occupant is said to have been a giant. And when, in 709 AD, Saint Aubert, the bishop of Avranches, completed the construction of the Mont Saint-Michel sanctuary, it was to 'Mount Gargan' in Italy that he sent his monks to seek out the archangel's 'relics' after the latter had manifested his presence there. Indeed, the Italian Monte Gargano is the centre of Saint Michael's and Saint Nicholas' cult. And if the first of the two — in whom some have longed to see not only the successor of Mercury or Wotan but also the 'national saint' of the Lombards (See Olga Rozhdestvenska's *Culte de saint Michel et le Moyen Âge latin.*[17] Augustin Picard, 1922) — is regarded as a fighter, an 'arch-strategist' of the celestial militia and, owing to his very name, even God's rival (Michael = *Quis ut Deus*), it is Saint Nicholas, whose heavenly

16 TN: Meaning 'Mount Tomb'.

17 TN: The Cult of Saint Michael and the Latin Middle Ages.

sled takes over from the 'wild hunter' 's retinue at Christmas time, that has clearly inherited the sac borne by Gargantua the giant.

And there is one final clue — Bayart, the horse attributed to Gargantua in the *Great Chronicles*, is the very same horse encountered in the geste[18] of the sons of Aymon and other medieval poems including *La Chanson de Maugis* and *La Chanson de Renaud de Montauban*. This solar animal, however, bears a name which, derived from *baillar*, also means 'Belenic'. Mr Dontenville writes:

> Despite displaying a bay colour, he belongs to the family of the sacred Germanic horses, which were all white. He is also part of the family of the white horses of *Rosmersholm* mentioned by Ibsen[19] and perpetuated by the memories of the *Schimmel* celebrated by Theodor Storm.[20] Yet he is equally the kindred of the white horses of Gallic France, which have been identified everywhere.

Gargantua seems to have become, thereafter, a sort of 'mythical hero'. Tradition has it that at the end of the Hundred Years' War, in 1453, it was he who drove out the English on the Dordogne, at Castillon.

Due to a bizarre sort of historical coincidence, it was Rabelais, a church man without any vocation, who would claim the privilege of restoring the honour of Gargantua, a fallen god that had been fought by Christianity (which then proceeded to extend some of his attributes to Saint Nicholas and Saint Christopher), turning him into the hero of the famous adventures known to all school children since 1532.

Histoire et géographie mythique de la France[21], an essay by Henri Dontenville. G.P. Maisonneuve et Larose (11 Victor-Cousin street, 75005 Paris, France), 379 pages.

---

18 TN: Also spelt gest, geste is a story of achievements or adventures. Among several famous medieval collections of gests are Fulcher of Chartres's *Gesta Francorum*, Saxo Grammaticus's *Gesta Danorum*, and the compilation known as the *Gesta Romanorum*.

19 TN: Henrik Johan Ibsen (20th March, 1828–23rd May, 1906) was a Norwegian playwright, theatre director and poet.

20 TN: Commonly known as Theodor Storm, Hans Theodor Woldsen Storm (14th September, 1817–4th July, 1888) was a German author. He is considered one of the most significant figures of German realism.

21 TN: The Mythical History and Geography of France.

Arnold Van Gennep, créateur de l'ethnographie française[22], an essay by Nicole Belmont. Payot, 187 pages.

Mythes et croyances de l'ancienne France[23], an essay by Nicole Belmont. Flammarion, 187 pages.

Mythologie française[24], an essay by Henri Dontenville. Payot, 269 pages.

Established by Mr Dontenville, the *Société de mythologie française* (SMF) has been publishing a quarterly bulletin known as 'Mythologie Française' (Lycée Félix-Laure, 60021 Beauvais) since 1950. Around a hundred issues have been released, all under the management of Mr Henri Fromage, a professor at Beauvais. The SMF has also edited three albums of figurative documents relating to France's 'mythical' heritage.

During these past years, French ethnography has experienced some important developments, as testified by the success of various books including those of Mr Pierre-Jakez Helias (*Le cheval d'orgeuil*,[25] Plon, 1975) and those of Mr Emmanuel Leroy-Ladurie (*Paysans de Languedoc*,[26] Flammarion, 1969; *Montaillou, village occitan*,[27] Gallimard, 1975). In the field of rural ethnography and historiography, alongside some excellent photo books such as the one by Mr Jean Carrière and Michel José entitled *Joseph, Noémie, Célestin et autres paysans d'Ardèche*[28] (Chêne, 1976), one must also mention the highly remarkable *Histoire de la France rurale*[29], published in four volumes by Seuil editions (in a collective compendium, 1975–77). Another wave of books focusing on the topic of 'holidays' has allowed us to gain a better understanding of the origins of French popular traditions and myths: Rosemonde Sanson's *Les 14 juillet, 1789–1975. Fête et conscience nationale*[30] (Flammarion, 1976); Mona Ozouf's *La fête révolutionnaire, 1789–1799*[31] (Gallimard, 1976); Michel Vovelle's *Métamorphoses de la fête en Provence*[32] (Aubier-Montaigne, 1976); Yves-Marie Bercé's *Fête et révolte*[33] (Hachette, 1976); and others. For further reading, see also the *Ethnologie française*[34] journal, which acts as the

22 TN: Arnold Van Gennep, the Creator of French Ethnography.

23 TN: Myths and Beliefs in Ancient France.

24 TN: French Mythology.

25 TN: The Horse of Pride.

26 TN: The Peasants of Languedoc.

27 TN: Montaillou, an Occitan Village.

28 TN: Joseph, Noemi, Celestine and Other Peasants of the Ardèche Region.

29 TN: The History of Rural France.

30 TN: The Fourteenth of July 1789–1975: Celebration and National Consciousness.

31 TN: The Revolutionary Celebration, 1789–1799.

32 TN: The Metamorphoses of Provençal Holidays.

33 TN: Celebration and Revolt.

34 TN: French Ethnology.

organ of the French Ethnology Society (Musée des arts et traditions populaires,[35] 6 route du Mahatma Gandhi, 75116 Paris, France) and is published by Berger-Levrault.

FRENCH TOPONYMY

'TOPONYMY HAS LONG BEEN THE Cinderella of literature', Albert Dauzat[36] once said.

At the very borders of history, archaeology, linguistics and ethnology lies toponymy, a science that deals with the names of places in relation to the soil's population and that was, for a long time, compelled to seek a scope of its own.

Its precursors in France were represented by Quicherat, a mediaevalist, and d'Arbois de Jubainville, a Celticist. Next came Georges Dottin (*La langue gauloise*[37]), Camille Julian (*Gallia*[38]), Joseph Loth and Antoine Thomas.

In 1922, Albert Dauzat decided to reinstate the teaching of place names into his course. Ten years later, he created a 'chronicle of toponymy' in the *Revue des études anciennes*[39] and, in 1938, presided over the very first International Congress of Toponymy in Paris.

Having become the studies director at the *Ecole pratique des hautes études*[40] and attained worldwide fame soon thereafter, Albert Dauzat wrote numerous books including *Tableau de la langue française*[41] (Payot) and some essays on *Linguistic Europe* (Payot), *Linguistic Geography* (Flammarion), *The Phonetics and Grammar of the French Language* (Larousse), etc.

In *La toponymie française*,[42] he retraces both the history and the evolution of our language.

---

35 TN: The Museum of Popular Arts and Traditions.

36 TN: Albert Dauzat (4th July, 1877–31st October, 1955) was a French linguist specialising in toponymy and onomastics.

37 TN: The Gallic Language.

38 TN: Latin for 'Gaul'.

39 TN: The Journal of Ancient Studies.

40 TN: Literally 'The Practical School of Higher Studies'.

41 TN: A Depiction of the French Language.

42 TN: French Toponymy.

MIGRATIONS AND CONQUESTS

French is a Romance language largely stemming from the 'popular' Latin that was spoken in the northern part of Gaul at the beginning of our era but which underwent a considerable transformation, particularly under the influence of Germanic languages; this makes 'Francien' the most Germanic of all Romance languages. In his *Tableau de la langue française* (which was reedited in 1967), Albert Dauzat gives the following indication in this regard:

> The mixing of the native population with non-native ones resulted in a simplification impacting not only the delicate phonetism of the Latin language but, above all, the complex flexion system, which almost completely collapsed. The tendency towards the analytical type, which already manifests itself in low Latin, is due to other causes: it is the result of a growing change of mentality.

The names of places are the fossils of human geography. And just like all fossils, they offer a testimony:

> They enlighten us with regard to the migrations of peoples, their conquests, colonisations, language changes, as well as the land's development and the successive stages of civilisation.

In his work entitled *Les Celtes*[43] (Albin Michel), Henri Hubert[44] was among the first to bridge archaeology and toponymy. As for Albert Grenier,[45] he also bestows great importance upon the names of places in his *Manuel d'archéologie gallo-romaine*.[46]

Here is an example given by Mr Dauzat:

> In the proximity of Royan, the so-called "Susac" consisted in a pine wood that had been planted (and quite late at that) on marine dunes: it seemed that the place had never been previously inhabited. And yet the toponymy hinted at a Gallo-Roman

[43] TN: The Celts.

[44] TN: Henri Hubert (23rd June, 1872–25th May, 1927) was a French archaeologist and sociologist of comparative religion who is best known for his work on the Celts.

[45] TN: Albert Grenier (22nd April, 1878–23rd June, 1961) was a French historian, theologian, and archaeologist who specialised in the history of ancient Rome and the Celts, especially the Gauls.

[46] TN: Manual of Gallo-Roman Archaeology.

type of name. And sure enough, when excavations were conducted, the ruins of a Gallo-Roman villa were unearthed.

In regions that are both mountainous and more or less arid, one encounters pre-Latin and even Indo-European names up to altitudes that border on 1000 metres.

It is indeed the vocabulary of mountainous areas that offers the highest number of archaisms: the word *cala* (i.e. 'stone', 'stone shelter' and, later on, simply 'shelter'), which has reached us from the depths of time, can still be recognised in the Savoyard 'chalet'.

Having come from Central and Meridional Germany, the Celts were the first to successfully achieve the linguistic unity of the future French Hexagon (with the notable exception of the South-West and a certain part of the Alps).

Their influence was not as great as was once supposed: when one sets aside some minor morphological and syntactic aspects, 80% of the 50,000 words of ancient French are of Latin origin, with 15% derived from a Germanic source. The remaining 5% are divided between the Continental Celtic, Greek, Etruscan and Phoenician languages.

Some cities owe their names to the Gallic tribes that established them: the Turones of Tours, the Bellovaci of Beauvais, the Namnetes of Nantes, the Atrebates of Arras, and the Carnutes of Chartres.

1200 Celtic roots and words have survived, most of which are, in fact, toponyms. *Renos* or *rinos* ('impetuous water stream') gave us the Italian *Reno*, as well as the words *Renne*, *Renon* and *Rhine*. *Noviento* ('new city') can be found in *Nogent*, and *nanto* ('vale', 'river') in *Nanteuil* and *Nantua*. Words with *duro* ('fortress') and *ialo* ('clearing'/'glade'), whose presence stretches from South Germany to the *Massif Central*, date back to the same epoch, as do superlatives with -sama (Uxisama: Ussel, Icolisama: Angoulême, etc.).

Some Greek influences are to be found in the South of France: *Massilia* (Marseille), *Nikè* (Nice), *Antipolis* (Antibes), *Monoïkos* (Monaco).

During the sixth century, the Gallic language completely disappeared; but the Latin *dunum* and Celtic *duno* (meaning 'hill' — see also the French word 'dune') combine to explain the origin of *Lyons* (Lug-dunum: hill of the god Lug), Belgrade (Sigi-dunum: the hill of victory), Melun (Meldunum), Châteaudun, Verdun.

THE FRANKS AND THE NORMANS

Soon enough, Europe underwent a change of religion, abandoning the old cults dedicated to Belenos (*Beaune*), Belisama (*Belime*, *Bellême*), Lug and even Jupiter (Fanjaux, from *Fanum Jovis*, 'temple of Jupiter') and shifting its focus towards hermitages (*cellae*: Seals) and 'small monasteries' (Moutier, Montreuil).

It was not, however, until the great upheavals brought about by the respective invasions of the Alans (Allaines), the Alemanni (Auménancourt), the Goths (Gueux) and the Marcomanni (Marmagne) between the sixth and the ninth century that French acquired its own physiognomy.

The Franks did not content themselves with giving our country its name, but also imposed their language in the north and the north-east. Their influence, which was thoroughly studied by Walther von Wartburg[47] (*Evolution et structure du français*.[48] PUF, 1935), was exerted by means of intense rural colonisation.

Toponymy certifies the existence of major domains in which the possessor's name is connected to the common one: Gondreville is thus the 'domain of Gondric'.

Mr Albert Dauzat reminds us that 'during the first centuries, swamps constituted an almost impassable obstacle to colonisation. As for the great forests, they were bypassed and barely ever damaged. Neither the Gauls nor the Romans ever cleared land'.

The ones who arrived next, by contrast, proceeded to reclaim and clear land on a vast scale. Hence the names ending with the suffix *-heim* and *-dorf* on the Alsatian plain.

In the Beauce region, for instance (the ancient Belsa, derived from Belisama), Celtic toponyms are spread along the periphery, ramifying around Chartres and Orléans: this testifies to the fact that the interior had not been penetrated. It was not until the sixth century, when the entire region was fallowed, that one witnessed the emergence of names ending with '-ville' and '-villiers', which are characteristic of the Frankish period.

---

47 TN: Walther von Wartburg (18th May, 1888–15th August, 1971) was a Swiss philologist and lexicographer.

48 TN: The Evolution and Structure of the French Language.

During the feudal period, the country was covered with fortified buildings: *Châteauneuf*, Castelnau, *Neufchâteau*.

In Normandy, during the tenth century, Scandinavian colonisation reached its highest density in the *Pays de Caux* and the *Nord du Cotentin* areas. *Le Havre* is of course reminiscent of the Germanic word for 'harbour' (German *haven*, Danish *havn*). Saint-Vaast-la-Hougue, which Hrolfr (known in French as *Rollon*) used as his general headquarters during the invasions, stems from the Norse *haugr*, i.e. 'knoll' or 'mound'. Almost everywhere, one encounters the ancient Scandinavian words or roots *holm* (Saxon *hoo*), i.e. 'islet' (Quettehou, Holmet); *bekkr*, meaning 'brook', altered into -bec (Bolbec, Caudebec); *thorp* (German *dorf*), i.e. 'a group of farms' or 'village' (Le Tourps in Val-de-Saire); *lundr*, meaning 'bocage' (Les Londes); *flodh*, i.e. 'tide' or 'flow', which then became -fleu(r) (Barfleur, Honfleur); *vik*, meaning 'cove', changed into -vy (Foulvy, Brévy); *topt*, i.e. 'foundation' or 'farm', which evolved into -tot (Ectot: the 'domain of the oak', Quartot, Yvetot, Maltot, Le Tot); *ham* (Ouistreham); *gate* (Houlgate); etc.

In the 12th century, France's toponymical map was set. A century later, the *langue d'oïl* of the northern barons triumphed once and for all over the *langue d'oc* used by the Cathars and the troubadours.

The history of place names reflects the history of our language and, through it, the history of all that we are:

'These names may mirror the first impression made by our fatherland, the land that all we live in and love, on the eyes and the souls of the men who inhabited it and slumbered in it before we came', Gaston Paris[49] once said.

La toponymie française, an essay by Albert Dauzat. Payot, 335 pages.
Histoire et guide de la France secrete,[50] an essay by J.P. Clébert and A. Michel. Planète, 461 pages.

---

49 TN: Bruno Paulin Gaston Paris (9th August, 1839–5th March, 1903) was a French writer and scholar. He was nominated for the Nobel Prize in Literature in 1901, 1902 and 1903.

50 TN: Secret France — A History and Handbook.

FRENCH INDIVIDUALISM

ALL PEOPLES HAVE THE QUALITIES of their own flaws. Mr de Lévis-Mirepoix[51] writes:

> If our public misfortunes are, more often than not, the result of our divisions and our excessive individual affirmations, our great successes are mostly due to individual affirmations directed towards the magnificence of our national destiny.

Published in 1957 and then reedited in 1973, the work which the duke of Lévis-Mirepoix dedicated to French individualism emphasises a constant facet of our national character.

In his essay on *European Peoples* (La Baconnière, Neuchâtel, 1946), Nicolas Lahovary remarked that 'France is the only one among the great European nations to include numerous representatives of Europe's three main races: the Mediterranean race, the Alpine race and the Celto-Germanic race'. Formed through successive enlargements of the royal 'private reserve', the French Hexagon comes across as a geographical and human crossroads. A Celtic language is spoken in it (Breton), as are two Germanic languages (Flemish and the Alsatian dialect) and five Romance languages (French, Occitan, Catalan, Italo-Corsican, and Franco-Provençal); not to mention Basque.

French people have different heritages, languages, histories and cultures and have difficulty perceiving what they could ever have in common; they are *individualists.*

It is this French heterogeneity that accounts for the fact that our national unity did not result from a slow ripening of popular consciousness but from a central authority that endowed it with an artificial and rigid framework. Just like in Spain or England, the *state* has preceded and *created* the nation in France, instead of only embodying its result, as is the case in Germany or Italy.

There is a French or Spanish nation and a civilisation. There is, likewise, a German or Italian culture and a people. And these terms correspond to one another as much as they are in contrast with each other: *people* and *nation*, *culture* and *civilisation*.

---

[51] TN: Antoine Pierre Marie François Joseph de Lévis-Mirepoix (1st August, 1884–16th July, 1981) was a French historian, novelist and essayist.

French individualism dates back to the Celtic era. It was a Gallic people, the Eduans, who called for the Romans to intervene in the hope of removing the Germanic threat. It was a naïve scheme on their part: having vanquished the Teutons, the legions undertook to conquer their 'allies'.

CIVIL WAR OR NATIONAL SPORT?

The above-mentioned conquest was accomplished using modest forces, as Caesar did not, in total, command more than 50,000 men; he did, however, take advantage of the Gallic divisions and disagreements.

'The Celts were mediocre citizens, and this represented one of the very principles of their weakness', observed Mr Henri Hubert (*Les Celtes*).

'What they lacked was political cohesion', specified Gonzague de Reynold[52] in *Le monde barbare vol. 1*.[53]

According to Fustel de Coulanges,[54] 'there is no doubt at all that the Gauls were indeed very profoundly attached to both their fatherland and their independence, yet this attachment was, for a period of six years, weaker than their dissensions' (*Institutions politiques, vol. 1*[55]).

When Vercingetorix undertook to unite those who resisted the Romans, he came up against both indifference and a diversity of passions.

Caesar's soldiers had little difficulty in seizing Avaricum (Bourges). At Dijon, the Gallic army suffered the consequences of its cavalry's lack of discipline, and the call of Alesia remained unheeded.

In a country where everyone criticises everyone else, civil war would become a national sport.

During the 18th century, it was Colbert,[56] who, in one of his memoirs, deplored the fact that 'the French, the world's most polite people, find it so unbearable to suffer each other's presence; that 'their union is so difficult to

---

52 TN: Gonzague de Reynold (15th July, 1880–9th April, 1970) was a Swiss writer, historian, and right-wing political activist.

53 TN: The Barbarian World, volume 1.

54 TN: Numa Denis Fustel de Coulanges (18th March, 1830–12th September, 1889) was a French historian.

55 TN: Political Institutions volume 1.

56 TN: Jean-Baptiste Colbert, Marquess of Torcy (14th September, 1665–2nd September, 1746), generally known as Colbert de Torcy, was a French diplomat.

achieve and their societies so inconstant'; and that 'the best affairs perish in their hands through some unfathomably unfortunate fate'.

In the aftermath of World War I (1914–18), an inquiry spanning across approximately sixty volumes and conducted by the National Association of Economic Expansion attributed the bad state of the French industry at the start of the century not to technological or financial causes but, instead, to psychological reasons.

Gustave le Bon[57] once bitterly remarked that 'in the German industry, banks, factories, and exports are interconnected so as to achieve a common goal. There is no fear of risks, since this interconnection allows for the division of burdens. All individual initiatives are encouraged because the local authorities set to exploit them are perfectly aware of their value'. He also denounced 'the lack of solidarity rendering us unable to undertake coordinated and disciplined collective efforts; the routine that prevents us from changing anything once the methods have been established; and the fear of risk-taking, timidity and lack of initiative which lead us to dread major undertakings' (*Psychologie des temps nouveaux*.[58] Flammarion, 1920).

The current situation surrounding French industry and agriculture, which is partly due to excessive fragmentation and the absence of collective equipment, proves that little has changed in our country over the course of half a century.

As far as military action is concerned, Mr Alexandre Sanguinetti[59] remarks:

> The moment the nation's or army's discipline becomes lax, it is the Gallic that resurfaces from under the French.

He goes on to add:

> Although we are an ancient *warrior* people, we are not a *military* one. We have retained our Gallo-Roman origins, but especially the former of the two, i.e. our taste for band turmoil; indeed, we prefer bands to the firmness of legions. This

---

57 TN: Charles-Marie Gustave Le Bon (7th May, 1841–13th December, 1931) was a French polymath whose areas of interest included anthropology, psychology, sociology, medicine, invention, and physics.

58 TN: The World in Revolt — A Psychological Study of Our Times.

59 TN: Alexandre Sanguinetti (27th March, 1913–9th October, 1980) was a French politician who contributed to the return of Charles de Gaulle in response to the May 1958 crisis.

> explains the great "thrashings" we suffered during the feudal age. On the eve of our greatest disasters, there is nothing we love as much as assembling irregular soldier units with prestigious names. It is in such troops that we feel most at ease. Our misfortune, however, dictates that these units of ours regularly encounter the 24th Bavarian, which, despite not having such an ostentatious name, remains far more solid and reduces them to a pile of rubble — for there are no miracles in war. (*Une nouvelle résistance.*[60] Plon, 1976)

As explained by the Duke of Lévis-Mirepoix, French individualism, which was controlled by the state under the Old Regime, prospered in the party system (i.e. the twenty-five governments of the Fourth Republic) and was simultaneously tempered by sudden and brief explosions of socialist anarchy (The Revolution of 1789, the Commune of Paris, May 1968) and a plebiscitary reflex that decorated militaries such as Bonaparte, Déroulède, La Rocque, Pétain, and de Gaulle took advantage of.

THE AMBIGUITY OF OUR NATIONAL HERITAGE

The continuity of our policies and institutions has, of course, suffered because of this.

> Any English diplomat that succeeds another will behave exactly as his predecessor did. With us Latin nations, it is the very contrary that applies. Our colonies had as many political systems as they had governors, and we all know how often the latter changed. A French diplomat practices *politics* yet is incapable of embracing *one* policy. (Gustave Le Bon, *Psychologie du socialisme.*[61] Félix Alcan, 1902)

Georges Pompidou[62] writes:

> Periodically, the wealthy uptown part of Paris grows fond of a certain man before turning away from him on an equally regular basis. General de Gaulle experienced this: idolised by Paris in 1947, he ended up being almost hated by the Parisians in 1953. Having reclaimed his idol status in 1958, he saw Paris — the same bourgeois Paris that I referred to earlier — gradually detach itself from him in a process that

60 TN: A New Resistance.

61 TN: The Psychology of Socialism.

62 TN: Georges Jean Raymond Pompidou (5th July, 1911–2nd April, 1974) was Prime Minister of France from 1962 to 1968 — the longest tenure in the position's history — and later became President of the French Republic from 1969 until his death in 1974.

> began in 1965 and culminated in the spring of 1968, which undoubtedly marked an extreme point in this evolution. (*Le nœud gordien.*[63] Plon, 1974)

Too often, nationalism in France has deviated towards xenophobia. It is more of a plain and simple rejection of difference than a favoured conception of man's relation to the universe.

Solidarity and sociability do not intersect. The English, who are highly solidary, are rather unsociable indeed. The French, who, by contrast, are very sociable, only become solidary in times of war and danger. In times of peace, it is the 'each man for himself' principle that prevails. Every social or professional category makes demands that suit its own interests, while in the Parliament, 'the parties that find themselves in a minority never refuse to ally themselves against the one who has triumphed', remarks Gustave Le Bon once again, before adding:

> There is a large number of revolutionary socialists who have only been elected to the current Chamber thanks to the assistance provided by the monarchists, who remain as lacking in terms of intelligence as they were at the time of the Revolution. (*La Révolution française et la psychologie des revolutions.*[64] Flammarion, 1913)

Irony, panache, politeness, witty remarks, elegance, eloquence, and a taste for style: these are all typically French traits. 'The French mistake *words* for *facts*', Moltke used to say.

We could characterise individualism in this manner in all domains. In war — the bravery of the partisan rather than the composure of a front-line soldier; in sports — the spirit of initiative rather than team spirit; in music — individual singing rather than choral singing; in matters of intelligence — a taste for analysis rather than a sense of synthesis; in the educational field — knowledge rather than discipline. And then there is this destructive form of mental activity embodied by *hypercritical irony*, this manner of being 'the one who is not to be duped', of not respecting anything and scoffing at everything and everyone (beginning with oneself): what it reveals is an extremely profound *division* affecting the personality (the one who shows respect is the one who

---

63 TN: The Gordian Knot.

64 TN: The French Revolution and the Psychology of Revolutions.

believes, because he is of a *single* moulding, finding in his own ideal the pure image of what he longs to be).

To the Celts, the state was evil incarnate. The Celtic empire perished due to a lack of authority. For the Latins, the state is everything. It was thus Machiavelli[65] who stated: 'I love the state more than my own soul'. In the eyes of Germanic nations, the state expresses and shapes the aspirations of the people.

As for Georges Pompidou, he also wrote the following:

> It is enough for one to observe the manner in which the French live to gain an awareness of their profound natural inaptitude to accept someone governing them. The natural reaction of the French towards both the state and its representatives is one of mistrust, a hostility paired with a sort of inferiority complex. To the Frenchman, the state comes across as an implacable and absurd machine that is foreign to him and of which no good could ever be expected to come out ... so much so that political crises almost inevitably turn into government crises; because, at the end of the day, it is the very foundation of the state's authority that finds itself constantly questioned. (Op. cit.)

Willingly statists when it comes to collective interests, the French remain fiercely individualistic as far as their personal interests are concerned. Ever favourable to nationalisations, the communist electorate still prefers the ownership of individual houses and shuns public transit.

The same ambiguity applies to the notion of 'liberty'. Mr Lévis-Mirepoix explains that when speaking of individual reality, 'the Latins conceive of it in the strict sense, as the primacy of the person over society, whereas the Anglo-Saxons perceive it very differently, namely as the defence of private life and natural rights and without any encroachment on what is the state's own due'. This is why England, which has undergone two revolutions and led a king to his death, has never rejected its past experiences and knowledge.

It was in the 19th century that the individual-versus-state antinomy arose in its sharpest form. One thus proceeded to oppose, without any nuances, a 'liberalism' bordering on anarchy and a 'statism' verging on dictatorship.

---

65 TN: Niccolò di Bernardo dei Machiavelli (3rd May, 1469–21st June, 1527) was an Italian diplomat, politician, historian, philosopher, humanist and writer of the Renaissance period.

This is because for any state that finds itself compelled to compensate for individual lacks, the temptation to infringe on individual prerogatives is great. Rudolf Stadelmann[66] once wrote:

> There is, on the one hand, a frivolous sort of individualism that barely condescends to receive support from the state and, on the other, a cynical perception of power which lowers the individual to playing the role of an instrument, to his use as cannon fodder.

He does add, however, that 'wherever balance is preserved, history will always be inclined to uphold a fertile equilibrium between statal necessity and the individual's right to freedom'.

THE VALUES OF PEOPLES AND MASSES

The ailments of statism are well-known. The state's inferiority in economic matters is as patently obvious as its superiority in political issues.

Gustave Le Bon explains:

> This inferiority relates to a very simple mental law, one that has been experimentally verified a thousand times over, according to which any man whose efforts serve a general sort of interest is far less valuable than the one who endeavours to act in his own personal interest. (*Psychologie des temps nouveaux*, op. cit.)

In 1861, Heinrich von Treitschke[67] celebrated productive liberty in the following manner:

> Blessed is any governmental action that gives rise to, encourages and purifies the citizen's initiative. All else is harmful.

In the preface of his book, the duke of Lévis-Mirepoix draws yet another distinction between 'doctrinal' and 'temperamental' individualism; he does not, however, give a clear definition of either. Furthermore, he covers the question of their origins rather hastily, a question that is, literally speaking,

---

66 TN: Rudolf Stadelmann (23rd April, 1902–17th August, 1949) was a German historian.

67 TN: Heinrich Gotthard von Treitschke (15th September, 1834–28th April, 1896) was a German historian, political author and National Liberal member of the Reichstag at the time of the German Empire. An outspoken nationalist, he favoured German colonialism and opposed the British Empire.

the 'primordial' one (and one is thus surprised, at times, when coming across evaluations or anecdotes whose connection to the subject matter is quite thin indeed).

What is highly evident, by contrast, is the persistence of a national temperament which, having attained stability, has succeeded in maintaining its presence across all eras and under all regimes.

Such permanency illustrates the difference between peoples and masses: within the former, the collective spirit retains a fixity that is unknown to the crowd's essentially *transitory* mindset. Only when it has lost its own consciousness and soul does a people become a 'mass', which the leaders and the *media* can manipulate and shape as they please.

Grandeur et misère de l'individualisme français à travers l'histoire,[68] an essay by the Duke of Lévis-Mirepoix. Librairie académique Perrin, 658 pages.

In *Le mal français*[69] (Plon, 1976), Mr Alain Peyrefitte,[70] a former minister, also denounces the French 'verbal engine' ('We admire words and despise facts'), our perpetual tendency towards civil war, as well as the manner in which French individualism finds its 'natural' compensation in bureaucracy, with the two feeding upon one another. Nevertheless, he does not restrict himself to describing the symptoms, striving, on the contrary, to identify the underlying and profound causes: beyond the 'statal ailment', what he detects is a 'societal affliction'.

For three centuries now, France has been an 'administrative society'. And throughout this time, the position occupied by France in the hierarchy of powers has never ceased to decline. 'Jacobinism' was born under the monarchy, somewhere between Richelieu and Colbert. The 'Great century' was actually the 'dazzling onset of decline'. While Northern European countries proceeded to endow themselves with a supple form of organisation allowing the instinct of transcendence present in a minority of men ('history's greatest force') to flourish to everyone's benefit, the administrative omnipotence pervading Latin countries, and especially France, only served to exacerbate 'convulsionary immobilism'.

The French have become both fractious and passive towards the state. On the one hand, they leave any and all initiative in the hands of the institutions, of which they expect nothing but services and gratifications, while, on the other, manifesting an incessantly bad temper towards these very same institutions, ever unable to perceive that they themselves are the

68 TN: The Grandeur and Misery of French Individualism Throughout History.

69 TN: French Evil.

70 TN: Alain Peyrefitte (26th August, 1925–27th November, 1999) was a French scholar, politician and a confidant of Charles De Gaulle. He had a prolonged career in public service, serving as a diplomat in both Germany and Poland.

source of the situation that they denounce. They thus oscillate continuously between submission and insubordination and are 'dissenting conservatives'. Behind these two seemingly contradictory attitudes, one encounters a common denominator: the rejection of difference. Frenchmen are 'uniformisers and egalitarians, thus driving the state to embrace its negative penchants'. The reign of impersonal power leads to a society of 'limitless irresponsibility'.

'The history of civilisations teaches us that their progress relies on difference. Monotony is synonymous with death itself', Mr Peyrefitte writes.

He then specifies that 'unitarian obsession results in egalitarian obsession, both of which are equally sterilising. And yet one cannot progress if one does not seek to transcend or, if one wishes, to equalise: although equality is an objective, it does imply the presence of inequality. For some inequalities are of a creative nature'.

'The day may come, as it did in England, when the quest for equality ends up exhausting the sources of a prosperity that would allow us to advance towards further equality. In France, the passions of inhibiting equality do not yet threaten our economy, but the ravages of envious egalitarianism are ever a menace to our society', he goes on to add.

Mr Peyrefitte also says that to understand the past is to understand oneself; but what is it that the past reveals to us? The disastrous influence of our Roman Catholic heritage. During the sixteenth century, all the necessary conditions were met for all of Europe to invent a genuine civilisation of development. In that same period, however, the Counter-Reformation triggered, in response to the Protestant rupture, an accentuation of the centralised system, which inhibits individual initiative.

This reaction was simultaneously religious and profane: the tendency to reinforce central power went hand in hand with the necessities of the struggle against 'heresy'. 'In all domains, the Counter-Reformation applied the brakes. It proceeded to create or protect hierarchies everywhere, discouraging novelties and establishing a society of distrust'. Still today, 'one encounters', through the bureaucratic reflexes of the state, 'the reflexes of dogmatism and Catholic clericature'. In Protestant countries, by contrast, individual religious commitment (where 'everyone acts as their own priest') has led to the principle of 'responsible autonomy'. The 'dynamic of polycentrism' was inscribed into both Luther's and Calvin's defiance.

Mr Peyrefitte states that 'a civilisation is fertile as long as it accepts, within itself, exchanges between differences. Protestant countries have implemented Erasmus'[71] lesson, evolving towards tolerance and polycentrism. In their unitarian obsession, Catholic lands have, on their part, hounded pluralism and constructed monocentrism'. Nordic societies are, nowadays, open societies, societies of mutual trust that bestow 'a clear conscience upon Prometheus'. On the other hand, Latin societies are closed ones, characterised by reciprocal defiance. So as to reduce this opposition and become (once again) a society of trust, what is necessary is a 'mental revolution'. Mr Peyrefitte does not deem the latter to be impossible and outlines the means that could enable us to achieve it.

---

71 TN: Known as Erasmus or Erasmus of Rotterdam, Desiderius Erasmus Roterodamus (28th October, 1466–12th July, 1536) was a Dutch Christian Humanist and the greatest scholar of the northern Renaissance.

NORTH AND SOUTH

DURING THE WEDDING OF CONSTANCE of Arles and Robert the Pious (996–1031), chronicler Raoul Glaber tells us, 'France found itself inundated by a certain kind of people, the vainest and shallowest among all men. They were all genuine histrions whose ridiculous shaved chins, breeches, ankle boots and entire ill-composed exterior heralded the disorder of their very soul'. These 'histrions' actually have a name: Meridionals.

Books, records, and newspapers: for a few years now, we have been witnessing the awakening of militant 'Occitanism'. The 'Oc' abbreviation flourishes almost everywhere these days; the red flag bearing the yellow cross clechée relates to all wine-growing manifestations. In Paris, the ultra-Left is discovering a new sort of exoticism and gleefully chanting slogans in a language that it does not understand: *Volem viure al païs! Gardarem lo Larzac!*[72] It seems that in May 1968, we were all German Jews. And lo and behold, we have now become Occitan shepherds.

In 1964, 165 baccalaureate candidates took the optional Occitan language exam. In 1973, the number was already close to 7,000 and today, it has risen to over 10,000.

> The Marquis appeared. Julien hastened to inform him of his departure. "Where to?", asked Mr de la Môle. "To the Languedoc", came the reply. "Do not do so, I beg of you. You are destined for higher accomplishments. If you must leave, it shall be northwards!"

When quoting this excerpt from Stendhal's[73] *The Red and the Black*, the Occitans claim that nothing has yet changed. A student who has obtained his diploma from the University of Toulouse or Montpellier is still compelled to travel to Paris for his 'consecration', a fact which Mr Jean Larzac of the Institute

---

72 TN: We want to live in this land! We shall keep the Larzac!

73 TN: Marie-Henri Beyle (23rd January, 1783–23rd March, 1842), known as Stendhal, was a 19th-century French author. His most famous novel is *Le rouge et le noir* (The Red and the Black).

of Occitan Studies expresses through a specific formula: 'To have luggage is to have to pack one's trunk!'

THE VISIGOTHIC KINGDOM OF TOULOUSE

The 'Occitan difference' is by no means a myth. Mr Jacques Vedel, a professor at Toulouse, writes the following:

> No matter how far back we go, France's historical substratum reveals a clear dualism.

The 'demarcation line' lies approximately across the Loire: the ancient border of the two Gallic dioceses, the lands of written law (urban consulates and public notaries) and customary law, of the *langue d'oc* and the *langue d'oïl*, of the ancient seneschalsies and the bailiwicks of the North.

The word 'Occitania' derives from the Latin word *Aquitania*. It designates all the ancient lands of the *langue d'oc*, thus thirty-five contemporary French departments belonging to ancient provinces: Poitou, Limousin, Manche, Dauphiné, Provence, Auvergne, Aquitaine, Gascogne, and Languedoc (the ancient Septimania), to which the Catalan domain is added. Their possible capital city? Toulouse.

Although the Occitan language belongs to the Romance family of languages, it has never been unified. It is subdivided into four dialects: Central Occitan, North Occitan, Catalan and Gascon.

According to Henri Espieux,[74] the Occitan man is comprised of 'two subraces of the White race — the Alpine race and the Mediterranean one'.

As early as in the year 1000 BC, the Celts, who made great use of iron, stood up against the Iberians and the Ligurians. Mr Jean Larzac writes:

> From the intermixing of the Ligurians, the Iberians, the Greeks, the Celts, the Romans and the Visigoths was born a type of man that bore no resemblance to the Gauls (who were blue-eyed and blond-haired) and whose physiological constants were defined on various levels, including, for example, that of blood groups: whereas the *Frankian* type is based on the balance between the A and O group, the *Occitan* type is marked by the predominance of the O group in the West and the A group in the East, with this diversity compensated for by a more pronounced

[74] TN: Henri Espieux or Enric Espieut (1923–1971) was a French author and poet who expressed himself in Occitan.

> proportion of the B aspect in the East compared to the West. (*Le petit livre de l'Occitanie*[75])

Francia (The Land of the Franks) was originally a region that stretched from the Elba to the North Sea and *la Manche* and whose boundaries were, in the sixth century, delimited by both the Visigoth state that had established itself south of the Loire and the Breton surge. It is this very kingdom which, by means of various treaties and conquests, gradually extended its domain until it became the France of today.

In 451, the king of Toulouse, Theodoric I, dies while fighting against Attila's army in the 'Battle of Catalaunian Plains'. Finding itself in need of the Western Goths, Rome proceeds to support them.

Saint Sidonius Apollinaris[76] describes this Visigothic Toulouse that visitors from all over the world swarmed to admire:

> In Toulouse, one witnessed the thronging of the blue-eyed Saxons accustomed to overcoming the ocean waves; the old Sicambri whose hair, cropped after their defeat, slowly rose upon their heads to cover their skulls now that peace had restored their freedom; the Heruli with their cheeks tattooed in blue and a complexion akin to sea water; the seven-foot Burgundians; the Ostrogoths, so proud of the support of the king of Toulouse, Euric, against the Huns; and even the envoys of the Persian king. Rome itself implored Toulouse to grant it its assistance against the men of the North that attacked it from all sides. The Garonne river thus protected the Tiber.

When entering into function, kings swear an oath of fidelity to the traditions and customs of the peoples that they govern. Such is the origin of local liberties: the 'fors' to the north of the Pyrenees; the Spanish *fueros*.

In 507, Clovis (Chlodowig) defeats the Visigoths at Vouillé and takes control of the *Gallia Romana*. The Church, which had already brought about the collapse of the Ostrogoth kingdom of Italy, triumphs. Against the Goths, Christianised a century earlier but ideologically uncertain, it had chosen to

---

75 TN: The Little Book of Occitania.

76 TN: Widely known as Saint Sidonius Apollinaris, Gaius Sollius Modestus Apollinaris Sidonius, (5th November of an unknown year, c. 430–August 489 AD) was a poet, diplomat and bishop and is often considered 'the single most important surviving author of fifth-century Gaul'.

support the Franks, who had, until recently, espoused pagandom. Salic Law proclaims: 'Praised be the Lord, who loves the Franks!' (Next, the Church directed its vindictiveness against the Visigoths of Spain, whose leader, Roderic, would meet his fate on 26th July, 711, in Jerez, on the banks of the Guadalete).

In 732, Charles 'the Hammer' Martel faces the Arabs between Tours and Poitiers. Among his adversaries' ranks, one finds a rather large number of superficially Islamised Visigoths. 'Occitan militias', some would go on to say.

THE LAND OF THE CATHARS

During the 12th century the literary movement of the troubadours surfaces. It proposes a novel genre: the *Chanson*. Having initially emerged in Limousin with the Ebles de Ventadour school, it soon triumphs at the court of Poitiers. Despite having perhaps originated from the Andalusian civilisation, one also detects Celtic and Germanic influences in it.

Mr Robert Lafont[77] writes:

> Whether in Occitania, the South of Spain or the Orient, sung poetry constitutes the common form of complimentary celebration.

'The troubadours' Occitan' quickly conquered the entire meridional region. One even witnessed the development of a 'troubadour civilisation' around Toulouse. In their books, Mr Pierre Bec[78] (*Nouvelle anthologie de la lyrique occitane du Moyen Âge.*[79] Aubanel, 1970) and Charles Camproux of the University of Montpellier (*Histoire de la littérature occitane.*[80] Payot, 1953) have demonstrated its literary wealth. Its tolerance, its 'liberalism' and the important position it bestows upon feminine values have all been praised as well. Unlike the barons of the North, who were rather supportive of 'male power', the troubadours proclaimed the futility of social principles in relation to

---

77 TN: Robèrt Lafont (16th March, 1923–24th June, 2009) was an Occitan intellectual from Provence. He was a linguist, an author, a historian, a literature expert and a political theoretician.

78 TN: Pierre Bec or, in Occitan, Pèire Bèc (11th December, 1921–30th June, 2014) was a French Occitan language poet and linguist.

79 TN: A New Anthology of Occitan Medieval Lyricism.

80 TN: The History of Occitan Literature.

amorous feelings. In contrast to chivalric love, Mr Jeffrey B. Russel[81] writes, 'courtly love is an adulterous love, meaning a heretical one' (*Courtly Love as Religious Dissent*, The Catholic Historical Review, Vol. 51, No. 1, 1965).

'The man proceeds to beg the woman, instead of imposing his desires upon her', Mr Larzac proudly specifies.

This civilisation developed on the fringes of the Church, which was a source of irritation for the latter, especially when considering the fact that, sheltered by the mountains anthe precipitous terrain of the South of France, heresies never ceased to flourish.

First came the Muslims and the Arians, then the Albigensians and the Cathars, and, at a later point, the Waldensians of the Alps and the Protestants of the Cévennes.

The 'land of the Cathars' is located between Albi, Toulouse, Foix and Carcassonne. The claim that the South of France was uniformly Cathar is therefore very far from being truthful. Hence these words by Mr Lafont:

> By welcoming Catharism, what Occitania acknowledged was much more the *right* to heresy than heresy itself.

Ever since the first centuries of our era, Mr Michel Roquebert[82] remarks, Manichaean dualism 'had never, in fact, ceased to seethe in the bosom of the Orient's religious communities'. Around the year 1000 of our era, it spilled out into the West, passing through Northern Italy and the Balkans. All around the West, it gave birth to sects that declared themselves against the established Church: the Paulicians of Armenia, the Bogomils of the Balkans, and the Albigensians.

In Occitania, Catharism was the religion of the land-owning aristocracy, ever in league with the people against Roman guardianship.

DESTROYING HERESY

In May 1243, on the road to Montferrier, a flicker allows one to surmise the presence of a compact mass of arms-bearing men. The night draws to its end

---

81 TN: Born in 1934, Jeffrey Burton Russell is an American historian and religious studies scholar.

82 TN: Born on 7th August, 1928, Michel Roquebert is a French author and historian.

and, in the still fresh dawn of this spring morning, the watchmen suddenly shake each other out of slumber. The sergeant-at-arms sounds the alarm. 500 Cathars, some simple believers and others 'Perfects' (i.e. members of the Cathar clergy), have fallen back into the citadel of Montségur. Facing them are 10,000 men that have come from the North.

The 'Franks' set up camp. The banner of the Archbishop of Narbonne, Pierre Amiel, flutters alongside that of Carcassonne Seneschal Hughes des Arcis. The siege of Montségur commences.

The conflict had already lasted for more than half a century, and it was Pope Innocent III, the count of Segni, that had initially triggered it.

Having ascended to the pontifical throne in 1198, Innocent III would, three years later, decree the 'domestic crusade'. Because of his predications, Arnaud Amaury, the Abbé of Citeaux, would mobilise the barons of the North. Mr Robert Lafont remarks:

> The critical fact is that the Church proceeded to modify the notion of crusade, no longer implementing it on infidels but, for the very first time, on heretics instead.

The purpose of the entire undertaking was to destroy the Cathar heresy by replacing the Occitan feudal rulers protecting it with lords devoted to Rome's cause.

From the Pope's perspective, however, the crusade also represented an opportunity to intervene in 'Frankish' matters. Mr Michel Roquebert writes:

> One must not forget that Philippe-Auguste[83] had deliberately delayed the crusade for about ten years. [...] At the very time when he begged Philippe-Auguste to lead the crusade himself, the Pope actually sought to use the king. Paradoxically perhaps, the latter did not actually reciprocate the intention.

In 1209, an army of crusaders had already invaded the lands of Toulouse. Its leader, Simon de Montfort, originally from Montfort-l'Amaury, was an ambitious and determined man driven by a cold sort of energy. A remarkable man, he would be killed during the siege of Toulouse, in 1218. The crusaders themselves originated from all northern regions. In contemporary texts, the 'French' are mentioned along with the Bretons, the Flemish, the Normans, the Burgundians, the (Swabian and Lorrain) Germans, the Picard people, the

83 TN: Philippe-Auguste, or Philip II, was the seventh king of the Capetian dynasty (1180–1223).

Champenois,[84] and the 'Tiois' (meaning northern Germans or 'theodisca'[85]). The Viscount of Béziers-Carcassonne was the first to oppose them. His troops were immediately crushed.

In November 1212, Simon de Montfort organises a sort of large parliament in Pamiers, whose members he instructs to 'wipe out the heretical filth' and 'ensure that common decency reigns over a land that has been claimed by the Holy Roman Church and has submitted to the latter'. Some 'statutes' restoring the Church's privileges and instituting the repression of the Cathars and the Jews are then put in written form.

The crusade would successively face the counts of Toulouse, Foix and Comminges, the Viscount of Béarn, and even the king of Aragon.

It is initially successful: during the battle of Muret, on 12th September, 1213, Peter II of Aragon is killed and the Occitan armies defeated. Soon enough, however, it is forced to retreat.

In 1224, the aggressors are compelled to leave the region and, once again, Catharism comes out into the open.

Two years later, a second crusade is led by the king of France, Louis VIII, the son of Philippe-Auguste.

This time around, Occitania falls. The treaty of Meaux, signed in 1229, consecrates its defeat. Its signatory, Raymond VII, Count of Toulouse, commits himself to purging his land of heresy, dismantling his city's fortifications, paying the Church an indemnification of 10,000 silver marks, and, last but not least, offering his daughter's hand in marriage to one of Saint Louis' brothers, Alphonse de Poitiers (Saint Louis[86] had, in the meantime, ascended to the throne), in exchange for which he would receive formal absolution on the main square of Notre-Dame, in Paris.

Catharism thus enters secrecy. At the Council of Toulouse, the Inquisition is established in the region. The 'Occitan issue', however, remains unresolved.

In 1240, the land of Carcassonne rises up and, in 1242, several Inquisitors are slaughtered in Avignonet (with the news of the massacre infuriating

---

84 TN: Those that are from the region of Champagne.

85 TN: 'Germanic people' in mediaeval Latin.

86 TN: Louis IX (25th April, 1214–25th August, 1270), commonly known as 'Saint Louis', was King of France, the ninth from the House of Capet, and is a canonised Catholic and Anglican saint.

Blanche of Castile[87]). Raymond VII, who had attempted to put together a new anti-French coalition, is vanquished once again. The Cathars seek refuge in the lands of Ariège and the Corbières. In 1243, the siege of Montségur begins.

THE FALLEN SOUL OF MONTSÉGUR

This bizarre citadel is a genuine hot spot. The *puy*[88] (*pog* in Occitan) is an enormous calcareous bloc leaning towards the east and situated amidst an impressive scenery. The château was built in 1204 in accordance with plans provided by the Cathar clergy, establishing mysterious alignments and spiritual formulas set in stone. In the donjon, the arrow slits that span across opposite walls are, strangely enough, decentred in relation to one another. The result is that the sun can only traverse them from side to side once a year: at the dawn of the summer solstice.

Mr Alain Hubert-Bonnal[89] points out:

> Nowadays, a small crowd still comes here to watch the sun rise, just as people did back then. Akin to their predecessors, several dozens of curious individuals spend the night inside the castle walls, reconnecting with the eternal solar tradition.

Isolated, starved, and bombarded by perriers, the besieged capitulate after being surrounded for ten whole months. The terms of their surrender are negotiated: those who choose to embrace the Church would be amnestied and the others burned alive.

During the last night of the siege, four men manage to break through the surrounding enemy lines. It is said that they succeeded in concealing what was most precious to the Cathars — their spiritual treasure. Was it the Grail?

On 16th March, 1244, at dawn, a long procession comes out of the château of Montségur. It is comprised of the Cathars that have opted for death, with bishop Bertrand d'en Marti leading the way. He is followed by approximately 200 people, including Ramon de Perelle, the Lord of Montségur, his wife Corba and daughter Esclarmonde. They all mount an immense pyre that has

---

87 TN: Blanche of Castile (4th March, 1188–27th November, 1252) was Queen of France by marriage to Louis VIII, acting as regent twice during her son's reign.

88 TN: *Puy* is a geological term used locally in the Auvergne, France in reference to a volcanic hill.

89 TN: A French author.

been erected at some distance, in a place that would henceforth be known as the *Camp dels Cremats*.[90] Torches are thrown upon the wood, which quickly catches fire. At the very moment when the flames rise, the army begins to chant the *Veni Creator*. Montségur is now history.

From this point on, the conquest is very quick. In 1252, Pope Innocent IV uses the *Ad Extirpenda* bull to grant Inquisitors permission to resort to torture. Arnault, the Pope's legate, would shout during the attack on Béziers: 'Kill them all, God will recognise his own!'. The last fortified Cathar bastion, Quéribus, would fall in 1255.

In 1258, Saint Louis has further prisons constructed under the City of Carcassone.

Today, a young Occitan woman affirms:

> While violating this land, now in his grasp, the man of the North also violates the woman of the South, a crossbreed of the Sarasin and a diabolical creature. Having been vanquished, the man of the South begins to desire the victor's blonde, evanescent and inaccessible woman.

In 1300, thirty-five Albigensian notables are accused of heresy. In 1321, a 'Perfect', Guillaume Bélibaste, is also burned alive. At this point, however, Occitan independence is already a mere memory: in 1271, upon Alphonse de Poitiers' death, the County of Toulouse is annexed by France once and for all.

At the start of the fifteenth century, Charles VII takes control of Bordeaux. Montpellier is purchased in 1439 and Montélimar in 1447. The annexation of the Aquitaine follows in 1453, after the battle of Castillon. Next, in 1481, Louis XI claims the Provence region. Finally, Béarn is incorporated into France. Henri IV then declares: 'Paris is well worth a Mass'.

The Occitan language declines as well. During the 13th century, at the time of the *Leys d'amors*[91] and the floral games[92], one still spoke Occitan below the

---

90 TN: The 'Place of the Burned'. Alternatively, *Prat dels Cremats* is used instead, referring to the 'Field of the Burned' (in Occitan).

91 TN: *Leys d'amors* ('Laws of Love') is a long Occitan treatise codifying rhetoric, prosody, and grammar, produced by Guilhem Molinier of Toulouse and his collaborators not during the 13th but the 14th century, in imitation of 12th and 13th century troubadours.

92 TN: Floral Games were any of a series of historically related poetry contests with floral prizes. Initially, the floral games were intended to keep alive the poetic language and style of the Occitan troubadours but, in time, this aim was forgotten.

line that connects Rochefort, Niort and Poitiers. During the fourteenth century, the *langue d'oïl* takes over the regions of Civray, Montmorillon and most of the lower Charentes. In 1539, the ordinance of Villers-Cotterêts replaces Latin with literary French as the official language of the ancient kingdom of the Franks. Clément Marot (1496–1544) declares 'the relinquishment of the maternal language to embrace the paternal one', for 'only the prince's language pays'.

In his *Essays*, Montaigne (1533–1592) writes:

> My French language finds itself altered, both in its pronunciation and elsewhere, by the barbarity that I myself have devised.

PARIS MAKES FRENCH

Around 1560, a wind of turmoil blows across the South once again, as one witnesses the rebirth of political and religious separatism. Established in the Provence and Dauphiné regions for several centuries, the Waldensians embrace the cause of reformation. In 1571, Protestantism becomes the state religion in Jeanne d'Albret's[93] Béarn. Three years later, a national synod gathers in Nîmes. Reformed churches were, at the time, proportionally more numerous in the South than in the North. Toulouse sinks into heresy again.

Many other 16th- and 17th-century movements attest to the persistence of Occitan particularism: the revolt of the 'Pétaults' of Guyenne (1548); the revolt of the 'Jacques' (1560); the tax strikes of 1580; the 'Croquant' rebellions of Limousin (1595); the Montmorency rebellion in Languedoc; the 'Casaveus' revolt of Provence; the proclamation of an independent republic in Marseille (1650); the revolt of the 'Sabreurs' of Béarn (around 1650); and the 1670 rebellion of the 'Camisards'(whose name is derived from the Occitan word *camisa*, meaning 'shirt').

In 1645, the Protestants are excluded from the states of Languedoc and, in 1663, their temples are razed to the ground. Then, in 1685, Louis XIV revokes

---

93 TN: Jeanne d'Albret (16th November, 1528–9th June, 1572), also known as Jeanne III, was the queen regnant of Navarre from 1555 to 1572. She married Antoine de Bourbon, Duke of Vendôme, and was the mother of Henry of Bourbon, who became King Henry III of Navarre and King Henry IV, the first Bourbon king of France.

the Edict of Nantes[94] and makes the necessary arrangements for the dreadful 'dragonnades'[95].

While on a trip in Valence, Racine[96] asked for a bedpan. Instead, the servant brought him a chafing dish. He writes:

> My need of an interpreter is as great as that of a potential Muscovite in Paris. (*Letters from Uzès*)

In the 18th century, Montesquieu[97] would declare:

> It is Paris that makes one French. In its absence, Normandy, Picardy, and the Artois region would be as German as Germany itself. As for the Guyenne, Béarn, and Languedoc regions, they would be just as Spanish as Spain.

In his *Historical Review of Occitania*, Mr André Dupuy[98] tells us that 'on the eve of 1789, 95% of the Occitan population only spoke the *langue d'oc*'.

Two Occitan men, acting as the delegates of the Third Estate, dominate the early hours of the Revolution: Abbé Sieyès[99] and the Count of Mirabeau. This does not prevent the revolutionaries from pursuing, with increased vigour, the unification undertaken under the monarchy.

The Capetians abolished the Treaty of Verdun (842), which had enabled the inclusion of Provence into Lotharingia. On its part, the night of 4th August,

---

94 TN: Signed in April 1598 by King Henry IV of France, the Edict of Nantes granted the Calvinist Protestants of France (also known as Huguenots) substantial rights in the nation, which was still considered essentially Catholic at the time. The purpose was to promote civil unity.

95 TN: The Dragonnades were a French government policy instituted in 1681 by King Louis XIV, the so-called Sun King, to intimidate Huguenot families into either leaving France or converting to Catholicism.

96 TN: Jean Racine (22nd December, 1639–21st April, 1699), was a French dramatist, one of the three great playwrights of 17th-century France (along with Molière and Corneille), and an important literary figure in the Western tradition.

97 TN: Charles-Louis de Secondat, Baron de La Brède et de Montesquieu (18th January, 1689–10th February, 1755), generally referred to simply as Montesquieu, was a French judge, man of letters, and political philosopher.

98 TN: André Dupuy (31st October, 1928–17th March, 2018) was a French historian.

99 TN: Emmanuel Joseph Sieyès (3rd May, 1748–20th June, 1836), most commonly known as Abbé Sieyès, was a French Roman Catholic Abbé, clergyman and political author, as well as one of the chief political theorists of the French Revolution.

1789 consecrated the disappearance of the province of Béarn. Abbé Grégoire, a passionate defender of human rights, dreamed of finding the right means to 'erase all traces of Patois[100]'. Through its struggle against local languages, what the Convention strived for was 'political provincialism'. This marked the birth of Jacobinism[101].

In 1792, three Occitan men, Guadet, Gensonné and Vergniaud, declare themselves in favour of a 'federative republic stretching from Lyons to Bordeaux'. This project triggers the quarrel between the Montagnards[102] and the Girondins.[103]

During the 19th century, the establishment of the road network and the subsequent installation of the railway system places Paris at the very centre of everything. The industrial momentum accelerates the rural exodus and compulsory recruitment inaugurates the intermixing of regional milieus. The Hexagon thus takes shape around its capital city, the 'eccentric donjon' of the northern half of the country and the soon-to-be development and emigration centre.

The divide, however, remains unchanged. One still contrasts the poor France with the wealthy one, the wine of the South with the wheat of the North, the olive tree with the oak, early fruit and vegetables with potatoes, the swing-plough with the plough, and the sheep with the cash cow; perhaps even the ant with the grasshopper.

On 10th December, 1948, at the time of Louis-Napoleon Bonaparte's election to the Presidency of the French Republic, voters in the Bouches-du-Rhône and Var departments only grant him a 23% and 25% support rate respectively,

---

[100] TN: *Patois* is speech or language that is considered nonstandard, although the term is not formally defined in linguistics.

[101] TN: The Jacobin Club was one of several organisations that grew out of the French Revolution. It was distinguished for its left-wing, revolutionary politics. Because of this, the Jacobins, unlike other sects such as the Girondins, were closely allied to the *sans-culottes*, who were a popular force of working-class Parisians that played a pivotal role in the development of the Revolution.

[102] TN: The Mountain (French: *La Montagne*) was a political group during the French Revolution whose members, called *Montagnards*, sat on the highest benches in the National Assembly.

[103] TN: The Girondins were members of a loosely-knit political faction during the French Revolution and initially part of the Jacobin movement, along with the *Montagnards*.

compared with 75% for the rest of the country. Three years later, the 2nd of December coup leads to turmoil in Toulouse, Limoges and the Languedoc. The movement takes on an insurrectional aspect and hundreds of suspects are deported to Algeria.

In 1860, the County of Nice becomes French once and for all. In 1870, the *Ligue du Midi*,[104] comprising thirteen departments of the South-East, proposes the 'federalisation' of democracy.

On 23rd March, 1871, Gaston Crémieux[105] proclaims the founding of the Commune of Marseille. On the 24th, it is an outcast from 1852, Emile Digeon, who follows suit in Narbonne, where the 52nd regiment allows the population to disarm its men after having delivered its own officers into the hands of the rebels (Marseille would only be reclaimed on the 4th of April).

While in Toulouse, Taine[106] writes the following in his *Carnets de voyage*:[107]

> My colleagues tell me that the South has always displayed less loyalty than the North.

Staying in the very same city, Michelet[108] notes in his *Tableau de la France*:[109]

> The well-off are Frenchmen; common people, on the other hand, are an entirely different matter, being either Spanish or Moorish.

As for author Huysmans (1848–1907), he rages against Southerners, 'those walnut-stained, glossy-eyed, chocolate-crushing and garlic-chewing beings!'

---

104 TN: Southern League.

105 TN: Born Isaac Louis Gaston, Gaston Crémieux (22nd June, 1836–30th November, 1871) was a lawyer, a journalist and a French author. He is famous for having stood up in defence of poor people.

106 TN: Hippolyte Adolphe Taine (21st April, 1828–5th March, 1893) was a French critic, historian, the main theoretical influence of French naturalism, a major proponent of sociological positivism and one of the first practitioners of historicist criticism.

107 TN: Travel Notebook.

108 TN: Jules Michelet (21st August, 1798–9th February, 1874) was a French historian.

109 TN: A Description of France.

A DEMARCATION LINE

The year of 1907 sees huge demonstrations against the viticultural legislation which had (already!) been judged unfavourable to an industry stricken with overproduction, as agitators channel the movement. On the 9th of June, more than 80,000 demonstrators gather in the streets of Montpellier. Monsignor de Babrières, the city's bishop, opens the cathedral's doors for them. The leader of the rebellion and the mayor of Narbonne, socialist Ernest Ferroul, boasts about having gone to spit on Simon de Montfort's grave as a student. Clémenceau[110] decides to have the army intervene. Composed of Béziers residents, however, the 17th territorial regiment refuses to open fire. It is on these events that Montéhus[111] bases a famous song entitled *Salut, salut à vous, braves soldats du 17ème!*[112] The Revolutionary Communist (Trotskyite) League would then add it to its repertoire.

At the time when Mistral[113] was awarded the Nobel Prize, the teachers of the Third Republic declared war upon all 'Patois'. Mr Gaston Bonheur[114] writes:

> During my childhood, if one partook in the religion of lost Alsace, it was to the detriment of the *langue d'oc*, which was deemed a kind of "patois" and banned in our schools. It was my mother who taught me the extremely syntactic and grammatical French that I speak. Fortunately, however, my grandmother held on and only spoke to me in "Patois". And it was through the lessons given to me by this old peasant of the Corbières region that all of Occitania lodged into me.

Mr Jean Cau, who comes from the Audes region, also remembers:

> My father and mother both addressed my grandparents using the equivalent of the formal French "vous" and only spoke to them using the *langue d'oc*. If my father

110 TN: Georges Benjamin Clémenceau (28th September, 1841–24th November, 1929) was a French physician, journalist and politician who went on to become Prime Minister of France during the First World War.

111 TN: Gaston Mardochée Brunswick, better known by his pseudonym Montéhus (9th July, 1872–December 1952), was a French singer and songwriter.

112 TN: Hail to thee, hail to thee, oh soldiers of the 17th!

113 TN: Frédéric Mistral (8th September, 1830–25th March, 1914) was a French author and lexicographer of the Occitan language who won the 1904 Nobel Prize in Literature.

114 TN: Gaston Bonheur is the pseudonym of Gaston Tesseyre (27th November, 1913–4th September, 1980), a French journalist and writer who achieved great fame for having written the screenplay for the 1955 film version of 'Lady Chatterley's Lover'.

> had ever dared to speak to my grandmother in French and had addressed her using the informal "tu", I think the ground would have opened up under my own two feet. The same did not apply at school, however; for the secular form of teaching, which was both compulsory and free, held us in check and compelled our minds to relinquish any and all notions of race by arousing shame for the language of our fathers. (*La Grande Prostituée*. Table Ronde, 1974)

In 1940, France is, once again, cut in half. Mr Henri Espieux writes:

> During the Occupation, the Franciens were separated from the Occitans by the famous "demarcation line". For a long time, we believed that the drawing of this line had been suggested to Hitler by the Romanists around him. Nowadays, however, it is our conviction that the line was actually imposed upon the occupier by the geopolitical realities which we are well familiar with. And it is no miracle if, owing to the very same imperatives, the Resistance's principal hotbeds (Limousin, Cévennes, Vercors) essentially surfaced across the entire Occitan territory, at a time when the demarcation line had already ceased to exist.

It was in Toulouse, on 27th May, 1943, that the National Resistance Council (CNR) met for the first time, presided by Jean Moulin, an Occitan from Béziers.

In London, the people around General de Gaulle grew increasingly concerned over the implantation of the FTPs (The *Francs-Tireurs et Partisans Français*) in the South of France — Guingouin, the head of the Resistance in Limoges, was a member of the French Communist Party, and so was Ravanel in Toulouse. There were even some elements that hinted at the creation of a 'Soviet Republic of the South of France'. In 1943, Simone Weil[115] went as far as to write:

> Current collaborators espouse the same attitude towards the new Europe which a German victory would forge as the people of Provence, the Bretons, the Alsatians and the people of Franche-Comté are required to embrace with regard to their past and their land's conquest at the hands of the king of France. (*L'enracinement*[116])

115 TN: Simone Weil (3rd February, 1909–24th August, 1943) was a French philosopher, mystic, and political activist.

116 TN: Deep-Rootedness.

A year later, the purge takes on particularly intense proportions in the South, where a sort of 'Popular Republic of the Maquis[117]' is established from the end of August to the end of November 1944. In Toulouse, Nimes, and Montpellier, certain animosities reach far back. It is a war involving the very same people.

It is a tradition of dissent has survived from this past. Mr Guy Héraud[118] writes the following in *L'Europe des ethnies*[119] (Presses d'Europe, 1963):

> It does seem to be the case that the specific voting preferences that surfaced in both the South and the Centre of France during the various referendums of the Fifth Republic are to be attributed to certain constants of the meridional personality.

THE OBSTINATE PERMANENCY OF THE 'REFRACTORY' SOUTH

The 'Red South' actually emerged as early as the general elections of 1849. Mr Michel Le Bris[120] specifies:

> If one were to examine the various French election results, one would notice that in 1849, 1871, 1965 and 1968, the South of France always displayed great obstinacy in shaping the very same red bloc upon the French map.

Of the twenty departments in which the majority voted against the proposed direct election of the President in the constitutional referendum of 28th October, 1962, a total of eighteen lie south of the Loire. Two others, namely the Indre and the Allier departments, are tangent to it. 'It was as if the lands of written law had displayed a more scrupulous sort of respect for constitutional laws than the lands of customary law'. The results of the 'Algerian' referendums of 8th January, 1961 and 8th April, 1962 were analogous.

Mr Robert Lafont asserts:

---

117 TN: The *Maquis* was the French Resistance movement during the German occupation (1940–45).

118 TN: Guy Héraud (29th October, 1920–December 2003) was a French politician and lawyer.

119 TN: The Europe of Ethnicities.

120 TN: Born on 1st February, 1944, Michel Le Bris is a French author.

> The Occitan hostility to the violent reconquest of Algeria was basically the negative film image of the consciousness of a colonised people that could not present itself as such. (*La revendication occitane*[121])

During the presidential elections of 1965, Mr François Mitterrand[122] was nicknamed the 'Occitan President'. In the first round, he claimed first place in twenty departments, of which seventeen were southern ones; in the second, the total was twenty southern departments out of twenty-four.

During the referendum of 27th April, 1969, which led to General de Gaulle's retirement, the departments that voted favourably were all situated in French Flanders, Brittany and Alsace-Lorraine. In June 1969, Mr Pompidou was the 'candidate of the North', where he only failed to obtain less than his first-round national average in twenty-seven departments out of sixty-two, compared to twenty-one out of thirty-two in Occitania.

This is all because the South and the North do not perceive political participation in the same manner. Liberal democracy originated from Northern Europe, but the 'party regime' was born on the shores of the Mediterranean. The South is more 'politicised', and people adhere more often to major political formations there, especially those of the opposition. The 'Nordic' electorate, by contrast, votes for specific men and abhors parties. The Gaullist movement remained in power for about fifteen years but, proportionally to its own electorate, never included a large number of adherents. The man of the North is a man of consent and 'monarchy'. The man of the South, on the other hand, espouses protestation and 'democracy'.

Mr Grosclaude[123] affirms:

> Everyone knows that there is a North whose votes are Right-oriented and a South where voters lean towards the Left.

He then adds:

---

[121] TN: The Occitan Demand.

[122] TN: François Maurice Adrien Marie Mitterrand (26th October, 1916–8th January, 1996) was a French statesman who served as President of France from 1981 to 1995, the longest time in office in French history.

[123] TN: Michel Grosclaude (1926–2002) was a French philosopher and linguist, in addition to authoring works on grammar, lexicography and Occitan onomastics.

> The reason for this is that the South of France is less inclined to trust one single man, even if his policy is, or seems to be, a Leftist one. One is under the impression that the North of France responds more readily with a "yes", whatever the question asked. The South, on the other hand, is more reticent and more rebellious when it comes to giving a favourable response, no matter what the question may be.

And here is Mr Philippe Sénart's[124] diagnosis:

> The South is refractory and, as we tend to say, antagonistic.

The workforces of the Socialist and Radical Parties are clearly 'regionalised' in Occitania. Mr Jean Cassou[125] has, in fact, traced the 'birthplace' of socialism to 'Jaurès' fatherland', which is also that of Gambetta, Louis Blanc, Jules Vallès, Elisée Reclus, Blanqui, Combes, Jules Guesde, Arago, Ramadier, Daladier, Paul Reynaud, Vincent Auriol, Gaston Defferre, Edgar Faure, Roger Garaudy, Georges Séguy and Jacques Duclos.

From the perspective of the electoral results of the past two decades, an 'Occitan Assembly' established within the framework of our federal institutions would have yielded, almost uninterruptedly, a parliamentary majority oriented towards the Centre-Left. In 1967, its ranks would have included twenty-five Gaullists, twelve Centrists, sixty-four Leftists and Centre-Leftists and fifteen Communists.

There is, of course, also a 'Southern Right', but it has hardly anything in common with the 'consenting' Right of the major electorates of French Flanders, Picardy, Alsace or Brittany. It is a *protesting* sort of Right that feels naturally at ease when in the opposition. Its representatives include Charles Maurras and Léon Daudet of Provence, Pierre Poujade of Quercy and Tixier-Vignancour of Béarn.

During the presidential elections of 1965, the first nineteen 'Tixierist' departments were all located in Occitania, a phenomenon that cannot be accounted for through the mere influx of repatriates.

---

124 TN: Philippe Sénart (1922–2013) was a French chronicler, journalist and historian.

125 TN: Jean Cassou (9th July, 1897–16th January, 1986) was a French author, art critic, poet, member of the French Resistance during World War II and the first Director of the *Musée national d'Art moderne* in Paris.

Every year, in Baux-de-Provence (previously in Montmajour), a royalist celebration is organised by the *Provençal Order*, attracting thousands of participants. Mr Philippe Sénart writes:

> Occitania's ultimate opportunity to claim its freedom may have been embodied by the ultra-royalist resistance of Toulouse against king Louis XVIII, in 1815. Did they not intend to proclaim the duke of Aquitaine king of Occitania?

It is against this backdrop that the Occitan Movement arose, a movement which, as a literary school, dates back to the *Félibrige*,[126] which was founded in 1854 by three Provençal authors: Aubanel, Roumanille and Mistral.

FROM THE FÉLIBRIGE TO THE OCCITAN MOVEMENT

The *Félibrige*'s primary purpose is to allow the Provençal language to reclaim its position of literary language. The 'Félibres' extol the Provence region, its folklore, popular celebrations and climate. When praising the sun, they sometimes undergo the existential experience of some sort of neopaganism (Mistral: 'The sun makes me sing'). What they also strive for, however, is to 'establish a national Provençal consciousness', as proclaimed by the *Armana prouvençau* of 1867.

Mistral, who won the Nobel Prize in literature in 1904, declares:

> I am not an ambitious man, yet my entire ideal lies in the resurrection of the Provençal fatherland, crushed by 500 years of Parisian centralisation.

In 1859, he writes the following in *Mireille*:

> Those who have never lived in the South, and especially amongst our rural populations, could never have the slightest idea of the incompatibility, insufficiency, and poverty of the Northern language with regard to the traditions, needs and organisation of Southerners. Born under a rainy climate, characterised by a primness that mirrors the etiquette of French courts and specially forged for higher social classes, this inflexible language is naturally averse to free attitudes, fiery temperaments, rustic customs and the Provençal people's vivacious and imaged speech. And nothing could ever change that.

---

126 TN: The *Félibrige* is a literary and cultural association established by Frédéric Mistral and other Provençal writers to defend and promote the Provençal language and literature.

In 1878, republican *félibres* would accuse Mistral of embracing separatism.

In 1887, a journal entitled *Occitania* is launched in Montpellier (this title would subsequently be readopted several times). In 1911, the Félibrige chooses to have the terms 'Occitania' and 'Occitan' respectively replace 'Provence' and 'Provençal' when referring to all *langue d'oc* regions. In 1919, an 'Occitan school' is established in Avignonet at baron Desazars de Montgalhard's, who then becomes its very first 'capiscol'[127]. In 1923, the *Almanach Occitan* becomes the organ of the League of the Meridional Fatherland, whose manifesto opens with the following words: 'What we want is the recognition of all that is Occitan'.

Nevertheless, the Félibrige, which was divided into 'maintenance units' and governed by a few 'majorals'[128] and a single 'capoulié',[129] soon came across as some sort of conservatory. Wearing Ascot ties and 'gardian'[130] hats, the *félibres* gathered on specific dates so as to sing the *Coupo Santo*[131]. During the war, they supported the state of Vichy, which fought against all kinds of autonomism but longed to resuscitate the 'old provinces'.

Upon the Liberation of France, the Occitan movement made a sharp left turn, breaking with folkloric and picturesque themes.

Mr Jean-Michel Franco, a student at the university of Aix-en-Provence, states that 'what is most harmful to the South are conventional ethnotypes: the ridiculous Gascons with their rough accent, the myth of Matamoros[132], the lazy

---

127 TN: It would seem that the word 'capiscol' relates to the dean of a chapter or religious body.

128 TN: High-ranking officials.

129 TN: The grandmaster of the Félibrige.

130 TN: A *gardian* is a mounted cattle herdsman in the Camargue delta in Provence, southern France.

131 TN: The *Coupo Santo* (Holy Cup), in full *La Cansoun de la Coupo* (The Song of the Cup), is the anthem of Provence, sung in Provençal, one of six Occitan dialects. It refers to a silver chalice the Catalan *félibres* offered their Provençal counterparts on 30th July, 1867 during a banquet held in Avignon to thank them for hiding Victor Balaguer, a poet from Barcelona who'd sought political asylum out of Spain. The cup is traditionally entrusted to the *capolièr* ('capoulié'), who presides over the Félibrige.

132 TN: Saint James the Moor-slayer (Spanish: *Santiago Matamoros*) is the name given to the representation of the apostle James, son of Zebedee, as a legendary, miraculous figure who appeared at the equally legendary Battle of Clavijo, helping the Christians conquer the Muslim Moors. The story was invented centuries after the alleged battle is said to have taken place.

Corsicans, the boastful people of Marseille, Marius and Olive,[133] Tartarin,[134] pastis and pétanque! Indeed, what are tall stories if not a colonial joke?'.

In 1945, René Nelli[135] and Ismaël Girard, the former director of *Oc* magazine (whose first issue came out in 1923), founded the Institute of Occitan Studies (IEO) in Toulouse. Inspired by a certain pre-war project (namely the Institute of Catalan Studies, established at the start of the 20th century), it originated directly from the Resistance. Its first president was Mr Jean Cassou, a writer, art historian and former commissary of the Republic in Toulouse, who, at the time, sympathised with the French Communist Party (P.C.). The second one was none other than Mr Robèrt Lafont, in 1951.

Displaying dishevelled hair and a 'Mao' collar, Mr Lafont, a professor at the Paul-Valéry University of Montpellier, is the author of a large number of essays and novels (*La phrase occitane*[136], *Mistral ou l'illusion*[137], *Phonétique Provençale*[138]). He has recently published *La révolution régionaliste*[139] (Gallimard, 1967), *Sur la France*[140] (Gallimard, 1968), *Renaissance du Sud*[141] (Gallimard, 1970), *Clefs pour l'Occitanie*[142] (Seghers, 1971), *Lettre ouverte aux Français d'un Occitan*[143] (Albin Michel, 1973), *La revendication occitane* (Flammarion, 1974), and others. Acting as the director of *Viure* magazine, he is one of the principal theoreticians of Leftist regionalism.

He declares:

---

133 TN: Marius and Olive are two fearless friends whose imaginary adventures are popular in France.

134 TN: Tartarin of Tarascon is a novel written by the French author Alphonse Daudet in 1872. In it, Tartarin's gullibility causes him to experience many misadventures until his return home, penniless but covered in glory (after shooting a tame, blind lion).

135 TN: René Nelli or, in Occitan, Renat Nelli (1906–1982) was one of the major Occitan authors of the 20th century.

136 TN: The Occitan Sentence.

137 TN: Mistral, or the Illusion.

138 TN: Provençal Phonetics.

139 TN: The Regionalist Revolution.

140 TN: On France.

141 TN: The Rebirth of the South.

142 TN: Keys for Occitania.

143 TN: An Occitan's Open Letter to the French.

> I am, indeed, the heir of both Jaurès and the Jacobins. Nowadays, however, the Jacobins would be in favour of autonomy.

He then adds:

> Around 1954–55, we found ourselves facing a necessity of rupture. The communists, for instance, used the argument of the elimination of Occitan nationalism to raise the issue of the "unity of the French nation" and reject what they termed "the economic impasse", meaning the interest that we attached to specific problems.

And yet, it was on the fringes of the IEO that the Occitan Nationalist Party (PNO) surfaced in 1959. Its founder, Mr François Fontan, made his debut in *Action française* before frequenting anarchist and Trotskyist milieus. During the war of Algeria, he took part in assisting the FLN[144] and the desertion networks. He then settled in Italy. A neo-Freudian disciple of Wilhelm Reich, he also sides with *ethnicism* and 'revolutionary nationalism'.

The PNO would be represented in Paris by P. Maclouf, the director of the *Lu Lugar* ('Morning Star') newspaper, who would then go on to join the 'Volem viure al païs' committees at the end of 1973.

In 1962, the IEO gives birth to an Occitan Committee of Studies and Action (COEA), which then undertakes to attack the PNO and Mr Fontan, whose 'reprehensible behaviour' and 'Gaullist tendencies' it denounces. Mr Robert Lafont becomes its Secretary General.

From 1963–64 onwards, this Committee presents an 'action programme' that it submits to various Leftist clubs. For this purpose, it participates in the creation of the Convention of Republican Institutions. In 1966, Mr Michel Rocard, then leader of the Unified Socialist Party (PSU), draws inspiration from its principles so as to formulate the contents of a brochure that he titles *Décoloniser la province*.[145] In it, he adopts the COEA's three watchwords: Occitania, regionalism, socialism.

---

144 TN: The National Liberation Front (French: *Front de libération nationale*, FLN) is a socialist political party in Algeria. It was the principal nationalist movement during the Algerian War and the sole legal and ruling political party of the Algerian state until the legalisation of other parties in 1989.

145 TN: Decolonising the Province.

In 1967, poet Robert Allan launches an Occitan Socialist Party (PSO) in attempt to find a middle path between the PNO and the COEA. The party would only last a few months.

'RESURRECTION'

The events of May 1968 trigger a series of 'realisations' in the Occitan Movement. One witnesses the emergence of Occitan Action Committees (CAOs) which, in turn, give rise to various newspapers and small groupings: *Lutte occitane*[146], *Fédération anarchiste-communiste d'Occitanie*[147] (which came about through a local scission of the Anarchist Revolutionary Organisation), *Esquerra catalana*[148], *Action régionale catalane*[149], Occitania nova[150], etc.

The most important one is Occitan Struggle ('Lucha Occitana'), which was founded in 1971 by elements originating from both the CAOs and the PSU and took over from the COEA in an almost official manner.

Its president, forty-two-year-old Mr Gaston Bazalgues, is a professor at the Faculty of Letters in Montpellier who is in 'touch' with the Parisian parties. It is also said that he has found in militarism a distraction from his own personal problems. One of his collaborators, Mr Roland Péquou, is the president of the movement's Coordination Committee. Very hostile to the PNO but rather favourable to the IEO, Occitan Struggle (O.S.) intends to fight against 'centrist regionalism' and keep 'all nationalistic contamination' at bay, while pronouncing itself in favour of both autonomism and a rather vague sort of 'class organisation'.

On 6th May, 1971, Occitan Struggle organised a 'march' on the Larzac plateau: 3,000 people responded to its appeal. Local actions have since multiplied. During the autumn of 1972, the peasants of Larzac brought their sheep to graze upon the *Champ de Mars*,[151] at the foot of the Eiffel Tower. Soon afterwards,

146 TN: Occitan Struggle.

147 TN: The Anarchist-Communist Federation of Occitania.

148 TN: The Catalan Left.

149 TN: Regional Catalan Action.

150 TN: New Occitania.

151 TN: The *Champ de Mars* (English: Field of Mars) is a large public greenspace in Paris, France, located in the seventh arrondissement, between the Eiffel Tower to the northwest and the *École Militaire* to the southeast.

they constructed a 'wild sheep pen'. On 24th July, 1973, on the summer solstice, Occitan Struggle gathered 5,000 youths on the slopes of the rock of Montségur in order to celebrate the 'Occitan resurrection', seven centuries after the Cathar surrender.

Bearing within itself highly heterogeneous tendencies, Occitan struggle has been the focus of several 'hijack' attempts, particularly on the part of Maoists and currents stemming from the PSU's Left.

During its Lille congress in 1971, the PSU had created a Commission of National Minorities headed by Serge Mallet. In July 1973, shortly before passing away, the latter came up with the project of forming a 'unified Occitan socialist party' that was meant to gather, on a common basis, the militants of Occitan Struggle, the PNO, the Communist Party's oppositionists, the Occitan sympathisers of Leftist parties, the members of the CFDT (French Democratic Confederation of Labour), former FTPs,[152] etc.

The group calling itself *Pòble d'Òc* was excluded from this gathering, since the Leftists accused it of bringing 'disguised fascists' together. Its main leader, thirty-seven-year-old solicitor Mr Richard Roudier,[153] declares himself in favour of a 'free Occitania' and opposed to 'class collaboration'. He is, however, reticent with regard to Marxism. The Algerian affair has left its mark on him. *Pòble d'Òc* identifies with a 'libertarian' Occitan tradition; which leads it to reject the 'traditional French Left'. It was the militants of this very group who, in 1974, assaulted and booed Mr Mitterrand on the Larzac plateau, labelling him a 'political hijacker'. The director of the *Pòble d'Òc* newspaper (formerly *Jeune Languedoc*) is Mr Jean-Louis Lin[154] from Montpellier.

ETHNIC PERSONALITY

In 1972–73, the viticultural movement also became an Occitan movement, and has remained so since. 'Not for political reasons, but ethnic ones', Mr André Dupuy specifies.

---

152 TN: *Franc-Tireurs et Partisans* members.

153 TN: Born on 20th June, 1947, Richard Roudier is a now famous for his political role.

154 TN: Jean-Louis Lin was an Occitan militant and revolutionary who later died under rather bizarre circumstances.

There is a certain newspaper that played a significant role in this evolution: The *Echo des Corbières* monthly, which presents itself as the 'opinion page' of the Viticultural Action Committees (CAVs). Its founder, Mr Henri Fabre, is a former partisan of French Algeria and someone who enjoys great popularity in the Aude department.

Another spokesman for the CAVs, Mr Emmanuel Maffre-Baugé, who also happens to be the grandson of a Félibrige 'majoral', declares:

> I am not an Occitan in the revolutionary sense of the word. I am, however, as much of an Occitan as I have been this land's son for centuries, through my own kin.

Standing before an immense crowd that had gathered on the Peyrou esplanade in Montpellier on 17th March, 1975, Mr Maffre-Baugé screams out, 'Awaken, Occitan people'! A few days later, 60,000 wine-growers invade the city of Sète and chant the *Coupo Santo.* Mr Maffre-Baugé continues:

> Oh, people of Oc! Mediterranean people! My people! The time will come when we shall claim the right to our own parliament and govern our own affairs!

Later on, in February 1976, he would write in *L'Echo des Corbières*:

> If it genuinely longs to become the focus of credibility, the Occitan land must confront and accept several thought currents. It must neither be the land of a minority of long-haired idealists nor a privileged place for notables to gather. It must bestow upon each of its sons the proof of his ethnic personality, the vocation of his specificity and a taste for community.

Beginning in 1974, it became obvious that the extreme Left, was, despite its efforts, unable to take charge of the viticultural movement. Occitan Struggle proceeded to direct itself towards 'Gramscian culturalism', while its centre of gravity shifted towards the regions of Provence and Nice. Leftists Daniel Chatelain and Pierre Tafani write:

> Despite espousing a different style compared to the COEA, Occitan Struggle has failed to become anything but a regional pressure group whose only pretence is to strive for "the intellectual and moral reformation of large masses" from the

> perspective of an enigmatic sort of cultural revolution. (*Qu'est-ce qui fait courir les autonomistes?*[155] Stock, 1976)

Faced with Occitan Struggle's failure and supported by P. Maclouf, Mr Robert Lafont attempts to appropriate Serge Mallet's project. On the occasion of the presidential elections of 1974, he launches the 'Volem viure al païs' committees. The latter describe themselves as 'socialist, self-managing and autonomist Occitans' (one notices, however, that they do make certain concessions towards nationalism). An individual brought into the region from Paris itself strives to cleanse them, albeit unsuccessfully: Mr Michel Le Bris, the former manager of the *Cause du people* newspaper and a man who, in addition to his collaboration with *Libération*, acted as the organ of the former Proletarian Left (the 'Mao-Spontex' of May 1968). The book that he published through Gallimard (as part of the 'Savage France' collection run by Mr Jean-Paul Sartre) is entitled *Occitanie: volem viure!*[156] and ends with a quote by an unexpectedly Occitan figure: Mao Zedong.

In 1975, an Occitan Popular Movement (MPO) is launched in Agen. Its purpose is to unite all the tendencies, without 'imposing upon anyone any sort of ideology with the potential to weaken the great momentum of ethnic solidarity'.

Free from political action in the strict sense of the word, what the Institute of Occitan Studies deals with henceforth are, above all, pedagogical and literary issues. Its current president is Mr Pierre Bec, a university professor and a specialist in Occitan medieval lyricism. Alongside him, one encounters Mr Yves Rouquette, a forty-one-year-old history professor and the Institute's vice-president, as well as his brother, Mr Jean Larzac, a clergyman in Viviers.

THE AMBIGUITY OF OCCITAN 'NATIONAL REGIONALISM'

Considering linguistics to be 'the foundation of Occitania's legitimacy' (R. Lafont), the IEO publishes an informational bulletin and strives to unify all Occitan languages. Mr Rouquette explains:

---

155 TN: What Is It that Draws Autonomist Crowds?

156 TN: Occitania: We Want to Live!

> A language is not solely a literature. What it represents instead is the very breath of a people. And as for the famous "southern accent", it is merely a matter of pronouncing French words with the accent of another language — Occitan. The words have been lost, but the *musicality* remains!

Questioned by Jacques Chancel[157] on 1st February, 1974, Mr Rouquette had this to add:

> What constitutes my personality is not French. My parents, incidentally, made love in Occitan, and I see no reason not to imitate them.

On his part, Mr Lafont attributes the sterilisation afflicting Occitan culture to 'conquest'. Besides, '*Oc* literature is largely reactionary', he declares.

In Toulouse, Privat Editions' second youth came about through its publishing of books with a focus on regionalism. Mr Michel Roquebert runs the 'Occitan Domain' collection there. As for the IEO, it has launched a collection of paperbacks written in Occitan, with fifteen volumes released each year. There are also other publishing houses — *4 Vertats* ('Four Truths') and *Cap e cap* ('One on one').[158]

It is, however, in the music sector that the Occitan rebirth has particularly been felt.

Small, dark and stocky, thirty-eight-year-old Claude Marti is the most famous of the new troubadours. He has published, through Stock editions, a book entitled *Homme d'Oc*.[159] His Leftist wife is said to have influenced him. This is what he sings:

> One does not hunt crows with a butterfly net.

There is also Patric, a thirty-year-old student in Montpellier who began a successful life in Paris; thirty-six-year-old Pèire-Andrièu Delbeau, who sings in Gascon and has lived in a resin collector's hut; Mans de Breish, a former employee of the *Crédit Agricole* of Carcassonne; as well as Beltramme, Morcheoine,

---

157 TN: Born Joseph André Jacques Régis Crampes, Jacques Chancel (2nd July, 1928–23rd December, 2014) was a French journalist and author.

158 TN: Literally, 'Head to Head'.

159 TN: Man of Oc.

Broglia, Los Caminaires, Longamai, Mauris, Gérard Franco, Miquela, Daniel Daumas, Maria Roanet, Toni Rodriguez, Bramaric, and many others.

It was with them in mind that the IEO created the 'Ventadour' cooperative; indeed, there are who some live in dread of being 'hijacked'.

The Occitan movement is nowadays the most markedly Left-oriented of all regionalist movements; or, to be more precise, the one in which the Leftist faction of regionalism enjoys the greatest representation. Will this always be the case? The issue arouses numerous comments.

Some 'ultra-Marxists' have criticised the 'interclass ambiguity' of regionalism. Paul Alliès, a member of the Communist Revolutionary League in Montpellier, states:

> It is impossible to grant Occitan awareness a reality of its own without a class basis. If it does exist, of course, it will be formulated by the workers themselves, within their organs of power.

Likewise, Mr Chatelain and Tafani, both of whom are ferociously opposed to 'national-regionalism', denounce the persistence of a 'national ideology' within *ethnicist* demands. They point out the fact that Mr Lafont has been labelled by Emmanuel Le Roy-Ladurie[160] as 'a Maurras of the extreme Left'!

They remark that 'at the very moment when the nationalistic and chauvinistic history taught in state schools faces its own demise, it commits itself to the (hi)stories that regional ideologists tell both small and big children' (op. cit.).

The term 'regional colonialism' surfaced in December 1961, during the miner strike of Decazeville (Aveyron). The event caused quite a stir. Robert Lafont writes:

> It is in Decazeville that … both the Félibrige and the series of ideological defeats suffered by Occitanism genuinely came to an end.

The term is, however, far from having gained unanimous acceptance. A young doctor from Toulouse declares:

160 TN: Born on 19th July, 1929, Emmanuel Bernard Le Roy Ladurie is a French historian whose work is mainly focused on Languedoc in the *Ancien Régime* (Old Regime), particularly the history of the peasantry.

> This expression is absurd. The members of extreme Left parties use it for the purposes of amalgamation and in order to awaken the memory of anticolonial struggles; but the problem that arises here is different.

The opportunity to conduct a struggle 'against tourism' has also given rise to polemics. In 1967–68, the development of the Languedoc-Rousillon coast (the 'Great Clod' complex in Fos-sur-Mer) was supported by a slogan — 'A New Florida to Be'. The Occitans responded to it in a most abrupt manner:

> Industrial Europe will have to find another region for people to tan their arses!

Mr Lafont writes:

> Not being a productive sort of activity, tourism does nothing to alter the structural inferiority of underdeveloped regions. Instead, it reinforces their economic "deadweight" by diverting investments, sedating regional consciousness, weighing down the inactive proportion of the population, and keeping the workforce busy with unproductive tasks which, at times, are parasitic.

A young engineer from Marseille declares.

> Provençal drumming, garlic mayonnaise and farandole — it's all past now. We will not have anyone come and look at us the way they do with the Indians that dance in their reserves. When folklore turns into a *show*, it's because tradition is dead.

In his *Nouveaux Cathares pour Montségur*,[161] novelist Saint-Loup remarks:

> Folklore embodies the shame of an ethnic group that is still alive yet no longer dares affirm its own sovereignty.

Mr Jacques Ressaire, the PNO's secretary for the Provençal region, says:

> We are not xenophobic. We do not wish to reject foreigners. You must, however, understand our situation. In the summer, our cities become the theatre of demonstrations that express the loss of our culture, attracting a clientele that is completely unaware of our problems.

In the eyes of a second-year student from Montpellier, however, 'such events constitute genuine provocations'. He expands on things:

---

161 TN: New Cathars for Montségur.

> The tragedy that has struck the Occitan movement lies in the fact that it has fallen into the hands of extreme-Left militants who hope to dominate public opinion through it. If they rely on Occitania, it is only for tactical reasons: the smaller the political ensembles, the easier they are to control. In point of fact, excesses always feed off each other — Jacobinism plays right into the hands of separatism and vice versa. What is necessary is for us to break this vicious circle and impose a third solution.

In Bordeaux, a faculty assistant adds:

> When we say "Volem viure al païs", what we mean is that we want the Occitan personality to be recognised. The fact that some believe this can be achieved by embracing such a depersonalising doctrine as Marxism is paradoxical. Occitanism is what makes us *different* from one another. Marxism, on the other hand, represents universalism and internationalism. Between the two currents, there is a contradiction that some conceal but none can reduce.

ANARCHY WITHIN ANARCHY

Mr Robert Lafont has also written that 'although there is no great bourgeoisie in Occitania, middle classes abound. If Leftists find themselves unable to propose a socialistic regional project, there could still be a fascist Occitania'.

In order for this to happen, the South would have to achieve unity, a unity that remains completely out of reach. In spite of all efforts, of the 'regional Jacobinism' pervading autonomist movements, the Occitan unrest is still limited to the areas surrounding Toulouse and Montpellier. Catalonia, the Basque region and especially Corsica have their own specific issues. The inhabitants of Bordeaux, on their part, seem to have other concerns. As for the people of Provence, who were, at first, successively conquered by the Romans, the Visigoths, the Burgundians, the Ostrogoths, the Franks of Neustria and Austrasia, and the Teutons, then once again by the Burgundians, who were followed by the counts of Barcelona, Toulouse and Anjou, it is rather unlikely that they would now wish to find themselves under the control of the heirs of Catharism.

Born in Pertuis (Vaucluse), Mirabeau described his region in the following manner:

Disorder within disorder, incoherence within incoherence, anarchy within anarchy.

Clefs pour l'Occitanie, an essay by Robert Lafont. Seghers, 269 pages.

Lettre ouverte d'un Français aux Occitans, an essay by Robert Lafont. Albin Michel, 224 pages.

Le Sud et le Nord. Dialectique de la France[162], a series of essays edited by Robert Lafont. Privat, Toulouse, 249 pages.

Renaissance du Sud. Essai sur la littérature occitane au temps de Henri IV[163], an essay by Robert Lafont. Gallimard, 312 pages.

Histoire de l'occitanie[164], an essay by Henri Espieux. Cap e cap, 247 pages.

Occitanie: volem viure!, an essay by Michel Le Bris. Gallimard, 366 pages.

L'Occitanie et la lutte des classes,[165] an essay by Paul Alliès. Maspéro, 48 pages.

Petite encyclopédie occitane,[166] an essay by André Dupuy. Saber, 293 pages.

Nouveaux cathares pour Montségur, a novel by Saint-Loup. Presses de la Cité, 382 pages.

Albigeois et cathares,[167] an essay by Alain Hubert-Bonnal. Lieu dit, 128 pages.

L'épopée cathare,[168] an essay by Ferdinand Niel. PUF, 126 pages.

Occitanie libre!,[169] an essay published by the PNO. Cap e cap, 70 pages.

Le petit livre de l'Occitanie, a series of essays edited by Jean Larzac. 4 Vertats, 250 pages (second edition by Maspéro, 213 pages).

Historique de l'Occitanie,[170] an essay edited by André Dupuy. Alain Nouvel (P.O. Box 129, 34004 Montpellier Cédex), 159 pages.

In his *Procès de l'Occitanisme*[171] (L'Astrado, Toulon, 1975), Mr Louis Bayle, the manager of 'L'Astrado provençal' magazine (2 Vincent-Allègre street, 83100 Toulon), strongly objects to the separatist tendencies of the current Occitan movement; all from a regionalist and 'Mistralian' perspective. He contends that the 'Occitan nation' is an illusory viewpoint, specifying that the words 'Occitania' and 'Occitan' are, in themselves, 'pure barbarisms' from the Languedocian phonetical point of view. In the conclusion, he expresses his wish for the Félibrige to 'reclaim its initial vocation' (and 'sacrifice its amusements') and for Occitanism to 'renounce all political, partisan or Jacobine activity'. The book also comprises a circular by

162 TN: The South and the North — The Dialectic of France.

163 TN: The Rebirth of the South — An Essay on Occitan Literature in the Age of Henry IV.

164 TN: The History of Occitania.

165 TN: Occitania and Class Struggle.

166 TN: A Small Occitan Encyclopaedia.

167 TN: Albigensians and Cathars.

168 TN: The Cathar Saga.

169 TN: Free Occitania!

170 TN: Historical Review of Occitania.

171 TN: Judging Occitanism.

Mr Pierre Bonnaud and Jean-Claude Rivière whose purpose is to create an Association of Langue d'Oc Teachers.

THE FLEMISH

IN 1973, THE MUNICIPALITY OF Dunkerque proceeded to rename about twenty streets. We now have a Leughenaer Street (the street of the 'lying' beacon), a Dyck Street (Dyke Street), a Bazennes Street (the street of the *Baas*' wife, i.e. the seafaring fisherman-skipper's wife), a Michiel de Swaen Street, and many others.

A Lille student explains:

> This constitutes a sort of return to the sources. All of it, however, has come rather too late, because the Flemish language has been losing ground incessantly. Our region has even lost its own name! One speaks of Normandy, Provence and Béarn, but around here, all we are is the "North", meaning a mere point on a map.

As an indirect consequence, the term 'French Netherlands' is making a comeback into our everyday language. Taken in its general meaning, what it designates is French Flanders, as well as the Artois, Hainaut, Boulon and Cambrésis communes and regions.

It is a 'flat land' with houses of remarkable cleanliness, market places and belfries, pediments with stairs, brick buildings whose colour is reminiscent of dry rust and ripe fruit, a pervading smell of beer, countryside canals, and grass-covered dunes.

The area has been inhabited since prehistoric times, but it was during the 6th century that Germanic populations established themselves there.

Mr Henri Platelle, a professor at the Free University of Lille, writes:

> The Germanisation of the western part of Pas de Calais and Flanders is particularly accounted for by the invasions that swept in from overseas, and not by the impact of the Salian Franks who, from within their encampment of Campine, chose to head towards Tournai and Cambrai and then lower, towards the Somme river. They were tribes who originated from the coastal areas of the North Sea in Germany or immigrants who had come from England during the seventh century and Germanised the Flanders and Boulon regions. The name *litus saxonicum*

("Saxon coast"), which this coastline bore around 400 A.D., is a sign of the very pressure that lasted for a long time. (*Histoire des Pays-Bas français*[172])

The names given to the area attest to massive settlement. It was Saint Eligius[173] who, around 646, built the church around which Dunkerque would be born — *duyne*, meaning 'hill' (Celtic: *duno*, Latin: *dunum*), and *kerke*, i.e. 'church' (German: *kirche*).

The new arrivals brought with them a Frankish dialect comprised of Frankian, Frisian and Saxon elements and related to the 'Low German' (*Nederduitsch*) family of eastern and southern Germanic languages. This group includes the now extinct Lombardic language, the *Plattdeutsch* spoken on the northern plains of Germany, the Dutch language, Afrikaans and Flemish.

During the 7th century, the Frankish language reached the banks of the river Seine.

'Louis the Debonair[174] was forced to put the Bible into Teuton verses and Charles the Bald[175] sent monks from Ferrières to Pruym so that they could familiarise themselves with the Germanic language', Louis de Baecker[176] reminds us (in *Les Flamands de France*[177]).

The backward surge commenced in the 9th century with evangelisation. When, in 912, Viking leader Rollon (Hrolfr), to whom Charles the Simple[178] had handed over control of the Duchy of Normandy, presented himself before the king and exclaimed '*By Got!*' (meaning 'By God', an expression that resulted in the word 'bigot' in the French language), the king's assistants all burst into laughter. An interpreter had to be brought in. Mr Platelle adds:

---

172 TN: The History of the French Netherlands.

173 TN: Saint Eligius (also Eloy or Loye) (11th June, 588–1st December, 660) is the patron saint of goldsmiths, other metalworkers, and coin collectors.

174 TN: Louis the Pious (778–20th June, 840), also called the Fair and the Debonair, was the King of the Franks and co-Emperor (as Louis I) with his father, Charlemagne, from 813 onwards.

175 TN: Charles the Bald (13th June, 823–6th October, 877) was the King of West Francia (843–877), King of Italy (875–877) and Holy Roman Emperor (875–877, as Charles II).

176 TN: A French solicitor and erudite.

177 The Flemish People of France.

178 TN: Charles III (17th September, 879–7th October, 929), also called the Simple or the Straightforward, was the King of West Francia from 898 until 922 and the King of Lotharingia from 911 until 919–23.

> During the eleventh and twelfth centuries, Romanisation was a *fait accompli* all the way to Calais, Andres, Ardres, Audruicq, Eperlecques, and Saint-Omer.

In the 15th century, the Great Netherlands represented a political, cultural and ethnic unit that comprised the seventeen provinces (including the contemporary North and Pas-de-Calais) as well as the north-west of the Somme. To designate this common linguistic sphere, the word *diets* (Low Dietsch dialects) was used. According to A. Van Loey[179] (*La langue néerlandaise au pays flamand.*[180] Office de publicité, Brussels, 1945), the word 'Dutch' did not surface until 1514, as part of a book published in Anvers.

The son and successor of John the Fearless,[181] Philip the Good[182] allows Burgundian power to enjoy extraordinary progress. In 1428, he is acknowledged as the *ruwaert*, meaning the governor of Hainaut, whose countess he forces to abdicate in 1433. In 1477, however, the death of Charles the Bold[183] puts an end to the dynasty's astonishing ascent.

Two centuries later, the Treaty of Münster separates the North of the Netherlands from the South; whereas the former becomes independent, the latter remains under Spanish domination.

Professor Meijer of the University of London states:

> The North then evolved into the independent Dutch Republic, experiencing a well-defined national identity as well as a flourishing culture in an atmosphere of liberty and relative tolerance. In the South, on the other hand, the Counter-Reformation smothered the Dutch culture, so to speak. A northern, heretical and rebellious language, Dutch was relegated to a background position and became the language of the household. It was replaced by French in terms of literary and cultural language in the broad sense of the word. (*Septentrion* number 1, 1975)

---

179 TN: Adolphe Van Loey (14th July, 1905–6th March, 1987) was a Belgian linguist and philologist.

180 TN: The Dutch Language in the Flemish Region.

181 TN: As John I, John the Fearless (28th May, 1371–10th September, 1419) was Duke of Burgundy (the second of the House of Valois) from 1404 until his death.

182 TN: Philip the Good (31st July, 1396–15th June, 1467) was Duke of Burgundy from 1419 until his death.

183 TN: Charles the Bold (10th November, 1433–5th January, 1477), baptised Charles Martin, was Duke of Burgundy from 1467 to 1477, the last from the House of Valois.

Through the Treaty of Aix-la-Chapelle in 1668, Louis XIV proceeded to annex coastal Flanders once and for all. Jean Baert (Bart), a 'privateer' of the 'Royal Navy', is ennobled in 1694. He had previously served under admiral De Ruyter, the commander of the Dutch fleet.

In 1830, with the failure of William I's[184] attempt to bring about the reunification of the Great Netherlands, the South (i.e. Brussels and its region) rebels and embraces secession. Belgium is thus born.

LANGUAGE AND CUSTOMS

From the perspective of customs and language, the situation took much longer to evolve. Spoken in most of the Artois region and far to the south of the Lys in the Middle Ages, the Flemish language was driven back north, mainly after the Revolution. The examination of inscriptions carved into gravestones even leads us to believe that the higher social classes were not fully francised until the 19th century.

In the middle of the previous century,[185] Louis de Baecker, two of whose 'classical' works have recently been reedited, undertook to identify the 'archaisms' that are still observable today; his harvest was plentiful. He writes:

> We, the Flemish of France, have preserved intact the language of our Frankish ancestors, the old language of the founders of the ancient French monarchy. This Germanic idiom has remained constant in our region and retained its vivaciousness on our soil, despite all the changes in territorial conscription that politics have subjected it to. (*Les Flamands de France*)

Not having undergone the consonantal mutation of High German (Dutch: *paard*, German: *pferd*—both meaning 'horse'), the Flemish language is reminiscent of English in its consonants but closer to German in its vowels, vocabulary and syntax. It allows for the creation of diminutives on the basis of adverbs (to speak *zoetjes* or *stilletjes*: to speak in a hushed or low voice). With its four dialectal groups (Western, Eastern, Brabant and Limburgish), it is a

184 TN: William I (Willem Frederik, Prince of Orange-Nassau; 24th August, 1772–12th December, 1843) was a Prince of Orange and the first King of the Netherlands and Grand Duke of Luxembourg.

185 TN: The 19th century.

complete language that is highly similar to Dutch. In the French Netherlands, there are approximately 120,000 people who use it on a daily basis.

Referring to customs, Louis de Baecker also quotes the words of Tacitus, according to whom Germanic people had the habit of measuring time in terms of nights, and not days, and, on the other hand, harboured a 'mad passion' for dice games. He adds:

> Well, the habit of counting things in nights and the passion for dice games were perpetuated by our fathers until the fourteenth century. Joanne of Constantinople had already banned the inhabitants of Bergues and Bourbourg from playing dice under penalty of a twenty-sol fine.

In the religious domain, pagan survivals are numerous in a land where the name of the god Thor is encountered in the names of the cities of Tongres, Turnhout, Tournay, Tume, and Tourcoing. Mr de Baecker writes:

> The custom of lighting fires on the occasion of the summer and winter solstices has been preserved in certain Flemish cities of France. In Bergues and Dunkerque, on both Saint John's Day and Saint Peter's Day, children roam the streets, asking for firewood and singing: "Wood, wood, we come for Saint John's wood; give us a little, a little wood, and then a little more still for Saint Peter!"

There are also carnivals, kermesses, Saint-Martin's Vigil, the 'bouhours' or fires of the first Sunday of Lent (the commencement of spring), the procession of giants, the *Visscherbende*, May trees (which Saint Eligius tried to ban), the 'Papegaults' (cardboard birds placed at the top of a tree or a pole — in Beauvais, during the 19th century, those that managed to shoot them down would be exempted from their tax duty for a whole year!), and so on.

'PROHIBITED FROM THROWING PEBBLES AND SPEAKING FLEMISH'

Politically speaking, having been the first to free itself from servitude, the French Netherlands gave France two men whose actions and personal relations had a profound impact upon our century: Philippe Pétain, who was born in Cauchy-à-la-Tour (Pas-de-Calais) and Charles de Gaulle, born in Lille.

Nowadays, the French Netherlands has new vocations. Exchange routes have replaced invasion routes and some axes have surfaced — the one that connects England to the Rhineland (through Wallonia and the Manche) and the one that joins Paris to Holland. The 'region of the North', which is located at the very heart of the 'golden delta' (an economic space that covers almost all of continental north-western Europe, with a 'peak' in Bâle and a coastal base stretching from Ijmuiden to Calais), intends to take advantage of things.

The Dunkerque agglomeration rose to the level of an urban community in 1969. In February 1968, the guiding ideas of a regional management plan had been expressed in a White Book, which was then followed by a Green Book for rural management.

On the linguistic level, the situation is a source of concern. The Flemish language is hardly spoken at all these days in the 'Westhoek', meaning in the Hazebrouck and Dunkerque arrondissements. Some people have found themselves wondering 'why the ORTF,[186] which dedicates half an hour of its radio broadcast time to the Polish language every three weeks (to cater to immigrant workers), has never been willing to reserve as little as a few minutes for a Dutch language programme to be broadcasted once or twice a week, whether in its radio or television transmissions'.

And yet the University of Lille lies at a mere twenty-six-kilometre distance from the Flemish University of Courtrai (Kortrijk) in Belgium. Additionally, the Dutch language is used by more than twenty million people worldwide (in the Netherlands, Belgium, South Africa, and the former Dutch Indies). In spite of these facts, there is not a single primary or secondary educational establishment that would provide Dutch language lessons in the North. And despite the Guichard Law of 1972 and the Deixonne Law of 11th January, 1951, which introduced regional languages into primary school programmes, there are only two Dutch language professors receiving their salaries through our National Education system.

One of the hosts of the Michel de Swaen Circle bitterly remarks:

> It was not such a long time ago that one could read the following words on the walls of certain schools: "Pupils are prohibited from throwing pebbles and speaking Flemish". It was the time of the *signum*, a shoe that would be suspended around

---

186 TN: The *Office de Radiodiffusion-Télévision Française* (ORTF) was the national agency charged, between 1964 and 1974, with providing public radio and television in France. All programmes, and especially news broadcasts, were under the strict control of the national government.

> the neck of any child caught speaking Flemish (meaning his or her own language) on the school playground. This shoe would be transmitted by the "guilty" to any other schoolmate who they, in turn, would catch speaking Flemish. At the end of the break, the last pupil to wear the *signum* would be punished.

The Michel de Swaen Circle is fighting for bilingualism. It has adopted the name of the most famous Flemish author of the French language, Michel de Swaen (1654–1707), a doctor of medicine who translated *El Cid* into Dutch and whose major works include, alongside *La botte couronnée,*[187] a theatre play entitled *L'abdication de Charles-Quint.*[188]

ETHNOPLURALISM

Founded in October 1971 under strictly apolitical circumstances, the Michel de Swaen Circle has set itself the objective of defending the character and heritage of the French Netherlands, as well as that of promoting the cultural values of the Dutch language. It is headed by Jaak Fermaut, Nick Neirynck and Dominiek Hardebolle (who all stem from the federalist milieus that published the *Courrier lillois*[189] in 1970–73). Its honorary president, Mr Nicolas Bourgeois, has authored a book entitled *Hexagons* and is the former chairman of the Bar Council.

The Circle is continuing the work undertaken by Abbé Gantois, who, having established the *Lion de Flandre*[190] magazine before the war, passed away in 1968. Back in the 1950s, it was *La Nouvelle Flandre,*[191] run by Doctor Jan Klaas and formerly known as *Notre Flandre,*[192] that had taken charge of this endeavour.

Today, the Circle organises excursions to the Flanders region, popular song evenings, farm and old house restoration workshops, and conferences/debates. Its managerial staff offers free Dutch courses attended by approximately

---

187 TN: The Crowned Boot.

188 TN: The Abdication of Charles V.

189 TN: Lille Courier.

190 TN: Lion of Flanders.

191 TN: The New Flanders.

192 TN: Our Flanders.

200 people. Its correspondent in Belgian Flanders is Mr Wido Bourel, the co-founder of *Hekkerschreeuwen*.

Mr Neirynck declares:

> In a world where individuals are increasingly subjected to standardisation and egalitarian trends, and human groups to assimilation, acculturation and levelling, what we propose is a new path — that of enabling our cultural values to achieve deep-rootedness through promotion.

On 25th June, 1975, a member of the Circle represented the French Netherlands during the traditional *Tour de l'Yzer* pilgrimage in Dicksmuide,[193] where 100,000 Flemish people from all three lands meet every year to honour the memory of the Flemish soldiers who fell during World War I. On the occasion, he specified the following:

> The French Flemish movement shuns any and all extremism and strives to respect the open-mindedness and "pluralism" that characterise the peoples of the North; which is why it rises up against the uniformisation and egalitarian trends that human groups are nowadays subjected to. A universal melting pot would only serve to impoverish humanity, for it is indeed true that the existence of a just society does not entail a disappearance of differences. It is only by remaining rooted into their own culture that the men and women of our land will regain confidence in the future.

In 1976, the Michel de Swaen Circle published a file on regionalism. In it, it declares its hostility to both Marxism and the values of the mercantile bourgeoisie, while simultaneously proclaiming its support for *ethnopluralism*. Furthermore, it also rejects separatism, which it contrasts with autonomism:

> Just like any other movement, regionalism has its limits, and it must strive, above all, to avoid contributing to Europe's weakening; for dividing Europe could only serve American or Russian interests.

Ever since October 1976, the *Tÿl* monthly bulletin run by Mr Nick Neirynck has been added to the *notebooks* and documentation published by the Circle.

---

193 TN: The *Ijzertoren* (Dutch for 'Yser Towers') is a memorial along the Belgian Yser river in Dicksmuide.

There are also other organisations, such as the *Komitee voor Frans-Vlaanderen*[194] (KFV) headed by Mr Luc Verbeke in Belgium, and the *Comité flamand de France*,[195] whose creation in 1853 was actually a response to a decree issued by the Academic Council prohibiting the teaching of the Flemish language in all schools located in the Nord department of France (one of the founders of this committee was musicologist Edmond de Coussemaker, whose *Popular Flemish Songs of France*, collected in 1856, are part of the repertoire of our contemporary French Flemish singers).

In 1972, the *Ons Erfdeel* Foundation launched its *Septentrion* trimonthly, a magazine of Dutch culture published in French and edited by Mr Jozef Deleu and André Demedts. Since 1976, it has also been publishing a *Yearbook of the French Netherlands*.

Barrès[196] once wrote:

> Each day, we destroy what is undoubtedly the best in us — our smallholder farmers. One carelessly commits to loosening or breaking all the bonds which tie today's children and tomorrow's men to their soil. They can no longer speak their own maternal language and are taught to despise it. While behaving this way, one fails to notice that what one destroys are not actually the words, but the vivacious attachments and profound ways of feeling things.

As for Gromaire, the painter who was born by the Sambre river, he stated the following:

> Individuality is as important to countries as it is to men. The more one is themselves, the more one experiences the inner continuity of a civilisation, and the more one finds themselves capable of perceiving the values of eternity beyond the fleeting fantasies of the picturesque and the imitative.

Les Flamands de France, an essay by Louis de Baecker. Ed. Gérard Monfort (Le Portulan, Manoir de Saint-Pierre de Salerne, 27 Brionne), 408 pages.

---

194 TN: The French Flanders Committee.

195 TN: The Flemish Committee of France.

196 TN: Auguste-Maurice Barrès (19th August, 1862–4th December, 1923) was a French novelist, journalist and politician.

De la religion du Nord avant le christianisme,[197] an essay by Louis de Baecker. Ed. Gérard Monfort, 354 pages.

Histoire des Pays-Bas français,[198] a collection of essays edited by Louis Trénard. Privat, Toulouse, 582 pages.

The former editor-in-chief of *Courrier Lillois*, Mr Alain Walenne (Marc Wattiez), is currently in charge of a Nordic Cultural Institute (ICN, Maison de l'Europe, 219 bis boulevard de la Liberté, 59000 Lille), which has organised several public events during the past months: a Viking workshop, a visit to the outdoor museum of Bokrijk (near Gand), a conference by Mr Henri Fromage on the mythology of the Artois region, a sculpture exhibition (Maurits de Maertelaere), an exhibition of popular craftsmanship (Frank Seydlitz), etc.

The Flemish Committee of France, long headed by Monsignor Dupont and then taken over in 1973 by the curator of the *Hospice Comtesse de Lille* museum, Mr Philippe Jessu, seems to be slumbering these days. On its part, the KFV publishes some 'Mededelingen' (communications) in the shape of a trimonthly magazine (Vanderhaeghenstraat 46, 8790 Weregem, Belgium).

The twenty-ninth *Frans-Vlaamse Kultuurdag* was held in Waregem on 19th September, 1976, and the ninth *Frans-Vlaamse Dag* in Hulst, Zeeland on 2nd April, 1977. As for the fiftieth Yser pilgrimage, it took place on 3rd July, 1977.

Michel de Swaen Circle, P.O. Box 5, 290, 59379 Dunkerque Cedex — 'Tÿl', P.O. Box 5, 266, 59379 Dunkerque Cedex — 'Ons Erfdeel' /Jozef Deleu, Murissonstraat 160, 8530 Rekkem, Belgium.

THE BRETONS

DURING THE MONTH OF APRIL 1973, the Breton *Strollad ar Vro* party (SAV) banned the television airing of a film entitled *Tout va très bien, Madame la Marquise*.[199] Released in 1936 and starring Noël-Noël, the film focuses on a Breton servant who 'journeys northwards' to Paris, where his foolish and naïve actions accumulate — which is why it is 'an insult to the Breton people'.

Back then, the SAV party was one of the emanations of a polymorphous entity, the *Emsav* (pronounced 'emsao'), a term that can be likened to the Italian *Risorgimento*[200] and is used to designate the Breton Movement.

197 TN: On the Religion of the North Prior to Christianity.

198 TN: History of the French Netherlands.

199 TN: All Is Well, Lady Marquess.

200 TN: A movement for the unification and independence of Italy, which was achieved in 1870.

The Parisian public opinion seems to have never clearly grasped the movement's purpose — for although its history reaches back into the 19th century, it still evades traditional political labelling. In his book entitled *Breiz Atao*, Mr Olier Mordrel[201] writes:

> One is struck by the biased attitude of French officials towards a handful of idealists whose selflessness and courage should, at the very least, elicit a comprehension effort.

Historically, the issue relates to several important dates.

'THE ANCIENT LAND OF MY FATHERS'

In 1499, the matrimonial contract of Duchess Anne and Louis XII guarantees Brittany a certain level of autonomy. Governance of the duchy is meant to fall to the king's second son, with the duke being crowned in Rennes. In 1515, however, François d'Angoulême, who had married Claude, Anne of Brittany's daughter, is crowned as François I and seems to put Breton rights at risk.

In August 1532, the Breton states gather in Vannes and deliver a petition to the king. A month later, the famous Franco-Breton treaty known as the Plessis-Macé Edict is signed, guaranteeing Brittany's autonomy within the kingdom of France and promising to preserve its Parliament and local customs, while exempting its inhabitants from all military and fiscal obligation. Although the treaty would never be abolished, it would never be respected either, a fact that is mentioned by Breton autonomists when justifying their own actions.

The first Breton Association, founded by a group of Breton liberals, dates back to 1829. A second one bearing the same name surfaces in 1834. Napoleon III, however, abolishes it by means of a decree.

In 1898, writers such as François Botrel and Anatole Le Braz launch a Regionalist Breton Union (URB) strongly inspired by the Gaelic League. Two years later, future grammarian François Vallée creates, with the help of poet François Jaffrenou, the Bardic College or Gorsedd of Little Brittany.

---

201 TN: Olivier Mordrelle (29th April, 1901–25th October, 1985), known in Breton as Olier Mordrel, was a Breton nationalist and wartime collaborator with the Third Reich who founded the separatist Breton National Party.

That is when Taldir-Jaffrenou proceeds to compose a Breton national anthem entitled *Bro goz ma Zadou* ('The Ancient Land of My Fathers'), all to the tune of the Welsh anthem *Hen Wlad vy Nhada*.

In 1905, Abbé Yann-Vari (Jean-Marie) Perrot, a small yet well-built man with the large head of a stubborn bloke, undertakes to regroup 'Bretonising' Catholics. He founds the *Bleun-Brug* ('Heather Flower') Association, whose name, he says, 'symbolises the tenacity of the Breton race'. He also launches the *Feiz ha Breiz* magazine and proclaims: *Ar Brezoneg hag ar feiz a zo breur ha c'hoar e Breiz* ('In Brittany, the Breton and his faith are brother and sister').

Later on, communist teacher Yann Sohier would engage in an analogous effort targeting non-religious people. In 1933, he would establish the *Ar Falz* ('The Sickle') newspaper and strive to free the teaching of the Breton language from the influence of clericalism. In passing, he would state that to the Bretons, 'the example set by the Soviets is of immense value' (*Ar Falz*, April 1933). Upon Mr Sohier's passing in 1935 (at the age of thirty-four), Abbé Perrot would attend his funeral alongside Marcel Cachin.[202] As for his work, it would be continued by a linguist called Kerlann.

The 'real' policy commences in 1911, when a monument celebrating the Franco-Breton Treaty of 1532 and depicting Duchess Anne kneeling at the feet of her lord and master, French King Charles VIII, is inaugurated in Rennes. During the ceremony, a prolonged whistling is heard, causing a scandal. The whistler is none other than author and poet Camille Le Mercier d'Erm, who would go on to write an *Anthology of the National Bards and Poets of Armorican Brittany* (1922). He makes no secret of his 'pro-independence' sentiments.

A few weeks later, during the Saint-Renan congress, the most active elements of the Breton Regionalist Union split off from it and, led by Jean Choleau, found the Regionalist Breton Federation, which would soon morph into the Breton Nationalist Party (PNB).

A year later, Yves Le Diberder launches *Brittia* magazine, whose purpose is to turn Celtic culture into the very foundation of Breton rebirth. Then, in October 1912, Le Mercier d'Erm publishes a *separatist manifesto* and releases the *Breiz Dishual* ('Liberated Brittany') journal. In his eyes, just like those of

---

[202] TN: Marcel Cachin (20th September, 1869–12th February, 1958) was a French politician.

Marie de France,[203] 'Brittany is poetry'. Among other things, what he suggests is that the date of Brittany's national day be moved from the 14th of July to the 19th of September, which marks the anniversary of the crowning of the first Breton king, *Nominoë*. On his part, Emile Masson[204] (Ewan Gouesnou Brenn) creates the *Brug* journal, which advocates a socialist-revolutionary sort of syndicalism (and whose texts would be reedited in 1972 through Maspéro). World War I, however, puts an end to these endeavours.

TO RE-ESTABLISH A SPIRITUAL FAMILY

The first to leave for the front, the Bretons fight with exceptional tenacity. They leave 240,000 casualties on the battlefields, totalling an average of one inhabitant out of fourteen (compared to one inhabitant out of twenty-eight for the rest of France).

When the armistice is signed, the 240,000 dead men weigh heavily on the public opinion. Many Bretons are under the impression that Paris only shows interest in them when spilling their blood. *Bécassine*[205] and her blunders, the 'yokels' and the 'Mahauts'. 'The potatoes go to the pigs, the peels to the Bretons'. 'Alcoholism and round hats'. All the old clichés are now outdated.

The foremost event of the year 1919 is the emergence of the *Breiz Atao* ('Brittany Forever') journal, a title that would soon become a war cry and even a label: 'Now that bloke is a real *Breiz Atao*!'.

This is what the people running *Breiz Atao*, namely Job de Roincé (who would later drift towards Maurrassian reformism), Olier Mordrel and Morvan Marchal, declare in a most straightforward manner:

> The three ailments which Brittany suffers from are tuberculosis, alcoholism and French domination.

---

203 TN: Marie de France (fl. 1160 to 1215) was a medieval poet who was probably born in France and lived in England during the late 12th century.

204 TN: Émile Masson (1869–1923) was a Breton writer and thinker who used the pseudonyms Brenn, Ewan Gweznou, and Ion Prigent.

205 TN: *Bécassine* is a French comic strip and also the name (or rather the *nickname*) of its heroine, a Breton housemaid. The nickname itself is derived from the French word for a number of birds of the snipe family and is often used as a way of saying 'fool' in French.

Swotting up on the books of bards, heroic tales and the writings of Arthur Griffith (the man who created the Irish *Sinn Fein*), they proclaim the right of peoples to draw from their own heritage the necessary inspiration for self-governance.

Soon, the journal becomes famous for its original standpoints. Through Morvan Marchal, it considers the francophone 'Gallos' inhabiting Eastern Brittany (the High Bretons) to be fully-fledged Bretons, despite the fact that they reside 'beyond Vannes and Guingamp'. It also rejects the stereotyped image of a touristic and 'bagpipe-bearing' Brittany. And above all, what it imposes is the following formula — *Na ruz, na gwenn, Breizhad hepken* ('Not red, not white, only Breton!').

Mr Olier Mordrel says:

> We maintained that one could indeed be a free-thinker or a Protestant, a proponent of Druidism or materialism, a Free-Mason or a Capuchin, while simultaneously remaining an outstanding Breton.

He then adds

> Our primordial concern lay in not allowing ourselves to be confined to the capitalism-Marxism dilemma, since the essential purpose of Breton nationalism was to re-establish a spiritual family.

On the linguistic level, the situation has never ceased to deteriorate ever since that day in 1845 when, addressing teachers, a deputy prefect declared:

> Above all else, gentlemen, remember that your only role in this establishment is to kill the Breton language.

Mr Mordrel recounts:

> I remember a farm in Plouguerneau where the grandparents, unable to speak a single word of French but prohibited from using the Breton language to communicate with their grandchildren, who had come to spend their school holidays with them, addressed the children using gestures punctuated with "erm, erm" sounds, as if they were both deaf and dumb. The children responded to this behaviour by treating them harshly, as if the grandparents were simple-minded beasts.

At the start of the 1920s, the *Breiz Atao* team proceeds to create the *Unvaniez Yaouankiz Vreiz* ('Union of Breton Youth'), which, in 1927, turns into the Breton Autonomist Party (PAB).

Its first congress is held on 11th September, 1927 in Rosporden, under the fluttering *Gwenn ha Du* ('The White and the Black'), the new flag of the Breton people drawn by Morvan Marchal. Whereas its five black bands represent the 'Gallo' dioceses (Dol, Nantes, Rennes, Saint-Malo and Saint-Brieuc), the four white ones symbolise the Breton language dioceses — Trégor, Léon, Cornouaille and Vannes. As for its ermine canton, it is taken from the coat of arms of the historical duchy of Brittany.

Gathered in Châteaulin in 1928, the PAB elects a triumvirate comprising Olier Mordrel as the CEO of propaganda, Maurice Duhamel as the editor-in-chief of *Breiz Atao*, and Fransez Debauvais as its Secretary General. Yann Brickler is appointed as its treasurer. In contrast to the old Nationalist Party, the PAB, which chose the four-spiral hevoud[206] as its emblem (a symbol later replaced by a triskelion), is not essentially separatist. The following is stated in its programme:

> We believe that, account taken of the current state of both Europe and the world, the severing of all ties between Brittany and France would only be a source of incomplete solutions to the problems faced by our land. We do, however, reject any harmful *assimilation* of our material and moral interests.

It is not nostalgic either:

> The old Brittany of our kings and dukes has vanished, never to return. We respectfully hail its memory but do not seek to reconstitute it as such. A people cannot go back to its origins any more than a river can return to its source. We are modern Bretons.

Contact is made with the other regionalist organisations. On 12th September, 1927, a Central Committee of French National Minorities is created. There would also be a journal, *Peuples et frontières*,[207] including Breton, Alsatian, Flemish, Occitan, Catalan and Basque columns.

---

206 TN: A hevoud is a kind of four-spiral swastika. A triskelion, by contrast, only has three.

207 TN: Peoples and Borders.

On the linguistic level, the *Breiz Atao* team launches the *Gwalarn* journal; Roparz Hémon is entrusted with its management. Here is what he declares:

> We have always been Nordics. As soon as we detached ourselves from France, it was towards the north that we directed our gaze, just as a compass needle immediately determines the right direction once it has been cleaned of rust.

In 1929, *Breiz Atao* becomes a weekly publication. The following year, the PAB participates in partial elections in the second circumscription of Guingamp, receiving 400 votes. Soon, however, it undergoes its first crisis. A 'Leftist-federalist' tendency comprising Maurice Duhamel secedes and founds the *War Zao* movement.

On 15th August, 1932, Daniel Renoux writes in *l'Humanité*:

> The fact that the Breton people enjoys its own ethnic particularity is beyond all discussion. Faithful to the right of peoples to shape their own destiny, the French Communist Party shall defend the claims voiced by Brittany's popular masses. (Mr Marchais[208] would qualify this declaration as 'absolute nonsense'.)

In 1932, the PAB reorganises itself and adopts the name of Breton National Party (PNB).

At the end of 1933, it already includes sixty-two active sections. Membership is on the rise, and 6,000 copies of *Breiz Atao* are published. The party organises some of its meetings on historical sites: at Saint-Aubin-du-Cormier, where the troops of La Trémoille vanquished the Duchy's army in 1488; and in Ballon, near Redon, where Nominoë crushed Charles the Bald's 'Franciens' in 845.

THE DOCTRINE OF BRETON NATIONALISM

A few months later, the PNB launches the theoretical journal *Stur* ('Helm'), whose very first issue comes out in July 1934. Mordrel is in charge of its management. It is there that, in the space of a few years, the doctrine of Breton nationalism formulated in *Breiz Atao* finds itself deepened and 'universalised'.

---

208 TN: Georges René Louis Marchais (7th June, 1920–16th November, 1997) was the head of the French Communist Party (PCF) from 1972 to 1994 and a candidate in the French presidential elections of 1981.

Stur strives to achieve the synthesis of Celtic Romanticism and the ethics of old Prussia. In it, R. Glémarec (Roger Hervé) turns himself into the exegete of both Spengler and Brocéliande's[209] *enchanted* myth. Olier Mordrel writes:

> What we affirm is a new principle, yet one that is as old as our own race: the right of the best to sit at the Round Table and the right of the weak to be granted the protection of the strong.

Heroism is contrasted with sheer force:

> The notion of absolute force excludes that of heroism, for the latter is nothing but the intervention of superhuman energies that arise to modify the balance of brutal forces in a most unexpected manner. The hero's presence comes into play and upsets the predictions of the strong. Our vocation lies in countering the prejudice of quantity with our faith in quality.

Mordrel also writes poetry:

> The motherland does not lie before our eyes,
> To be picked like a blossoming woman that yearns
> And cannot resist;
> Nowhere does she await us today,
> And one shall have to carve her way
> With one's own fist;
> A queen on the rise
> Is she who loves all places clear;
> We all belong to those that forgotten lay,
> And how we must now struggle and fear
> Until to us she returns!

Simultaneously, the PNB 'lads' target 'Paris-Babylon', as *Breiz Atao* publishes the following headline:

> Paris, a City of Light? Yes, Indeed, Inside a Red Lantern!

---

209 TN: Brocéliande (also known as Breselianda, Bersillant, Berthelien, Berceliande, Brecheliant, Brecilien, Broceliande) is a legendary enchanted forest that had a reputation of magic and mystery in the medieval imagination. Brocéliande is featured in several medieval texts mostly related to the Arthurian legend and the characters of Merlin, Morgan le Fay, the Lady of the Lake, and some of the Knights of the Round Table.

Forty years later, Glenmor, the singer, would express the very same idea through his lyrics:

> So beautiful are our countryside's maids
> Arriving to Paris in the early morn,
> Their distant Brittany none yet mourn;
> Still their child-like laughter never fades,
> Though by Paris they have been reduced
> To harlots that men have seduced.

Being moderate regionalists, Le Cam and Yann Fouéré (born in 1910) establish a movement for the teaching of the Breton language known as *Ar Brezoneg er Skol* ('The Breton language at school'). The movement has already attracted a certain audience. In June 1937, in the National Assembly, the Teachers' Commission would choose to support its demands.

Some cultural journals have also seen the light of day — Loeiz Herrieu's *Dihunamb*, Yves Le Moal's *Breiz, Studi hag Ober*, and others.

VIOLENT ACTIONS

There are, however, other Bretons who prefer rougher means and clandestine struggle.

On the night of 7th August, 1932, an explosion shakes the city of Rennes. In front of the *Hôtel de Ville*, the famous monument commemorating the Act of Union that attached Brittany to France had just been blown up. Edouard Herriot was supposed to arrive on the next day from Paris to celebrate the fourth centenary of the 1532 Union Treaty. Talk about a waste of efforts.

A few months later, the very same Herriot (a 'symbol of radical, Southern and parliamentary France') is delayed on his way to Nantes. The railway that his train was meant to take had been dynamited.

A mysterious organisation calling itself the *Gwenn ha Du* (just like the Breton flag itself) claims responsibility for both attacks. No one would ever be arrested.

The leader of the *Gwenn ha Du* is a man named Célestin Laîné. He is a member of the PNB and a long-time supporter of violent action. Olier Mordrel, who was involved in sharp disagreements with him, describes him as 'the prophet of his own made-to-measure Celtic religion'. Soon, he establishes an embryonic Breton army, the *Kadervenn* ('Combat Trench'). Military marches, target shooting, and the manufacturing of explosives ensue. Mordrel states:

> With his *Kadervenn*, Laîné created a new type of man among us — the soldier of the cause, devoted to the death. The obligation of absolute secrecy taught participants never to ask questions, even when something seemed bizarre to them, and exempted the leader from giving any kind of explanation. In this regard, it was quite a big thing.

In May 1933, a secret meeting is held on the heathland of Bréhec, which overlooks the sea and is located near Saint-Quay. Five men (two PNB delegates, two representatives of the *Gwenn ha Du*, and a member of the *Bleun-Brug*) decide to coordinate their activities. They thus form a clandestine council — the *Kuzul Meur*. The opposition between Laîné's 'activists' and the 'politically inclined' members of the PNB would, however, persist.

As the war draws closer, the authorities begin to feel concerned about the activities conducted by the autonomists. On 23rd May, 1938, a law-decree proclaims that anyone 'who undertakes to violate the integrity of the national territory' would be prosecuted. The PNB's main leaders, Mordrel and Debauvais, are brought before the criminal court of Rennes. Upon hearing the presiding judge remark that he was born in Paris, Mordrel responds by saying:

> I am the son of Bretons. Even if I had been born in China, I would still not be Chinese.

A few months before war is declared, the PNB is prohibited, as is *Breiz Atao*.

When the hostilities erupt, Mordrel and Debauvais make a grave and especially ambiguous decision, crossing the border and travelling to Berlin. On 12th October, 1939, they release a manifesto written in six languages where they proclaim that 'Brittany must remain neutral in this global conflict'. This declaration would result in their being condemned to death (in absentia) by a French military tribunal on 7th May, 1940.

Mordrel explains:

> And yet, if there was one thing which we dreaded, it was the fact that we could be passed off in France as the mere agents of a foreign power. In actual fact, what weighed on our minds was the example of Masaryk and Benes, moulding their national government in America and Paris with the help of the enemies of their

> official fatherland; that of Pilsudski and his Poles, unremittingly attempting to find allies to combat their oppressors; or also that of the Irish and the Scots offering king Louis of France entire regiments to fight against the English enemy. Our people had no fewer reasons and no fewer motivations than they did.

Their hopes would soon be disappointed. Despite keeping the autonomist card handy, the Reich was reluctant to use it. Rather than a Europe with a hundred flags, what it had in mind was a Great Germany. Having tried, without great success, to rally Breton prisoners to their cause, Olier Mordrel and Debauvais return to Brittany, where, once again, they cross paths with Célestin Laîné.

THE DRAMATIC YEARS OF WAR

On 3rd July, 1940, a Breton National Council (CNB) gathers in Pontivy. It is Debauvais who chairs its executive committee. On his part, Mordrel suggests expanding movement and 'transcending the *Breiz Atao* phase'.

At the same time, the dissolved PNB launches another weekly publication, *L'heure Bretonne*,[210] and proceeds to reorganise itself, with Fred Moyse acting as its Secretary General and Ronan de Fréminville (i.e. writer Jean Merrien) as the journal's editor-in-chief.

Four months later, two moderate organisations, the Breton Association and the Regionalist Breton Union, submit to the Vichy Government a *Briefing on the Legitimate Demands of the Province of Brittany.*

This reawakening of Breton activities is not met with much appreciation in the higher spheres of the French state. In 1940, Marshal Pétain mentions the 'thousand-year-old' French unity (despite the fact that in 940, neither Lyons and Arles, nor Cambrai and Verdun were actually French, and Dreux was but an enclave in the county of Blois). In Paris, the Germans are equally reticent. Otto Abetz,[211] who married a French woman, is very hostile towards the Bretons. In Rennes, the 'Collaboration' movement is sponsored by a Corsican.

---

[210] TN: The Breton Hour.

[211] TN: Heinrich Otto Abetz (26th March, 1903–5th May, 1958) was the German ambassador to Vichy France during the Nazi era.

And whereas Maurras viewed the Celts as 'a vague group of root-gnawers and solitary carnivores', it was Marcel Déat[212] who declared:

> The more Breton the Bretons become, the more French they will be.

In the end, PNB members would not be looked upon favourably in either Vichy or London, nor even in Paris or Berlin.

On 14th July, 1940, the Bishop of Quimper, Monsignor Duparc, publishes a warning 'against a Breton separation campaign organised by men that have already been condemned by French courts'.

Tensions peak at the end of the year, when the Germans order Mordrel and Debauvais to renounce their activities. Arrested by the German police in Quimperlé, Mordrel finds himself being offered the position of Celtic language lecturer at the University of Tübingen. Forced to accept the offer, he returns to Germany.

Mr Paul Sérant[213] writes:

> This German intervention undoubtedly stemmed from the political orientation that was decided upon following the meeting between Hitler and Pétain in Montoire. (*La Bretagne et la France.*[214] Fayard, 1971)

Neither Célestin Laîné, the hard-line member of the PNB, nor brothers Yves and Raymond Delaporte, who represent the 'Rightist' tendency within the party, are not upset by Mordrel's departure. They even make the most of his absence to trigger a 'palace revolution' that crystalises an already old rivalry. It is Raymond Delaporte, the former president of the *Bleun-Brug* and the Catholic students of Angers, who is then entrusted with running the PNB, thus bestowing upon the movement a more traditional sort of orientation.

Morvan Marchal remarks:

---

212 TN: Marcel Déat (7th March, 1894–5th January, 1955) was a French socialist politician until 1933, when he initiated a spin-off from the French Section of the Workers' International (SFIO). During the occupation of France by Nazi Germany, he founded the collaborationist National Popular Rally (RNP).

213 TN: Paul Sérant is the pen name of Paul Salleron (19th March, 1922–2nd October, 2002), a French journalist and author. He was a great lover of the French language, as well as a lover of regional diversity, supporting the preservation of local cultures such as Breton, Occitan and Basque.

214 TN: Brittany and France.

> What happened in Brittany was the same as in Vichy — the Church took over the movement.

In order to avoid a wait-and-see attitude, the PNB creates some *Bagadou Stourms* ('Combat Groups'), which are then placed under the authority of Yann Goulet, the head of the party's youth organisations.

The 'Bagadou' would end up recruiting more than 500 people, who would periodically be involved in physical clashes with both French police and fascists.

In the meantime, Breton cultural life remains active. In November 1940, linguist Roparz Hémon, who had already become the director of the *Arvor* weekly, takes charge of a Celtic institute known as *Framm Keltiek*, in which he would do a considerable amount of work (especially through his successful creation of a unified form of Breton spelling that would later impose itself within the *Emsav)*. While Robert Le Helloco proceeds to publish *Galv* ('The Appeal'), Yann Fouéré launches the *La Bretagne*[215] daily, while also taking control of *La Dépêche de Brest*,[216] which would soon print as many as 110,000 copies. He additionally serves as the secretary of the Breton Advisory Council, under the authority of the regional prefect, Jean Quénette, originally from the Lorraine region.

Olier Mordrel spends five months in Germany. Having been allowed to return to Paris in May 1941 (under the condition of not establishing any contact with the PNB and 'not entering Breton territory'), he exerts himself to have *Stur* published again, an endeavour he would not be granted permission for until June 1942.

Dedicating himself henceforth to theoretical tasks, he publishes a series of essays in which he denounces the 'myth of the Hexagon'. In contrast with the 'soft separatism' advocated by the 'rump PNB', he simultaneously adopts a resolutely European position. The Franco-Breton conflict is, in his eyes, 'outdated' (*Stur*, July–August 1942). He thus writes:

> The impassable divide dug by intolerance between the Parisian Region and the Peninsular Armorican Massif is not a natural law. … It is not a matter of "freeing" Brittany, but of asserting its presence. (Stur, autumn 1942)

---

215 TN: Brittany.

216 TN: A French newspaper.

That is when blood began to flow in Brittany. On 4th September, 1943, Yann Brickler, the head of *Stur* and the *Emsav*'s pillar in Quimper, is assassinated in his office by three members of the Maquis Resistance. On the 12th of December, having celebrated Mass, sixty-six-year-old Abbé Perrot, the founder of *Bleun-Brug*, is shot dead by unidentified assailants while traveling on foot to an isolated chapel, five kilometres from Scrignac. 'They had been granted permission by the radio of London', Robert Aron would state in his *Histoire de l'épuration*[217] (Fayard).

The death of Abbé Perrot, considered one of the most striking figures of the Breton Movement, arouses considerable emotion. It triggers a new crisis within the PNB, one which, this time, involves a face-off between the Delaporte brothers and Célestin Laîné.

Indeed, the latter believed that the hour of reprisal against 'terrorists' had come. For this purpose, he proceeded to form a new paramilitary group, the *Bezen Perrot* ('Perrot Formation'), in which one encountered the former members of the *Kadervenn*, which had, in the meantime, been transformed into 'Special Services' and subsequently into a 'Breton Army'.

Used by the Germans, this small-sized militia would participate in the battle against the Maquis before being placed under the command of the *Sicherheitsdienst*.[218] The result was an infernal circle of vengeance and hatred. And yet the *Bezen Perrot* would never comprise more than seventy people.

Olier Mordrel writes:

> It was still too much, because this formation allowed Brittany's enemies, who had returned to Paris in full force, to crucify the movement with the support of the Breton people.

Following the Liberation, passions are indeed unleashed, and around a thousand summary executions are carried out in Brittany. Some people attract suspicion for having merely played the bagpipes. On their part, most former members of the PNB proceed to disperse or escape.

Fransez Debauvais dies in Colmar in March 1944, following a prolonged illness. His brother-in-law, Jos Youénou, is shot dead by a commander of the

[217] TN: History of the Purge.

[218] TN: The *Sicherheitsdienst* or SD was the intelligence agency of the SS and the Nazi Party in Nazi Germany.

Alsatian gendarmerie at the Struthof concentration camp. Mordrel, Goulet and Laîné are all sentenced to death in absentia, with Yves and Raymond Delaporte respectively given a ten- and twenty-year hard labour sentence. Having been acquitted by the Court of Justice of Rennes, Roparz Hémon would go on to become a professor at the School of Advanced Studies in Dublin. Laîné also moves to Ireland, as do Yann Fouéré and Yann Goulet, while others choose to leave for Italy, Spain, Brazil and Canada.

POPULAR ART AND MUSIC

In his book entitled *Au village des condamnés à mort*,[219] Ronan Caerléon describes the case of a Breton militant named Geffroy, who remained shackled in his death row cell for a period of 618 days.

Olier Mordrel, who decides to present himself to the Anglo-American authorities in an effort to initiate a procedure in favour of Breton nationalists, ends up incarcerated in the English prison of Cinecitta, near Rome, from which he would then escape before being transferred to Rennes. Later on, he would be located in Argentina.

The Resistance comprised some autonomists as well, of course. Alongside the more famous figures such as Henri d'Estienne d'Orves, whose deeds would be recounted by Mr Christian Durandet in *Les maquis bretons*[220] (France-Empire, 1973), there were also others, including Jacques Le Maho, a member of both the PNB and the *Bagadou Stourm* and a man who would first shine in the French Forces of the Interior[221] and the Rhine and Danube army before moving on to a militant role in the ranks of the Breton Liberation Front (FLB). The Breton association of the FFL,[222] *Sao Breiz*, includes several hundred adherents; and yet, in 1945, of the eighty members appointed under the Resistance at the Provisory Consultative Assembly, not a single one was a Breton.

---

219 TN: Capital Punishment Village.

220 TN: The Breton Members of the Maquis.

221 TN: The phrase 'French Forces of the Interior' (French: *Forces Françaises de l'Intérieur*) refers to French resistance fighters in the later stages of World War II.

222 TN: During the Second World War, the Free French Forces (FFL) were the armed forces of Free France (the French government-in-exile) under the aegis of General de Gaulle.

Following the Liberation, the Breton Movement thus found itself dismantled. A new beginning was in order, one that would essentially concern the cultural domain, impacting both the Breton language and popular music.

It was a time when authors such as Youen Olier, Alain Guel, Pér Denez, and Ronan Huon all attained fame, but also one when various brotherhoods of 'music players' flourished. In 1954, Brittany comprised more than a hundred Celtic Circles, as well as some 2,000 bagpipe players gathered around the *Bodageg ar Sonerion* (BAS) and its *Ar Soner* ('The Player') newspaper.

CULTURE AND SONGS

Around thirty new 'Bretonising' publications surface between 1946 and 1950, of which *Ar Vro*[223] must be mentioned in first place. Lay teachers publish *Skol Vreiz*,[224] as *Al Liamm*[225] continues the efforts undertaken by *Gwalarn*. Children read *Wanig ha Wenig*[226] and *l'Appel d'Ololé*,[227] run by Henry Caouissin (*Ololé* had already been one of the newspapers that enjoyed the greatest number of readers during the war).

1963 sees the birth of the *Strollad Deskadurezh an Eil Derez* (SADED), a secondary level teaching organism which offers correspondence courses and commits itself to translating the faculty's main courses into the Breton language, while relying on a journal entitled *Preder* ('Reflection').

In 1965, the Celtic League — an inter-Celtic organisation headquartered in Dublin and represented in Nantes by Mr Jakez Derouet — sends the United Nations a memorandum on 'the rights of three Celtic lands to self-determination': Brittany, Wales and Scotland.

In May 1967, an apolitical organisation known as *Emgleo Breiz* gathers 150,000 signatures supporting the teaching of the Breton language. Its leader,

---

223 TN: *Ar Vro* was a Breton bimonthly journal with close ties to the Breton autonomist movement, written mainly in French and published from 1954 to 1974.

224 TN: *Skol Vreiz*, or 'Breton School', is a pedagogical guidebook.

225 TN: *Al Liamm* (Breton for 'The Link') is a bimonthly magazine of culture and literature in the Breton language.

226 TN: Inspired by Christian notions, *Wanig ha Wenig* was a children's magazine.

227 TN: *Ololê* or *O-lo-lê*, the call of Breton shepherds, was the name of an illustrated Breton newspaper which targeted young people and was published from 1940 to 1944; it then resurfaced from 1970 to 1974 under the name of *Appel d'Ololê*, meaning 'Call of Ololê'.

a teacher named Keravel, is committed to pursuing the work of *Ar Falz* and Yann Sohier.

One thus gradually witnesses the re-emergence of Breton literature (Xavier Grall, Alain Guel, Youen Olier); Breton theatre (Tanguy Malmanche, Jakez Riou, and Paol Keineg, who authored *Printemps des bonnets rouges*[228]); Breton cinema (Britta-films and René Vautier, the creator of *Avoir vingt ans dans les Aurès*[229] and *La folle de Toujouane*[230]); and Breton publishers (Kelenn, Presses universitaires de Bretagne). In Quimper, the *Nature et Bretagne*[231] publishing house is born of the efforts of an economic interest group formed by seven Breton writers.

Simultaneously, thanks to the articles and books written by journalists and authors such as Jean Bothorel (*La Bretagne contre Paris.*[232] Table Ronde, 1969); Yann Poilvet (*Armor*); Morvan Lebesque (*Comment peut-on être Breton?*[233] Seuil, 1970), a former member of the *Breiz Atao* and the first editor-in-chief of *L'Heure Bretonne*, who went on to become a columnist at *Canard enchaîné*;[234] Yann Fouéré (*L'Europe aux cent drapeaux.*[235] Presses d'Europe, 1968); Renan Caerléon; Hervé Le Boterf; Yann Poupinot; and others, the French — or Parisian — public opinion is gradually becoming better informed about Breton issues.

Since the end of the 1960s, Breton culture has thus reclaimed its legitimate place both in Brittany and Paris.

The Breton flag, which had, until 1950, been considered seditious, is now accepted everywhere. The 'Bzh' abbreviation of *Breizh* ('Brittany'), which was officially banned on 7th August, 1967, is sprouting up in increasing numbers on the rears of cars. And since 1966, Breton parents have been free to call their

---

228 TN: Red Bonnet Spring.

229 TN: To Be Twenty in the Aures Mountains.

230 TN: The Madwoman of Toujouane.

231 TN: Nature and Brittany.

232 TN: Brittany Versus Paris.

233 TN: How Can One Be Breton?

234 TN: Literally 'Shackled Duck', *Canard enchaîné* is a satirical weekly newspaper in France whose title also translates as 'Shackled Paper', since *canard* is French slang for 'newspaper'.

235 TN: Europe of a Hundred Flags.

child Gwenola or Goulven, just as they were once allowed to choose Glacette or Clémenceau.

Breton song (*An Alarc'h, Pontcallek*) now enjoys newfound radiance thanks to Glenmor in particular, but also Alan Stivell, Gilles Servat, *Gweltaz*, the *Tri Yann an Naoned* ('The Three Yanns of Nantes'), Youenn Gwernig, *Gwalarn*, *Kerrien*, *Diaouled ar Menez*, and others.

Despite beginning his career in the Bleimor Scouts (whose leader, P. Géraud-Keraod, has since created the Scouts of Europe), Alain Stivell (*Cochevelou*) periodically declares himself to be a 'communist' (September 1975). In 1970, he was awarded first prize in the folk song category at the Pan Celtic Festival of Killarney.

Gilles Servat (*L'hirondelle*,[236] *Les Bretons typiques*,[237] *Koc'h ki gwenn ha koc'h ki du*), who rages against 'Breton leukaemia' and considers himself to be Left-oriented, declares that 'under current circumstances, singing in Breton is revolutionary' (*Armor-Magazine*, March 1974). In his song entitled *White Ermine*, however, what leftists Daniel Chatelain and Pierre Tafani perceive is an 'involuntary synthesis of the national and patriarchal worldview of the reactionary bourgeoisie of the nineteenth century' (*Qu'est-ce qui fait courir les autonomistes?* Stock, 1976).

In the French capital, which was already home to a Breton mission and numerous associations, the newspaper entitled *La Bretagne à Paris*[238] became a weekly publication. The *Ker-Vreiz* cultural centre, headed by Mr Simon-Pierre Delorme, celebrated its thirtieth anniversary in May 1968. As for the *Elysées-Bretagne* centre, which opened in 1967, it received around 4,000 visitors a day until it burnt down.

FROM THE MOB TO THE UDB

Political action resumed more discreetly with the 1947 release of *Le peuple Breton*,[239] a federalist European newspaper established by former Resistance member Joseph Martray. This attempt was, however, not followed up on

236 TN: The Swallow.

237 TN: Typical Bretons.

238 TN: Brittany in Paris.

239 TN: The Breton People.

(during that same year, two clandestine issues of *Breiz Atao* written in Ireland were circulated in the Netherlands).

The month of July 1950 saw the birth of the *Comité d'études et de liaison des intérêts Bretons*[240] (CELIB), also headed by Mr Martray. Mr René Pléven acted as its long-time chairman before being replaced by Mr Lombard, the senator-mayor of Brest. It was a sort of officious regional council whose ambition was to compensate for the state's shortcomings. Although it would be targeted with reproach for being 'reformistic', it did play a significant role in the 1950s.

In 1955, Yann Poupinot, the former secretary of the *Ker-Vreiz*, joins forces with Yann Fouéré, who had returned from Ireland specially for the occasion; together, they found the Movement for the Organisation of Brittany (MOB), the first genuine Breton party of the post-war period.

No sooner had it been created than the MOB demanded autonomy for the financial management of a Breton regional assembly elected through universal suffrage, while also proposing a redefinition of the 'Breton nation' within a federalist European framework and protesting against the inclusion of the Nantes region in an alleged 'central-western region'. Last but not least, it rejected traditional distinctions and adopted the *Breiz Atao* slogan *Na ruz na gwenn* ('Neither red, nor white'). Right-wing populism, its adversaries would claim.

Around a hundred municipal advisors accepted this programme, including some who were once part of the PNB. Mr Olier Mordrel writes:

> Without the MOB, the Breton scene would have been a huge void, one that the CELIB was not meant to fill. Whereas the latter established economic recovery programmes, the MOB vulgarised them and strived to encourage the public opinion to grant them the necessary support. Brittany thus reclaimed a political consciousness of its own.

The MOB made a political breakthrough around 1960–62, but was soon weakened by an internal crisis. During the Brest congress held at the end of 1963, a faction of the movement led by Le Prohon and Vieillard adopted a more radically Leftist position under the impact of the Algerian events. The faction,

240 TN: The Liaison Committee for the Study of Breton Interests.

whose ranks included a majority of UNEF[241] students from Rennes, chose to embrace secession and create the Democratic Breton Union (UDB).

The UDB still exists today and publishes the *Pobl Vreiz* and *Peuple breton* newspapers. It has also sponsored the Progressive Youths of Brittany (*Yaouankizou Penn-a-raog Breiz*), which have since drifted towards the Left.

An extreme-left organisation that practices 'democratic centralism' with a sectarianism that is every bit as pronounced as that of the French Communist Party, the UDB likens the Breton issue to class relations. It thus rejects any sort of alliance with Rightist Bretons, just as the *Bleun-Brug* did with leftist Bretons at the start of the 20th century when attempting to tie the *Emsav* to clericalism. It alleges that 'what is Breton expresses an ethical system and civilisation that are actually those of the proletariat'. It also proclaims:

> If it were but a matter of replacing the French Right with a Breton one, we would see no point in our struggle. (*Le Peuple breton*, November 1976)

In 1970, the release of Morvan Lebesque's book entitled *Comment peut-on être Breton*, which was praised in Parisian cenacles, seemed to set the seal on the alliance between the French Left and the Breton movement.

Mr Mordrel remarks:

> Our Breton publications followed suit, just like Panurge's sheep, without realising that by offering their adherence to the party of French Leftist intellectuals, they identified with a generation that no longer had any belief or home base, a generation of uprooted cosmopolitans that had nothing in common with that of young Bretons, who are all strong in their blood and filled with their region's vigour.

The UDB also attempted to exploit social conflicts — Michelin in Vannes, CSF in Brest, the Breton Foundry Society in Lorient, and especially the *Joint français*[242] strike, which began in March 1972 in Saint-Brieuc.

This tactic did not meet everyone's approval. Olier Mordrel writes:

> The Breton employers who struggle against external competition from a position of inferiority and all too often succumb to the situation, declaring their own bankruptcy, must be defended by the *Emsav* not only because they provide Bretons

241 TN: The UNEF is a student support association in Rennes, France.

242 TN: The *Joint français* strike was a strike involving the workers of the so-called 'Joint français' plant, a subsidiary of the General Electricity Company.

> with work and allow them to avoid emigration, but also because they embody the indispensable economic frameworks of tomorrow's autonomous Brittany. [...] Class struggle is not the battle for national liberation. Even if we had been unaware of this at some point, the French Resistance, which our communists are so keen on, would have taught us the lesson. For within the Resistance, all classes fraternised in order to drive out the occupier. What was advised back then is still advised now.

The UDB only comprised 190 adherents in 1969, compared to fifty-eight in 1965. With great difficulty, this number reached 215 in 1971 (figures provided by J.C. Lecorre and Nicolas in *L'Union démocratique bretonne. Contribution à l'étude de l'Emsav.*[243] DES de sciences politiques, UER de sciences juridiques de Haute-Bretagne, 1973). Today, its members are fewer than 500, mostly consisting of students regionalised particularly in the Finistère and Ille-et-Vilaine departments.

During the events of May 1968, the UDB aligned itself with the positions of the French Communist Party, which led it to experience its own leftist scission.

In February 1970, the leftists led by Guiomar and Le Guyader, who had almost overrun the movement's leadership during the Guidel congress of November 1969, were indeed purged; and not in a very democratic manner either. In the journal entitled *La Taupe bretonne*[244], they would denounce the 'nationalist hijacking of class struggle' and state that 'the UDB is a tiny Breton bureaucracy whose ideology is national-reformistic' (*La Taupe Bretonne*, issue number 1). In 1972, Guiomar would release *Les Bretons et le socialisme*[245] through Maspéro.

During that same period, one actually witnessed a proliferation of Leftist groups: the Breton Communist Party (PCB), *Sav Breizh*, *Stourm Breizh*, etc.

Born in 1971, the Breton Communist Party (PCB) publishes the *Bretagne révolutionnaire*[246] newspaper. It is headed by Y. M. Gefflot and the Count of Gouyon-Matignon. The *Sav Breizh* ('Breton Resistance') journal aimed to 'open a new revolutionary path for the Breton struggle, one that takes the 1968 mutation into account'. However, it vanished after several years of efforts to define

243 TN: The Democratic Breton Union — A Contribution to the Study of the *Emsav*.

244 TN: The Breton Mole.

245 TN: The Bretons and Socialism.

246 TN: Revolutionary Brittany.

a doctrine that never ceased to be vague. *Stourm Brezh* ('Breton Struggle') was an 'autonomist revolutionary' organisation whose alleged inspiration stemmed from the Ukrainian and Catalan anarchist experiences. It was led by a former paratrooper of the Eighth Marine Infantry Parachute Regiment of Carcassonne who had embraced Leftism under Occitan influence.

The ultra-Left was also represented by *APL-Nantes* (which had ties to *Libération* magazine), the pro-Chinese *Rennes-révolutionnaire*,[247] *Politique-Bretagne*[248] (a local emanation of *Politique-Hebdo*[249]), *Test* (connected to *Tempêtes*,[250] the successor of *L'Idiot international*[251]), (Trotskyist) *Bretagne rouge*,[252] and so on.

POLITICAL MEANDERINGS

On its part, the MOB pursued its activities until around 1969, when it entered a more or less slumbering state; meanwhile, its leaders continued to express themselves through Yann Fouéré's newspaper entitled *L'Avenir de la Bretagne*.[253]

On 2nd February, 1969, while in Quimper, General de Gaulle announces his intention to hold a referendum on regional reform. He declares:

> Every region whose existence is justified by both its size and its value must have the will and be given the necessary means to play its rightful role within the entirety of our national effort.

This declaration kindles great hopes. From his Argentine exile, Olier Mordrel adopts a 'favourable' position. A few months later, however, de Gaulle exits the political scene.

In 1972, a French industrial, Mr Jean Le Calvez, launches the *Strollad ar Vro* (the 'Land's Party' or *SAV)*. With seemingly quite significant financial means at its disposal, the latter comes across as the MOB's successor in the eyes of the public opinion. In fact, it proceeds to elaborate its own doctrine on

---

247 TN: Revolutionary Rennes.

248 TN: Breton Politics.

249 TN: A Leftist weekly magazine with a general focus.

250 TN: Tempests.

251 TN: *L'Idiot international* was a lampoonist French newspaper.

252 TN: Red Brittany.

253 TN: Brittany's Future.

the basis of the *Breiz Atao*, and Mr Le Calvez buys out *L'Avenir de la Bretagne*, where Mr Yann Fouéré continues working as a columnist.

No sooner had it been created than the SAV came up against the hostile attitude of Ms Anne-Marie Kerhuel, the former head of the Informational Committee on Breton Emigration. In the *Douar Breiz* ('Soil of Brittany') bulletin, which acts as the organ of the 'Adsav 1532',[254] she accused it of being an 'emanation of the authorities'.

This accusation would be adopted by Patrice Chairoff (Ivan D. Calzi), who claims, in his *Dossier B... comme barbouzes*[255] (Alain Moreau, 1975), that Mr Le Calvez, a former employee of the Francexpa Society (whose director is Mr Gilbert Beaujolin, a founding member of the 1958 Left-Wing Gaullist Movement), has been continuously paid out of the funds of various trade companies that served as a 'façade' for parallel policing activities whose implementation depended on Mr Beaujolin and Colonel Barberot. These 'revelations' would cause quite a stir in the *Emsav*.

The SAV's first congress is held in Saint-Servan on 27th May, 1973. The participants decide to campaign in the legislative elections, as Le Calvez declares:

> Tomorrow, we shall be the elected representatives of the Breton people.

The results, however, are beyond mediocre. With twenty-seven candidates, the SAV only gathers a total of 30,166 votes. The UDB, with merely five candidates, obtains 6,062.

In the aftermath of this electoral setback, the SAV initiates a sudden shift towards the Left. In 1974, the editorial staff of *L'Avenir de la Bretagne* undergoes complete transformation. Having become a supporter of a 'pro-self-governance Breton Left', journalist Lucien Raoul, known as Fanch Tremel, replaces Jean-Pierre Le Méleder in the role of secretary general. Siding with Lenin and Bakunin,[256] he launches a full-scale attack against the Breton Right, apparently in the hope of obtaining a place within Leftist milieus. With an amused look in their eyes, UDB members scornfully reject him.

---

[254] TN: Movement for the Implementation of the Treaty of 1532.

[255] TN: The S Files — As in 'Spy'.

[256] TN: Mikhail Alexandrovich Bakunin (30th May, 1814–1st July, 1876) was a Russian revolutionary anarchist and the founder of collectivist anarchism.

During the presidential elections of 1974, the SAV chooses to support Mr François Mitterrand, who represents the French Left, against Mr Guy Héraud, the federalist and regionalist candidate.

In the spring of 1975, during the congress of Guerlédan, the party's Left-wing rids itself of Mr Le Calvez, who vanishes as quickly as he had once appeared. Mr Yann Fouéré dissociates himself from this new orientation. *L'Avenir de la Bretagne* ceases to be published, as Mr Raoul-Tremel's decides to express himself solely through a confidential newsletter entitled *Combat Breton*,[257] published in Paris and specialising in the peddling of gossip. The SAV thus finds itself completely eliminated.

Since then, the last fragments of SAV number 2 have merged into the Socialist Front for the Autonomy and Self-Governance of Brittany (FASAB), a conglomerate where the survivors of *Sav Breizh* and *Stourm Breizh* rub shoulders with the representatives of the Breton Action Committees (CAB), born of the transformation of bodies that had previously supported the detainees of the Breton Liberation Front. It is there that one encounters Mr Alain Guillerm, who co-authored *Clefs pour l'autogestion*[258] (Seghers, 1975) together with Mr Yvon Bourdet. The FASAB participates above all in the organisation of *Festou-noz* (popular music evenings). Its spokesman is Doctor Guy Caro, a psychiatrist who formerly acted as the general counsellor of the Côtes-du-Nord department and the head of the PSU's 'national minorities' commission.

At present, the *Emsav*'s Right wing is only represented by *La Nation bretonne*[259] and the team behind the Young Bretons' Movement.

AUTONOMISM VERSUS SEPARATISM

Having adopted the title of an ephemeral publication created by singer Glenmor and writers Xavier Grall (*Keltia Blues*) and Alain Guel (*L'homme de pierre*[260]), *La Nation Bretonne*, run by Mr Hervé Glot, mainly publishes theoretical studies that are rather reminiscent of *Stur*'s first version.

---

257 TN: Breton Struggle.

258 TN: The Keys to Self-Governance.

259 TN: *La Nation Bretonne*, meaning 'The Breton Nation', is a newspaper.

260 TN: The Man of Stone.

Jeune Bretagne,[261] which replaced the *Bretagne-Action*[262] newspaper in 1971 (a newspaper whose initials coincide with those of *Breiz Atao*), had had close ties to the SAV during the period that preceded its transformation. In agreement with Yann Fouéré, its leaders had undertaken to give *L'Avenir de la Bretagne* a new lease of life. Shortly afterwards, the Brest section that opposed the SAV's electioneering policies chose to secede. Mr Eric Le Naour (Georges Abhervé-Guéguen) was among those who decided to leave. He would then write a book about the Breton language under the pseudonym of Jorg Gwegen. Since 1975–76, *Jeune Bretagne* has regained momentum, publishing a newspaper entitled *Breizh Yaouank*, whose subheading is: 'For Brittany, for Europe'.

Just like *La Nation Bretonne*, *Jeune Bretagne* rejects the separatist temptation, while simultaneously dismissing simple decentralisation:

> The independentist dream is a dangerous one. On the eve of the establishment of a peoples' Europe, Breton separatism would leave an infected wound upon our continent's side. Autonomy lies in the domain of more readily accessible matters, where the price to pay is not as great. (*Breizh Yaouank*, October–November 1976)

Jeune Bretagne also criticises insurrectional or terrorist action, stating that the 'archetypal example' of Northern Ireland 'is not to be followed'.

It is nonetheless a fact that clandestine struggle has found some new partisans. From 1966 to 1976, a total of more than sixty bomb attacks signaled the rebirth of Breton activism. The first one was carried out on 18th October, 1966 against a tax office in Saint-Brieuc. Next came the destruction of a CRS barracks garage in April 1968, and then, in 1974, that of a television relay station located on Roc'h Tredudon.

CLANDESTINE STRUGGLE AND THE FOUR VERSIONS OF THE FLB

Initially, the Breton Liberation Front (FLB), which declared itself 'nationalistic and independentist above all else', claimed responsibility for these acts. This 'first' FLB was organised into *Kevrenns* (regional sections), *bagadou*[263] and

261 TN: Young Brittany.

262 TN: Action-Brittany.

263 TN: Plural of *bagad*, apparently meaning band or group.

strolladou.[264] It also had connections to the Committee of Free Brittany (CBL), headed in Ireland by Mr Yann Goulet.

In 1969, the police, acting upon information received from a trustworthy source, conduct an entire wave of arrests. About fifty people suspected of belonging to the FLB find themselves behind bars, including three members of the clergy, journalist Jean Bothorel of *Bretagne-Magazine*, and two members of the UDB (who are immediately excluded from the latter). In both Brittany and Paris, committees are established, offering their support to the detainees. The latter, however, would be amnestied following the election of Mr Georges Pompidou.

A few weeks later, a 'second' FLB attempts to take legal action. Unlike the first, it advocates extreme-Leftist opinions, but still relies on the *Skoazell Vreizh* ('Breton Rescue'), whose treasurer, Mr Raymond Jégaden, is a former member of *Bezen Perrot*. In November 1969, a meeting held at the *Mutualité* gathers various figures ranging from Abbé Aimé Lebreton, the rector of Gommenec'h, to Reverend Father Cardonnel, through the likes of Doctor Guy Caro and Mr Jean-Pierre Vigier. The *Internationale* is sung there more often than the Breton anthem. This entire undertaking would, however, not be followed up on (although its inspirers would later resurface in *Bretagne révolutionnaire* and the CABs).

In 1971, it is a third FLB, one that is prone to 'spontaneity', that carries out its own series of attacks. Soon enough, it ends up being dismantled. In December 1972, eleven Bretons are tried in Paris. The debate is rekindled.

The end of 1973 marks yet another FLB rebirth. The latter, however, splinters into two branches corresponding to two distinct tendencies — on the one hand, the FLB-ARB (Breton Republican Army), which takes its orders from Ireland and is said to have rather close ties to the *Strollad ar Vro* (SAV); and on the other, the FLB-LNS (For National Liberation and Socialism), which declares its support for a 'national bloc managed by the Breton working class, from which none but the Breton bourgeois oligarchy would be excluded'. The leaders of the FLB-LNS are then rumoured to be in touch with the 'hardliners' of the Basque ETA movement. One of them, however, Mr Serge Liégeard, would be denounced as a 'spy'.

264 TN: Seemingly 'Parties'.

On 20th October, 1975, Mr Yann Fouéré, the former head of *L'Avenir de la Bretagne*, is arrested in Saint-Brieuc. Twelve other Breton militants are brought before the State Security Court. Mr Fouéré, who is accused of being one of the FLB-ARB's inspirers but against whom not a single shred of evidence can be brought forth, would be detained for several months. A remarkable fact: the (leftist) FASAB refuses to intervene in his defence, highlighting the fact that it has 'nothing in common with him politically speaking'. In an effort to secure his release, however, a committee would be launched by Mr Jean-Jacques Mourreau (Hans Zorn of the Alsatian Autonomist Movement) and, during the month of December, his case would be mentioned to the European Parliament by English socialist MP Mr Tom Ellis. He would eventually be released.

Having compromised its position in relation to the 'pro-self-governance' Breton Left, the FLB-LNS seems to have vanished today. Only the FLB-ARB subsists, along with it 'external Irish lungs'.

On 29th September, 1976, a twenty-two-year-old Breton, Yann-Mikaël Kernaléguen, is killed by the blast of an explosive charge that he himself had planted in Ti-Vougeret (Dinéault), but which chose to collect upon realising that the targeted premises were home to a family.

THE *EMSAV*'S CHANGE OF ESSENCE

All in all, the 1968–1976 period was therefore characterised by a complete atomisation of political organisations, yet also by ever intensifying cultural renewal.

As for Mr Olier Mordrel, who benefited from the statute of limitations in 1968, he returned shortly afterwards from Argentina, passing through Spain on the way. His exile had lasted twenty-two years, a period during which he had regularly expressed himself through the notebooks of *La Bretagne réelle-Keltia*,[265] a newsletter published in Merdrignac since 1953 by Mr Jacques Quatre-Boeufs (Jacques Gallo) and intended to serve as an opinion column for all tendencies encountered in the *Emsav*.

Olier Mordrel is now seventy-six years old, yet he has not aged for half a century. Tall, well-built, with a razor-sharp voice and thin lips, he still decides, settles and arguments like a twenty-year-old dialectician. He speaks seven

265 TN: The True Brittany-Keltia.

languages — but most of all Breton. The publication of his book entitled *Breiz Atao* caused quite a stir in the *Emsav*, and the local authorities have been a source of trouble to him as well. This is what he writes today:

> The *Emsav*'s spiritual and intellectual tradition has been broken. Not only has the former been adapted to suit current tastes (which has always been the case), but it has undergone a change of essence, which is an infinitely graver development.

And yet 'it is enough for one to open a newspaper published in Brest or Rennes on any day of the year to discover that, far from being moribund, Brittany seethes with youths eager to break their fetters and experience their own truth'. Hence this reminder:

> Following the crushing of the Dublin revolt in 1916, the crowd insulted the prisoners dragged by the English through the streets and spat in their faces (we ourselves experienced this in 1944). Twenty years later, however, the main railway station in Dublin had been named after their leader, Patrick Pearse. And it took thirty years for the Irish government to repatriate with pomp and circumstance the ashes of Roger Casement, the "traitor" who, in 1915, did the very same thing in Berlin that two Breton men would do there in 1940 and was later hanged in London.

More forthright than ever, Olier Mordrel proclaims:

> A genuinely national Breton party can only exist outside the leftist spectrum, as well as outside any Right which, regardless of its French or Breton character, only offers us development.

He adds:

> If *Breiz Atao* were reborn, it would be entirely different from anything it has ever been. The Breton question must be rethought, and Breton nationalism must undergo a genuine and "heart-rending" revision.

And here is his conclusion:

> *Breiz Atao* has been anything but a minority-based nationalism moulded in harmony with the nineteenth century. In a land caught in the throes of death, it has acted as an inexhaustible and unfaltering source of life whose birth and emergence one must familiarise themselves with if one is to have a clear idea of what is happening and will occur in Brittany. It does indeed happen that the very old returns

with the intensity of the very new, displaying a strength whose secret is unknown to anyone else.

Breiz Atao. Histoire et actualité du nationalisme Breton,[266] an essay by Olier Mordrel. Alain Moreau, 557 pages.

La voie bretonne. Radiographie de l'emsav,[267] an essay by Olier Mordrel. Nature et Bretagne, Quimper, 235 pages.

Le mouvement Breton,[268] 1919–1945, an essay by Alain Deniel. Maspéro, 450 pages.

Plus de pardons pour les Bretons,[269] a narrative by Saint-Loup. Presses de la Cité, 574 pages.

Le révolution bretonne permanente,[270] an essay by Ronan Caerléon. Table ronde, 346 pages.

Les Bretons le dos au mur,[271] an essay by Ronan Caerléon. Table ronde, 218 pages.

Au village des condamnés à mort, an essay by Ronan Caerléon. Table ronde, 380 pages.

Le rêve fou des soldats de Breiz Atao,[272] an essay by Ronan Caerléon. Nature et Bretagne (38 Jeanne d'Arc street, 29000 Quimper, France), 235 pages.

Fransez Debauvais de "Breiz Atao" et les siens,[273] an essay by Anna Youenou (2 volumes). Self-published, 412 and 431 pages respectively (with a third volume expected to come out some time in 1977).

La Bretagne dans la guerre,[274] an essay by Hervé Le Boterf (3 volumes). France-Empire, 335, 332 and 763 pages respectively.

La question bretonne,[275] an essay by Renaud Dulong. Presses de la Fondation nationale des sciences politiques, (27 Saint-Guillaume street, 75341 Paris cedex 07), 207 pages.

La langue bretonne face à ses oppresseurs,[276] an essay by Jorg Gwegen. Nature et Bretagne, Quimper, 313 pages.

Bretagne: re-naissance d'un people,[277] an essay by Jean-Pierre Le Dantec. Gallimard, 314 pages.

266 TN: Breiz Atao — The History and Topicality of Breton Nationalism.

267 TN: The Breton Path — Radiography of the Emsav.

268 TN: The Breton Movement from 1919 to 1945.

269 TN: No More Excuses for the Bretons.

270 TN: The Unremitting Breton Revolution.

271 TN: The Bretons — Backs to the Wall.

272 TN: The Insane Dream of the Soldiers of Breiz Atao.

273 TN: 'Breiz Atao' 's Fransez Debauvais and His Supporters.

274 TN: Brittany During the War.

275 TN: The Breton Issue.

276 TN: The Breton Language in the Face of Its Oppressors.

277 TN: Brittany — The Rebirth of a People.

At the end of 1976, the Liaison Centre for the Study of Breton Interests (CELIB) undertook to publish a monthly letter whose aim is to 'comment on regional, national or European events' (22 Hoche street, 35000 Rennes, France).

'La Nation bretonne', P.O. Box 26, 56200 La Gacilly, France; 'Breizh Yaouank', P.O. Box 2, 44590 Derval, France'; 'Douar Breizh', 9 du Port street, 22530 Mur-de-Bretagne, France; 'La Bretagne réelle-Keltia', 44 Philippe-Lemercier Street, 22230 Merdrignac, France.

THE COLONIAL NOTION IN FRANCE

> When making the decision to take control of Algiers, the government of Charles the Tenth had no intention whatsoever to undertake the conquest of a vast North African empire: it was only a matter of conducting a small-scale operation whose basic purpose was to boost the monarchy's prestige.

PARADOXICALLY, EXPLAINS MR GIRARDET, THE first adversaries of 'colonisation' were the masters of liberal thought, namely Adam Smith in the United States, Cobden in England, and Jean-Baptiste Say in France.

> Their reasoning was simple: the fact of having colonies is only advantageous to a small minority of individuals — soldiers, officials, and certain traders. On the other hand, it imposes considerable military and administrative burdens upon the metropolis' budget; due to the resulting heavy taxation, it represents an obstacle to the general development of industrial and commercial activity.

A professor of contemporary history at the Institute of Political Sciences in Paris, Mr Raoul Girardet had previously published books dealing with the political Right (*Le nationalisme français, 1871–1914.*[278] Armand Colin, 1966) and the army (*La crise militaire française, 1945–1962.*[279] Armand Colin, 1964). At the start of the 1960s, he was part of the *Esprit Public*[280] team. His study of the *Colonial Notion in France from 1871 to 1962* constitutes a novel and remarkable contribution to the history of French national sentiment. It is a depiction of a *mentality*, an *idea*-based novel. What one discovers in it is that colonial

278 TN: The French Nationalism of 1871–1914.

279 TN: The French Military Crisis of 1945–1962.

280 TN: *Esprit Public*, or 'Public Spirit', was a French political and literary journal.

expansion was not due to the presence of a specific party but was rather the result of an era.

Indeed, Mr Girardet remarks, observation leads one 'to relativise or, should I say, almost de-sacralise the obsessive *Right-Left* opposition within which an entire school gradually acquired an ever-pronounced tendency to restrict the moral history of contemporary France'.

SCHOLARS AND MISSIONARIES

In 1871, when the smoke of the Commune had already dissipated, France's overseas possessions represented a total of one million square kilometres, scattered across four continents and inhabited by some five million people.

With regard to these possessions, the public opinion had thus far been indifferent. French sovereignty had, incidentally, only affirmed itself as a result of random circumstance. There was no colonial *intent*, nor was there any colonising *settlement*. There were barely 200,000 Europeans in Algeria, half of whom were not even French:

> Just like the 20,000 Parisian workers deported by the Second Republic, many of those settlers had been primitively recruited among elements that were deemed asocial — the unemployed, the rebellious, and the rootless suburbanites for whom that era's conformism had no tendency to manifest sympathy.

It takes minds a few years to evolve. Three rarely associated currents combine to give rise to what would (wrongly) be termed *imperialism*: the highly scientistic ideal of a new humanity that remains ever open to progress; missionary renewal; and people's bitterness in the face of an amputated national territory, combined with a desire to reinstate a larger and stronger France.

'Scientism' puts a new spin on the optimism inherited from the Enlightenment. Both geographers — who are often rationalistic — and 'explorers' rush to the forefront of the 'discoverer' wave. Clergymen are, however, not to be outdone. While scientists depart to combat 'superstitions', evangelisers uproot foreign beliefs so as to impose the Christian faith everywhere.

France sets the example: twenty-two missionary congregations see the light of day between 1816 and 1870. This leads to martyrdom in both Black

Africa and Tonkin, as elderly ladies collect stamps and *La Semeuse*[281] coupons to 'redeem the little Chinese'.

Monsignor Miché, the vicar apostolic of Saigon, writes:

> For a long time, rebels managed to curb the conversion growth. Now that the French authorities have finally exacted a cruel revenge against the rebellious, peace is gradually re-establishing its presence; and as confidence re-emerges, so does our religious movement.

In 1802, Monsignor Guillaume Mauviel, the bishop of Saint-Domingue, addressed the inhabitants of the eastern part of the island, which had recently become a French colony. This was his message:

> Do not doubt, my very dear brothers, that it is the Lord that has enabled your transition from the domination of your former suzerain to the guardian empire of the laws of the French Republic.

To which he then added:

> Be wary of the fact that Christians must never ponder how or why a country passes from one government to another, unless their sole purpose is to acknowledge in these changes the eternally present hand and will of God.

And here is what the bishop of Évreux declared in the spring of 1830, when Charles X launched the Algiers expedition:

> It is not a matter of spilling Christian blood, but a question of repressing the insolence of a barbaric nation, the enemy of all that is Christian. It is to the audacity and rapacity of a nation of pirates that we must now put a stop. (As quoted by Pierre-Marie Dioudonnat[282] in *Les ivresses de l'Eglise de France*,[283] Sagittaire, 1976.)

Following the collapse of the Second Empire, France finds itself robbed of both Alsace and Lorraine. 'One must not forget', however, 'that France's borders are

---

281 TN: *La Semeuse de Paris* was a consumer credit company owned by the *La Samaritaine* department store in Paris. It sold coupons to working class consumers, who paid in installments.

282 TN: Born on 24th March, 1945, Pierre-Marie Dioudonnat is a French editor.

283 TN: The Inebriations of the French Church.

not limited to the Vosges', Gabriel Charmes[284] reminds us. In 1871, Monsignor Lavigerie invites the refugees of Alsace-Lorraine to travel to Algeria and discover 'French Africa'.

Jules Ferry justifies the colonisation by contradicting the traditional liberal doctrine and says:

> The colonial policy is the very daughter of the industrial one. In the eyes of wealthy states, where capital abounds and rapidly accumulates and the manufacturing system is in a state of continuous growth, exports represent an essential factor of public prosperity; and just like labour demand, the capital's employment field is measured in relation to the very size of the foreign market.

LEFTIST COLONIALISM

In 1874, a historic book entitled *De la colonisation chez les peuples modernes*[285] is published. Its author, Paul Leroy-Beaulieu, affirms:

> The nation that colonises most is the most supreme one. And if this is not the case today, it shall be so tomorrow.

He then adds:

> The establishment of colonies is the best business in which the capital of a rich and ancient country can be employed.

The Left approves with a vengeance. In the Chamber, the 'progressivists' and 'Leftist republicans' represent the majority of those who adhere to the 'colonial parliamentary group' founded by 'pied-noir'[286] Eugène Etienne, a group which, in 1902, comprised 200 elected representatives.

The socialists are not to be outdone either. So as to praise 'France's civilising role', Fourier, Enfantin and Cabet use the very same words as Francis

---

284 TN: Gabriel Charmes (7th November, 1850–19th April, 1886) was a French journalist and explorer.

285 TN: On Colonisation Among Modern Peoples.

286 TN: The term 'pied-noir' is used in reference to a person of European (and particularly French) origin who lived in Algeria during French rule and, in most cases, returned to Europe after Algeria was granted independence.

Garnier, the man who conquered Tonkin. In the *Temps modernes*[287] issue dedicated to *National Minorities* (number 324–26, August–September 1973), Mr Yves Person[288] reminds his readers that Karl Marx himself had rejoiced at Algeria's annexation.

By contrast, the Right displays greater reticence and is very loath to undertake such 'distant adventures'. It also feels concerned to see 'the best of its sons' set off towards 'the lands of the tropical sun'. In 1920, Maurras emphasises the fact that instead of following the path of conquest, France had better 'devote its strength to the struggle against German hegemony in Europe'. On his part, Barrès would write in 1911:

> Gambetta has embraced anticlericalism and colonialism so as to divert our army's elite from the Rhine region.

A pink stain spreads across geographical atlases — the French Empire. It compensates for the 'lost departments', which are all marked in black. Senegalese riflemen, however, cannot replace good-natured Alsatian women. Déroulède[289] shouts:

> I have lost two sisters, and what you are offering me are twenty servants!

Incidentally, within the French Hexagon, ethnic cultures and regional languages also fall prey to that same republican and universalistic ardour.

In parallel, however, a more original kind of criticism develops. In 1899, Léopold de Saussure publishes a book entitled *Psychologie de la colonisation française*.[290] In it, he criticises our 'erring colonial ways'.

> Adopting and developing some of Gustave Le Bon's ideas on the hereditary aspect of mental characteristics, he bases his view on the principle which states that since man's nature is neither identical on a spatial nor on a temporal level, in no way could human societies be equated to one another. Account taken of the fact that

[287] TN: *Les Temps modernes* (Modern Times) is a French journal whose first issue came out in October 1945.

[288] TN: Yves Person (1868–1975) was a French Africanist who worked as a professor at the Sorbonne.

[289] TN: Paul Déroulède (2nd September, 1846–30th January, 1914) was a French author and politician, and one of the founders of the nationalist League of Patriots.

[290] TN: The Psychology of French Colonisation.

> the elements of a civilisation are "intimately linked to a certain stable and hereditary mental constitution", the institutions, cultures and languages of European peoples could never be imposed on others without causing severe damage to both the colonisers and the colonised. If worse comes to worst, assimilation may even occur in the opposite direction to the one officially preconised.

Of anti-egalitarian thought was thus born 'the original and fertile idea that the European progress model is not the sole conceivable one and that there is a plurality of possible development paths for human societies to take'.

The conquests, however, follow each other in quick succession. Annam, Tonkin, Madagascar, the Congo, Morocco, Laos: so many names that begin to inspire imaginations. Crowned with laurel wreaths on July afternoons, schoolchildren enjoy their holidays as they carry thick, red books with golden spines bearing the most delightful titles: *In Search of the Castaways*, *The Swiss Family Robinson*. The last balloons, the first cars, the first planes. Jules Verne's books are widely read, as is *Le Journal des voyages*[291]. Minds drift towards desertic continents and impenetrable forests, where mysterious animals and menacing 'savages' lurk.

During the Great War, the colonial troops suffer 205,000 fatal casualties. The Tonkinese and Senegalese thus become 'French by spilt blood'. In implementation of the Treaty of Versailles, the government would send them to occupy the Ruhr.

Little by little, colonies are populated and North Africa is divided into departments. Snobbisms begin to play their part. In Paris, one witnesses the triumph of negro art, which would later come to influence cubism. A colonial administrator, Maurice Delafosse, writes:

> One must readily admit that the inhabitants of the Sudan have their own civilisations that are worth studying and describing.

[291] TN: *Le Journal des voyages et des aventures de terre et de mer*, i.e. 'The Journal of Voyages and Land and Sea Adventures', was a French weekly that was published between 1877 and 1949.

A new genre thus surfaces: colonial literature. In *Sang des races*[292], Louis Bertrand[293] glorifies the work of the Algerian settlers. In the cinematic field, this would result in *Pépé le Moko*[294] and *La Bandera.*[295]

'THE GENUINE GRANDEUR OF FRANCE'

This entire movement culminates during the bitter spring of 1931. At the edge of the woods of Vincennes, Paul Reynaud, the Minister of the Colonies, inaugurates the Colonial Exhibition. The Church is represented by the Pavilion of Missions. Monsignor Serrand, the bishop of Saint-Brieuc, declares that 'the colonies are extensions of the mother country'. Paris is in line with exoticism. President Doumergue travels to North Africa, and picturesque images are published in *L'Illustration*: explorers are shown wearing caps, their cartridge belts strapped across their shoulders as they sit enthroned amidst the 'natives'. The 'greatest France' comprises one hundred million inhabitants. The dream passes.[296]

On 4th January, 1939, while in Tunis, Daladier[297] is heard to cry:

> It is in North Africa that one can truly measure the genuine grandeur of France!

At that point, opinions had already evolved. Having failed to seize power in Paris, the 'nationalists' took to watching the proliferation of French flags across the globe, in a display of great emotion. Leftist 'anticolonialism' had

---

292 TN: Blood of the Races.

293 TN: Louis Bertrand (20th March, 1866–6th December, 1941) was a French novelist, historian and essayist.

294 TN: *Pépé le Moko* is a 1937 French film depicting a gangster nicknamed 'Pépé le Moko'. *Moko* is slang for a man from Toulon, derived from the Occitan *amb aquò* ('with that'), a term which punctuates sentences in Provence and which, in Toulon, is pronounced *em'oquò*.

295 TN: Released in the United States as 'Escape from Yesterday', *La Bandera* is a 1935 French drama film that tells the story of a Frenchman who flees to Barcelona, where he enlists in the Spanish Foreign Legion. He is sent to fight in Morocco where he unexpectedly bonds with his comrades and marries a local woman before his past begins to catch up with him.

296 TN: *Le rêve passe*, i.e. 'The Dream Passes', is a traditional French song in which French soldiers fighting for a given cause eventually awake from their dream of glory.

297 TN: Édouard Daladier (18th June, 1884–10th October, 1970) was a French 'radical' (i.e. centre-left) politician and the Prime Minister of France at the start of the Second World War.

taken over from the Rightist one. Following the example of Jules Guesde[298] and Jean Jaurès,[299] who had risen up against 'colonial buccaneering' at the start of the 20th century, Henri Barbusse[300] and Félicien Challaye[301] increase their sharp criticisms. Léon Bloy[302] condemns the colonial principle in the name of the very same Christian tradition that had seemed to justify it a few decades earlier (other theologians, however, attempt to define the subtle concept of 'just colonisation', while Mr Joseph Folliet, the head of the *Semaines Sociales de France*,[303] makes the following declaration: 'The anticolonial argumentation is shattered in the face of the sheer size of one single fact: the very existence of colonisation'). In 1927, an Anti-Imperialist League is founded in Brussels; Albert Einstein is entrusted with its presidency.

Beginning in the 1920s, one witnesses the first rebellions of indigenous peoples. The Tunisian Destour[304] party is established in 1920, and riots break out in Indochina in 1930 and 1931. In 1925–26, the Rif War[305] offers the Communist Party the opportunity to strongly commit itself to supporting Abd el-Krim.

---

298 TN: Jules Bazile, known as Jules Guesde (11th November, 1845–28th July, 1922) was a French socialist, journalist and politician.

299 TN: Auguste Marie Joseph Jean Léon Jaurès (3rd September, 1859–31st July, 1914) was a prominent French socialist. Initially a moderate republican, he later became one of the first social democrats and, in 1902, the leader of the French Socialist Party, which opposed Jules Guesde's revolutionary Socialist Party of France.

300 TN: Henri Barbusse (17th May, 1873–30th August, 1935) was a French novelist, a member of the French Communist Party and a lifelong friend of Albert Einstein.

301 TN: Félicien Challaye (1875–1967) was a French philosopher and human rights activist who founded a human rights organisation for the indigenous people of the Congo in 1908.

302 TN: Léon Bloy (11th July, 1846–3rd November, 1917), was a French novelist, essayist, pamphleteer, and poet.

303 TN: *Semaines Sociales de France*, or 'Social Weeks of France', is a project founded in 1904 whose aim is to tackle social issues from a Christian point of view.

304 TN: The Constitutional Liberal Party, most commonly known as *Destour*, was a Tunisian political party whose ambition was to liberate Tunisia from French colonial control.

305 TN: The Rif War was an armed conflict fought from 1920 to 1927 between Spanish colonial forces (who were later joined by France) and the Berber tribes of the Rif mountainous region. Led by Abd el-Krim, the Riffians initially inflicted several defeats on the Spanish military. Only after France's intervention against Abd el-Krim's forces and the major landing of Spanish troops at *Al Hoceima* did Abd el-Krim finally surrender to the French.

In February 1925, Jacques Doriot, the then Saint-Denis communist MP, scandalised his colleagues when uttering the following words in the gallery of the House of Commons:

> It is for a task of expropriation and murder that our army is being used.

And this is what he added four years later in *Les colonies et le communisme*[306] (Aubier-Montaigne):

> The power of the Soviets has radically suppressed the colonial exploitation policy. There is thus no other solution to the national question but proletarian revolution.

Rare were the Leftist parties, however, which questioned the legitimacy of our conquest. During the Human Rights League congress of May 1931, two influential members of the Radical Party, Albert Bayet and Maurice Viollette, strived to justify the soundness of the colonial expansion. Albert Bayet declared:

> Owing to its very past, the country that first proclaimed the existence of human rights has the duty to spread, wherever possible, the ideas responsible for its very grandeur.

His contention was approved by a large majority.

In 1939, the French journal *Volontés* published the first texts written by Aimé Césaire, a twenty-six-year-old Martinique national. He would soon become the talk of the country.

During World War II, the 'close union between mainland France and overseas France' is glorified simultaneously in London and Vichy. While General de Gaulle proceeds to establish his temporary government in Algiers, the members of the African Phalange volunteer to go and fight in Russia.

On 25th May, 1945, Mr Gaston Monnerville, a man of Guyanese origin, declares before the Consultative Assembly:

> Without the Empire, France would only be a liberated country today. Thanks to its Empire, however, France is now a triumphant country.

Still in May 1945, the French Communist Party denounced the nationalist insurrection of Constantine as being an 'act of provocation by Hitlerian agents'.

---

306 TN: The Colonies and Communism.

As for Caballero, the Secretary of the Algerian Party, he wrote the following in *L'Humanité*:

> Those who long to separate themselves from France are the conscious or unconscious agents of another imperialism.

THE RIGHT TO DIFFERENCE

Two years later, during the eleventh congress of the French Communist Party, Maurice Thorez would state:

> Our party did not endorse the French Union's disaggregation policy in Indochina.

Trotskyist Jacob Moneta specifies that 'on 19th March, 1947, the central committee of the French Communist Party actually expressed its approval of the fact that communist ministers, including the then Defence Minister, Mr François Billoux, had voted in favour of the loans that were meant to finance the war in Vietnam' (*Le PCF et la question coloniale, 1920–1965*[307]. Maspéro, 1971).

Decolonisation thus began amidst the greatest possible confusion. A highly significant case is 'that of Pierre Mendès France, who acted as the president of the Council of Ministers in 1954, negotiated the Geneva Agreements that put an end to the war in Indochina, and was also a proponent of the Carthage Agreements that granted Tunisia its internal autonomy. Faced with the onset of the Algerian insurrection a few weeks later, he unequivocally affirmed his government's will to resist, as well as his own intention to keep intact the integrity of our national territory'.

In his speech to the Assembly on 12th November, 1954, Mr Mendès France would make the following declaration:

> Several MPs have drawn parallels between the French policies in Algeria and Tunisia, but I say to you that no correlation could ever be more erroneous, and no comparison more mistaken. We are still in France here.

Strangely enough, this decolonisation was conducted in the name of a certain conception of 'blood and soil'. Indeed, the 'indigenous populations' were eager to take charge not only of their own fate, but also of their own *land*, simply because it is theirs, because 'they were there first' and because they are *home*

[307] TN: The French Communist Party and the Colonial Issue, 1920–1965.

there. Today, we still watch as the universalist partisans of global civilisation are consumed by their passion for the 'right to difference' which colonised peoples are entitled to, with internationalists asserting that 'settlers' are to vacate the lands that 'do not belong to them' and the U.N. *simultaneously* proclaiming the 'unity' of the human species and the necessity for (different) peoples to be the *masters* of their own destiny.

ILLUSORY ASPIRATIONS

Colonialism was ultimately a certain *era's* response to both permanent data (the 'biological' propensity for expansion, people's taste for discovery, and the Promethean West's winning spirit) and a series of conjectural phenomena (the industrial boom, the increase of new technologies, and the birth of global commerce); in no way was it due to a specific political current. Despite displaying some 'Rightist' aspects, it remained fundamentally 'Leftist' in its illusory aspiration to create an 'overseas France' whose inhabitants, considered *similar*, would somehow chant 'our Gallic ancestors' in unison.

This era of 'old-fashioned' colonialism is now over. What is positive is that Europe has learnt to perceive the value and specificity of other cultures. It is henceforth aware of the fact that there are different *ways of thinking* that characterise humanity, which entitles it to hope for *mutual* decolonisation.

There is, however, another kind colonialism that subsists today—*neo-colonialism*. It is an insidious and subtle form of colonisation whose restrictive element is not necessarily visible and is accepted, and at times even *desired*, by the neo-colonised.

This colonisation is sometimes of an economic nature; among its causes, one can mention the need of developed societies for both raw materials and a cheap workforce. It can, however, also be spiritual, moral, ideological, cultural or religious. The persistence of the Soviet colonial empire in the East (accompanied by the forced *Russification* of the elites) and the degrading dissemination of the *American way of life* in the West (which goes hand in hand with perhaps even more intense *deculturation*) are two of its most striking examples.

Compared to these contemporary realities of ours, the 'old' type of colonisation seems very primitive indeed; but it did comprise a certain share of *adventure*, one that may yet fuel some bouts of nostalgia.

There is no doubt, Mr Girardet concludes, that 'the colonial idea enjoys its own posthumous history within the French national consciousness. So many children have, over the past few French generations, indulged in daydreams as they flicked through the pages of *Le Journal des voyages* or *La croisière noire*.[308] On the quays of Bordeaux and Marseille, so many young men have, likewise, experienced the emotions of their own departure, the waving handkerchiefs, the whirling of the seagulls and the sudden roar of the machines, before being surrounded by the sea as the waves broke over the stem'.

L'idée coloniale en France, 1871–1962,[309] an essay by Raoul Girardet. Table ronde, 332 pages.

[308] TN: The Black Cruise.

[309] TN: The Colonial Notion in France from 1871 to 1962.

ON THE 20TH CENTURY

BAYREUTH AND WAGNERISM

MEN IN DINNER SUITS PARADE alongside women in evening dresses, flooding all of the city's streets in mid-afternoon. In long and silent queues, they head for the *Festspielhaus*, the 'theatre of celebrations'. A certain contemplation emanates from their procession.

'Genuine pilgrims travel on foot', one of them declares.

In Bayreuth, a small German city in Franconia, the Wagner festival has, since its very birth, taken on all the aspects of a cult.

For all three cycles of the performance, around 60,000 tickets are sold on an annual basis; with more than 30,000 ticket applications ending up rejected.

No other musical festival ever experiences such a turnout. Whereas Salzburg and Vienna, to use the words of orchestra conductor Karl Boehm, are 'flooded with tourists', the Bayreuth festival targets devotees driven by true passion.

There are some who book their seats years in advance, and others who, despite having spent five years unsuccessfully attempting to reserve theirs, still refuse to give in. One encounters them in Bayreuth, trudging about in front of the reservation office every morning in the hope of benefiting from some last-minute rescission. The Society of Friends of Bayreuth, to which a certain number of seats are assigned ex officio, informs its members that it cannot guarantee its ability to provide them with the desired number of tickets.

Every year, the audience comprises a large number of French people. The latter, incidentally, represent the second largest group among the Friends of Bayreuth, second only to the Germans: 'French Wagnerism' has a long-established tradition of its own.

It was during his stay in Paris from 1859 to 1962 that Richard Wagner first addressed an audience that was, at the time, more familiar with Meyerbeer[1] or Rossini[2] and that particularly revered the 'Rossinian' Chadeuil and Azevedo.

The first great 'convert' was none other than Charles Baudelaire, whose 1974 Bayreuth programme booklet was actually a reproduction of the beautiful letter he wrote Wagner on 17th February, 1860:

> First of all, I would like to tell you that it is to you that I owe the greatest musical pleasure I have ever experienced. The characteristic that struck me most was your work's grandeur. It represents the magnificent and drives one towards magnificence. Throughout your works, what I have encountered is the solemnity of great sounds, the great aspects of nature and man's greatest passions. Since the very first day I heard your music, I have never ceased to make the following wish, especially at times of misfortune — "If only I could listen to some Wagner tonight!"
>
> P.S: I shall not include my address, for fear of having you think that there might be something that I would ask of you.

One year later, Napoleon III would give the order to have *Tannhäuser* staged at the *Opéra de Paris*.

The premiere, held on 13th March, 1861, caused quite a row. On the eve of the performance, the 'gentlemen' of the Jockey-Club, who had purchased a supply of hunting whistles, organised a monstrous sort of commotion. Wagner himself attributed this hostility to the influence exerted by Meyerbeer (who he would end up portraying in *The Mastersingers* through the character of Beckmesser).

Soon, however, a Wagnerian school is founded in Paris. Symbolist poets are among its representatives, as well as Catulle Mendès, Judith Gautier, Léon Leroy, Edouard Schuré, Gérard de Nerval, Auguste de Gaspérini, Villiers de

---

1 TN: Born Jacob Liebmann Beer, Giacomo Meyerbeer (5th September, 1791–2nd May, 1864) was a German opera composer of Jewish birth who has been described as perhaps the most successful stage composer of the 19th century.

2 TN: Gioachino Antonio Rossini (29th February, 1792–13th November, 1868) was an Italian composer who wrote 39 operas, in addition to some sacred music, songs, chamber music, and piano pieces.

l'Isle-Adam, and Champfleury. From 1885 to 1888, they all gathered around the *Revue wagnérienne*,[3] established by Edouard Dujardin (to whom we owe, among other things, an essay on H. S. Chamberlain[4]). In it, Verlaine[5] sings the praise of 'Valhalla', while Mallarmé[6] celebrates 'the god Wagner radiating a consecration, hardly silenced by the very ink of cryptic weepings' (January 1886).

In 1890, Péladan[7] publishes *Wagner's Complete Theatre*. One witnesses the emergence of an increasing number of 'Wagnerian' tragedies and novels. Marcel Proust[8] and even Zola[9] take part in the movement.

In Bayreuth, the alphabetical list of Frenchmen who attended the festival between 1876 and 1896 includes no fewer than 3,000 names. Among those who had come from Paris for the first ever performance of the Tetralogy, the

---

3 TN: Wagnerian Magazine.

4 TN: Houston Stewart Chamberlain (9th September, 1855–9th January, 1927) was a British-born German philosopher who wrote works about political philosophy and natural science. He has been described by some as a 'racialist writer'. Chamberlain married Eva von Bülow, Wagner's daughter, in December 1908.

5 TN: Paul-Marie Verlaine (30th March, 1844–8th January, 1896) was a French poet associated with the Decadent movement. He is considered one of the greatest representatives of the *fin de siècle* in international and French poetry.

6 TN: Born Étienne Mallarmé, Stéphane Mallarmé (18th March, 1842–9th September, 1898) was a major symbolist poet and critic. His work anticipated and inspired several revolutionary artistic schools of the early 20th century, including Cubism, Futurism, Dadaism, and Surrealism.

7 TN: Joséphin Péladan (28th March, 1858–27th June, 1918) was a French novelist and Martinist who established the *Salon de la Rose + Croix* for painters, authors, and musicians that shared his artistic ideals, particularly the Symbolists.

8 TN: Valentin Louis Georges Eugène Marcel Proust (10th July, 1871–18th November, 1922), known simply as Marcel Proust, was a French novelist, critic, and essayist. He is particularly famous for his monumental novel *À la recherche du temps perdu* (nowadays translated as 'In Search of Lost Time') and is regarded by both critics and authors as one of the most influential writers of the 20th century.

9 TN: Émile Édouard Charles Antoine Zola (2nd April, 1840–29th September, 1902) was a French novelist, playwright, journalist, the best-known figure of the literary school of naturalism, and an important contributor to the development of theatrical naturalism. He also played a pivotal role in the political liberalisation of France and the exoneration of the falsely accused and convicted army officer Alfred Dreyfus. His writing skills led to his nomination for the Nobel Prize in Literature in 1901 and 1902.

names of Vincent d'Indy, Catulle Mendès, Judith Gautier, Gabriel Monod and Edouard Schuré are the most striking.

Wagner paid homage to them when writing:

> What my French friends had already understood but my German brethren and critics labelled a ridiculous delusion dreamt up by my own pride was, in fact, a work of art which, clearly separate from opera and modern drama, rose above both, while borrowing from them their most outstandingly special tendencies so as to lead them towards the right goal, moulded into an ideally free sort of unity.

Subsequently, one reproached Wagner for having written a 'comedy in antique style' entitled *The Capitulation*, in which he allegedly 'ironised' the ordeal of the Parisians that found themselves besieged in 1870. In a letter dated 25th October, 1876 and addressed to Gabriel Monod, Wagner offered an explanation, declaring:

> All that I wrote with regard to the French spirit was written in German and solely for Germans to see. It is thus clear that I never intended to offend or provoke French people; my intention was, instead, to simply divert my compatriots from imitating France and to encourage them to remain faithful to their own genius, if any good was to come out of their actions.

Later on, he would state:

> It was in Paris that I became fully conscious of this thirst for ideals which had already manifested its presence in me and was, at a later stage, to lead me back to my homeland and my homeland back into me.

Strangely enough, it was Houston Stewart Chamberlain who, in a letter to Antoine Lascoux,[10] formulated a genuine apology of Francophile Wagner, an unexpected attitude penned by this fierce defender of the Germanic. He writes:

> This incredible mental mobility, the staggering speed at which his ideas followed each other in quick succession and formed a sequence, all of it came from a Parisian rather than from someone Germanic! It is just as Goethe tells each of us: "What you are, you must desire! And do not desire anything but that!" As for Wagner, it is nations that he addressed in such a manner.

10 TN: Antoine Lascoux (3rd October, 1839–1st October, 1906) was a French magistrate.

The criticisms targeting Wagner would resume at the time of World War I, reaching extremes that bordered on the absurd. One would witness authors denouncing 'the music of our fatherland's enemies'. And in a book stating that 'ever since Schumann, German musicians have remained premeditatively German', Camille Saint-Saëns[11] would not hesitate to describe Wagner's music as 'an incredibly well-equipped machine for gnawing upon patriotism in France' (*Germanophilie*,[12] Dorbon-Ainé, 1916).

In the 1920s, anti-Wagnerism would be represented on a musical level by Darius Milhaud (France), Emmanuel de Falla (Spain), George Gershwin (USA), Bela Bartok (Hungary), Paul Hindemith and Igor Stravinsky.

Nothing would, however, ever manage to curb the success of Wagner's music, as testified to by the existence of today's National Richard Wagner Circle, headed by Ms Catherine Devraigne, the daughter of Doctor Pierre Devraigne, the former president of the Municipal Council of Paris.

'ARTISTIC VOYAGE'

> The artists who, a good month in advance, flock to Bayreuth from all corners of Germany, and even from abroad, so as to cooperate in the great work begin to animate the usually silent streets with their presence. Hotels are cleaned, and all private residences intended to serve as accommodation for foreigners organise themselves as best as they can. Soon, the chosen date for the first performance is upon us at last: everyone is at their post, armed and ready. This is because one does not visit this place the way one would the *Opéra de Paris* or a similar location in some other city, bringing yesterday's concerns or their mundane indifference with them; or, at least, one *should* not go there in such a state of mind, for to enter the Bayreuth celebration hall without being in a mental state becoming of what one has come to listen to is to voluntarily deprive oneself of one of the most intense artistic emotions anyone could ever have the opportunity to experience.

These lines date back to 1896 and are comprised in Albert Lavignac's *Le voyage artistique à Bayreuth*.[13] Not a single word can be removed from them. During

---

11 TN: Charles-Camille Saint-Saëns (9th October, 1835–16th December, 1921) was a French composer, organist, conductor and pianist of the Romantic era, a musical prodigy by any standards.

12 TN: Germanophilia.

13 TN: In addition to having been a minor composer, Alexandre Jean Albert Lavignac (21st January, 1846–28th May, 1916) was a French music scholar known for his essays on theory,

the entire summer, the city of Bayreuth, which is located in one of Germany's most beautiful regions, organises its life in harmony with a henceforth immutable rhythm.

In accordance with Wagner's own wishes, the performances commence every day at 16:00, the sole exception being *The Rheingold* (the first part of the Tetralogy), which starts at 18:00. They all end around 22:00, with none of the intervals lasting more than an hour each.

Shortly afterwards, artists and members of the audience meet for supper in restaurant halls which are always filled to capacity and where Franconian wine flows in torrents.

On the days when no performances are held, foreigners are seen enjoying their trips to Bamberg, Nuremberg and the villages of the *Fichtelgebirge*.

One also visits the (*Wagner-Gedenkstätte*) museum, where the stage production scale models, the couch on which Wagner passed away, his manuscripts and portraits, and the (French) letters which Liszt sent his daughter 'Cosimette' (who would later become Cosima Wagner) are all kept. A comical exhibit can also be seen there — the letter sent by the management of *Der Spiegel*, the German weekly, to 'Mr Richard Wagner, Bayreuth', dated 31st July, 1974.

Wagner himself proclaimed that Bayreuth was indispensable when it came to the accomplishment of his work's 'mystery', an opinion that is shared by all of today's Wagnerians.

In an essay on *Post-War Bayreuth*, Mr Hans-Jürgen Nigra[14] writes:

> It is solely in Bayreuth, or, at least, through the latter, that the Wagnerian *myth* exerts its most profound fascination and evokes most intensely a world and humanity that remain at odds with our current world and humanity.

Historically speaking, no musician has ever aroused as many polemics and passions as Wagner himself did. Both during his lifetime and after his passing, his adversaries and defenders have never ceased to clash in a display of extraordinary violence. This is specifically due to the fact that Wagner was not merely a musician, but also a poet, a playwright ('The greatest theatrical

---

including *Le voyage artistique*, i.e. 'The Artistic Voyage'.

14 TN: 'Hans-Jürgen Nigra' is a pseudonym used by Giorgio Locchi, one of the founders of Alain de Benoist's GRECE.

genius of all time', according to Egon Friedell[15]), and a philosopher, and even the herald of *time's regeneration*.

MUSICAL PATH

A dramatic poet — that is precisely what Wagner was already in his youth, before even desiring to become a musician. He would later state:

> In my case, the *poetic* ("male") element has fertilised the *musical* ("feminine") element.

To which Houston Stewart Chamberlain adds:

> What I maintain is that in Wagner's works, one cannot truly comprehend the music, the poetry, the stage production, the character interaction, or anything at all unless one first consents to consider the whole from the perspective of dramatic action.

This action, however, is not a matter of pure entertainment, as is the case with Italian opera, whose music only acts as a sort of support or prop. Indeed, it constitutes a *whole* in itself, one that *precedes* the actual musical composition.

On 19th January, 1859, Wagner penned the following words:

> My poetic conceptions have always taken place at such a distance from experience that I find myself compelled to consider them the very source of my spirit's entire moral development. *The Flying Dutchman*, *Tannhäuser*, *Lohengrin*, *Die Nibelungen*, and *Wotan* had all been present in my mind before the actual visual experience.

On 21st December, 1861, he makes the following declaration to Mathilde Wesendonck:[16]

> All I see are inner images, images that long to be realised through sound.

---

15 TN: Born Egon Friedmann, Egon Friedell (21st January, 1878–16th March, 1938) was a prominent Austrian philosopher, historian, journalist, actor, cabaret performer and theatre critic. He has also been labelled a polymath.

16 TN: Mathilde Wesendonck (23rd December, 1828–31st August, 1902) was a German poet and author. The words that she used in five of her verses served as a basis of her friend Richard Wagner's *Wesendonck Lieder*. It is quite possible that Wagner was, at least at some point, her paramour.

There are some who have perceived Wagner's Tetralogy as the musical equivalent of both the *Iliad* and the *Odyssey*, works whose recitation had also enjoyed a *sacred* sort of character in ancient Greece. Such a comparison may sometimes be rather farfetched, since the Wagnerian drama constitutes the 'culmination' of all Western music, just as Homer's work represents the 'culmination' of epic poetry during the period of classical antiquity.

There is, in fact, a musical path in European history that stretches from Bach to Wagner and whose counterpart in the mental domain begins with Luther and extends all the way to Nietzsche.

Jean-Edouard Spenlé[17] writes:

> Bayreuth is the symbol of a certain Germanic Reformation of Art. Just like Luther's religious Reformation, Wagnerian art acts as the artistic protest of German consciousness against a corrupt sort of tradition, as the protest of living Faith against dead works, routine repertories and a sacrament offered for a miserable price. What Bayreuth symbolises is mankind's Regeneration and Redemption through German Art. (*La pensée allemande.*[18] A. Colin, 1934)

This 'German notion', however, of which Wagner is the representative figure, bears no connection to nationalism in the modern sense of the word. On the contrary, it originates from the conviction that it is henceforth necessary to guide *all of humanity* towards a new adventure.

Faithful to a tradition that dates back to Fichte,[19] Wagner dismisses any and all preoccupation with nationalism and, what is more, defines every man 'who acts strictly in accordance with his own convictions' as 'German'.

Schopenhauer perceived the world as '*realised* music', adding:

> What results from the fact that music lies at the very heart of things and feeds on their essence is that it has a hold over all objects, whatever they may be.

With both Wagner and Nietzsche, the Kantian discovery of the limits of pure reason undermined the 'Socratic illusion'. By the same token, it has brought to

---

17 TN: Jean-Édouard Spenlé (20th January, 1873–21st March, 1951) was a French Germanicist.

18 TN: German Thought.

19 TN: Johann Gottlieb Fichte (19th May, 1762–27th January, 1814) was a German philosopher who went on to become a founding figure of German idealism, the philosophical movement which resulted from the theoretical and ethical writings of Immanuel Kant.

light the radical powerlessness of language to attain and describe the 'thing-in-itself' (*Ding an sich*). Hence one's recourse to *music*, to this 'language of languages', this 'Sanskrit of the soul', this metalanguage that retains the unique ability to express the thing-in-itself of phenomena, without, however, rooting them in any kind of present.

In Wagner's case, Music, Drama (meaning *tragedy*) and Myth are all closely related. Music, he says, 'is an *idea of the world*, more specifically an idea of the world that encompasses everything'.

Tragedy is *born* out of music, as if it were a maternal bosom. It *re-presents*, i.e. *realises* (on stage) this 'idea' of music; and it does so by regenerating the myth, which is the only possible form that allows us to reach and reclaim the purity of the origins. This is what Wagner calls the 'purely human' (*Rein-Menschlichen*).

Wagner does not explain *this idea of the world*; instead, he *realises* it by means of the *Wort-Ton-Drama*, meaning the association of words and musical tones within dramatic action. This *idea* consequently organises space-time in a radically novel manner, by instituting mankind's historical becoming in the shape of a *tragedy* governed by the law of Return. *At every given moment*, the past, present and future *coincide* with one another. The Becoming is *at hand*. Only its centre is subject to change, and along with it all resulting perspectives. Wagner replaces the unilinear conception of time, which he rejects, with *tri-dimensional* time, which represents the *specific* time of humanity's becoming.

Mr Giorgio Locchi writes:

> Within the Wagnerian drama, scenic "representation" constitutes a scenic realisation of both the present's tridimensionality — meaning the simultaneous presence of the past, present and future — and the change of perspective established by each present upon the entire represented becoming. (*L' "idée de la musique" et le temps de l'histoire*[20], in *Nouvelle école* number 30, winter 1976–77)

The image of the Nibelungen Ring, the very Ring that gave the Tetralogy its name, is the living symbol of this 'spherical' conception of history, of this music of Eternal Return. And the perfect E-flat major chord, unfolding over

20 TN: The 'Idea of Music' and Historical Time.

136 measures[21] and opening the prelude of *Rheingold*, is, to use the words of Thomas Mann[22], the musical representation of the very 'idea' of time's birth.

THE IMMENSITY OF THE WAGNERIAN MYTH

In his effort to represent the *idea* of music, Wagner does not solely require the support of the audial element; for he resorts to *all* forms of art. What he aspires for is 'total art', which he almost views as the religion of the new age.

Not only does he connect notes, words, music and poetry in an indissociable manner, thus discouraging in advance any and all translation efforts, but by resorting systematically to *chromatism*, also breaks with the diatonic system, an excessively 'analytical' system that *affirms* more than it *generates* genuine musical emanations. Last but not least, he demands the presence of the 'fusion of timbres' which once led Abel Gance[23] to ask, when referring to the cinema:

> Who shall be able to orchestrate, within the seventh art[24], the music of sounds?

In Bayreuth, the covered orchestra pit would be specifically designed to facilitate such 'mixing': redirected towards the stage thanks to the presence of a resonant ceiling, the music subsequently reaches the hall in unison with the singers' voices. That is how the '*infinite* melody' comes into being, a melody that is responsible for making the Wagnerian drama the very opposite of a 'classical' opera.

This 'total art' is heir to an ancient tradition. Indeed, already the Middle Ages, German music strived to attain an 'integral art' that would achieve both the *synthesis* and the *transcendence* of the various forms of expression.

---

21 TN: In music, a 'measure' represents a segment of time corresponding to a number of beats, determined by tempo.

22 TN: Paul Thomas Mann (6th June, 1875–12th August, 1955) was a German novelist, short story author, social critic, philanthropist, and essayist who was awarded the Nobel Prize in Literature in 1929.

23 TN: In addition to being a film director and producer, Frenchman Abel Gance (25th October, 1889–10th November, 1981) was an author and actor.

24 TN: In 1911, Ricciotto Canudo wrote *The Birth of the Sixth Art*, arguing that Cinema was the sixth artform. At a later point, he redefined dance as artform number six, making cinema the seventh. The term 'seventh art' is nowadays much more common in French than in English.

In old German, the word *Leich* (corresponding to the French 'lai') bears the simultaneous meanings of 'music', 'dance', 'singing' and 'sacrifice'. The Wartburg Tournament, which dates back to 1207, marked a parallel development of poetry and melody which Wagner glorified in *Tannhäuser*. The very same phenomenon would be encountered in popular ballads and songs. Heinrich Heine[25] writes:

> One would have to have lived in Germany to comprehend the popularity of poetry through that of singing, as well as the intimate alliance which unites the two.

Experiencing a brief deceleration in the 18th century as a result of the spreading *Aufklärung* and the simultaneous dominance of the analytical way of thinking, this march towards the fusion of artforms would once again triumph during the Romantic period with Hölderlin, Eichendorff and Novalis.[26]

Ever identical yet constantly renewed, Wagnerian *discourse* is structured around a certain number of 'guiding images' or *Leitbilder*: the affirmation of Becoming (in contrast with Being), a foreboding of a 'rupture' in historical time (*Zeit-Umbruch*), a withdrawal into a *mythical* past associated with an impetus towards the future, a prescience of the necessary connection between the people and the 'genius', nostalgic desire (*Sehnsucht*), and others.

What corresponds to these different images are *Leitmotivs* (i.e. 'guiding motifs'), which act as the former's musical transpositions, with the overture already offering us a certain *prefiguration*. Thanks to them, the 'idea' can be felt not only as an impression of the present, but also as a 'memory' (*Erinnerung*) and a 'premonition' (*Ahnung*).

There is a number of key-figures that return on a regular basis: the god-father; the master-sovereign of the world (Wotan); the hero, symbolising the warring function (Parsifal, Tannhäuser, Siegfried); choirs (*Tannhäuser*'s knight-singers, the *Master-Singers* and their craft, the knightly brotherhood of *Parsifal*, the Valkyries of the Tetralogy); and so on.

25 TN: Christian Johann Heinrich Heine (13th December, 1797–17th February, 1856) was a German poet, journalist, essayist, and literary critic. He is most famous outside of Germany for his early lyric poetry, which was set to music in the form of *Lieder* (art songs) by composers such as Robert Schumann and Franz Schubert.

26 TN: All of whom were key figures in the Romanticist movement.

As for the themes, they undoubtedly lie beyond good and evil: the theme of inner tragedy (whose outer conflicts are but the *reflections*), the theme of superhuman desire, the theme of the popular genius, the theme of nightly truth and the power of destiny, the theme of contradictory loyalties, and the theme of the beginning and end of a time that is to undergo an eternal return.

The Wagnerian myth thus attains a power of extraordinary immensity, a power so great that it would lead Nietzsche to harbour a secret jealousy of it and reproach Wagner for having only given rise to 'superhuman feelings' so as to channel them towards the realm of the imaginary, while preventing the specific *realisation* of an *idea* that was henceforth to remain restricted to the fictions of the stage.

A SECRET ETCHED IN STONE

It is, however, also because of the essentially 'mythical' aspect of Wagner's work that the Bayreuth *Festspielhaus* has managed to become a sanctuary.

This stately building stands tall alongside a wood, on the 'green prairie' (*die grüne Wiese*) so often evoked by Wagner. At its foot lies a shaded park. The Master's bust is displayed there, in white marble sculpted by Arno Breker (a second bust created by Breker and depicting Franz Liszt was inaugurated in 1976). A flag can be seen fluttering outside, bearing a red 'W'. On the balcony of the main building, a marching band performs, three times before the start of each act, a *Leitmotiv* indicating the resumption of the performance.

Wagner laid its very first stone on 22nd May, 1872, on the day of his fifty-ninth birthday. Enclosed within the stone is a metallic cylinder containing a roll of parchment inscribed with the following words:

> Herein have I enclosed a secret — may it rest for many centuries to come. As long as it remains protected by stone, it shall reveal itself to the world.

Owing to a lack of funds, the construction process was a long and difficult one and was only completed in 1874 thanks to the aid provided by Ludwig II, the young king of Bavaria, one of the most surprising figures of the Romantic saga and a sovereign who had been supporting the construction financially since 1864.

During that same period, Wagner had the 'Wahnfried' villa constructed, moving into it a little more than a century ago, on 28th April, 1874. The importance he attached to it was as great as in the case of the theatre itself. It is a two-storey house built in Renaissance style and surrounded by a vast garden. A fresco depicting Wotan surrounded by his two ravens can be seen on the pediment.

The very first performance of the Tetralogy took place on 13th August, 1876 (on the same day, Wagner wrote: 'My final wish is for you, my dear friends, to remain faithful to me!'). So as to honour the Master's directives, the stage director, Carl Brandt, had unfolded several treasures of the human imagination. Lying across boards that had been positioned at the end of five-metre flexible poles, the daughters of the Rhine could be seen soaring into the air with the help of 'floating chariots' that transported them from one side of the stage to the other. Likewise, Valkyries were depicted on galloping horses and projected onto a given background using a magical lantern. What resulted was a triumph; and a financial deficit of 148,000 marks. Indeed, the festival has remained ever since under the twofold sign of success… and the gold's curse.[27] Today still, it only succeeds in balancing budget thanks to a thirty percent subvention rate.

THE CIRCLE OF BAYREUTH AND ITS INFLUENCE

Wagner passes away in Venice on 13th February, 1883. A few months earlier, with *Parsifal* being performed at the *Festspielhaus*, he had surreptitiously entered the orchestral pit so as to conduct the end of the drama. The last text we would ever write is entitled *On the Feminine in Humanity*. Its closing words? 'Tragic love'.

Wagner is interred in the proximity of 'Wahnfried', in a tomb that is now covered with leaves and ivy.

Following his passing, it is his wife, Cosima (1837–1930), who first takes charge of directing the festival, before being replaced by their son, Siegfried

27 TN: This is a rather witty allusion to the gold of the Nibelungs and the curse that lies upon the hoard. It would seem that, on a financial level, the performances of Wagner's dramas have been burdened with a similar fate.

(1869–1930), in the aftermath of World War I. In the process, both of them exhibit exemplary faithfulness to his work.

It is also during this period that Wagnerian cenacles attain their greatest importance. Attracting a crowd of writers and artists during the 19th century, the 'Circle of Bayreuth' (*Bayreuther Kreis*) plays a considerable role in the intellectual and political existence of a German nation that had, at long last, achieved its own unity. What it contributes to, in particular, is the rise of nationalist thought, which reaches all the layers of the German population.

In an award-winning university thesis published at the University of Münster in 1971, Mr Winfried Schüler describes the history of the Circle from its origins to the end of the Wilhelmine Era, i.e. at a time when its ramifications reached all the way into France, Italy, England and Scandinavia.

In Bayreuth, the Circle's organ is embodied by the *Bayreuther Blätter*, whose first issue is published in 1878. Its founder, Hans (Paul) von Wolzogen (1848–1938), who authored *Von deutscher Kunst* (1906) and *Germanisierung der Religion* (1911), would take charge of its management until his own death. Considered one of the fathers of the 'German modern cabaret', his brother, Ernst von Wolzogen (1855–1934), also penned poems and novels of nationalistic inspiration.

The principal ideologists of 'Wagnerism' were, back then, Heinrich von Stein; Carl Friedrich Glasenapp, to whom we owe a significant biography of Wagner; Ludwig Schemann, who, in 1894, established the Gobineau-Vereinigung and, in 1906, the Gobineau Museum at the University of Strasburg; and, most of all, H. S. Chamberlain.

Born in 1855 in the vicinity of Portsmouth, England, Houston Stewart Chamberlain had already published an essay on Wagner (*The Wagnerian Drama*, 1892), an essay which was translated into French two years later. It was followed, in 1895, by a text entitled *Richard Wagner*, which would be repeatedly reedited. Chamberlain had also engaged in a long correspondence with Cosima Wagner from 1888 to 1901. His fame was, however, mainly the result of his *Grundlagen des Neunzehnten Jahrhunderts*, a translation of which was released by Payot editions in 1913 under the approximative title of *La genèse du XIXème* siècle.[28]

---

[28] TN: When translated into English, the French title is 'The Genesis of the Nineteenth Century', which, although merely approximative and not entirely faithful to the original

In 1908, he marries Eva Wagner, the daughter of Richard and Cosima. During that same year, he settles in Bayreuth, where he obtains German citizenship. He would subsequently publish numerous philosophical and political essays, before passing away in 1927.

Introduced by Alfred Rosenberg in the summer of 1923, Adolf Hitler travels to Bayreuth for the first time, where he is received by Siegfried Wagner and his wife, Winifred. All of this takes place a few weeks prior to the *Feldherrnhalle*[29] putsch. Having become the Chancellor of Germany, the Reich leader would return to 'Wahnfried' on more than one occasion.

With the passing of Siegfried Wagner in 1930, it was to his thirty-three-year-old widow, Winifred, that the formidable task of ensuring the staging of the Bayreuth performances fell during the 1930s. The general consensus is that she conducted herself quite brilliantly and fostered the objective and scientific study of Wagner's work.

In 1933, Hans Tietjen is entrusted with the festival's artistic direction. Spurred on by Pretorius, the stage design reaches unequalled heights. Ten years later, the scenery of the *Master-Singers* would be created by Wieland Wagner, Richard's great grandson.

In the aftermath of the war, the festival met with a peculiar fate. The performances were initially prohibited. And yet, while the 'Wahnfried' villa had been partially destroyed by a bomb, the *Festspielhaus* remained intact. The occupation authorities, however, perceived it as a 'temple' of German nationalism and, in order to desacralise it, entrusted it to the American army, which then had various jazz bands settle in so as to distract the GIs. A series of musicals and cabaret spectacles was performed there over the course of several years.

Convinced that the 'mythical' ideology with which Wagnerian *Musikdramen* are imbued was in some way responsible for the aberrations committed by National Socialism, certain milieus declared themselves hostile towards the resumption of the performances. Some even went as far as to claim that the theatre should be destroyed.

German title, does manage to capture the contents of the work itself. In the English language, the German title is rendered as 'The Foundations of the Nineteenth Century', which has the merit of being both fully faithful to the original title and accurate content-wise.

29 TN: Otherwise known as the 'Beer Hall Putsch' or the 'Munich Putsch' in English.

During that same period, several of Wagner's adversaries found themselves unable to dismiss their unbounded admiration for that 'infinite melody' which, having been silenced, was all the more present around them. A recent film by Ken Russel[30] described the ambiguous fascination exerted by Wagner upon Mahler.[31] The very same ambiguity was encountered in the sentiments that people expressed towards Bayreuth. 'Since I am so fond of Wagner, I shall deny him': was it not Debussy[32] who once stated this?

Thomas Mann, who, at the start of his political evolution, had praised Wagner to the heavens (*The Sufferings and Greatness of Richard Wagner*. Fayard, 1933) went as far as to write (in *Reflections of an Apolitical Man*, Grasset, 1975):

> Rarely has Wagner's influence been, in my view, greater and more decisive upon a non-musician than it was on me. All that I know is owed to his art.

In 1945, he makes the following declaration:

> The Germans have granted the West its most profound and meaningful music. The Occident, however, has been overcome by an enduring feeling that is now felt more intensely than ever, the feeling that such musicality of the soul is paid for all too direly in another domain, namely the political domain of the common life of the world's peoples.

There were others who thought, in a simpler manner, that the time had come for them to 'deify' Wagner by pitting themselves against this troublesome dead man. In the end, one thus decided to restore the festival in its rights. Winifred, who was accused of having served the Third Reich, was, however, banned

---

30 TN: Henry Kenneth Alfred Russell (3rd July, 1927–27th November, 2011) was an English film director famous for his pioneering work in both television and film, as well as for his extravagant and controversial style. Generally speaking, his films were liberal adaptations of existing texts or biographies, notably of composers of the Romantic era.

31 TN: Gustav Mahler (7th July, 1860–18th May, 1911) was an Austro-Bohemian Late-Romantic composer and one of the leading conductors of his generation. Although his music was subjected to a ban during the Nazi era, it achieved great popularity in the years that followed.

32 TN: One of the most influential composers of the late nineteenth and early twentieth centuries, Achille-Claude Debussy (22nd August, 1862–25th March, 1918) was a French composer who is sometimes considered the first Impressionist composer, although he himself rejected the term.

from taking charge of it again, and the production duties thus fell to his two sons, Wieland and Wolfgang.

A VAUDEVILLE[33] FOR THE CENTENARY

The 'new Bayreuth' was born, and what began to take shape was the ceaselessly expressed desire — particularly on the part of Wieland Wagner in his book entitled *Richard Wagner und das neue Bayreuth*[34] — to reach a 'new public' that would have been led to forget the nature of the dramas performed at the *Festspielhaus*, thus coming to Bayreuth to listen to music 'like any other'.

One first proceeded to 'de-Germanise' a work that had been constructed using exclusively Germanic materials, while simultaneously stressing its 'universal' significance.

From there, Wieland Wagner went on to introduce an entire sequence of innovations, one that strived to strip the performance of all its 'visual' aspects or those that were too blatantly symbolic.

Under the pretext of eliminating superfluous elements, one soon reached a stage[35] where the entire essence had been modified. Thanks to an appropriate choice of theatrics (lights, costumes, etc.), one erased the plot's very tragic character. Several textual fragments found themselves amputated and removed from the Tetralogy. One exerted themselves to minimise the importance of the opening scene of *Lohengrin*, as well as that of the closing part of the *Master-Singers*. One gave the audience permission to applaud at the end of *Parsifal*, although Wagner himself had prohibited any and all applause so as to highlight the performance's *sacred* character. Soloists were discretely encouraged to come up with personal innovations. Furthermore, an effort was made to render *Tristan* more 'erotic', while in *Tannhäuser*, the role of Venus was given to an African singer. And in 1956, one simply removed Nuremberg from the staging of the *Master-Singers*.

---

33 TN: A vaudeville is a comedy without psychological or moral intentions, based on a comical situation. It was originally a kind of dramatic composition or light poetry, usually a comedy, interspersed with songs or ballets.

34 TN: Richard Wagner and the New Bayreuth.

35 TN: Pun intended on my part.

The process peaked in 1976, when, on the occasion of the festival's centenary, Mr Pierre Boulez[36] was entrusted with directing the Tetralogy (Mr Boulez had previously only been in charge of *Parsifal*), with the production duties resting in the hands of Mr Patrice Chéreau.[37]

Modifying all the musical *tempi* in a most insensitive fashion, Pierre Boulez set the example of an *analytical* sort of direction: he granted each instrument a large amount of autonomy, separated the orchestral tones from the singers' vocals and strived, above all, to *allow* the sounds *to settle* throughout, thus going against the formal notice left by Wagner, who never ceased to insist on the necessary fusion of all the elements of the musical discourse within the 'mystic abyss' of the orchestral pit.

As for Mr Chéreau's staging, which lies halfway between Offenbach's[38] Olympia and Brechtian[39] patronage, the only thing it led to was the simple fact of turning Wagnerian drama into a sort of 'committed' vaudeville. The kingdom of Alberich was a mine into which Wotan descended using a ladder. In *The Valkyrie*, the wooden hut leaning against the world's ash tree, so perfectly described by Wagner, suddenly became a factory, and Wotan was depicted wearing a frock coat with a dressing gown on top. In short, everything was 'deformed, not to say caricaturised', Mr Jean Mistler[40] writes (*L'Aurore*,[41] 14th-15th August, 1976).

In the bulletin published by the Richard Wagner National Circle, one could read the following statement:

---

36 TN: Pierre Louis Joseph Boulez (26th March, 1925–5th January, 2016) was a French composer, conductor, author, and the founder of several institutions. He is considered to have been one of the dominant figures of the post-war classical music world.

37 TN: Patrice Chéreau (2nd November, 1944–7th October, 2013) was a French opera and theatre director, filmmaker, actor and producer. Best known for his work for the theatre, he attained international fame for his staging of the *Jahrhundertring*, the centenary Ring Cycle at the Bayreuth Festival in 1976.

38 TN: The son of a synagogue cantor, Jacques Offenbach (20th June, 1819–5th October, 1880) was a German-French composer, cellist and impresario of the romantic period.

39 TN: Known professionally as Bertolt Brecht, Eugen Berthold Friedrich Brecht (10th February, 1898–14th August, 1956) was a German theatre practitioner, playwright, and poet.

40 TN: Jean Mistler (1st September, 1897–11th November, 1988) was a French author.

41 TN: Aurora.

> It does seem to be the case that the less familiar with Wagner's work each audience member was, the more the 1976 production of the Ring managed to appeal to them. (October–December 1976)

In Bayreuth, tickets were returned for the very first time, and owing to their rage and indignation, some people even found themselves in tears.

Mr Georges Liébert, the former head of *Contrepoint* magazine, passed the following judgement upon the performance:

> The very same French mindset reigned, in fact, over both the stage and the pit, a mindset which Stendhal would have immediately recognised based on its most irritating trait: a fear of duped, one which turns the sublime into a game and targets all grandeur with resentment. From Voltaire to *Canard enchaîné*, it is understood that the French are not to be taken for fools; Patrice Chéreau's winking is proof of this, as is the jeering smile with which he welcomed the great honour of being booed. For more than two centuries, Shakespeare has been suffering from this national shortcoming of ours in France, and it is now Wagner's turn to fall victim to it, despite having previously encountered, from Baudelaire to Lévi-Strauss, through Proust, Claudel and Julien Gracq, the most poetic and most convincing comprehension he could ever have hoped for. (*Le Quotidien de Paris*, 26th August, 1976)

There were also other performances, of an even more political nature, that had already experienced a certain success, particularly in East Germany, where it is customary for one to contrast the 'young Wagner', who authored and composed both *Rienzi* and *Art and Revolution*, with the mature Wagner.

'CRITICAL' PSYCHOANALYSIS

In 1938, in his *Perfect Wagnerite*, George Bernard Shaw[42] had already indulged in a socialist and humanitarian 'reading' of the *Ring*. At a later stage, one reminded the world that in 1848, Wagner had sided with the revolutionaries of Dresden, while also pretending to believe that the revolution he had wished for had actually not been very different from Marx's. The Tetralogy was then depicted as a 'striking' tableau of the birth and fall of capitalism, which, in *Twilight of the Gods*, succumbed to its own internal contradictions.

---

42 TN: George Bernard Shaw (26th July, 1856–2nd November, 1950), known at his insistence simply as Bernard Shaw, was an Irish playwright, critic, polemicist and political activist.

On its part, a 'new critique' inspired by Freud and Marx displayed its intention to 'restore' Wagner's thought in all its truth by venturing 'beyond' the interpretations of Wagner's entourage and of those faithful to him, interpretations which all were deemed 'abusive'. Whenever such interpretations had been expressed by Wagner himself, one specified that 'in fact', what the Master had wanted to say was the opposite of what he had expressed and that the very fact of having been so 'eager' to make a certain declaration betrayed his 'unconscious desire' to be understood differently (such second-rate psychoanalysis had already been conducted on Nietzsche's work).

Mr Hans-Jürgen Nigra writes:

> With Wieland interpreting Richard in contrast with Richard, this criticism undertook to "demonstrate" that Richard had been wrong about himself and that it was, in fact, Wieland who, at long last, put things back in their proper place. (As stated in the previously mentioned text.)

One of the most significant and, simultaneously, most intelligent attempts to neutralise the very sense of Wagnerian drama was the work of Theodor W. Adorno.

A disciple of Alban Berg, the former musical advisor of Thomas Mann for *Doctor Faustus*, Adorno is, along with Ernst Bloch and Max Horkheimer, the principal representative of the neo-Marxist Frankfurt School. His *Essay on Wagner*, written in 1937–38 in London and New York, came out after the war. In it, he presents an analysis of the Tetralogy conceived from the angle of the 'ruse of reason'.

Attacking the very conception of *Wort-Ton-Drama* head-on, Adorno perceives it as a 'phantasmagoria' and, in the final analysis, a *mystification*. By illustrating the 'spherical' conception of history using a music of *Eternal Becoming*, Wagner is alleged to have strived to 'delay' the triumphant march of 'progress' and the advent of the proletariat. 'Suspended' between the past and the future, Adorno writes, 'Wagner does not dare to wage the revolution'. Furthermore, while being conscious of his 'lie', Wagner is said to have attempted, by means of a contempt-worthy subterfuge (the *Wort-Ton-Drama*), to make people forget that any work of art is but a 'fabricated product' (one that is due to the division of work, to the separation of intellectual work from the manual kind). His intentions are thus purported to be 'morally reprehensible'.

On the basis of such claims, Adorno proposes a novel interpretation of the *Ring*, one in which Siegfried becomes an allegorical representative of the 'proletariat' who, as the story goes on, 'transforms into a fantasy of an immediate humanity that has not been corrupted by history'. Initially a socialist (just like Wagner himself), Wotan 'betrays the rebellion' by compromising with the world instead of transforming it. As for the dwarves Alberich and Mime, as well as the despicable Beckmesser of the *Master-Singers*, Adorno declares that he perceives them as 'caricatures of the Judaic kind', the incarnations of a rational world from which any and all non-quantitative values are excluded (Adorno justifies this point of view by referring himself to the famous essay entitled *Judaism in Music*, published by Wagner in 1850).

It is this interpretation that probably prevailed in Israel, where, ever since 1948, people have been banned from listening to the works of Wagner and Richard Strauss (on 22nd June, 1974, the Municipal Council of Tel Aviv asked the Israeli philharmonic orchestra and its conductor, Zubin Mehta, to renounce its intention to play a few segments of Wagner's music during a certain concert. The press had revealed that most of the tickets had been purchased by people whose purpose was the prevent the orchestra from playing this music. What is more, the ushers had decided to go on strike).

Today still, the theories of Theodor W. Adorno exert a strong influence on an ill-informed public, in addition to voicing a complicit sort of criticism.

In 1974, during the staging of the *Master-Singers*, the audience watched clerk Beckmesser return to the stage after his setback in the third act. In the original text, however, Wagner made him melt into the crowd and disappear. This seemingly insignificant detail reflects a specific intention.

In the programme booklet published by the festival that same year, author Walter Jens specifically quotes Adorno and, indeed, explains that tolerating any sort of 'discrimination' against the unfortunate Beckmesser would contradict the spirit of the times. He writes:

> Every conceivable reproach has been used to afflict this mangy sheep, this lacklustre voice amidst the singers, this Black man lost among the Whites, this Jew that has strayed among the Christians.

THE ETERNAL MELODY

It is then explained that, in the end, Beckmesser is but an 'unconscious' projection of Wagner himself and that the defects that characterise him actually reveal, through their very excess, Wagner's 'fear' of being 'identified'; in short, that in contrast with Hans Sachs, 'a bourgeois fraught with good intentions' but dreaming of an impossible 'social reconciliation', his dissenting mindset is absolutely necessary. Hence this conclusion:

> It is impossible to accept Beckmesser's complete disappearance at the end of the play. He must remain on stage, for he is still needed.

Not all post-war Wagnerians have been stricken with the 'Beckmesser complex', however.

Towards the end of the 1950s, two publics existed side by side in Bayreuth: on the one hand, a festival-going and mundane public and, on the other, a 'celebrative audience' whose members went to the *Festspielhaus* in silence, like pilgrims reaching for a source of hope within secret catacombs.

Back then, whenever Hans Sachs asked the residents of mediaeval Nuremberg to put their trust in the 'holy German art' (*heil'ge deutsche Kunst*) in times of great tribulation, it was the latter public that shared in the mastersinger's famous apostrophe. All that its members needed was to close their eyes to once again experience the eternal melody.

Wieland Wagner died in 1966; and since 1967, the management of the Bayreuth festival has been in his brother Wolfgang's hands. The Wagner family has, incidentally, never stopped growing. Instead of Wieland, we now have his widow, Gertrud, and his four children Wolfgang Siegfried ('Wumi'), Iris, Daphne and Nike, as well as Wieland's and Wolfgang's sisters, Friedelind and Verena.

In order to avoid excessive complications, the Wagner legacy has been turned into a foundation. A contract signed in 1973 between the public authorities and the Wagner family guarantees the Festival's material continuity.

The Society of Friends of Bayreuth (*Gesellschaft der Freunde von Bayreuth e.V.*), whose president is Doctor Ewald Hilger and secretary Mr Adolf Hopf, is the partner of the organisation of representatives. Its 2,600 supporters participate in its funding (sometimes considerably) and include the Aga Khan, the

BASF corporations, Bahlsen, Thyssen, Mannesmann, the Krupp factories, the Munich House of Culture, and others.

Now eighty-one years old, Winifred Wagner has kept her proud bearing and glittering eyes. As a sign of protest against the spirit of the 'new Bayreuth', she had previously renounced her place in the *Festspielhaus*'s theatre box before returning to it after Wieland's death. She did not, however, attend the Centenary Festival and now resides in the proximity of 'Wahnfried', in the 'Siegfried-Haus'.

In 1941, Paul Viereck[43] wrote:

> Wagner's originality consists in the adaptation of Romantic values to a different era; not to the past, nor to his own time, but to the age of complete spiritual and material mechanisation which his sensibility allowed him to predict.

It is this very age that we have now entered.

❧

L'enchanteur et le roi des ombres,[44] a collection of selected letters by Richard Wagner and Ludwig II of Bavaria presented by Blandine Ollivier. Libr. Académique Perrin, 379 pages.

Wagner l'enchanteur,[45] an essay by Jean Matter. La Baconnière, Neuchâtel, 281 pages.

A Bayreuth avec Richard Wagner,[46] an essay by Jean Mistler. Hachette, 324 pages.

Der Bayreuther Kreis, Wagnerkult und Kulturreform im Geiste völkischer Weltanschauung, an essay by Winifred Schüler. Aschendorff, Münster, 293 pages.

Cosima Wagner, an essay by Alice Sokoloff. List, München, 341 pages.

La famille Wagner et Bayreuth, 1876–1976,[47] photos presented by Wolf Siegfried Wagner. Ed. du Chêne, 160 pages.

Wagner au jour le jour,[48] a chronology established by Martin Gregor-Dellin. Gallimard, 315 pages.

Wagner et l'esprit romantique,[49] an essay by André Coeuroy. Gallimard, 380 pages.

Essay on Wagner, written by Theodor W. Adorno. Gallimard, 214 pages.

Richard Wagner, an essay by Michel R. Hofmann. Pierre Waleffe, 216 pages.

---

43 TN: Paul Viereck (22nd January, 1865–9th February, 1944) was a German classical philologist, epigraphist, papyrologist and high-school teacher.

44 TN: The Enchanter and the King of Shadows.

45 TN: Wagner the Enchanter.

46 TN: In Bayreuth with Richard Wagner.

47 TN: The Wagner Family and Bayreuth, from 1876 to 1976.

48 TN: Wagner from Day to Day.

49 TN: Wagner and the Romantic Spirit.

Numerous works on Wagner were published in 1976, on the occasion of the centenary of the Festival of Bayreuth. *Éditions d'aujourd'hui* (14, rue de Grenelle, 75007 Paris, France) have notably reedited Wagner's complete prose works in a total of thirteen volumes published in 1928 through Delagrave. The *Nouvelle école* magazine has also released a special issue (number 30, winter 1976–77).

Cercle national Richard Wagner[50] (6, Square de l'Aveyron, 75017 Paris, France); Gesellschaft der Freunde von Bayreuth e.V. (Festspielhügel 6, 8580 Bayreuth, Germany).

VON SALOMON'S GERMANY

THERE IS A VERY BEAUTIFUL house located in Elbdeich (Stöckte), between Schleswig and Hamburg — it includes a wooden barrier, two large buildings with a thatched roof, and a garden with trees. A white, brown and green vision. This is where writer Ernst von Salomon passed away on 9th August, 1972. On the previous evening, he had voiced his concern over a storm whose end he would never see.

'It is never the fact of taking action that dishonours, but the fact of suffering the actions of others', Walther Rathenau[51] wrote in his *Reflections*. Ernst von Salomon and his friends did not wish to suffer; they thus killed Walther Rathenau.

The work of von Salomon is the story of his life; and, simultaneously, the (hi)story of Germany itself. The two overlap, and neither could ever be mentioned separately, for they both began in the aftermath of the Great War.

THE SCHOOL OF CADETS

29th October, 1918, North Germany. The third squadron of the imperial fleet, located in Kiel, has entered a state of insurrection. The crews have formulated

50 TN: The Richard Wagner National Circle

51 TN: Walther Rathenau (29th September, 1867–24th June, 1922) was a Jewish statesman who served as German Foreign Minister during the Weimar Republic. Although he was actually a moderate liberal who openly condemned Soviet methods, some nationalists accused him of being a revolutionary. Admittedly, he did initiate the Treaty of Rapallo, which removed major obstacles to trading with Soviet Russia. Two months after signing the treaty, he was assassinated in Berlin.

revolutionary demands and have threatened to gun down some officers. It is a Spartacist (and German) *Potemkin*[52]. Soon, the rebels take control of the city. On the 5th of November, a first Council of Sailors and Soldiers sees the light of day. The movement then spreads to the old cities of the *Hanse*[53], one after the other: Hamburg 'the red', Lübeck, Wilhelmshafen, Bremen, and ultimately Berlin.

Wilhelm II abdicates on the 9th of November, and on the same day, Social-Democrat Scheidemann proclaims the birth of the Republic. A few hours later, Spartacist Karl Liebknecht announces the creation of a 'Socialist Republic'. Then, on the 10th, a Council of People's Commissars is elected in Berlin by a plenary assembly of workers and soldiers.

Mr Gilbert Badia[54] writes:

> In the morning hours of 10th November, 1918, actual power is, throughout Germany, in the hands of the councils of workers and soldiers. And yet, although there are more than 10,000 of them in the entire country, these councils are comprised of highly disparate elements. They are rather analogous to the Committees of Liberation that surfaced in France in 1944 and include the most active militants. To claim that their birth had been the result of elections would be a fallacy. (*Histoire de l'Allemagne contemporaine*[55], volume 1. Ed. Sociales, 1962)

A wave of anti-militarism floods the country, as officers are attacked in the street. Von Salomon, who wore the uniform with pride, recounts at the start of his *Outlaws* how he himself was subjected to a beating:

> I suddenly found myself surrounded by a number of people, including some women. A man wearing a bowler hat brandished his umbrella above my head; another began to laugh, and many were those that imitated him. Yet all I could think of were my shoulder-pieces. Everything depended on them: my honour

52 TN: The Russian battleship *Potemkin* was a pre-dreadnought battleship built for the Imperial Russian Navy's Black Sea Fleet. It became famous when the crew rebelled against the officers in June 1905 (during that year's revolution), an event that is now regarded as a first step towards the Russian Revolution of 1917.

53 TN: *Hanse*, later spelt *Hansa*, was the Old High German word for a convoy. The word was subsequently applied to bands of merchants traveling between the Hanseatic cities — whether by land or by sea.

54 TN: Gilbert Badia (11th September, 1916–5th November, 2004) was a French historian.

55 TN: The History of Contemporary Germany.

> (a ridiculous thought by any means — what importance did my shoulder-pieces have?), everything. I therefore grabbed my bayonet; and that is when a fist landed on my face.

He had only just turned sixteen.

Ernst von Salomon was born in Kiel on 25th September, 1902 to a family originally from Venice and France. A certain Louis-Frédéric Cassian de Salomon had already participated in the Pichegru plot against Napoleon. Von Salomon's father had been born in England and died fighting on the front; as for his mother, she was born in Russia. They were all Prussian by affinity: 'Had I not been born a Prussian, I would have become one by choice' (*The Questionnaire*).

Initially raised in an institution in Karlsruhe, von Salomon joins the Emperor's School of Cadets at a very young age. A Prussian Prytaneion. His education there would be an unforgettable experience, one which he would recount in *The Cadets*. The defeat of 1918, however, shatters his universe. Like a bullet, the news of the armistice's signing hits him in the face: all of imperial Germany's traditions seem to collapse, and he makes the decision never to recover from it.

Then, one day, the soldiers return, haggard. They enter the cities in utter silence, as if they were ghosts.

> They were men who heeded an inner calling, a secret call of blood and spirit; one way or another, they were volunteers. They were men who had been taught the rough code of fraternity and who had learnt to perceive what lies beyond things. Fatherland, people, nation — those were great words, but whenever we uttered them, they sounded wrong. For the fatherland was within them, and within them was the nation.

The only thing that henceforth subsists is the mystique of war, heroism and death. And this *idea* is only exemplified by the 'outlaws' (*Geächteten*), the outcasts of the Freikorps whose gaze the vanquished Germany is reluctant to meet because they long to keep a certain notion of the fatherland alive at a time of defeat. Von Salomon sets off to fight at their side.

THE FREIKORPS SAVIOURS OF THE REPUBLIC

In a book that has become almost a classic and entitled *Die deutschen Freikorps, 1918–1923*[56] (F. Bruckmann, 1936), F. W. von Oertzen[57] explains that the Freikorps actually had a twofold origin — they had, on the one hand, stemmed from the troops that had been formed in 1918–1919 to struggle against the Bolshevik agitation and, on the other, from the ones that had been brought back from the Baltic countries after the war.

Mr Droz, a professor at the Sorbonne, reminds us:

> In December 1918, the regular army, undermined by Spartacist propaganda, was unable to reclaim Berlin, which remained in the hands of the revolutionaries. General Lequis' troops had been contaminated and the government chaired by Ebert, the new chancellor, seemed to be their prisoner. (*Le nationalisme allemand de 1871 à 1939*[58]. CDU-SEDES, 1967)

It is under these conditions that a secret agreement with the military staff is reached. So as to counter the 'ultras' of the extreme Left, the army commits itself to supporting the socialist government.

At the start of his *Outlaws*, Ernst von Salomon recounts how, with the support of Social-Democratic minister Noske, General Märker undertook to unite, within a single formation, volunteers whose task was to re-establish order and protect the borders.

A long-overdue decision on his part. During the night of 7th-8th November, 1918, the Republic is proclaimed in Munich. King Ludwig III escapes to Tyrol and is replaced by a socialist government headed by agitator Kurt Eisner,[59] who had come out of prison a month earlier. Under the latter's authority, Bavaria would experience weeks of madness. On 21st February, 1919, however, Eisner is assassinated by a young monarchist, Count Arco-Valley.

---

56 TN: The German Freikorps, 1918–1923.

57 TN: Friedrich Wilhelm von Oertzen (5th October, 1898–8th July, 1944) was a German journalist and publicist.

58 TN: German Nationalism from 1871 to 1939.

59 TN: Kurt Eisner (14th May, 1867–21st February, 1919) was a journalist and theatre critic who organised the Socialist Revolution that overthrew the Wittelsbach monarchy in Bavaria in November 1918. He was cited by Max Weber as an example of charismatic authority.

A month later, Béla Kun establishes Bolshevik dictatorship in Hungary. Soon, the movement reaches Bavaria and Austria. On the 7th of April, the Commune of Munich is born. A neurotic poet, Ernst Töller, becomes the leader of a 'Council of People's Commissars', whose members also include Russian-born Levien, Axelrod and Leviné. Daftness gives way to terror. Common law detainees are released; one proceeds to arrest suspects, imprison people and organise firing squad executions.

In the meantime, on the 2nd of March, Lenin creates the Third International. On the 28th of June, the Treaty of Versailles is signed and accepted by the Weimar Republic.

The first Freikorps surface in Westphalia. At the end of 1919, they comprise more than 300,000 men. Thanks to them, order is reinstated and Berlin reclaimed. Communist uprisings are crushed in Saxony, Thuringia and Hamburg. In Weimar, the constituent assembly meets under the protection of General Märker's Hunters.

In Munich, the Freikorps units of Görlitz and Colonel Ritter von Epp are involved in fierce clashes with Rudolf Eglhofer's Red Army. On the 30th of April, communist militiamen proceed to slaughter hostages, most of whom are members of the Thule Society. On the 2nd of May, the Mathöser brewery, which served as the revolutionaries' headquarters, is attacked. The city is liberated. On the 6th, the Freikorps withdraw from Munich. In recognition of services rendered, each member receives ten marks, two sausages and two bread rolls, with no rank distinction.

Ever since the assassination of Karl Liebknecht and Rosa Luxemburg (15th January, 1919), the Spartacists had lost control of the workers' councils. Social-democracy thus gains the upper hand and the Republic of Weimar establishes itself in a climate of treacherous tranquillity.

It is a time of contrasts. Von Salomon writes:

> Sweating and breathless as a result of our march, we perceived the sounds of negro chanting coming from the bars and clubs where people were having fun. We crossed paths with profiteers and drunk and noisy tarts. We saw the bourgeois, whose protection we were entrusted with, sitting in chic cabarets in the company of girls who they tightly embraced, with entire tables of shiny bottles and glasses before them, or indulging in sensual and intoxicating dances on the mirror-like

> floor. Yet in the distance, one could still hear the muffled sound of some of our comrades' rifles.

Further ahead lay the *Baltikum*,[60] home to the *desperados* of the fatherland.

'BALTIKUM'

In the aftermath of the armistice, Germany is allowed to maintain its presence in the Baltic countries, as the Allies fear the possibility of a Russian take-over. That is when General Rüdiger von der Goltz, the former leader of the United Patriotic Associations of Germany, comes up with the idea of counterbalancing his country's recent losses on the western front with achievements in the east. Appointed to Livonia and granted extensive powers, he adopts and modernises the policy of the Teutonic Knights.

Mr Dominique Venner[61] recounts:

> His plan is quickly outlined: to attract to Courland all the demobilised soldiers that have been unable to find employment, and to transform the region into a vast military-agricultural colony whose soldiers-labourers, supervised by their own officers, would always be ready to jump to their feet and pick up their weapons.

Demobilised soldiers begin to flock together. Von Salomon writes:

> The presence of the fatherland still burnt silently within some courageous minds.

In February 1919, von der Goltz has 20,000 men at his disposal. He would write the following in his memoirs:

> There were four enemies for me to combat: the Bolshevik army, soldier soviets, the Germanophobic Latvian government, and the Allies. Abiding by the sound precepts of the Warfare School, I chose not to take them on all at once, but rather one at a time, starting with the Bolsheviks (*Meine Sendung in Finnland und im Baltikum.*[62] Leipzig, 1920).

---

60 TN: The Baltic states or countries.

61 TN: Dominique Venner (1935–2013) was a French writer, historian, and political activist who also cooperated with Alain de Benoist's 'New Right' organisation, GRECE.

62 TN: My Mission in Finland and the Baltic States.

The offensive is launched at the beginning of the month of March. Libau, Mouravievo and Mitau[63] are taken following murderous combat. On the 22nd of May, the Freikorps take control of Riga. Once there, they discover the bodies of hundreds of prisoners that had been slaughtered by the Bolsheviks.

This adventure would not have any repercussions. In 1920, France and Germany decide to foster the creation of a Latvian government. The Allies then demand the repatriation of the Freikorps from the Baltic region.

The decision is greeted most negatively. A large number of officers refuse outright to obey. The Freikorps of lieutenant Gerhardt Rossbach, which had reclaimed the city of Culmsee in East Prussia from the hands of the Poles, declares that it has 'no intention to disband' (Rossbach would subsequently transform his unit into a working community in Pomerania). Other volunteers opt for the Russian nationality and establish a kind of White Army, one which would continue to wage war in the Riga region. Others still settle in the Baltic countries. The majority, however, returns to Germany, disgruntled and embittered.

In the space of a few months, the anger felt by the young von Salomon and his friends is refocused on the Republic that they had saved from Bolshevism, a Republic that now longs to rid itself of its most turbulent allies.

General von der Goltz exclaims:

> I had not discerned that what lay in my hands was a broken sword and that my worst enemy would actually be my own people and government!

On his part, Mr Dominique Venner writes:

> In the German chaos, amidst the confrontations of classes and parties, it was the Freikorps that came across as the sole embodiment of the state. They alone enjoyed strength; they alone had displayed indifference towards any and all conflicts of interest; they alone had enabled life to resume. They shared the state's primitive harshness, and thus were they sought by all and welcomed by none. Yet whenever they passed through, disorder would be smothered, cities pacified and the Reich maintained. And still they went on, their clothes in rags. Being extremely poor, they knew nothing of the temptations of the bourgeois lifestyle, nor of its constraints, peacefulness and comfort. Although reluctant to form ideas themselves,

---

63 TN: These names, used by the author, are all German. Due to the absence of adequate English renditions, I have decided to keep them unchanged.

> they were the ones who had done what others had failed to achieve — in spite of their plethora of ideas.

In addition to a repugnance for both humanism and bourgeois institutions, what many bore within themselves was bitterness, a taste for war and a nostalgia for action:

> War gripped them; it dominated them and would never let them escape. Warfare would always remain in their blood, with death lurking close, alongside horror, drunkenness and iron.

Mr Droz remarks:

> What is particularly worth studying is the mentality that developed within the Freikorps, a mentality characterising people who were completely uprooted and disinherited and who could see no salvation for themselves outside a persistence of hostilities. Many of these Freikorps members had previously belonged either to the Youth Movement (*Jugendbewegung*) or the shock troops. They shared the conviction that the army had been betrayed and Germany backstabbed, and that the army was not responsible for the defeat. Numerous were those among them who, incidentally, knew nothing of life but war, and it was therefore natural for them to feel ill at ease in a world of peace.

THE RANCOUR OF 'LOST SOLDIERS'

To any soldier that loves what he does, the *hunt* is always worth more than the *prey*. Von Salomon writes:

> We did not know what we wanted, and what we knew, we did not want. We did, however, feel happy amidst confusion, for we felt that we were one with our time. (*The Outlaws*)

Ideology mattered little, if at all:

> To act, act any old how, while keeping one's head low; to revolt by principle and extend our energies using all available means and every conceivable boldness — never is blood spilt in vain.

Later on, the hero of *The City* would utter decisive words:

> What one thinks is of little importance. What does matter is the *manner* in which one thinks.

As in all situations involving 'lost soldiers', this led to a putsch. The Kapp-Lütwitz putsch of March 1920 corresponded to the culmination of the Freikorps' rancour.

The Allies had demanded the dissolution of the Ehrhardt brigade. Established by a corvette captain and a hero of the Imperial Marine, this corps had previously played a significant role and thus came across as a centre of nationalist agitation. Its leader, captain Hermann Ehrhardt, enjoyed a great popularity of his own, and his men had taken on a song of rage and fury: *Hakenkreuz am Stahlhelm!*[64]

With its very existence under threat, the Ehrhardt brigade decides to respond. On the 12th of March, the Freikorps claim Berlin, and chancellor Ebert is forced to flee the city. Two officers, Kapp and von Lütwitz, attempt to 'bring down' the Reichswehr, but the members of the officer corps hesitate. Soon, the situation deteriorates, and a general strike paralysing the capital puts an end to this undertaking.

Ernst von Salomon himself participated in the putsch. He describes the disgust felt by his companions towards any and all 'legalist' political activity. So as to eliminate those that have betrayed their fatherland (*Vaterlandsverräter*), only radical means will do, he decrees.

Rendered 'unemployed', some activists integrate into the small army of 100,000 men that the Allies had allowed Germany to keep; others join the *Einwohnerwehren*,[65] which act as an auxiliary to the Reichswehr and constitute a sort of local police that would officially be dissolved on 1st January, 1921. Most of them become members of veteran associations, shooting clubs, and sport or cultural societies.

Within a climate that one could hardly imagine today, one witnesses a multitude of (secret or official) parties and movements sprouting out everywhere: the *Wikingbund*, the Friends of the Edda Bund,[66] the Bund of Franconia, the

---

64 TN: Swastikas on Our Steel Helmets!

65 TN: The Citizens' Defence.

66 TN: Although some may find it surprising, the word 'bund', referring to a (political) association, is widely used in the English language.

Bund Arminius, the Aryan *Wandervogel*,[67] and others. Von Salomon himself joins around eighteen of these associations.

In August 1920, several secret Bavarian societies merge together to form the Escherich Organisation, commonly known as Orgesch. In it, one encounters some veterans of the *Stahlhelm* ('Steel Helmet'), the *Oberland Korps*, the *Jungdeutscher Orden*, etc.

Shortly afterwards, the *Organisation Consul* (O.C.), established almost everywhere by captain Ehrhardt and secretly run by the Munich chief of police, Pöhner, sees the light of day. Its watchword is the following: 'No negotiations — simply open fire'.

Von Salomon writes:

> The image that one had of the O.C. resulted in people believing that it was actually involved in every single affair. What is both strange and troubling, however, is that, all too often, loud indignation mingled with secret joy, and fearful anguish was accompanied by a sort of wicked satisfaction. There have been moments when, even in the heart of the most modest and most loyal minor official, the fantastical rumours spread in connection to the O.C. caused enthusiasm to surface as quickly as foam tends to reach a beer mug's rim.

In 1921, a new adventure begins. Forcing the Allies' hand, Poland attempts to seize control of a certain part of Upper Silesia, although the population had, by means of a referendum held on the 4th of March, declared itself in favour of being incorporated into Germany. Warsaw, however, refuses to submit. German civilians are kidnapped, tortured and killed. General Le Rond, the president of the Inter-Allied Commission, sides with the Poles. Once again, conflict turns out to be necessary. Gathered under the command of General Höfer, 15,000 men belonging to the Freikorps proceed to form self-defence groups (*Selbstschutze*). They organise the defence of cities, as well as the protection of the inhabitants.

That is when Weimar disavows them and the Reich's border is closed behind their backs. On the 24th of November, the Minister of the Interior orders the dissolution of the *Selbstschutze* and the disarming of the volunteers. It is the *Baltikum* affair all over again.

---

67 TN: Literally 'migratory/wandering bird', but close in meaning to the English 'rolling stone', i.e. someone who is reluctant to stay in one place for an extended period of time.

Von Salomon writes:

> To those who threatened the Poles with universal reprobation and us with imprisonment, we offered victory with our sacrifice-ready hands, as if it were a precious cup. Yet they let it fall to the ground, and it broke to pieces at their feet.

Having returned from Upper Silesia, Gerhardt Rossbach re-enters his Pomeranian dens. From 1922 onwards, he would begin creating cells within the Reichswehr: the *Reichswehrblock Rossbach* (RWBR). The 'outcasts' disperse once again.

SCHLAGETER AND RATHENAU

One encounters them again in the Ruhr region, a region occupied since January by French and Belgian troops under General Degoutte's command. This occupation faces unanimous opposition, stretching from workers to master ironworkers. The Freikorps organise a movement of resistance whose symbol would be embodied by Leo Schlageter.

Just like von Salomon, Schlageter had participated in the Kapp putsch and the Silesian conflicts. A member of the Havenstein corps, he had also joined the NSDAP (*Nationalsozialistische Deutsche Arbeiter Partei*[68]) as early as 1922. In March 1923, he blows up a railway bridge near Calkum, paralysing the traffic organised by the occupiers, and is arrested by the French. On the 26th of May, following a summary judgement, he is executed by firing squad on the Golzheimer heathland, north of Düsseldorf (at the age of twenty-eight). His companions are sent to the isle of Saint-Martin-de-Ré, before being deported to Cayenne.

Ten years later, Schlageter would be declared a national hero, with monuments to his memory erected all over Germany. His grave is nowadays located in Schönau.

Mr Venner specifies:

> For a certain time, communists would also celebrate Schlageter, presenting him as a misled hero. At the time, Soviet foreign policy desired an alliance with Germany against Poland, France and the West in general. The idea of an agreement between these two outcast nations, perhaps even that of a German national-Bolshevik

[68] TN: The National Socialist German Workers' Party.

> revolution, made headway. As a result of their own despair, certain Freikorps combatants surrendered to it. This environment seemed to favour a new communist attack against the Weimar Republic.

In parallel to this, the Freikorps proceed to establish secret tribunals, drawing inspiration from the Holy Vehme, the mysterious institution that arose in Westphalia during the 12th century, at a time when the Holy Roman Empire of the German Nation was crumbling. (In a chapter of *The Outcasts* specifically entitled *Holy Vehme*, von Salomon recounts the — failed — execution of a spy.)

From 1919 to 1922, around 354 political assassination attempts are recorded. On 26th January, 1920, Matthias Erzberger, the Minister of Finance and head of the (Catholic) *Centrum*[69] who ceaselessly demanded the strict implementation of the clauses of the Versailles Treaty, is severely wounded. On 26th August, 1921, he is shot dead by two members of the Organisation Consul, marine lieutenants Heinrich Tillesen and Heinrich Schulz. Upon their arrest, the two 'outcasts' proudly claim responsibility for the act.

Next in line is the Rathenau affair, which would mark von Salomon for life.

On 24th June, 1922, Walther Rathenau, the Foreign Affairs Minister in the Second Wirth Cabinet, leaves his Grünewald villa — in the vicinity of Berlin — by car. Another car soon catches up with him. Marine lieutenants Kern and Fischer fire a few revolver shots and throw a grenade at him. Rathenau is killed on the spot.

Rathenau was, however, not a man of the Left. Germanist Edmond Vermeil even classified him among the doctrinaires of the German national revolution, alongside Thomas Mann, Oswald Spengler and von Keyserling.

This multi-faceted humanist and avid reader of both Bergson and Nietzsche dreamt of a 'kingdom of the soul' in which mechanised man, the *Zweckmensch* (a man that only pursues ends that lie *outside* his own life), would be brought back to his rightful place. He subordinated 'genuine democracy' to the establishment of the *Volkstaat* (a state attuned to the substantial life of the people). He even founded an entire philosophy on a bizarre opposition between a 'dark and intellectual race of fear' and a 'brave, spiritless and dominating blonde race'.

This is what he said:

---

69 TN: Centre Party.

> One must be wary of demonstration-based ideas and only allow oneself to be guided by the *inner* voice which, despite holding a tone of severity, only ever utters the truth. (*Où va le monde?*[70] Payot, 1922)

Simultaneously, Rathenau confessed that he was fraught with contradictions. Attracted by capitalism at times, by communism at others, and dreaming of both a rational world founded upon economy and an age that would put an end to countries, he never ceased to adopt seemingly contradictory standpoints.

In the eyes of German nationalists, he was, above all else, a symbol of both defeat and the latter's consequences. A member of the German Democratic Party, he consented to taking charge of the Ministry of Reparations. Having moved on to the Foreign Affairs sphere, he signed the German-Soviet Treaty of Rapallo, through which Germany resumed its diplomatic relations with the USSR and renounced the upholding of its nationals' rights in relation to Soviet authorities (the very same agreement also inaugurated a collaboration policy between the Reichswehr and the Red Army).

Having been informed of Rathenau's assassination, Chancellor Wirth let out his famous invective:

> There he is, the enemy that secretes poison into our people's wounds! There he is, this enemy! He is part of the Right — of that there is no possible doubt!

Already on the next day, Kern and Fischer are hounded by the police. First one million, then four and a half million marks are offered for their capture. In the end, they find themselves surrounded while in a castle belonging to writer Hans Stein. One of them is killed, and the other commits suicide — 'Fischer sat on the second bed. Raising his gun, he pressed it against his own temple, against the very same place where Kern had been shot, and squeezed the trigger'.

Ernst von Salomon had supplied the car used by the two officers to carry out the assassination. Following the murder, he had also sought out his companions to provide them with passports. Wanted and, in his turn, arrested, he is sentenced to five years' imprisonment for 'active participation' and to three

---

70 TN: '*Où va le monde?*', i.e. 'Where is the World Heading?', seems to be a book published by Rathenau in 1917 and originally titled *Von kommenden Dingen*, whose appropriate English rendition is 'Of Things to Come'.

further years for assault and battery (it is only in 1928 that he would finally be amnestied and released). After three years of 'incommunicado detention', he is granted permission to receive a book. He asks for Stendhal's *The Red and the Black*, after which he begins to outline his first great book, *The Outlaws*.

THE SUCCESS OF THE 'OUTLAWS'

As soon as it is published through Rowohlt in 1929, *The Outlaws* begins to exert genuine fascination on its contemporary world. Long before reading Malraux's *Man's Hope*, political militants of all stripes discover in it the eternal romanticism of action. In his *Notes for Understanding the Century*, Drieu la Rochelle[71] would mention, with a hint of nostalgia, 'the combatant of the Great War, once trained in the *Sturmtruppen* or the aviation and now a fierce member of the Freikorps, the terrorist-assassin of Rathenau, a boy-scout, a *Wandervogel* that moves from youth centre to youth centre until reaching the other side of Europe, advancing towards unknown salvation'.

Around the 1960s, equally outlawed and abandoned militants or putschists would passionately re-read those pages from which the fraternal faces of the past's great activists emerge:

> We were mad, and well aware of it. We knew that we would be struck down by the wrath of all the peoples that surrounded our foolhardy cohort, ever in a state of unrest. Yet if madness had ever been endowed with method, ours would have been the one. We refused to submit to an era whose daily motto was embodied by submission itself. We said "no" to the Germany of the day because our tongues already bore a "yes" for the one whose coming was at hand. Our madness was thus nothing but prideful obstinacy, an obstinacy whose consequences we were prepared to endure. No man could ever do more than that.

For as long as half a century, von Salomon lived in Rathenau's shadow. A few weeks before his passing, on the occasion of the assassination's fiftieth anniversary, radio stations were still asking him the same questions. With his rather drawling voice, Ernst Jünger had been the first to ask him, 'Why did you lack

71 TN: Pierre Eugène Drieu La Rochelle (3rd January, 1893–15th March, 1945) was a French writer of novels, short stories and political essays and a well-known collaborationist during the German occupation.

the courage to admit that Rathenau had been killed because he was Jewish?'. To which von Salomon always responded by saying: 'Because it is not true'.

Barely out of prison, von Salomon gets back in touch with his companions. He works for various insurance companies and as a 'free' stockbroker.

In 1932, he visits France and spends sixteen months in the Basque region, traveling to Lourdes and Saint-Jean-de-Luz and conversing with Claude Farrère.[72] This stay would give birth to a novella fraught with irony and entitled *Boche in Frankreich*,[73] which would later be (partly) annexed to the text of his *Questionnaire*.

Ernst von Salomon writes:

> All the Frenchmen that hear me speak French begin to smile, for my speech is marked by the accent of the French South. I thus speak French more or less in the same manner as my friend, the police commissioner of Saint-Jean-de-Luz, who spent four years in a war prisoner internment camp, speaks German. I swear that I shall never misuse my knowledge of the French language for the purpose of hearing the sacred soil of France scrape against the sole of my marching boots.

At the time, the Weimar Republic was running out of steam. In Berlin, the cabarets were always full, yet there were six million unemployed people. A society in a state of collapse. On 30th January, 1933, Adolf Hitler becomes the country's chancellor.

'FROM AUTHORITY TO TOTALITY'

Numerous former members of the Freikorps joined the National Socialist Party. As early as 1920, specifies Mr Uwe Lohalm in *Völkischer Radikalismus*[74] (Leibniz, Munich, 1970), the Protection and Defiance Federation (*Schutz und Trutzbund*) erected a sort of 'bridge' between the Freikorps and the NSDAP. Furthermore, the programme espoused by the *Wikingbund*, a semi-legal emanation of the Organisation Consul, was, from the very outset, modelled in harmony with that of the Hitlerian movement.

---

[72] TN: Claude Farrère was the pseudonym of Frédéric-Charles Bargone (27th April, 1876–21st June, 1957), a French author of novels.

[73] TN: A Boche in France.

[74] TN: Popular Radicalism.

Reinhard Heydrich himself, the future head of the SiPo,[75] was once a member of the *Schutz und Trutzbund*. His immediate superior, Himmler, formerly belonged to the *Einwohnerwehr* of Munich. As for Rudolf Hess, he spent some time in the Regensburg Freikorps. On his part, Martin Bormann was the treasurer of the Rossbach working community in 1922. Sepp Dietrich, the organiser of the *Leibstandarte Adolf Hitler*,[76] came from the Oberland Freikorps, and Constantin Hierl, the head of the Reich's Labour Service, from the Augsburg Freikorps.

One would, however, be mistaken when only perceiving the Freikorps as a Nazi 'breeding ground', for one also encounters, among the volunteers of 1919 and 1921, a considerable number of (rightist) members who opposed the National-Socialist regime.

No sooner had Hitler seized power than he ordered the arrest of Count Arco-Valley, the member of the Thule Society who had assassinated Kurt Eisner. On 30th June, 1934, during the 'Night of the Long Knives', several former Freikorps leaders are executed—Karl Ernst, Edmund Heines, Oskar Stable, August Schneidhuber, Hans Peter von Heydebreck, Hans Hayn, Fritz von Krausser, and even Werner von Fichte, the great-grandson of the author of *Addresses to the German Nation*, formerly stationed in the Baltic and Upper Silesian regions. Others still, such as Wilhelm Canaris or Wolf Heinrich Helldorf, would later be among the conspirers of the 20th July, 1944 plot. Already in 1923, Captain Ehrhardt chose to break with Hitler. Openly declaring himself an adversary of Nazism, he was compelled to seek refuge in Switzerland during World War II. In 1938, Friedrich-Wilhelm Heinz, a former member of the O.C., devised an assassination attempt against Hitler, and Gerhardt Rossbach, likewise, only narrowly evaded execution.

As a good North German man himself, Ernst von Salomon shares his countrymen's defiant attitude towards the 'beer drinkers'. The 'Cathedrals of Light' of Nuremberg hold his attention yet fail to exhilarate him. Just like Ernst Jünger and the supporters of 'Prussian socialism', he prefers to keep his distance from a movement that strikes him as excessively plebeian, one that is additionally marked by its southern, Bavarian origin. Rather than

---

75 TN: *Sicherheitspolizei* or Security Police.

76 TN: *Leibstandarte SS Adolf Hitler*, or LSSAH, was the full name of Adolf Hitler's 1st SS Panzer Division.

revolutionary nationalism, what he professes is a rigid sort of aristocratism. He would thereafter state:

> I regarded Hitler's attempt to shift the decisive weight from the state to the people, and from *authority* to *totality*, as a despicable betrayal of the real goal.

His brother, Bruno von Salomon, was meant to go even further. Having participated in the launching of the *Aufbruch* journal, he would join the Communist Party during the Republic's final years. His state of mind matched that of a number of German intellectuals who violently broke with the bourgeoisie around 1930 and, taking the view that no vengeful war could ever be waged westward without the backing of the Soviet Union, chose to turn to national-Bolshevik groups (Ernst Niekisch, Karl-Otto Paetel), Strasser's 'Nazi Left' or the Communist Party.

Franz Pfeffer von Salomon, the author's nephew and a former member of the Freikorps, barely manages to evade his own killing on 30th June, 1934. From 1941 onwards, he would find himself interned in a concentration camp.

In spite of all the offers made to him, Ernst von Salomon refuses to 'play a role' under the Third Reich. He decides, instead, to work as a manuscript reader at the Rowohlt publishing house, before becoming a scriptwriter.

At the Writers' Union presided by former expressionist Hans Johst, the only people that he associates with are Blunck, Ernst Wiechert, Agnes Miegel, Hans Carossa, Emil Strauss, Jünger, Kolbenheyer, and especially Hans Grimm, the man who authored *Volk ohne Raum* (A People Without Space). Some of his texts (*Die Front kehrt heim*,[77] *Putsch*, and *Die Verschwörer*[78]) are then re-edited, particularly by Rudolf Ibel and Walter Machleidt at Moritz-Diesterweg editions.

On 8th September, 1935, Pierre Drieu la Rochelle is in Berlin. He writes the following to a friend:

> Yesterday, I spent the evening with the German writer that I like most — Ernst von Salomon, who spent years in prison for having taken part in Rathenau's murder. He spoke to me with both elegance and power. How beautiful it is to see a man rise above the events! He has done everything to establish this regime, yet he rejects

77 TN: The Front Returns Home.

78 TN: The Conspirators.

> all the resulting honours: a true aristocrat by any means. We got on marvellously well with one another.

Thirty years later, National Socialism was but an indistinct memory in von Salomon's mind. In a conversation that took place shortly before his passing, he did celebrate the Waffen-SS's military exploits, but added:

> Those men were valiant; they thus had nothing to do with Nazism.

In *The Questionnaire*, the former Cadet Guard acknowledges both his incapability to form an opinion of this bizarre 'Austrian corporal' who had come to collect twenty centuries' worth of history in the space of two decades (the struggle for power, the imperium, the twilight of the gods) and his inability to scrutinise this 'Führer who arose from the shadows' and 'will never find his own place in history'.

We are now in 1945, at the time of the purge. Ernst von Salomon is once again arrested — by the Americans this time. He is accused of having belonged to the *Volkssturm*, in which all non-mobilisable 'territorials' had been enrolled, then mistakenly imprisoned and subsequently released.

At the time, the Allies had created no fewer than 262 denazification commissions. So as to accurately determine the responsibilities borne by each of the seven million members of the Nazi Party, they organised the distribution of twelve million copies of a printout containing 125 detailed questions. Such was the famed 'questionnaire'. Providing the necessary answers allowed the respondent to obtain a ration card and a work permit.

Unexpectedly, von Salomon fills in his printout and turns it into the content of a thick, lengthy and verbose book. In the latter, he outlines his own past again, displaying an almost amused kind of detachment that would scandalise some of his readers (after his death, the German weekly *Der Spiegel* would also denounce the book's 'stiffness' and insufficient humility).

Translated into French in 1953, *The Questionnaire* enjoyed tremendous success in Germany itself, with a total of 60,000 copies sold in the space of six months. There are some in whose eyes the book constitutes a sort of deliverance, just like Virgil Gheorgiu's[79] *Twenty-Fifth Hour*.

79 TN: Constantin Virgil Gheorghiu (15th September, 1916–22nd June, 1992) was a Romanian writer. Arrested at the end of World War II by American troops, he eventually settled in

THE PEASANT REVOLT OF EARLY 1929

After his *Questionnaire*, von Salomon publishes *Die Stadt*,[80] his sole genuine novel alongside *Die Schöne Wilhelmine*[81] (Corrêa, 1965).

As if it were a window, the book opens to a view of the Schleswig-Holstein regions located to the north of the Elbe, with their dunes, dykes, and meadows reclaimed from the sea. It is a landscape where polders abound, just like in Friesland and the Netherlands; a rural land where the uplands — the plateau (*Geest*) — contrast with the *Marschen*.[82]

> Farms are what dominates the area. The brick buildings, with their immense thatched roofs, tiny windows and a door that holds virtually all of the façade, rise amidst the narrow rectangular pastures separated by draining trenches. Grass abounds on the rich soil and is regularly mowed by cattle. More often than not, the stables and the dwellings are united under the same vast roof, and the warm and overpowering smell of tethered animals invades the entire house.

History crops up again, acting as a backdrop. Under the Weimar Republic, the indebted petty peasantry finds itself unable to pay taxes and, most of all, the enormous annual interest rates (1.5 billion marks). The prices of industrial products rise on a regular basis, whereas those of agricultural goods never cease to diminish. At the beginning of 1929, revolution is already brewing. A group of peasants led by a man named Klaus Heim advocates a tax strike. Heim is a 'stocky man, as strong as any one of his oxen, with greyish blond hairs on his square, red face'.

'What shall we do?', the peasants ask Klaus Heim, the first among equals. To which Heim responds: 'It is you who must help yourselves'.

The National Socialists make the most of the peasants' revolt and settle into the North of the country. Von Salomon reminds us that this had not been a smooth process.

On 7th March, 1929, in the small village of Wöhrden, the communists attack a 'brown shirt' procession, leaving two people dead and twenty-three injured.

France in 1948. A year later, he published the novel *Ora 25* (French: *La vingt-cinquième heure*; English: *The Twenty-Fifth Hour*), written during his captivity.

80 TN: Literally 'The City', but translated into English as 'It Cannot Be Stormed'.

81 TN: The Beautiful Wilhelmine.

82 TN: Marshes or marshlands.

6,000 people attend the funerals, including Hitler himself, accompanied by SA[83] leaders and Gauleiter[84] Lohse. The following week, 500 peasants join the NSDAP. During the elections of July 1932, the Nazi Party claims 76% of all votes in the south of the Dithmarschen and 95% to the north.

The hero of *The City*, Ive, takes part in Klaus Heim's movement. He then travels to Berlin in the hope of 'toppling the world of pavements'. His quest, however, remains fruitless. He ends up being killed by a policeman during a workers' demonstration.

Another character in the book, Hinnerk, is simultaneously a national socialist and a communist. He says: 'We must establish comradery, the sole decent Law, as our land's supreme Law'. To which he then adds: 'You can call it socialism or nationalism, I couldn't care less!'

In 1960, *Das Schicksal des A.D.*[85] is published; it is a true story, according to von Salomon. A.D. was born in 1901. A Reichswehr officer, he is wrongly accused of having communist sympathies. Arrested and imprisoned, he ends up actually joining the Communist Party — which he had not done so far. He is then transferred by the Nazis to a concentration camp. In 1945, however, it is the Americans' turn to target him with suspicion. Once again, he finds himself condemned and incarcerated, and is subsequently released. Throughout his entire life, therefore, A.D. never ceases to be judged for acts that he has not actually committed, living 'in the shadow of history' and never resisting it.

Von Salomon recounts A.D.'s story in a most impassive and cold manner, one that is in no way reminiscent of the style used in *The Outlaws*. This is because it took some time for him to acquire the skill of self-observation.

'We believe in those moments when an entire life finds itself upraised; we believe in the happiness that stems from a prompt decision', he wrote in his *Outlaws*. Considered a man of action at times, von Salomon was, in actual fact, no more than a 'passionately committed observer'. This is why A.D., who never *experienced* any of the adventures he participated in, ultimately resembles

83 TN: The *Sturmabteilung* or SA, literally translated as 'Storm Detachment', was the Nazi Party's original paramilitary.

84 TN: A political official that governed a district under Nazi rule.

85 TN: Literally 'A.D.'s Destiny', the book is one of von Salomon's less famous works.

him just as much as Garine, the protagonist of *The Conquerors*,[86] resembles Malraux.

OVERCOMING THE PAST

Ceaselessly accused and always at the most inopportune moments, von Salomon himself seems to have only led an exceptional life because the latter merged with events that were indeed so. Having been born too late, or too early perhaps, he was the perfect embodiment of all the contradictions and plights that tore the old, imperial Germany apart. His own existence was nothing more than the reflection of an *era*, and if he has indeed been the focus of so much controversy, it is only because one strived to judge an entire era through him.

In *Portrait d'un aventurier*[87] (Grasset, 1965), Mr Roger Stéphane[88] associates Ernst von Salomon with T. E. Lawrence[89] and André Malraux, considering him the period's foremost German writer alongside Ernst Jünger. One reads the following at the end of *A.D.'s Destiny*:

> Whosoever meets A.D. these days will certainly not suspect that the man standing before him was, for as long as twenty-seven years, the expiatory victim of our time's sins; a man who, in the midst of our "unovercome past", has perfectly managed to overcome his own; an ageing man discreetly dressed in grey, with a plastic hearing aid in his right ear, fastened to his horn-rimmed glasses. He walks his average-sized dog of undefinable breed, patiently stopping at each street corner.

In 1972, Ernst von Salomon had, likewise, 'overcome his past'. He was a small and slightly corpulent man with a pair of keen eyes and a scarf tucked into his shirt. Raising his index finger, he burst into laughter and said:

---

[86] TN: *Les Conquérants*, i.e. 'The Conquerors', was Malraux's first ever novel.

[87] TN: Portrait of an Adventurer.

[88] TN: Roger Stéphane (19th August, 1919–4th December, 1994) was the name used by writer Roger Worms. He originally chose it in September 1941, when he joined the 'Combat' Resistance group. After the Liberation, he became a literary critic, author and journalist, acknowledged during his final years as a member of the Parisian left-wing intellectual establishment.

[89] TN: Colonel Thomas Edward Lawrence (16th August, 1888–19th May, 1935) was a British archaeologist, military officer, diplomat and author.

> I am a German without his Germany, a Prussian without his Prussia, a monarchist without a king, a socialist without socialism, and would also be a democrat if any sort of democracy actually existed. War, revolution, and the struggle of ideas — that is what my century has been filled with, and I have drunk it all up as if it were alcohol.

Ernst von Salomon passes away in a house in Elbdeich, amidst a thunderstorm that has yet to end.

Baltikum. Dans le Reich de la défaite, le combat des corps-francs, 1918–1923,[90] an essay by Dominique Venner. Laffont, 366 pages.
La pensée politique d'Ernst von Salomon,[91] an essay by D. Apostopoulos. Didier, 72 pages.
Die Geächteten, a narrative by Ernst von Salomon. Plon, 378 pages (first edition, 1931).
Der Fragebogen,[92] a narrative by Ernst von Salomon. Gallimard, 650 pages.
Das Schicksal des A.D., Ein Mann im Schatten der Geschichte,[93] a narrative by Ernst von Salomon. Gallimard, 263 pages.

INTELLECTUALS IN THE FACE OF FASCISM

THE YEAR IS 1930. HAVING already published *Candide*,[94] Fayard decides to launch a major weekly publication with a general focus. Soon, the title is specified: *Je suis partout*.[95] The first issue comes out on the 29th of November. Mr Pierre Gaxotte is its editor-in-chief and Mr Georges Blond its editorial secretary. It is an overnight success.

Five years later, *Je suis partout* had already turned into one of the principle organs of the nationalistic Right.

A decade later, under the Occupation, it acted as the mouthpiece of the partisans of the collaboration policy.

90 TN: Baltikum — In the Reich of Defeat. The Freikorps Struggle, 1918–1923.

91 TN: The Political Thoughts of Ernst von Salomon.

92 TN: The Questionnaire.

93 TN: A.D.'s Destiny — A Man in the Shadow of History.

94 TN: *Candide* was one of the main literary and political weeklies of the inter-war period.

95 TN: I Am Everywhere.

It is to the history of this journal that thirty-one-year-old Pierre-Marie Dioudonnat has dedicated one of the most interesting theses of the past few years.

A young historian educated at the School of Political Sciences and a former member of team behind *Contrepoint* magazine, Mr Dioudonnat was first drawn to the topic more than ten years ago. His thesis, which he defended in June 1972, was a long-term undertaking. Upon reading it, what one notices immediately is the large number of documents that he consulted, and he summarises them all with both precision and objectivity.

Mr Dioudonnat ties *Je suis partout* to a 'second' fascism, the first having been that of Georges Valois' 'Faisceau'.[96] In connection to this second fascism, he writes the following words:

> Its essence is due to its origin. Indeed, it was a response to the economic crisis of 1929, which spread without allowing borders to impede its progress. This permeability of national boundaries had a profound impact upon people's minds: being a universal phenomenon, the crisis seemed to call for an equally universal solution.

It is only gradually that *Je suis partout* turns into a journal geared towards struggle.

On 21st June, 1937, Robert Brasillach is appointed as its editor-in-chief. An entire crowd of authors and brilliant journalists gravitates towards it: Lucien Rebatet, Pierre-Antoine Cousteau, Alain Lambreaux, Charles Lesca, Claude Jeantet, Claude Roy, etc., not to mention the less-committed intellectuals who were led by the event to the very edges of fascism.

It was then that, upon returning from Mussolini's Rome in 1934, Sacha Guitry[97] exclaimed, 'I had seen a village, but discovered a city!'. On his part,

---

[96] TN: *Le Faisceau*, i.e. 'The Fasces', was a short-lived French Fascist political party. It was founded on 11th November, 1925 by Georges Valois.

[97] TN: Alexandre-Pierre Georges 'Sacha' Guitry (21st February, 1885–24th July, 1957) was a French stage actor, film actor, director, screenwriter, and playwright of the Boulevard theatre. A strongly patriotic man, he was accused of collaboration with the German occupiers once France had capitulated.

Jean Giraudoux[98] writes in *Pleins Pouvoirs*:[99] 'We are in full agreement with Hitler when it comes to proclaiming that no policy can attain its superior form unless it is of a racial essence'.

In yet another work of more unequal value, Mr Alastair Hamilton[100] insists on the appeal exerted by fascism on authors that had not previously seemed particularly 'predisposed' to espouse it — Pirandello, Bronnen, Heidegger, T.S. Eliot, William Butler Yeats, Hilaire Belloc, Roy Campbell, Ezra Pound, and others.

'A JUSTICE THAT REIGNS THROUGH FORCE'

Analysing 'fascism' is, indeed, rendered all the more difficult by the very fact that the term itself covers, from one country to another (and even within a single one), entirely diverging worldviews. In France, fascism has, in a number of respects, never been more than a negative epidermal reaction. 'A sort of anti-antifascism', Brasillach used to say.

What actually defines the 'fascism' of the 1930s most accurately is a state of mind, a sensibility that feeds upon formulae: power in the hands of the youth, the end of the 'old world', the dawning of a 'new age', and the rejection of the omnipotence of money (these topics would later resurface among certain Leftists).

In *Histoire égoïste*[101] (Table ronde, 1976), Jacques Laurent[102] remarks:

> Many writers were seduced by fascism as a lyrical movement in which song and will mingled. For Drieu la Rochelle, who, just like any other Barresian, was obsessed with the empire of decadence, fascism represented the spirit that he initially expected to come out of Moscow; the mysterious drive that would suddenly suspend the very course of decline. In Brasillach's eyes, fascism was not a political operation but a vast current of symbols stemming from a secret culture that was

98 TN: Hippolyte Jean Giraudoux (29th October, 1882–31st January, 1944) was a French novelist, essayist, diplomat and playwright. He is regarded as one of the most significant French dramatists of the interwar period.

99 TN: Full Powers.

100 TN: Born 20th May, 1941, Alastair Andrew Hamish Hamilton is an English historian.

101 TN: Selfish History.

102 TN: Jacques Laurent or Jacques Laurent-Cély (6th January, 1919–28th December, 2000) was a French author and journalist.

> truer than that of books. What he did was transform fascism into national poetry and Mussolini into a cantor who, having awakened the immortal Rome, sent new galleys across the *Mare Nostrum*. There are also other poets-magicians: Hitler, who, accompanied by an escort of young, braided women picking bilberries and engaged to S.S. members who all came from Venusberg, celebrated the nights of Walpurgis, the May holidays, and seemed to Brasillach like a garland of marching songs and forget-me-nots, one that also comprised the tough branches of firs. Even Codreanu is a poet thanks to the Legion of Archangel Michael. The Rose and the Sword embrace each other around the warriors of Primo de Rivera, and even Belgium acquires a poetic aspect thanks to Degrelle, through whom the fresh Ardennes breeze of inspiration blows. Battered by the winds of history, the dark foliage of both Venusberg and the Ardennes and the swell of Spanish olive trees now ripe to become laurels all shiver and heave, just as the oak of Saint-Louis, the cedars of the crusades and the Atlantic waves swallowing Mermoz[103] once did.

The fascists long to transform man and live without any dead time, Brasillach writes in *Les sept couleurs*:[104]

> They call for a justice that reigns through force, knowing that it is of this very force that joy can be born. Behold the young fascist that leans against his own race and nation, proud of his vigorous body and lucid mind, pouring scorn upon the coarse goods of this world; the young fascist that remains in his own camp, amongst his comrades-in-peace who may yet become his comrades-in-war; the young fascist who sings, marches, works and dreams! What he is, above all, is a joyous being.

French fascism, however, does not preach one's complete surrender to *vital* forces. Instead, it remains 'civilised', Mr Dioudonnat specifies.

> No matter what they say about it, fascists remain both individualistic and rationalistic.

Having attended the Nuremberg congress, Robert Brasillach is initially enthusiastic. Soon, however, he realises that he has not understood much:

> Yes, indeed, when one attempts to remember those very busy days, the nocturnal ceremonies transversally lit by the light of torches and spotlights, the German children playing like wolves around their memories of civil war and sacrifice, and

---

103 TN: Jean Mermoz (9th December, 1901–7th December, 1936) is a famous French aviator who disappeared while flying over the Atlantic.

104 TN: The Seven Colours.

> the leader using his plaintive cries to incite the subjugated crowd to rise up in massive swells, the only conclusion is that this country is, profoundly and eternally, foreign to us. (*Les sept couleurs*)

All of this is marked by a complete, or virtually complete, absence of ideology; for *Je suis partout* is not a school. In it, one identifies, in a most disorganised fashion, with Péguy, Georges Sorel, Barrès, and Drument. As for Nietzsche, Drieu is the only one to quote him.

Maurras' influence is still the strongest, which accounts for the subheading used by Mr Pierre-Marie Dioudonnat in his book: 'The Maurrassians in the Face of Fascist Temptation'.

Many of *Je suis partout*'s readers first went through the *Action française*, which Emmanuel Berl[105] described in 1932 as the 'grumbling party'. Ever since 6th February, 1934, these readers have held the view that, 'far from being a threat to the Republic, the "A.F." acts as the latter's safety valve'. They have, however, retained certain memories and ideas. Shaped by Maurras, they share both his sympathy for Mussolini and his distrust of the 'Eternal Germany'. Mr Hamilton reminds us that Maurras' antisemitism originally served as 'evidence of Germanophobic patriotism', since 'a major part of the Jewish immigrants that came to France after 1870 had German names'.

On 14th July, 1906, at the height of the Dreyfus affair,[106] the *Action française* used the following headline: 'Death to the Jews — by any means necessary!'

'EVERYONE IS UNDER THREAT'

Some of *Je suis partout*'s editors would remain 'anti-German at heart', while simultaneously becoming 'national socialists through reason'.

Brasillach continues to publish articles in the *Action française*'s literary section until almost the start of the war. As for the cinema column, it is in the hands of Rebatet: on 16th April, 1938, the royalist daily praises him for the special issues of *Je suis partout* dedicated to *The Jews* and *The Jews of France*;

---

105 TN: Emmanuel Berl (2nd August, 1892–21st September, 1976) was a French journalist, historian and essayist.

106 TN: The Dreyfus Affair was a political scandal that revolved around the wrongful conviction of Captain Alfred Dreyfus, a young French artillery officer of Jewish descent who had been accused of treason. He was eventually cleared of all charges and released.

Maurras would also speak out in his defence (in *L'Action française*, 12th January, 1940) when Henri de Kérillis[107] accused him of being a 'German agent'. Mr Dioudonnat highlights:

> Even if Maurassism does not necessarily lead to fascism, there is no doubt whatsoever that a fascicising interpretation of Maurras' thoughts does indeed exist.

Hence the following formula:

> The history of *Je suis partout* is that of a possible Maurassism.

From 1938–39 onwards, *Je suis partout* becomes simultaneously pacifistic and revolutionary, as Brasillach proclaims: 'We are not the S.A. of conservatism'. He suggests celebrating a national Labour Day on the 1st of May; this Labour Day would then be instituted by the Vichy government and maintained by the regimes that would succeed the French state.

At the same time, the 'fascists' return to the camp of traditional patriotism. On 24th March, 1939, Pierre-Antoine Cousteau[108] declares:

> Germany has become an all-too-powerful beast, too fearsome not to elicit the necessity of our rendering it powerless. Germany must be stopped, for everyone is under threat.

---

107 TN: Henri Calloc'h de Kérillis (27th October, 1889–11th April, 1958) was a right-wing, conservative and profoundly nationalistic French politician. A hero of World War I, he travelled widely in the 1920s, and wrote several books about his adventures. He then became a journalist before entering politics as an independent Republican. He was hostile to the parties that advocated an appeasement policy towards Germany in the time leading up to World War II, and eventually went into exile to avoid being arrested after the armistice of July 1940.

108 TN: The brother of famous explorer Jacques-Yves Cousteau, Pierre-Antoine Cousteau (18th March, 1906–17th December, 1958) was a French 'far right' polemicist and journalist who had previously worked for left-wing papers such as *Regards* and *Monde* and was initially associated with pacifism and the Anti-Stalinist Left.

On 18th May, 1940, Paul Reynaud[109] appoints Georges Mandel[110] to the Interior Ministry. On the 24th of May, *Je suis partout* expresses its approval:

> There are none who could deny his working qualities, his sense of authority. Mr Mandel is not a man to evade his own responsibilities. The forces of disorder and treason will now face a real opponent.

However, the week had not yet passed when Mandel had a series of raids organised against the journal's main editors. Searches and detentions ensue, as Alain Lambreaux and Charles Lesca are incarcerated.

In *L'Action française*, on the 7th of June, Maurras is the only one to protest. He writes:

> When it comes to Lesca, never have I spied as little as a hint of divergence in our notions of national policy.

Je suis partout resurfaces in occupied Paris. This time around, the editing team no longer hesitates and endorses Collaborationism. It thus finds itself at the very centre of intellectual life in the northern zone (with newspapers *Candide* and *Gringoire* no longer being published). Towards the end of 1944, its print run reaches an approximate number of 300,000 copies per week.

The daily publishes the writings of Marcel Aymé, La Varende, Jean de Baroncelli, Morvan Lebesque, Serge Jeanneret, Maurice Bardèche, Max Favalelli, Pierre Daye, Claude Roy, François-Charles Bauer (the future François Chalais), Michel Mohrt, René Barjavel, Jean Anouilh, Drieu la Rochelle, Abel Bonnard, and others.

Having been appointed as the head of the Jewish Affairs Commission, Maurassian Xavier Vallat implements the antisemitic laws promulgated in Vichy in October 1940.

Maurras himself demands that hostages be taken from the families of Resistance members and subsequently executed. This does not prevent him, however, from separating himself, with equal sincerity, from those

---

109 TN: Paul Reynaud (15th October, 1878–21st September, 1966) was a prominent French politician and lawyer in the interwar period and a man famous for both his positions on economic liberalism and his militant opposition to Germany.

110 TN: Georges Mandel (5th June, 1885–7th July, 1944) was a French journalist, politician, and French Resistance leader.

collaborators who write in the 'German press'. In February 1942, he declares that he no longer has anything in common with Brasillach.

In July–August 1943, the latter resigns from his editor-in-chief position at *Je suis partout* due to personal differences with Lesca. Furthermore, on the ideological level, he distances himself more and more violently from both Rebatet and Cousteau. He is replaced by a 'soviet' of journalists.

The French Liberation takes place at a time when *Je suis partout* is attempting to reconcile Jacques Doriot and Marcel Déat. On 16th August, 1944, the newspaper is still published, with the Allies already in Chartres. On the 25th, Resistance members make the following mocking comment:

> It is no longer *Je suis partout*, but *Je suis parti*.[111]

The 'JSP' trial takes place in November 1946. Brasillach had already been executed by firing squad, on 6th February, 1945. Cousteau and Rebatet are sentenced to death (but later pardoned). Claude Jeantet is sentenced to life imprisonment. As for the others, they must make a choice between being banned from writing (i.e. sentenced to a 'dry death') and being exiled.

Looking back thirty years, the writings of the 'fascists of the 1930s' often come across as old-fashioned and outdated. What one perceives in them is more a matter of talent than rigour, more courage than discernment. Within this mixture of literary impatience and naïve enthusiasm, one does find some admirable pages, pages which have, however, lost all power and especially significance.

Mr Hamilton says that 'the disunion of French fascists was the main cause of their failure'; the truth is that there was nothing, neither man nor doctrine, to compensate for their mental divides.

In the end, all that one can say is that there never was such a thing as French fascism, only a few men who believed themselves to be fascists and paid a dire price for their own delusion.

Je suis partout, 1930–1944. Les maurassiens devant la tentation fasciste,[112] an essay by Pierre-Marie Dioudonnat. Table ronde, 471 pages.

---

[111] TN: I Am Forever Gone.

[112] TN: *Je suis partout*, 1930–1944. The Maurrassians in the Face of Fascist Temptation.

The Appeal of Fascism: A Study of Intellectuals and Fascism 1919–1944, an essay by Alastair Hamilton. Gallimard, 334 pages.

In his *Sociology of Revolution* (Fayard, 1969), Mr Jules Monnerot[113] rightfully remarks that the word 'fascism' is nowadays used in a number of very different meanings. Indeed, depending on the discourse, what it reveals is 'the imprecatory designation of a terrifying myth, an ideological entity fabricated by Marxists using their own fact-filtering dogmas, or a sociological fact of the twentieth century'; in short, 'a reflex, a dogma or a kind of fact'.

As far as the sociological reality is concerned, one must still distinguish those who restrict the term 'fascism' to its sole description of the Italian phenomenon from those who use the word to designate the 'model' to which the various common traits of certain parties and nationalist-authoritarian regimes of the 1930s belong.

According to Mr Dioudonnat, there have been 'three ages of French fascism'. The first was that of the 'Faisceau' created by Georges Valois in 1925. Indeed, it was the first to present the equation 'nationalism + socialism = fascism'. It, incidentally, laid claim to its labelling by exploiting the Italian example. Its specific traits included the glorification of both technological progress and productive activity and the remembrance of victory. Mr Dioudonnat writes that 'Valois' ambition was to unite, against parliamentary plutocraticism, the combatants frustrated with their victory and the manufacturers frustrated by the benefits which stem from economic growth and which they feel entitled to'. What he thus wanted was to rally all the discontents within the Right and the Left; all those who dreamt of 'marching on Paris'. Just like all reactions of the 'Poujadist'[114] type, the 'Faisceau' was rather quick to disperse. Its leaders would not be involved in any other 'fascist' undertakings. As for Valois himself, he died while in deportation, in 1944.

The second fascism, that of the 1930s, emerged in the aftermath of the 1929 economic crisis and relates to the political and intellectual fermentation that resulted from that crisis. It was an international and essentially volatile movement, not a doctrine. It is defined in relation to the 'Front Populaire', just as the first fascism is with respect to the Russian Revolution.

The third fascism was born of the French defeat of 1940, a defeat that resulted in a great deal of mental distress. Following that disaster, 'not a single truth acknowledged by the entirety of the French people was safe from being called into question'. Parliamentary democracy seemed to have been discredited once and for all, as were all strictly 'national' solutions. The formula of a single party led by one single 'leader' exerted an ever-increasing attraction upon people's minds. Under the Occupation, this fascism split into two kinds: on the one hand, an essentially nationalistic fascism of 'national retraction' encountered in the southern zone and, on the other, a 'crumbled' sort of fascism, one that was violent, made exaggerated promises, and feigned to revere Pétain while simultaneously accusing the Vichy government

113 TN: Jules Monnerot (28th November, 1909–4th December, 1995) was a French essayist and journalist.

114 TN: Poujadism was the political philosophy and methods advocated in the France of the 1950s by Pierre Poujade, who, in 1954, established a populist right-wing movement for the protection of artisans and small shopkeepers.

of 'laxness and weakness' in the occupied zone. This third fascism vanished alongside the situation that had given rise to it. A 'fourth generation' would perhaps have emerged on the Eastern Front, among those who experienced a war that was not merely one of words, but it was nipped in the bud.

On his part, Mr Monnerot proposes a politological definition. Fascism, he writes (op. cit.), is a 'monarchy of discontinuity'. It is essentially a response to a 'situation of distress' in the face of a movement of social destruction that arouses both fear and an aversion to chaos in the minds of the most homogeneous social elements. For this reason, fascism is doubly reactive: on the one hand, it responds to a (real or alleged) threat of chaos and, on the other, to the (actual or purported) weakness of the policy makers whose state or government faces this menace. Mr Monnerot writes:

'Fascism responds to a distress situation within a people or political unit which, despite having reached relatively great heights from the perspective of industrial development, science, culture and civilisational quality, retains a weak social mobility. This distress situation translates into a decentring of society and the mobilisation, in the etymological sense of the word, of its most stable component; the classes that identify with ultimate social stability and upon whom political order rests are thus afflicted with insecurity and incertitude and cast into psychological dispositions that give rise to revolutionary categories. This change in conditions does not alter but, instead, exasperates the basic aspiration of these homogeneous elements—the presence of order. [...] Unlike the revolutionaries who have already been certified and catalogued as such, society's homogeneous and central elements only choose to rebel when those in power are no longer (sufficiently) powerful'.

That is when the bankruptcy of the oligarchies in control of the state creates a 'demand for power' which is then answered by having a historically different type of men take centre stage (Mr Monnerot specifies that 'there is a link between the re-creation of power in response to the distress situation in question and the advent of men belonging to a new historical species').

In the face of such circumstances, fascism and communism find themselves in an automatic state of rivalry, which accounts for both their ideological differences and their methodological similarities. The anti-communism propagated by fascism presents itself, in fact, as an alternative: it is either 'them or us'. 'To the fascists, communism is not a subversion that attacks the existing order but a rival in the establishment of power'. This also explains why in the face of fascism, which is active in the same field, communism tends to lose one of its most efficient weapons against bourgeois democracies—emotional blackmail, meaning intimidation and guilt-tripping through the creation of incapacitating myths.

In Mr Monnerot's eyes, fascism is dated and belongs to the early 20th century, just as orthodox communism belongs to the end of the nineteenth: 'It is, so to speak, "post-socialistic", i.e. posterior to the 19th-century phenomenon involving the great encounter of utopias and masses and the birth of "secular religions" and political messianisms' (an increase in social mobility would nowadays prevent any rebirth of fascism).

In a striking essay on 'Fascist Style' (in Gerd-Klaus Kaltenbrunner, *Konservatismus international.* Seewald, Stuttgart, 1973), Doctor Armin Mohler[115] proposes another typology, one that is founded neither on sociology nor ideology, but on style. Indeed, the sociological theory fails to convincingly account for the rapid sequence of social upheavals that arose between 1919 and 1945; it is this very theory that led Mr Ernst Nolte[116] (*Fascism in Its Epoch*, published in 3 volumes by Julliard in 1970) to draw an absurd sort of parallel between the Action française, Italian fascism and national socialism.

From Doctor Mohler's perspective, 'fascist style' is essentially 'nominalistic': it implies a 'categorical rejection of commonplaces that have been drained of all substance, as well as the rejection of any and all universalism'. Fascism is 'existentialistic': in the face of the break-up of generalities and systems, it implements a 'withdrawal into existence'. It attains its most perfected form through a 'tension between youth and death'. The fascist thinks exclusively in terms of struggle, not in terms of commitment — it is a role that he longs to play, not a mission that he strives to fulfil. He despises any and all systems, including one that would justify his actions. He feels closer to an adversary in whom he discovers an equal than to a 'half-hearted' member of his own camp. He willingly sacrifices to violence, as long as it is personal, 'visible', symbolic and, if at all possible, pointless.

Based on this, Armin Mohler contrasts 'fascism' with two further components of 'right-wing totalitarianism': National Socialism and statism. From this perspective, men such as Brasillach, Drieu la Rochelle, Montherlant, Gottfried Benn, Ernst Jünger and others could be described as 'fascists'. As examples of (French) statists, Doctor Mohler mentions Bichelonne and Borotra, with Louis-Ferdinand Céline acting as a national socialist.

Recently, the argument centred around the interpretation of fascism was revived by the publication of an interview with Mr Renzo De Felice (R. De Felice and Michael A. Leeden, 'Intervista sul fascismo'.[117] Laterza, Bari, 1975), which aroused considerable emotion in Italy. The author of a monumental biography of Mussolini (in six volumes published by Einaudi), Renzo De Felice, who comes from socialist milieus, believes that fascism has fundamentally been a leftist phenomenon, thus contrasting with National Socialism on this level. This thesis has been the focus of passionate commentaries, as testified to by the publication of Marina Addis Saba's essays (*Il dibattito sul fascismo.*[118] Longanesi, Milan, 1976), Denis Mack Smith's and M. A. Leeden's *Un monumento al duce? Contributo al dibattito sul fascismo*[119] (Guaraldi, Firenze-Rimini, 1976), Michele Rallo's *Il caso De Felice e il problema di una nuova interpretazione del fascismo*[120] (Thule, Palermo,1976), and so on. See also the special issue of *La Destra*

115 TN: Armin Mohler (12th April, 1920–4th July, 2003) was a Swiss-born political writer and philosopher associated with the *Neue Rechte* (New Right) movement.

116 TN: Ernst Nolte (11th January, 1923–18th August, 2016) was a German historian and philosopher.

117 TN: An Interview on Fascism.

118 TN: The Debate on Fascism.

119 TN: A Monument to the Duce? A Contribution to the Debate on Fascism.

120 TN: The 'De Felice' Case and the Issue of a New Interpretation of Fascism.

(number 1/1976. Il Borghese, Rome) on 'Le nuove interpretazioni del fascismo',[121] published under editor Claudio Quarantotto.

In his book on the *Interpretations of Fascism* (General Learning Corp., Morristown, 1974), A. James Gregor, a professor of political sciences at the University of Berkeley, also dismisses most of the classic explanations of the fascist phenomenon (fascism as the result of a 'moral crisis', a 'psychological deficiency', class struggle, etc.). According to him, what fascism corresponds to, in a highly classic fashion, is a transition stage to modern economic structures; and it is in the Third World that one allegedly encounters its most characteristic manifestations today. An analogous thesis was advocated by sociologist Rolf Dahrendorf with regard to National Socialism (in *Gesellschaft und Freiheit.*[122] Munich, 1963).

The most complete bibliography on the interpretations of fascism is the one comprised in Ernst Nolte's book entitled *Die Krise des liberalen Systems und die faschistischen Bewengungen*[123] (Munich, 1968; pages 389–431). For an exposition of theories, see Ernst Nolte's essays (*Theorien über den Faschismus.*[124] Kiepenheuer u. Witsch, Cologne-Berlin, 1970) and Wolfgang Wipperman's *Faschismustheorien*[125] (Wissenschaftliche Buchgesellschaft, Darmstadt, 1972 and 1975–76). The latter two titles give leftist theses a prominent position. This can be rectified by reading Renzo De Felice's *Le interpretazioni del fascismo* (Laterza, Bari, 1971) and Klaus-Peter Hoepke's *Die deutsche Rechte und der italienische Faschismus*[126] (Düsseldorf, 1968).

THE HITLERIAN ENIGMA

IN 1933, FRENCH WRITER FRANÇOIS Le Grix attends Hitler's speech in Berlin. His impression is that Hitler has this 'indescribable quality to him, a striking and bold aspect that characterises both his face and his gait and that would have some ladies, especially in France, describe him as a "handsome man"' (*Vingt jours chez Hitler,*[127] Grasset).

121 TN: The New Interpretations of Fascism.

122 TN: Society and Liberty.

123 TN: The Liberal System Crisis and the Fascist Movements.

124 TN: Theories on Fascism.

125 TN: Theories Regarding Fascism.

126 TN: The German Rightists and Italian Fascism.

127 TN: Twenty Days with Hitler.

In 1937, Alphonse de Châteaubriant[128] has the opportunity to observe Hitler:

> His eyes have the same deep blue colour as the waters of his beloved Königssee. His body vibrates; the movements of his head are youthful, his nape warm. His back has not been battered by the filthy passions of politics — it is as solid and smooth as an organ pipe. One of his characteristics is his immense kindness. Yes, Hitler is kind, immensely kind indeed. (*La gerbe des forces,*[129] Grasset)

During that same year, novelist Maurice Bedel writes:

> I do not know whether it is pleasant to be a citizen in a totalitarian state; personally, I would find it unbearable. What I do know, however, is that there is more joy to be found in shackled Germany than in free France. (*Monsieur Hitler,*[130] Gallimard)

As for Nietzsche, he said that 'history is always written from the victor's perspective'.

THE GOLDEN MEAN

After 1945, indictments replaced apologies. Hitler became, depending on the author in question, a 'former house painter', a 'stupid and stubborn political beast', a great lunatic, a sick or impotent man, a sadist, the archetype of the 'authoritarian personality', the embodiment of evil, a high-calibre gangster, a puppet manipulated by industrialists, etc.

Most of the theories one encounters can be classified into two categories. Some of them offer 'external' explanations, in which Hitler is said to be a child of circumstance; the result of coincidence and necessity, one could say. Others, by contrast, offer 'internal' justifications: he was a madman, a criminal, etc. On the one hand, we are treated to a social analysis, with Hitler's person the mere logical result of a process; on the other, we are presented with an intimist biography ending in an unpredictable catastrophe.

---

128 TN: Alphonse Van Bredenbeck de Châteaubriant (25th March, 1877–2nd May, 1951) was a famous French writer who became a passionate advocate of Nazism after visiting Germany in 1935.

129 TN: The Wreath of Strength.

130 TN: Mister Hitler.

Displaying flat hair, a pale complexion, thin lips and high cheekbones, fifty-one-year-old Joachim Fest views all these theories as different attempts to evade the real issue. There is, indeed, one question that acts as an obstacle to such claims — if Hitler truly was all that he has been said to be, how could German people have been seduced by such a character? How could they have brought to power such a handful of brutes and imbeciles before supporting them, in an almost unanimous fashion, all the way to the fires and death of the 'twilight of the gods'? And last but not least, due to what secret human perversity do people still seem to foster an indescribable and dangerous nostalgia for his presence now that they have been freed from dictatorship?

In 1965, Joachim Fest published a series of portraits depicting the principal dignitaries of the National Socialist regime and entitled *Das Gesicht des Dritten Reiches: Porträt einer totalitären Herrschaft*[131] (Grasset). Initially a member of staff at the German weekly *Der Spiegel* (800,000 copies beginning in 1968), and then the head of the *Frankfurter Allgemeine* Zeitung,[132] he has never strayed from his topic. As a good disciple of Max Weber,[133] he avoids both simplistic responses and Manichaean formulae. What he seeks is the golden mean, an attitude that has resulted in a voluminous essay on *Hitler*, one that is twice the size of the latter's *Mein Kampf*.

The book, which has been the focus of an intense advertising campaign (with 300,000 copies sold in Germany and translations spanning across thirteen languages), strives, above all else, to act as a reflection on grandeur, on the very *idea* of grandeur and the notion's 'dreadful' dimension.

History allows peoples to *shape themselves*. Hitler, Stalin, de Gaulle, Roosevelt and Mao Zedong were not only the artisans of their own era but also its result. Joachim Fest writes:

---

131 TN: In France, the book published by Grasset bore the title *Les maîtres du IIIème Reich* ('The Masters of the Third Reich'). The English title is *The Face of The Third Reich: Portraits of The Nazi Leadership*.

132 TN: A renowned German newspaper.

133 TN: Maximilian Karl Emil Weber (21st April, 1864–14th June, 1920) was a German sociologist, philosopher, jurist, and political economist whose ideas had a profound influence on both social theory and social research.

> Hitler's ascension was only made possible by a unique convergence of individual and collective conditions, as well as by a hard-to-decipher correspondence between man and his era.

There is no doubt whatsoever that Hitler was in tune with his time, yet it is equally beyond doubt that the German *soul* bears within itself a sentiment which Hitler gave shape to and set aflame, a sentiment that has now been extinguished but shall necessarily be rekindled, whether tomorrow or in a thousand years.

> The seriousness with which Hitler switched between his own existence and the realm of the imaginary was genuinely German.

Mr Fest writes that this mental attitude consists in refining reality in the name of 'idealised revolutionary concepts'. He then adds:

> Whatever the German spirit was, it owed to him. Yet unlike what many believe, not all the paths that stem from this mental disposition lead to Auschwitz.

RIGHTIST CRITICISM

To equate German nationalism with National Socialism would indeed be a mistake. In his book on the 'conservative revolution' (*Die konservative Revolution in Deutschland*, 1918–32. Wissenschaftliche Buchgesellschaft, Darmstadt, 1974), Doctor Armin Mohler highlights, on the contrary, the opposition to Hitlerism clearly manifested by a considerable number of representatives belonging to the nebula of political movements, spiritual currents and thought schools that the German Movement (*Deutsche Bewegung*) actually was; an opposition that sometimes cost those representatives their very lives.

Mr Dominique Venner remarks:

> At a time when the Left was surrendering, the Right became the implacable adversary of triumphant fascisms. In 1943, it was the Right, and not the Left, that joined forces to assassinate Mussolini. Under the Third Reich, the sole conspiracies that

threatened Hitler came from the German Right, from Canaris[134] to Stauffenberg.[135] (*Item*, February 1976)

Published in July 1933, three years prior to its author's passing, Oswald Spengler's *Jahre der Entscheidung*[136] is highly revelatory in this regard. Anton Mirko Koktanek[137] sees it as 'the sole manifesto of the domestic conservative resistance ever published under the Third Reich' (*Oswald Spengler in seiner Zeit.*[138] C. H. Beck, Munich, 1968). As for Mr Gilbert Merlio,[139] he goes as far as to say that 'in Germany, *Jahre der Entscheidung* owed its success to the Rightist criticism of Nazism that had developed there' (*Oswald Spengler et le national-socialisme*,[140] in *Recherches germaniques*,[141] issue number 6, 1976).

Already in 1930, Alfred Rosenberg had attacked Spengler in his most famous work entitled *Der Mythus des 20. Jahrhunderts*[142] (Hoheneichen, Munich). Later, the national socialists would bestow upon Spengler the title of

---

[134] TN: Wilhelm Franz Canaris (1st January, 1887–9th April, 1945) was a German admiral and head of the *Abwehr*, the German military intelligence service, from 1935 to 1944. Initially a supporter of Hitler, he had, by 1939, turned against the Nazis as he felt Germany would lose another major war. During World War II, he was among the military officers involved in the clandestine opposition to Nazi leadership. He was subsequently found guilty of high treason and executed in Flossenbürg concentration camp, at a time when the Nazi regime was collapsing.

[135] TN: Claus Philipp Maria Schenk Graf von Stauffenberg (15th November, 1907–21st July, 1944) was a German army officer and one of the leading members of the failed 20th July, 1944 assassination plot against Adolf Hitler, otherwise known as Operation Valkyrie. Along with Henning von Tresckow and Hans Oster, he was one of the central figures of the German Resistance movement within the Wehrmacht. Shortly after the failed attempt, he was arrested and executed by firing squad, along with several of his co-conspirators.

[136] TN: The Decisive Years.

[137] TN: Anton Mirko Koktanek seems to have been an author who focused extensively on Spengler.

[138] TN: Oswald Spengler in His Era.

[139] TN: A Germanist and a professor emeritus at the Sorbonne, Paris 4.

[140] TN: Oswald Spengler and National Socialism.

[141] TN: Germanic Research.

[142] TN: *Der Mythus des 20. Jahrhunderts*, or *The Myth of the Twentieth Century*, is a 1930 book by Alfred Rosenberg, one of the most prominent ideologists of the Nazi Party and the editor of the Nazi paper *Völkischer Beobachter*. The titular 'myth' is 'the myth of blood, which, under the sign of the swastika, unchains the racial world-revolution'.

Untergangsmelodramatiker[143] (E. Günther Gründel, *Jahre des Ueberwindung*.[144] Korn, Breslau, 1934).

In the eyes of Oswald Spengler, who had already proclaimed this in his *Decline of the West*, it is not race that creates the nation, but on the contrary, history, culture, and idea-forces (such as the Prussian *idea*) that shape race (the Prussian officer *type*, for instance). It is the *soul* (spiritual energy) that forges the physical and is one with the latter. Man constructs himself from *within*, not merely from *without*. He does *have* a race of his own, but does not *belong* to it.

In 1932, when the NSDAP had become the prevailing force in Germany, Spengler declares in his *Politische Schriften*[145] that the national revolution is in need of 'statesmen, not party leaders', before adding: 'I do not see a single one these days'.

What he discerns in National Socialism is a variant of the 'revolution from below' (*Revolution von unten*), one that would result in levelling. He perceives it as an example of 'herd mentality'. 'It is insofar as Nazism seems humanitarian, socialistic and fraught with an excessive number of democratic aspects that he resists it and denounces its dangers', Mr Merlio writes (in the above-mentioned text). Due to this fact, Spengler encourages Hitler to free himself from the socialist layer that envelops his movement. He contrasts the plebiscitary (and acclaimed) leader with the genuine representative of Prussian ascetism, the *Herrenmensch*,[146] the charismatic leader whose power does not stem from the masses but solely from his own transcendence of the principle of authority.

Hitler, however, does not sever his ties to the 'mass'. Raymond Cartier[147] observes:

> The Marxist explanation that longs to turn Hitler into an invented instrument, one that is financed and imposed by the capitalist forces that alone govern the world, does not stand up to our knowledge of the facts. If Hitler was indeed an

143 TN: The Melodramaticist of Downfall.

144 TN: Years of Overcoming.

145 TN: Political Writings.

146 TN: The term *Herrenmensch* refers to a member of the 'master race'.

147 TN: A French journalist.

instrument (all historical figures are, to some extent), then he was an instrument of the German masses (*Le Crapouillot*,[148] issue number 31, July 1974).

Throughout the two volumes that make up his book, Joachim Fest quotes the words of architect and former minister Albert Speer[149] quite extensively. Speer's memoirs, published in 1971 (*Erinnerungen*,[150] Fayard), have caused quite an uproar, a fact which may, incidentally, conjure up a smile. Has it not been whispered, on the other side of the Rhine, that Joachim Fest was not foreign at all to the drafting of these memories? (Ever since, Albert Speer has been encouraging people to vote for Willy Brandt's party, a party whose leader allowed Speer to reclaim all the possessions that had previously been confiscated.)

According to Fest, Hitler had more than just 'set ideas'; for he had also understood how to accomplish them. In this regard, what he represented was 'an exceptional case of an intellectual who enjoyed a practical understanding of power'.

The formula has startled some people. Hitler, explains Joachim Fest, has 'refuted the experimental principle according to which all revolutions swallow up their children'. Indeed, he was his own revolution's Rousseau, Mirabeau, Robespierre and Napoleon, its Marx, Lenin, Trotsky and Stalin. This proves that he perfectly understood the forces that he was unleashing'.

During an interview, Fest specified the following:

---

[148] TN: *Le Crapouillot*, i.e. 'The Little Toad', was a satiric French magazine launched by Jean Galtier-Boissière during World War I.

[149] TN: Berthold Konrad Hermann Albert Speer (19th March, 1905–1st September, 1981) was a German architect and, for most of World War II, Reich Minister of Armaments and War Production for Nazi Germany. At the Nuremberg trials, as well as in his memoirs, he stated that he accepted moral responsibility for his complicity in the crimes of the Nazi regime, yet insisted that he had been ignorant of the Holocaust. As the Reich's General Building Inspector, however, Speer was responsible for the Central Department for Resettlement and was thus involved in the eviction of an estimated 75,000 Jews.

[150] TN: Although the German title should be translated as 'Memories', the French rendering is *Au coeur du IIIème Reich* ('In the Heart of the Third Reich'). In English, it is rendered as 'Inside the Third Reich'.

> It is an unpleasant realisation, but it was time to depict the Hitlerian phenomenon as it ultimately was and to put a stop to the travesties. Hitler was not Chaplin's dictator;[151] he was, in fact, the very opposite.

'Grandeur belongs to the very needs of the most dreadful eras', Jacob Burkhardt[152] once said. As for Joachim Fest, who declares himself a Christian Democrat, he is inclined to think that any 'great man' partakes of Evil in some way; that there is Evil in all grandeur. Hitler was a truly great man because he bore a great deal of Evil within himself. He states:

> I believe that although great men exert great influence, their grandeur is measured in accordance with the degree of independence that they maintain in relation to the circumstances. And it does seem to be the case that, on this level, the "action range" available to them is ever on the decrease. It is in this respect that Hitler was, perhaps, the last man to have attempted to make history.

In 1970, Mr Rudolf Augstein[153] had already remarked in *Der Spiegel*:

> Today, the individual that stands at the top no longer enjoys any genuine decision scope, tempering, at best, his own decisions. Only long-term projects are worked on. One thus has every right to think that Hitler was, indeed, the last representative of *great politics* in the classical sense.

'The phenomenon of great men is of an *aesthetical* nature and is hardly ever *moral* in essence', notes Mr Fest. This claim is a far-reaching one. The 'meta-moral' character of any and all exceptional historical deeds does, of course, seem obvious; but it is particularly pronounced in the case of National Socialism due to the great significance that one attached in this system to both *style* and *spectacle* (which observers have always considered a striking feature), as well as to its leader's very personality.

---

151 TN: As we all know, Charlie Chaplin's famous cinematographic portrayal of Hitler was a very mocking one and strived to depict the *Führer* as a sort of buffoon.

152 TN: Carl Jacob Christoph Burckhardt (25th May, 1818–8th August, 1897) was a Swiss historian of art and culture and an influential figure in the historiography of both fields. He is known as one of the major founders of cultural history.

153 TN: Rudolf Karl Augstein (5th November, 1923–7th November, 2002) was one of the most influential German journalists. He was also the founder and a part-owner of *Der Spiegel* magazine.

THE ABILITY TO HARMONISE COMPLETELY IRRECONCILABLE NOTIONS

In yet another book dedicated to the founder of National Socialism (*Prénom: Adolf. Nom: Hitler*[154]), German historian Werner Maser writes:

> Hitler viewed his Führer and Reich chancellor functions, as well as both politics and political power, as mere means enabling the realisation of his own artistic ideas.

He then goes on to say:

> Prior to becoming an orator, a politician, a soldier, a warlord and a party leader, what Hitler was (or wanted to be) was, above all, an artist. The values that governed his own worldview were "aesthetical" ones, those of an aesthetic that *belonged* to him. In his eyes, the supreme purpose behind political action lay not in the accomplishment of the common good but in a "total" sort of undertaking in which the darkest notion of beauty merged with the most savage desire for grandeur.

It is in this regard, as affirmed by Fest, that Hitler was an 'inhuman character, one that had the ability to harmonise, without the slightest hint of moral conflict, notions that were completely irreconcilable'.

Had he not undertaken, to use the words of his childhood friend August Kubizek, to 'tranquilly invert millennia'?

Already in 1909–10, at a time when he resided in Vienna, the 'city of Phaeacians' (of 'happy mortals'), as is stated in *Mein Kampf*, Hitler makes a living by selling his paintings and drawings. The few paintings that he did from life, says Maser, 'reveal an exceptional talent'. At a later point, while on the battlefront, he would paint some aquarelles.

At the time, his favourite German painters were Carl Spitzweg (1808–1885) and Eduard Grützner (1846–1925). What he valued above all else, however, was Graeco-Roman statuary art. Once he had attained the peak of power, painting, sculpture, architecture and music would continue to fascinate him beyond all expression. In January 1942, he declares:

---

154 TN: This French title, which can be rendered as 'First Name: Adolf. Surname: Hitler', seems to be a translation of Maser's *Adolf Hitler: Legende, Mythos, Wirklichkeit* ('Hitler: Legend, Myth & Fact', published in 1973).

> Politics is but a means to me. There are some who say that I shall, one day, have great difficulty in abandoning the active life that I now lead; but they are mistaken! Wars come and go, and the only thing that remains are cultural values.

The former Viennese aquarellist, who knew the *Opéra de Paris* inside out and never grew weary of listening to Wagner, invested as much passion into architecture and art as he did into military operations and the running of the state. One day, upon hearing one of his subordinates discussing the price of a sculpture that he had commissioned, he immediately interrupted him and said: 'Nothing is ever too expensive for an artist!'.

Werner Maser writes:

> At times, one might be led to believe that Hitler had only chosen the political path so as to achieve his gigantic and immoderate architectural projects.

The fact is that architects Paul Troost, Paul Giesler and Albert Speer spoke to him as if he were their 'colleague', and André François-Poncet, the French ambassador, once wrote that, in some respects, Adolf Hitler reminded him of Ludwig II of Bavaria.

BOOKS, NOTHING BUT BOOKS

> Today, I consider it a sign of my destiny that fate chose Braunau-am-Inn to be my birthplace; for this small town is situated just on the border of the two German states whose reunification represents, at least to us, the new generation, the objective to which we should devote our entire existence and in pursuit of which all the means at our disposal should be employed.

Such are the first lines one reads in *Mein Kampf*. Hitler did not believe in God. What he did believe in, however, was Providence (*Vorsehung*), the *providentia* of the Ancients which shaped people's destinies and saw to their fulfilment.

Hitler perceived history as 'the summary of everyone's struggle against everyone else'. His 'conception of the world', in fact, was set as early as 1918. It was the result of an entire series of reflections in which Maser detects the respective influences of Plato, Hegel, Schopenhauer, Schiller, Stewart Chamberlain, Leopold von Ranke, Treitschke, Goethe, and Dietrich Eckart, perhaps even Ibsen and Zola. He specifies:

> Schopenhauer was one of the thinkers to whom Hitler referred most often. He recommended him in terms of style and readily quoted entire passages he had memorised from his books.

His historical doctrine reflects his reading of the works of Malthus, Darwin, Carlyle, Ploetz, and Edward Gibbon, all of whom belonged, save for Gibbon, to the 19th century, a century he viewed as that of 'the heroes of the spirit'.

As for his military conceptions, they largely stemmed from his intensive studying of Clausewitz.[155] On 8th November, 1934, he hurls the following at his opponents of the *Bürgerkellerbraü*, in Munich:

> You have not read Clausewitz! And even if you have, you still do not know how to apply his doctrine to the present!

His reading experiences, which reached into the most various domains, were supported by an extraordinary sort of memory and accounted for the knowledge that the Führer's interlocutors were always struck by.

His childhood friend, August Kubizek, recounts:

> I cannot imagine Adolf without any books. At home, he always stacked them up around himself. Whenever a book obsessed him, he felt the need to always have it on hand, and even if he was not reading it, he insisted on having it close by. Such was my friend's life — books, nothing but books!

Werner Maser adds:

> However, he never studied anything *sine ira et odio*.[156] To him, it was always a matter of accepting or dismissing, and he always read precisely what he needed to support his own concepts.

Among those who exerted some influence upon Hitler, a special position must be reserved for writer and publicist Dietrich Eckart (1868–1923), who adapted

---

155 TN: Carl Philipp Gottfried (or Gottlieb) von Clausewitz (1st June, 1780–16th November, 1831) was a Prussian general and military theorist who stressed the 'moral' (meaning, in modern terms, psychological) and political aspects of war. Due to his dialectical method, his thinking has often been described as Hegelian in essence.

156 TN: *Sine ira et odio* can be translated as 'without anger nor hatred'.

Peer Gynt[157] into German and ran the *Auf gut Deutsch* weekly before becoming the first editor-in-chief of the *Völkischer Beobachter*. In the closing lines of *Mein Kampf*, Hitler writes that Eckart had been 'the man who devoted his life to reawakening his people, our people, through both his writings and ideas and, ultimately, through his actions'.

Peppered with a huge number of references, charts, tables and maps, Fest's and Maser's works allow one to unquestionably gain a more accurate understanding of Hitler's life; yet in no way do they elucidate the 'enigma' of his personality. After reading more than a thousand pages, one is still left in the dark in this regard and, paradoxically, the whole's very vacuity stems from the wealth of details. For it takes more than such an amount of documentation to define a character. What this documentation depicts is a well-constructed dummy whose strings are pulled but which never comes across as being real. Hitler never surfaces, despite always being at the heart of the subject.

The fact is that one learns a great deal *about* Hitler, but it may still be too early for us to understand *who* he was.

AN UNTENABLE DILEMMA

With thousands of books dedicated to him over the past forty years, there is perhaps no other man that has been the focus of so much writing as the Führer of the Third Reich. Yet one has hitherto failed to shed light upon his person. We are all familiar with the events, with thousands of documents, letters and speeches having been discovered, leaving no missing details whatsoever. When one proceeds to assemble the lot, however, what emerges is an artificial figure; a figure that keeps its secret and is never understood. At times, one is under the impression that the more intense the light becomes, the more the shadow zone grows.

Is this due to the fact that history is only weaved by the unique and unexpected? That history is nothing more than *destiny*, and 'human sciences' are incapable of faithfully restoring the very being of an uncommon sort of man? Or is there another reason for it? Is it all simply the result of our lack of *objectivity*? Or do the attempts made by historians and their subsequent failures

---

[157] TN: *Peer Gynt* is a five-act play in verse by the Norwegian dramatist Henrik Ibsen published in 1867.

demonstrate the actual superiority of intuition over deduction, of the lively and comprehensive synthetic method over the analytical one, which gathers and classifies facts without ever managing to bring them to life?

Goebbels[158] once said to his aide de camp, the prince of Schaumburg-Lippe:

> I have been working with Hitler for years and meet him on an almost daily basis, yet there are moments when he is completely beyond my understanding. Who could ever claim to see him as he truly is? In the realm of absolute inevitability which he inhabits, nothing makes sense anymore, whether it be good, evil, time or space, and what people term success can no longer serve as a criterion. You will perhaps take me for a fool, but listen to what I am about to tell you: it is likely that Hitler will lead us to a catastrophe, but his transformed ideas will only gain new strength through it. Around the world, Hitler has enemies who sense his greatness, but I personally doubt that any of his friends are aware of it, apart from myself. And yet, in spite of all this, what he ultimately is, I do not know. Is he really a man? I personally could not swear to it. There are times when he gives me the shivers.

Hitler once made the following declaration to Hermann Rauschning, the former head of the National Socialist government of Danzig:

> Whosoever views National Socialism as a mere political movement does not, so to speak, know it at all. For our movement is even more than a religion: it is the will to bring about a new creation.

To which he then added:

> The immense significance of our long and hard struggle for power lies in the fact that it enables the birth of a new generation of masters that are called upon not only to take charge of the destinies of the German people, but also those of the entire world.

Based on all of this, could one undertake to explain Hitler without being Hitlerian oneself? To explain him is to understand him, i.e. to *enter his system*, his worldview. And how could one genuinely enter it without having first espoused it? It is an untenable sort of dilemma, one whose consequences are

---

158 TN: Paul Joseph Goebbels (29th October, 1897–1st May, 1945) was Reich Minister of Propaganda of Nazi Germany from 1933 to 1945. He was one of Adolf Hitler's close associates and most devoted followers, and was known for his skills in public speaking and his deep, virulent antisemitism.

of a grave nature. For by striving to ascertain things and shed light upon the matter, all one does is reinforce the darkness and give birth to a legend.

It is furthermore clear that one cannot discuss a phenomenon from a historical perspective until the phenomenon itself is *already* part of history, when it has ceased to arouse such immediate passions (Otherwise, any and every criticism will always comprise an *a priori* tendency to view the historian as a partisan). With regard to Nazism, however, we are not that far yet, and are even less so because the opponents and partisans of National Socialism find themselves united in the effort to prevent the phenomenon from being discarded into history, i.e. into an *anterior domain* which could be discussed objectively yet would, for this very same reason, no longer *resonate* so much in today's minds.

From this perspective, any book that is *currently* published on Hitler can only serve to reinforce the 'Hitlerian myth'. Not only that: any criticism, however violent it may be, implies an *updating* of the system, and thus the fact of turning the 'past' into an eternal present.

Author Golo Mann[159] once stated:

> In the space of ten pages, or a hundred, it is quite possible to demonstrate that Hitler was the most repugnant and the pettiest villain in our entire European history. The moment one scrutinises him across more than a thousand pages, however, as Fest himself does so as to study his hero's motivations and psyche, one is soon tempted to try and understand it. Once you have reached this point, justifying his behaviour, and perhaps even admiring it, is no more than a step away.

What results from this are the most contradictory sort of appreciations.

ACTION IN THE MILITARY DOMAIN

In the eyes of the Italian historian Renzo De Felice (*Intervista sul fascismo*. Laterza, Bari, 1975), National Socialism is the very archetype of *archaic* resurgence, with fascism, on the contrary, having to be considered a 'progressive' phenomenon, one that conveys the very spirit of the 'national Left'.

Robert Aron, by contrast, sees things differently:

---

159 TN: Born Angelus Gottfried Thomas Mann, Golo Mann (27th March, 1909–7th April, 1994) was a popular historian, essayist and author, and the third child of novelist Thomas Mann and his wife Katia Mann.

> One can safely say that Hitlerism represents the ultimate result of our *modern* times. It is not, as Hitler himself claimed, a response to rationalism, but instead, a corruption of the latter. It is the demented conclusion of the great human saga of technological crusading preached by Descartes and his successors for the past three centuries. Rarely has more effort and more faith, more intelligence and more courage, more glorious conquest and a more sensational *blitzkrieg* against routine and ignorance ever transformed the very shape of the world as during these 300 years. And rarely have the excesses stemming from these conquests ever threatened the Western civilisation more profoundly. (*Retour à l'éternel*[160]. Albin Michel, 1946)

On the military level, Hitler saw an alliance of three factors rise up against him, just as Napoleon once did — the resistance of conquered adversaries, Anglo-Saxon power and the Russian steppe.

If one is to believe Gert Buchheit[161] (*Hitler der Feldherr.*[162] Arthaud, 1961), Hitler's great weakness in the military domain lay, on the one hand, in his reliance on his sole intuition (the faith that he had in his own mission) and, on the other, in his constant refusal to engage in defensive warfare of the elastic type, one that involved voluntary — yet temporary — territorial relinquishments (at times, this fact led him to disagree most violently with Wehrmacht leaders).

In the preface he wrote for the shorthand reports of the conferences held by Hitler in his headquarters from 1942 to 1945 (*Hitler parle à ses généraux.*[163] Albin Michel, 1964), Mr Jacques Benoist-Méchin, who authored an authoritative *History of the German Army* (Albin Michel, 6 volumes, 1936–1966), expresses a completely different opinion. He quotes Helmut Heiber,[164] according to whom 'it is not true that the ever correct and promising conceptions elaborated by the military staff were always shattered by the ignorant stupidity of a dilettante whose abilities were restricted to making absurd plans and demanding the unreasonable'.

He adds:

---

160 TN: Return to the Eternal.

161 TN: Gert Buchheit (2nd June, 1900–31st May, 1978) was a German historian and Germanicist.

162 TN: Translated into French as *Hitler chef de guerre*, the title can be rendered in English as 'Hitler the Warlord'.

163 TN: Hitler Addresses His Generals.

164 TN: Helmut Heiber (22nd February, 1924–1st November, 2003) was a German historian.

> When the leader of the Third Reich ordered his divisions to invade Russia, it was not because he had chosen to ignore the risks involved in waging war on two simultaneous fronts, but because he wanted to avoid it.

This opinion is shared by the victor of Stalingrad, Marshal Andrei Ivanovich Eremenko, who has stated in his memoirs that Hitler had been right to stubbornly pursue the conquest of Stalingrad in 1942 and that if the Germans had persisted in the execution of their initial plan (a concentrated attack against the north), they would have succeeded in turning the events to their advantage.

On his part, Raymond Cartier declares:

> My own personal conclusion, one that is, I dare say, founded upon a very attentive study of the matter, is that Hitler was a great captain and must unreservedly be credited with the major victories achieved by Germany during the first phase of the war, including the Sedan manoeuvre. (As stated in the previously-mentioned text.)

On 23rd February, 1945, this is what Goebbels writes in the German weekly *Das Reich*:

> If the German people were to lay down their weapons, the Soviets would occupy all of Eastern and South-Eastern Europe, in addition to most of the Reich itself. A genuine iron curtain (*eisener Vorhang*) would immediately descend upon all of these territories, which would then form, together with the Soviet Union, a single, vast expanse.

In his final statements, compiled by Bormann[165] and published in 1959 (*Le testament politique de Hitler*,[166] Fayard), Hitler assesses his own actions, which, according to historian H. R. Trevor-Roper, clarifies many of his intentions retrospectively.

---

165 TN: Martin Bormann (17th June, 1900–2nd May, 1945) was a prominent official in Nazi Germany as head of the Nazi Party Chancellery. He gained immense power by using his position as Adolf Hitler's private secretary to control the flow of information and access to Hitler. He succeeded Hitler as Party Minister of the National Socialist German Workers' Party after Hitler's suicide on 30th April, 1945.

166 TN: Hitler's Political Legacy.

THE JAPANESE AND THE ITALIANS

Hitler asserts that the war was 'imposed' upon him and that it came about both too early and too late: too early, because it would have taken an additional twenty years to bring to full maturity the generation of officers and diplomats that had been educated in accordance with his own school of thought; yet too late, because the Reich's adversaries had taken advantage of the time that had elapsed since the Munich Agreement to 'arm themselves in a superior fashion' (the war, according to him, should have been launched in September 1938).

He declares that the reason why he chose to wage war against Stalin was, first of all, because the latter was preparing to attack him and, secondly, to compel England to acknowledge Germany's predominance over the European continent. He expresses his belief that had the English acquired the conviction that there no longer was a power in Europe capable of preventing him from implementing his own policy, they would have agreed to sign a 'white peace' with the Reich. He says:

> I made up my mind to seal Russia's fate as soon as I surrendered to the conviction that England would stubbornly refuse to make peace with us. (26th February, 1945)

In order to attain this objective, one had to take the initiative:

> The idea of a defensive war against the Russians was simply untenable.

Hitler retained the greatest respect for the Japanese. He stated that the future Germany would have to seek its friends among the Chinese, the Japanese and the Arabs. By contrast, he blamed himself for his own Anglophilia and his 'illusions' regarding Latin peoples.

With regard to the English, what he says is that he had underestimated the power which the 'Jewish domination' held over them. He declares:

> Whatever this war's outcome, we can prophesy the end of the British Empire, for it has been mortally wounded. The fate of the British people is to die of hunger and tuberculosis on that cursed island of theirs.

He expresses his belief that Italy had actually got in Germany's way almost everywhere and that it would have been preferable if it had not become involved in the global conflict at all. Furthermore, he specifies that the war against the USSR had been intended to commence in the spring of 1941, so as to end in autumn, and that it was the intervention of the Italian army in Greece, which Germany had not been informed of, that had caused the former to be delayed. Mussolini's Greek undertaking had been a disaster, for it led to the Yugoslavian about-turn, which then resulted in the establishment of a state of war in the Balkans, a state which the Germans had specifically wanted to avoid. As a result, the British sent a military expedition, and Hitler was compelled to rush to his ally's aid and was thus robbed of the possibility to implement the *Blitzkrieg* tactic he had planned against Stalin. Because of this, the German army found itself trapped in the dreadful Russian winter, which marked the beginning of the end. The entire war is thus said to have played out in the space of a few weeks.

Hitler also reproaches the Italians for having prevented him from playing the decolonisation card in the Mediterranean and from practicing a policy of anti-imperialistic alliance with Islam.

Regarding France, he considers his policy to have been completely wrong. He says:

> Our duty was to liberate the working class and assist French workers in accomplishing their revolution. We should have jostled the fossil-like bourgeoisie out of the way, a bourgeoisie that is as devoid of a soul as it is of patriotism. [...] By not liberating the French proletariat already in 1940, we have failed to do our duty and to recognise our own interests.
>
> The same is true of our failure to liberate the French protégés in overseas regions. The French people would certainly not have held it against us if we had relieved them of the burden of the Empire. In this domain, the people of this country have always manifested more common sense than its alleged elites and are more endowed with the genuine instinct of the nation than the latter. Under both Louis XV and Jules Ferry, the French people rebelled against the absurdity of colonial undertaking. To my knowledge, Napoleon did not become unpopular for having rid himself of Louisiana. What is incredible, by contrast, is the disaffection which his incapable nephew brought upon himself by going to war in Mexico. (15th February, 1945)

Last but not least, Hitler gives a depiction of what will, in his view, become of the world once he is gone:

> In the event that the Reich is defeated, and in anticipation of the rise of Asian, African and perhaps even South American nationalisms, only two powers capable of legitimately confronting each other shall remain in the world — the United States and the USSR. The laws of history and geography condemn these two powers to be the adversaries of Europe. Both of these powers will necessarily be driven by the more or less short-term desire to ensure the support of the sole great European people that shall subsist after the war — the German people. I loudly proclaim that under no circumstances must the Germans agree to play the part of a pawn in the American or Russian game.

He then goes on to add:

> It is very hard to specify, at this very moment, what could be more pernicious for us on the ideological level — Jew-controlled Americanism or Bolshevism. Under the weight of the events, the Russians may indeed rid themselves completely of Jewish Marxism and henceforth only embody eternal Pan-Slavism[167] in its most ferocious and most savage form.
>
> As for the Americans, if they do not succeed in freeing themselves from the yoke of New York Jews, they shall soon decline, without even having attained the age of reason. The fact that they combine such material power with such mental lability is reminiscent of a child stricken with gigantism. One could indeed wonder whether their civilisation is not mushroom-like, destined to come undone just as rapidly as it took shape.

TO SHED A SECRET TEAR

> If we are to be vanquished in this war, it is only a total defeat that we could suffer. Indeed, our adversaries have proclaimed their objectives far and wide, thus allowing us to understand that we must harbour no illusions with regard to their intentions. [...] This is a most cruel thought. It is with horror that I imagine our Reich being torn apart by the victors, as our populations are left at the mercy of the savage Bolsheviks and the American gangsters and are subjected to their excesses. This prospect does not, however, rob me of my unshakable faith in the future of the German people. The more we are made to suffer, the more resounding

[167] TN: Pan-Slavism is a political and cultural movement which initially emphasised the cultural ties between Slavic peoples but was later associated with Russian expansionism. Prevalent in the 19th century, its adherents believed that their lineal and linguistic ties should bring about a union of all Slavs. The term itself is said to have been originally coined by Slovak J. Herkel in his linguistic treatise of 1826.

the resurrection of the eternal Germany. The specificity of the German soul that allows it to enter a state of lethargy whenever its affirmation threatens the very existence of the nation shall one again be of use to us; but I, personally, would find it unbearable to live in the transitional Germany that would succeed our defeated Third Reich.

HITLER, 2nd April, 1945

Less than a month later, on 30th April, 1945, the fifty-six-year-old Reich chancellor, who had only just got married on the previous day, takes his own life amidst an apocalyptic sort of atmosphere. In his *Mémoires de guerre*[168] (Volume 3: *Le salut, 1944–46.*[169] Plon, 1959), General de Gaulle remarks that 'it was suicide, not treason, that put an end to his undertaking'. He then adds:

Seduced to its very core, Germany followed its Führer in a single surge, submitting to him all the way to the end — a gun crew member exerting more effort for his leader than any other people had ever done before.

And here is his conclusion:

Hitler's undertaking, which he upheld without respite, was both superhuman and inhuman. Until the final hours of agony inside his Berlin bunker, he remained undisputed, inflexible and merciless, just as he had been in his glory days. In honour of the sombre grandeur of his struggle and memory, he had chosen never to hesitate, compromise or retreat, for the Titan that strives to lift the world could never falter nor grow soft. Vanquished and crushed, however, he may have reverted to a human state, just to shed a secret tear as everything came to an end.

Hitler, an essay by Joachim Fest (2 volumes). Gallimard, 526 and 541 pages respectively.
Adolf Hitler: Legende, Mythos, Wirklichkeit, an essay by Werner Maser. Plon, 510 pages.

Werner Maser, who has dedicated himself to the study of National Socialism since 1949, published in 1977 a large dossier on the Nuremberg Trials entitled *Nürnberg — Tribunal der Sieger*[170] (Econ, Düsseldorf). The book was simultaneously released in England through

168 TN: War Memoirs.

169 TN: Salvation, 1944–46.

170 TN: Nuremberg — The Victor's Tribunal.

Penguin Books. Two further essays by the same author came out in France: *Naissance du Parti national-socialiste allemand*[171] (Fayard, 1967) and *Hitler inédit*[172] (Albin Michel, 1975).

Regarding Dietrich Eckart, see Alfred Rosenberg's *Dietrich Eckart. Ein Vermächtnis*[173] (Zentralverlag der NSDAP, Franz Eher Nachf., Munich, 1937), Margarete Plewnia's *Auf dem Weg zu Hitler. Der "völkische" Publizist Dietrich Eckart*[174] (Schünemanns Universitätsverlag, Bremen, 1970), and William Gillespie's *Dietrich Eckart* (Houston, 1975–76).

THE PATH OF ETERNITY

A BUDDHIST PRIEST AND A professor at the Imperial University, Reverend Shinshō Hanayama was, from 1945 to 1948, the chaplain of the Japanese military leaders condemned by the International Tribunal for the Far East and imprisoned at the Sugamo penitentiary centre. He writes:

> In those days, whenever a Japanese person heard someone utter the name of Sugamo, they were overcome with profound sadness. For they all viewed Sugamo (with the gibbets on one side and the prison on the other) as a theatre stage on which the tragedy of life and death, in all of its permanent horror, was regularly performed.

Hanayama initiated the condemned into the principles of Buddhism and supported them in the final moments of their lives. It is his chronicle of the period which he revives, in a most vivid fashion, in *La voie de l'éternité*.[175]

THE TOKYO TRIAL

According to the translator, Mr Pierre Pascal, what Hanayama presents in this book, which was published a few years ago in Italy, is an account of 'the manner in which the defeated awaited their own deaths by penning poetry and alternating various prayers, before finally marching towards an ordeal that would, at long last, allow them to die for their country and, in accordance with

171 TN: The Birth of German National Socialism.

172 TN: The Unpublished Words of Hitler.

173 TN: Dietrich Eckart — A Legacy.

174 TN: Towards Hitler. The 'Völkisch' Publicist Dietrich Eckart.

175 TN: *La voie de l'éternité*, or 'The Path of Eternity', seems to be the French title of Hanayama's *Way of Deliverance*.

their own faith, enable them to exit the world so as to return to it as gods. In their godly form, they would then watch over the fate of their lineage, a lineage that stretched across several millennia'.

In his *Wartime Journals* (Albin Michel), Charles A. Lindbergh recounts how he discovered, while on a mission to the Pacific in December 1943, that the Japanese men who were taken alive were executed with a bullet to the back of the neck and then decapitated with a dagger. Smoked or marinated in whiskey, the severed heads became an exportation item and were sold in the USA as 'souvenirs', he says.

On 9th March, 1945, a major aerial raid against Tokyo leaves more than 200,000 fatal casualties in its wake. Then, in early August, atomic bombs are dropped on Hiroshima and Nagasaki, with a respective death toll of 86,000 and 38,000 victims.

On the 15th of August, the Japanese rise to their feet as they listen to the radio — Emperor Hirohito announces his decision to surrender. The next day, Admiral Onishi eviscerates himself. In a testament calligraphed on silk paper, he writes the following:

> Life must be taken seriously. Even in defeat, our youths must be proud of being Japanese. Our children are our country's treasure.

Following his example, thousands of officers and soldiers commit seppuku (hara-kiri). What would life be worth if it no longer matched its purpose, they ask?

Organised by the Americans on 3rd May, 1946 and 12th November, 1948, the 'Tokyo Trial' results in a total of seven Japanese leaders being condemned to death, with an additional eighteen given prison sentences. All in all, 5,000 Japanese men are judged by tribunals established in Japan, Singapore and elsewhere. Around 9,000 of them would be executed.

The charges brought forth by the Allies entail the relinquishment of the old principle guaranteeing the non-retroactivity of laws: *Nullum crimen sine lege*.[176] Some of the accused are reproached for having violated the Portsmouth Treaty of 1905[177] and the Japanese-American Agreement of 1908.[178]

The acts of the 'Tokyo Trial' are found in the national archives of Washington and have never been disclosed.

Hanayama had to assist forty men who had been condemned to death. The main ones were Hideki Tojo, the sixty-four-year-old head of the Japanese government from 1941 to 1944; Kōki Hirota, who had acted as prime minister in 1936; Iwane Matsui, the seventy-one-year-old former ambassador to Moscow and the supreme commander in Central China from 1928 to 1938; fifty-seven-year-old Akira Muto, the head of the Operational Office at the War Ministry; sixty-year-old Heitaro Kimura, the supreme commander of the Japanese troops in Burma; Kenji Doihara, nicknamed 'Lawrence of Manchuria'; and sixty-four-year-old Seishiro Itagaki, the former Minister of War responsible for military operations in Korea, Manchuria and Singapore. They were all hanged.

Whatever side they belonged to, those sentenced to death for political reasons have always had the courage to face the gallows or the rifles that were raised against them. The undaunted serenity displayed by the Japanese leaders has, however, gone beyond anything one could ever have imagined.

---

176 TN: *Nulla poena* — or *Nullum crimen* — *sine lege* is Latin for 'There is no penalty, or crime, without a law'. It is a legal principle that states that one cannot be punished for doing something that was not, at the time of one's actions, prohibited by law.

177 TN: The Treaty of Portsmouth marked the official end of the 1904–1905 Russian-Japanese War. It was signed on 5th September, 1905.

178 TN: This seems to be a reference to the Root–Takahira Agreement between the United States and the Empire of Japan. Signed on 30th November, 1908, the agreement comprised an official recognition of the territorial status quo as of November 1908, an affirmation of the independence and territorial integrity of China, the maintenance of free trade and equal commercial opportunities, the Japanese recognition of the American annexation of the Kingdom of Hawaii and the Philippines and the American recognition of Japan's position in northeast China.

YUKIO MISHIMA'S MEMORY

During their detention, the condemned wrote poems — *haikus*[179] and *tankas*.[180] What supreme luxury it is for one to even-heartedly celebrate the fragility of flowers and the beauty of clouds a mere few hours before plunging into the void. Here is an example of *haiku*, one by the ineffable Matsuo Bashō:

> You must not surmise
> When faced with lightning-torn skies
> That time in vain flies

On his part, twenty-nine-year-old Captain Kaichi Hirate writes:

> And why should I torment myself? The world is no more than a dewdrop upon the surface of a bellflower.

And here are Sergeant Masakatsu Hozumi's words:

> When I cross the yellow current, what I would like to do is to turn the chaplet that I am wearing into a thousand dewdrops upon a thousand blades of grass.

Prior to his death, Iwane Matsui confided in his family:

> I have exposed Japan to the shame of defeat. It is thus entirely natural that I should make honourable amends for it with my own life.

Only one of the condemned was executed by firing squad: fifty-five-year-old Colonel Satoshi Oiye, the former commander of the garrison stationed on Negros Island. He writes:

> I was able to lead a perfectly happy life. I only blush with shame for not having rendered my Emperor anything but the meagrest services.

On 22nd December, 1948, General Akira Muto declares: 'My impression of the entire situation is that it concerns someone else, not myself'. In response, his wife uses a *tanka*:

> How I love to hear

179 TN: A Japanese poem of seventeen syllables, in three lines of five, seven, and five.

180 TN: A Japanese poem in thirty-one syllables, divided into five lines of five, seven, five, seven and seven.

the beautiful words spoken
by those unbroken — for a warrior knows no fear
even when his death is near!

Shortly before the Japanese capitulation, Hideki Tojo, who replaced Prince Konoye at the head of the imperial government, visited a doctor so as to have his chest marked with the point corresponding to his heart's location. On 11th September, 1945, he attempted to commit suicide as he was about to be arrested. The bullet did not end his life. In Sugamo, he was the sole prisoner to move about in shackles. His final poem states:

The sun and the moon are no more
than flickering fireflies,
Next to Amida's splendour,
lighting the path before my eyes.

'"War criminals" were the genuine embodiment of Japanese nationalism', Hanayama states. 'It was thus natural to suppose that they would die in harmony with the often-quoted words of old: "Seven times shall I reincarnate and seven times shall I offer my lives to the fatherland"'. Indeed, all of them took their leave of life 'not with love, but with gratitude' (Nietzsche), undoubtedly whispering the (pass)word 'ketsubetsu', which evokes both eternal separation and the courteous exchange of the very same bowl of pure water.

The American authorities refused to tell the families where the bodies had been put. The ashes of the execution victims were scattered to the wind of their native country.

A few months later, the executioner met his own demise through electrocution, having touched a high-voltage cable.

One can only comprehend the Japanese military ethic by connecting it to a certain conception of honour. Quoting a samurai precept, Montherlant once said:

One must, at all times, keep one's promise, even when the latter has been given to a dog.

As for Spengler, he specified the following:

> Honour is a matter of blood, not intelligence. If one needs to ponder its essence, it is because one has none.

During the last war, 4,600 kamikazes, most of whom were married and had children of their own, chose to revive the spirit of the samurai, according to which 'loyalty is greater than fire'. Their names are inscribed upon the rice paper rolls kept in Kannonji Temple, Tokyo.

At the end of the above-mentioned book, Mr Pierre Pascal evokes the memory of Japanese author Yukio Mishima, who took his own life in public on 25th November, 1970, on the very spot where the Tokyo Trial had previously been held. He did so because he could no longer bear to live in an age when the notion of fatherland had lost all meaning.

A few moments before killing himself, Mishima wrote the following lines: 'Within the narrowness of human life, I choose the path of eternity'. Hence the book's title.

His death inspired Mr Pierre Pascal to write a *haiku*:

> Northwards you must sweep!
> Winds shall sow your revolt deep — the harvests we'll reap!

The translator of several books by Julius Evola and the author of new editions of the Apocalypse and Omar Khayyam's *Rubaiyat* (éd. Du coeur fidèle, Rome), Mr Pierre Pascal is a western man of letters and a 'Japanese poet'. He has peppered Reverend Hanayama's account with a host of remarks and commentaries through which he enlightens the readers and takes position himself. He writes:

> To read and understand how honourable, vanquished men crossed the threshold of Eternity shall, for a brief moment, comfort many a profane soul. In this book, the last connoisseurs of stoicism shall find what they still dare seek.

At the naval base of Yokosuka, people still recite the following old saying:

> Duty is heavier than a mountain, and death lighter than a feather.

The Way of Deliverance: Three Years with the Condemned Japanese War Criminals, an account by Shinshō Hanayama. Guy Le Prat (5 rue des Grands-Augustins, 75006 Paris, France), 308 pages.

THE ETERNAL JAPAN

THE JAPANESE EXAMPLE APPEARS TO disprove Kipling's[181] following words: 'East is East, West is West, and the two will never meet.'

Indeed, Japan belongs neither to the West nor to the East. It is simply Japan — no more, no less.

In 1867, seventeen-year-old Meiji (Mutsu-Hito) ascends to the imperial throne in the Land of the Rising Sun. Europe discovers a world that had lived in isolation for an entire millennium, a world whose historical development, however, still displayed astounding similarities to its own.

The Japanese Middle Ages resemble the West's feudal period. The civil wars that smeared it with blood are reminiscent of the rivalries between the great French, German and Italian feudatories. The shogun generalissimos, the true holders of authority, played an analogous role to that of Merovingian 'palace mayors'.

The samurai era goes back to around 1160 AD, at a time when the Tairas and the Minamotos waged a merciless war against each other. Armed with daggers and short swords and covered in iron just like our knights, the samurai despise death. They progress towards the end of their tragic destiny and abide by an old motto — honour and loyalty.

The aristocratic spirit survives in Japan through a taste for geste and a sense for the *useless*, a virtue that lies beyond good and evil and considers the question of 'reason' — i.e. 'what purpose does it all serve?' — to be meaningless. The art of serving tea in five gestures and six expressions is still taught in schools, as is the art of gardening, wrapping and flower arrangement in bouquets. In the tea ceremony, the hand fan serves no purpose whatsoever yet is never forgotten.

To the Japanese, the centre of man's sensibility is not located in his brain but in his entrails. And that is where the short sword of any man who takes his

[181] TN: Born in India, Joseph Rudyard Kipling (30th December, 1865–18th January, 1936) was an English journalist, short-story author, poet, and novelist. He was, in fact, one of the most popular writers in the British Empire, in both prose and verse, in the late-19th and early-20th centuries.

own life through seppuku (hara-kiri) is plunged. This conception of suicide is reminiscent of both European antiquity and the Stoics.

In *Japan und die Japaner*[182] (Payot, 1937), Karl Haushofer[183] writes:

> The sacrifice made by a person in the name of a great principle, the state or the family is facilitated far more in a culture centred around an ancestral cult than in such a culture as ours, in which the individual plays the main role.

Author Yukio Mishima was once asked if he was faithful to his wife:

> I am faithful to her because I am convinced that therein lies the means to preserve her beauty. It is certainly not a means to render her wiser, however.

The warrior who commits *seppuku* will not even be given access to some sort of Valhalla. He will have lost everything; save for his honour.

Self-domination prevails in Japan. The soul's movements abide by carefully preestablished rules, and the Japanese language is poor in insults and swear words. As for politeness, it may seem exaggerated, yet it is permeated neither by embellishments nor metaphors. Poetry, which holds a prominent position not only in the literature but also the social life of the entire Far East, is of a purely descriptive nature and does not exude any idealism. It was not such a long time ago when young girls still had to beg the needles they had broken for forgiveness.

The most beautiful sort of elegance lies in suffering with a grin on one's face — when announcing the passing of someone close, for instance. This tactfulness with regard to death is summarised in this *haiku* penned by Matsuo Bashō:

> The sun has now dried
> the tiny kimono sleeves
> of the child that died.

---

182 TN: Japan and the Japanese.

183 TN: Karl Ernst Haushofer (27th August, 1869–10th March, 1946) was a German general, geographer and politician. Through his student Rudolf Hess, Haushofer's ideas impacted the development of Adolf Hitler's expansionist strategies, although Haushofer himself rejected any direct influence on the Nazi regime.

In this regard, what springs to mind is a film depicting the battle of Waterloo in which Wellington, upon being informed of a friend's death, simply says: 'Sad, is it not?'. It is his expression that tells the whole story.

The Japanese climate is characterised by its sleep-inducing mildness. Devastating catastrophes do, however, occur — whether tidal waves, cyclones, or earthquakes. Similarly, within the profoundly introverted temperament of the Japanese, the smiles and courteous bowing sometimes make way for sudden outbursts of violence. Political assassinations are as frequent in Japan as the common manners are refined. And the Americans are far from having forgotten about Pearl Harbour — it is said that on that day, the myth of *Mlle Chrysanthème*[184] suddenly collapsed. Mr Haushofer notes:

> The dualism pervading Japan's cultural history is expressed in this very manner, in the antithesis between a harmonious rhythm and the catastrophic disturbances arising from its territorial conditions.

Things are the same in Germany, where *furor teutonicus*[185] goes hand in hand with *Gemütlichkeit*.[186] This clearly accounts for certain affinities. In both Bonn and Tokyo, defeat + austerity = 'economic miracle'. Indeed, the Japanese have always been considered the 'Prussians of Asia'.

There are, however, no 'miracles' in economy. All that there is are cause-and-effect relationships. Just like all other Japanese achievements, the results recorded by the famous Ministry of International Trade and Industry (MITI) must, above all else, be regarded as the consequence of a certain mental structure, of a mentality (one must not, for instance, be surprised at the fact that the felt pen was invented in a land where writing is the mother of all arts).

---

184 TN: *Madame Chrysanthème* is a novel by Pierre Loti, presented as the autobiographical journal of a naval officer temporarily married to a Japanese woman while stationed in Nagasaki, Japan. It has been considered a crucial text in shaping western attitudes toward Japan at the turn of the 20th century.

185 TN: *Furor Teutonicus* ('Teutonic Fury') is a Latin phrase referring to the proverbial ferocity of the Teutones or, more generally, the Germanic tribes of the Roman Empire period.

186 TN: Friendliness.

THE BIRTH OF THE JAPANESE PEOPLE

Where do the Japanese come from, then? There are none who know. During the prehistoric period (*Jomon*), Japan was solely inhabited by the Ainu people. Their name means 'Men of the Bow' (the word 'Ainos' is a derisive nickname meaning 'son of a dog' in Japanese. Indeed, according to legend, the Ainu people are said to have stemmed from the mating of a Japanese princess and a dog). Their physical chatacteristics — including their wavy black hair, matt white skin, the absence of a Mongolian fold, dolichocephaly, a straight or concave nose, and so on — are proof of their belonging to the 'Caucasian' racial group. Mr George Montadon[187] writes that the Ainu people's massive build 'has turned them into an ideal representation of how one might imagine the least evolved descendant of a Palaeolithic primitive Europid' (*La civilisation aïnou et les cultures arctiques.*[188] Payot, 1937).

Other authors such as Renato Biasutti view the Ainu people as the descendants of a large and primitive Australo-Caucasoid group, one that allegedly gave birth to the Polynesians, the Ainu people and proto-Europeans.

The Japanese in the strict sense of the word only arrived at a much later point, surfacing in the central part of Japan during the 3rd century BC. From an ethnic perspective, they comprise a certain Mongoloid element which, in all likelihood, intermixed with Chinese and Korean genetic components, in addition to a Malay element resulting, in turn, from a crossbreeding of Mongoloid, Indonesian Europid and Melanesian Negrito groups.

The Ainu people were gradually subjugated by the Yamato race, as part of a process that is rather reminiscent of the manner in which the Wends and other western Slavic tribes were absorbed by German settlers. Today, these 'barbarians' do not comprise more than 100,000 people scattered across Yeso island, the Kurile islands and the north of Hokkaido. They can, however, be traced using toponymy.

Beginning in the 7th century AD, the Japanese population lived in complete isolation (after borrowing its writing notions, statal structures and a part of its philosophy from China). What resulted from this isolation was a

---

187 TN: George-Alexis Montadon (19th April, 1879–3rd or 30th August, 1944) was a Swiss-French doctor, anthropologist and explorer known for his racialist and antisemitic views and theories.

188 TN: The Ainu Civilisation and the Arctic Cultures.

remarkable sort of ethnic homogeneity, despite the population's mixed origin. In this regard, this is what Montadon wrote in 1933:

> The value of the Japanese somatic group is a future value rather than a past one. Shaped by various contributions (Ainu, Tunguzian, North-Mongolian, Chinese and Indonesian), it is a type that remains in formation and will only assert itself in future. (*La race, les races*[189]. Payot)

GROUP PSYCHOLOGY

Percival Lowell[190] once stated that impersonality is the very soul of the Far East — in Japan, the word 'individual' has a privative meaning. This impersonality is, however, of the active kind. Mr Raymond Charles writes:

> No national morality has ever surpassed the Japanese one in its glorification of energy. Driven to the point of sacrifice, the tenacity of one's efforts is considered, in itself, inspiringly pure. And what this virtue of ideals does on a practical level is polarise and concentrate to the desired degree the determination and self-sacrifice of an entire people.

Japanese psychology is group psychology. Business is dealt with by several people at once, and it is sometimes very hard to determine who the decision-makers actually are. Although this uniformity tends to trouble the European mind, it also accounts for how easily and quickly the Japanese adapt to new situations. The Meiji era is an example of this — back then, the entire Japanese people broke with a certain part of their past in a most disciplined fashion and without any regret.

A bus stops at the *Avenue de l'Opéra* in Paris; thirty Japanese tourists get off, dressed in white shirts and black jackets and carrying cameras in their sling bags. They enter a shop and check out a few shelves. A short dialogue and quick debate ensue, after which they all leave the shop with the very same purchased item.

On 26th January, 1948, a man appeared in a branch of the Imperial Bank (*Teikoku Ginkō*) in Tokyo, claiming to be an employee of the Ministry of

---

189 TN: Race and Races.

190 TN: Percival Lawrence Lowell (13th March, 1855–12th November, 1916) was an American businessman, author, mathematician, and astronomer who fueled speculation that there were canals on Mars.

Public Health. Having asked the manager to gather his staff, he gave each of them a cup and made them take 'an anti-dysentery vaccine'. He specified that it was necessary to swallow the liquid quickly, 'because the product blackens the teeth'. Sixteen employees, in addition to the manager, emptied their cups in one gulp. No sooner had they done so than they fell to the floor — the potion actually contained potassium cyanide. The murderer then took money from the cash register and calmly left the premises.

In Japanese companies, decisions always meet three basic criteria: they all require a certain amount of time before they can be taken; they are virtually never made by one single person; no one can be blamed for a mistake that occurs in the decision-making process.

One begins by eliminating all proposals likely to encounter strong opposition. Once a strategy has been chosen, meetings are held to clarify each person's position. The conclusions that are drawn give birth to a written project, which is then submitted to each department manager for approval before being presented to the board of directors.

Such a procedure is only possible because the risk of having someone block the project is precluded, with the people involved preferring to make concessions whenever a compromise allows them to reach a decision more easily (the exercise of democracy requires the relative mental homogeneity of all participants, as well as a spontaneous desire to give public interest priority over the triumph of one's personal opinion. In a heterogeneous society, or one in which the individualistic principle prevails, democracy is practically impossible).

With 18% of available incomes, net of tax (compared to 7% in the case of the USA), Japan enjoys the world's highest private savings rate. Social security, however, is entirely absent there, as are family benefits. And although paid leave is available, it is considered 'inappropriate' to make full use of it.

When a Japanese man introduces himself, he first points out his place of employment. He defines himself through his social activity, meaning through what he does *in life* rather than the sole fact of being alive. There are hardly any tramps in Japan, and tips are rarely given. A beggar is regarded as being unworthy of help, precisely *because* he begs in the street. In the past, samurais had every right to simply chop off a beggar's head.

Likewise, individual rights take a backseat to collective ones, and economic imperatives are in no way subordinate to social factors. Furthermore, increases in productivity are almost always superior to salary increases.

Until recent years, employment mobility and the circulation of elites were virtually inexistent in Japan. Today, one still joins a firm the way one previously entered a clan and, at a later point, the army. Desertions are inadmissible. Each major company has its own flag and anthem. Every morning, the following words are, for instance, sung before the entire staff at Matsushita:[191]

> Grow, industry, grow, grow, grow!
> Harmony and sincerity!
> Matsushita Electric.

Only when the anthem has been sung does everyone start working.

In feudal society, merchants were a necessary evil. Craftsmen, peasants and warriors gathered more public esteem than anyone else. At the beginning of the 20th century, the members of 400,000 samurai families found themselves compelled to seek new ways of earning their living and turned to commerce and the industry. They thus infused the latter with the qualities and values of their own caste. This fact accounts for the *shushin-koyo*, the Japanese practice of *permanent employment*. Mr Hubert Brochier[192] states:

> New employees can be confident that they will not be dismissed unless they have made a particularly serious mistake or the company faces exceptional circumstances. They themselves will not, on the other hand, seek to leave their current company in order to find a better-paid job elsewhere. Such an ambition is, in fact, foreign to them and the very idea of gaining a personal advantage by moving from one company to another remains unfathomable to the average Japanese employee. (*Le miracle économique japonais.*[193] Calmann-Lévy, 1970)

The term *oya-ko*, meaning 'parents and children', applies to all relations within a Japanese business; it would, however, be too easy to speak of paternalism. Indeed, the hierarchical system is not founded on any kind of authoritarianism. Just like in a feudal contract, the absolute respect enjoyed by senior

191 TN: 'Matsushita Electric' is the former name of today's Panasonic Corporation.

192 TN: Hubert Brochier (1923–2017) was a French economist.

193 TN: The Japanese Economic Miracle.

members, managers and the elderly demands, in return, both benevolence and protection. Mr Brochier adds:

> The devotion displayed by workers is both the expression of a vital sort of solidarity and a reflection of the Japanese blind abnegation towards all the social groups that they belong to — the family, the clan, the village, or the national community.

In Japan, companies are in charge of some tasks which, in France, are assigned to various social organisms (and, in the US, to individual initiative). They thus provide dormitories and accommodation, medical equipment, hotels, holiday homes, general knowledge courses, music lessons, and flower arrangement courses. Further guarantees are only necessary in countries where ageing individuals are left to fend for themselves and thus find themselves threatened. In Japan, no one is left to take care of themselves, as the Japanese constitute one single whole.

Tokyo residents are crammed into flats whose average size ranges from thirty-five to forty square metres. This density is tolerated rather well. Whether in the household[194] or at work, the word 'crammed' lacks the unpleasant connotation given to it in the West. Japanese people are actually fond of human contact. In *Living Japan* (Doubleday & Co., New York, 1959), Donald Keene[195] reminds his readers that the word 'privacy' cannot be translated into Japanese.

In the past, what this lack of privacy fostered was 'private espionage'. 'Neighbourhood associations' used to serve as auxiliaries to the police force. As for Tokugawa Ieyasu,[196] this is what he decreed in the 16th century: 'Anything out of the ordinary must be reported to the authorities'.

Nowadays, information flow has become one of Japan's main assets. Books and newspapers enjoy record-breaking print runs, and the Japanese give out

---

194 TN: Alain de Benoist uses the word 'Ibashi' to refer to a Japanese household, but I have found no sources that would confirm this usage. The word seems to have a different meaning and is mostly rendered in English as 'tongs'. 'Ibasho', by contrast, means 'the place where one belongs'.

195 TN: Born on 18th June, 1922, Donald Lawrence Keene is an American-born Japanese scholar, historian, teacher, writer and translator of Japanese literature.

196 TN: Tokugawa Ieyasu (30th January, 1543–1st June, 1616) was the founder and first shōgun of the Tokugawa shogunate of Japan, which effectively ruled the country from the Battle of Sekigahara in 1600 until the Meiji Restoration in 1868.

their business cards all day long. Cities are built around railway stations and it is crossroads, rather than streets, that are given a name.

One encounters all these characteristic aspects of the Japanese mentality in the religions of the ancient Empire of the Rising Sun.

Shintoism is the most ancient and most authentic religion in Japan. It is a pagan cult involving the worship of one's ancestors and the spirits of the dead, who continue to dwell among the living. It justifies the Japanese taste for sacrifice and especially Japanese national pride. The goddess Amaterasu is not an abstract and impersonal divinity but actually Mikado's ancestor. Banned in 1945, the Shinto cult resurfaced more vigorously than ever upon the end of the Occupation.

Buddhism accessed Japan around the 6th century BC, having arrived from India through China and Korea. It did, however, undergo some profound transformations. After struggling against one another, the two cults merged. It is not unusual for someone to opt for a Buddhist burial rite despite having 'lived the Shinto way'.

Originally, Buddhism was a doctrine of renouncement. Indeed, according to Buddha, one is expected to kill any thirst for existence within oneself, thus attaining the state of Nirvana, which represents the annihilation of any and all personalised life. Such a conception is, to some extent, encountered in Japan, but was greatly modified by the bonze Nichiren,[197] who emphasised its ethical aspects — honesty, courage, and disinterest. It is not life itself that is bad, says Nichiren. It is, instead, man's spirit that must ceaselessly be remodelled ('What must be changed in man is the very structure of his desires').

The powerful *Soka Gakkai* sect and its party, the Komeito, have drawn their inspiration from this sort of 'protestant Buddhism'.

Having also originated from the continent, Confucianism has only influenced a certain number of educated people. It is rather a 'theory of good governance' based on an almost positivistic philosophy than a mere religion — what purpose does it serve for one to concern oneself with heavenly

---

197 TN: A bonze can be defined as a Japanese or Chinese Buddhist religious teacher. Nichiren (16th February, 1222–13th October, 1282) was a Japanese Buddhist priest who founded Nichiren Buddhism, a branch school of Mahayana Buddhism. He remains, to this day, a controversial figure among scholars, who regard him as either a fervent nationalist or a social reformer with a transnational religious vision.

matters, which one can never know anything about, when earthly matters are already so complex?

These doctrines have several common features. Each of them represents a morality devoid of both revelation and punishment. Stemming from the very same ancestors, divinities, men and nature are each other's kin, and it is through one's ancestors that one honours their lineage.

Even when displaying respect for nature, Europeans manifest the constant will to transform their own living space. Professor Louis Rougier[198] writes:

> The myth of Prometheus prefigures all of Western history. (*Le génie de l'Occident.*[199] Laffont, 1969)

Communing with nature as part of an almost sensual connection, the Far East is founded upon the ability to restrict certain temptations. Instead of dramatising the cycle of life, it surrenders to it and respects the world's autonomous will, which then fuels its own fulfilment.

The innate naturalism characterising Japanese people accounts for their indifference to metaphysics. Despite the efforts exerted by the missions and all the means that the latter had at their disposal, Christians represent a mere 0.4% of the Japanese population.

In 1905, Félicien Challaye wrote:

> The Christian ideas which the Japanese mind regards as most repugnant are those of original sin and eternal punishment. The Japanese cannot acknowledge nature to be essentially bad. Already in the seventeenth century, they objected to Saint Francis Xavier's[200] words, using statements such as this: "Either God chose to create hell and is thus not merciful in any way, or he could not help creating it and is therefore not almighty". It seems that such objections were a source of great embarrassment to the first Christian missionaries. (*Au Japon et en Extrême-Orient,*[201] Armand-Colin)

---

198 TN: Louis Auguste Paul Rougier (10th April, 1889–14th October, 1982) was a French philosopher who made numerous significant contributions to epistemology, the philosophy of science, political philosophy and the history of Christianity.

199 TN: The Ingeniousness of the West.

200 TN: Francis Xavier, S.J. (7th April, 1506–3rd December, 1552), was a Navarrese Basque Roman Catholic missionary and a co-founder of the Society of Jesus. He was also the first Christian missionary to travel to Japan, Borneo, the Maluku Islands, and other areas.

201 TN: In Japan and the Far East.

The doctrine of individual salvation is just as perplexing to them. How could a Japanese person ever imagine that they would, all on their own, gain access to eternal life, with their ancestors — whose very flesh and blood they embody and who live on inside them and never leave their hearts — perhaps facing eternal damnation?

EVERYTHING HAS REPERCUSSIONS ON EVERYTHING ELSE

The principle of contradiction takes on a special sort of significance in the Far East. In order to comprehend this, one must consider the example of Taoism, the Chinese popular form of worship.

The Chinese concept of *Tao*, which is summarily translated as 'nature', has sometimes been likened to the Indo-Aryan *prakriti* and the Germanic *sköp*, concepts which, in fact, relate to the immanent basis of all that exists, to the cosmic forces of becoming and destiny. Another parallel between *Tao*, *Brahman* and *Logos* was drawn by Rudolf Otto[202] (in *Das Gefühl des Ueberwertlichen*,[203] 1932). All these words are connected to the idea of cosmic sequencing (*rta*, *asha*, *orlog*) encountered in the notion of *Tao*.

In Taoism, all things are connected and *cannot be separated from one another*. No boundary could ever be established between existence and non-existence, nor between the useful and the harmful or life and death. I could dream that I am a butterfly and then wake up and find that I am Zhuang Zhu.[204] But who, or what, am I really? Zhuang Zhu dreaming of being a butterfly or a

---

202 TN: Rudolf Otto (25th September, 1869–6th March, 1937) was an eminent German Lutheran theologian, philosopher, and comparative religionist. He is regarded as one of the most influential scholars of religion in the early-20th century and is best known for his concept of the numinous, a profound emotional experience he argued was at the heart of the world's religions. His most famous work, *The Idea of the Holy*, was first published in German in 1917 as *Das Heilige — Über das Irrationale in der Idee des Göttlichen und sein Verhältnis zum Rationalen*.

203 TN: The Feeling of Transcendence.

204 TN: Zhuang Zhu was an influential Chinese philosopher who lived around the 4th century BC, during the Warring States period, which corresponded to the peak of Chinese philosophy, i.e. the *Hundred Schools of Thought*. He is credited with writing — either in part or in whole — a work known by his name, the *Zhuangzi*, considered one of the essential texts of Taoism.

butterfly imagining itself to be Zhuang Zhu? The precept abided by here is that of 'obscuring the obscure'.

Lao Tzu[205] never conceived the idea of *law*, but solely that of its *model*. He never reasoned through *deduction*, only by *analogy*. In his famous work on *Chinese Thought* (Albin Michel, 1934), Marcel Granet[206] writes:

> When a philosopher undertakes to explain the invention of the wheel, he asserts that the idea itself was provided by the whirling seeds of the air. Dismissing mechanical explanations, Chinese thought does not seek to implement itself in the domain of movement and quantity. Instead, it confines itself most obstinately to a world of symbols, a world which it refuses to distinguish from the real universe.

Their entire social and military life is thus governed by such analogies. During the feudal period, the suzerain received his vassals as he stood upon a south-facing platform; 'for the South is akin to the sky, and therefore to what is high' (Granet). In the household, 'the wife spreads her mat across the corner where the grain, harvested in autumn and stored along the west side, is kept. She borrows the grain's fertility and offers her own in return'. During the summer, the left and front are considered *yang*, whereas the back and the right are *yin*. A fish served to a guest must have its belly turned rightwards in winter, leftwards in summer, etc.

In *The Decline of the West* (Gallimard, 1949), Oswald Spengler contrasts the all-natural and 'landscape'-based Taoist soul of traditional China with the entirely artificial and 'architectonic' Egyptian one. Furthermore, he demonstrates the fact that this acute sense of 'natural order' is not accompanied by a Promethean or Faustian will to act upon the world and transform it, as is the case in the West. He writes:

> The Chinaman wanders through his world; consequently, he is conducted to his god or his ancestral tomb not by ravines of stone, between faultless smooth walls,

205 TN: Lao Tzu was an ancient Chinese philosopher and writer who is regarded as a deity in religious Taoism and traditional Chinese religions. The founder of philosophical Taoism, he is believed to have authored the *Tao Te Ching*.

206 TN: Marcel Granet (29th February, 1884–25th November. 1940) was a French sociologist, ethnologist and sinologist. As a follower of Émile Durkheim and Édouard Chavannes, Granet was one of the first to bring sociological methods to the study of China.

> but by friendly Nature herself. Nowhere else has the landscape become so genuinely the material of the architecture.

By means of analysis and synthesis, the European man has mastered the art of grasping the unity of a concept through a series of particular cases, the invariance of a relation within a sequence of transformations, or the permanence of a structure. He formulates general laws on the basis of relative observations. He has, to use the words of Philolaus,[207] the ability to seek out 'the unity of the multiple and the harmony of disharmony'. The Near East, by contrast, aspires to reduction, to Being, to the Unique. As for the Far East, it exists within a perpetually changing and overdriven universe, whose every aspect is equivalent to the next. Nothing is separate from anything else, and everything has repercussions on everything else. One thus cannot look for the cause of a certain event at the sole level where this event took place. The idea of an efficacious and complete sort of Order engulfs both the notion of category and that of causality.

Where the Western mind perceives a succession of phenomena forming a single process, the Far East only detects aspectual alternations. And whenever it considers two of these aspects to be connected, it is not in terms of cause and effect but in the shape of naturally 'paired' elements — sound and echo, forwards and backwards, shadow and light. *Yin* and *yang* are not in contrast with each other the way Being and non-Being or the positive and the negative are (pursuant to the classical principle of contradiction which states that the same concept cannot simultaneously be defined, from the same perspective and in the same regard, as A and non-A). For they are 'paired'; they 'melt into one another' (*Cheng*). The principle of the harmony of contrasts (*Ho* signifies harmonic union) replaces the classical contradiction principle; one thus understands the influence exerted by Mao Zedong through the dialectical idea of a reconciliation of opposites.

The *Tao* has hardly had any direct impact upon the Japanese, yet one does come across a weakening of the contradiction principle in Japan.

---

207 TN: Philolaus (c. 470 BC — c. 385 BC) was a Greek Pythagorean and pre-Socratic philosopher who argued that what lies at the very foundation of everything is the part played by the limiting and the limitless, which combine together in harmony. Philolaus is also credited with having been the first to advocate the theory that the Earth was not the centre of the Universe.

Although very different in our eyes, public and private life do not contrast with one another in Japan, just as the cities, which abound in flowers, are not at variance with the countryside. One can separate neither forward movement from backward movement nor time from space. So as to point out the way that allows one to reach a place, the Japanese actually begin with the destination; and in the streets, houses are not numbered in accordance with their logical order of succession but according to the order in which they were constructed.

The Japanese language, which belongs to the Ural-Altaic family, is an agglutinative language devoid of flexion. The notions of gender, number and person are foreign to it. Rarely does it distinguish between the singular and the plural and only offers ambiguous possibilities when it comes to conjugating verbs. Alongside a 'certain' tense generally known as the 'present' and an 'uncertain' one often referred to as the 'future', it no longer includes more than a single past tense, one which, during the 20th century, replaced other, more ancient forms of 'close', 'middle' and 'distant' past, etc.

THE OLYMPIAD OF INDUSTRIAL PRODUCTION

Illogicality and rationality; hyper-effectiveness and a pronounced taste for the useless; 'communist capitalism': what Japan calls for at any given moment are the most contradictory qualifiers. Lafcadio Hearn, an American author of the early-20th century, once said:

> When, after several years, you notice that you are completely unable to understand the Japanese, that is when you begin to understand them a little.

Floating like motionless ships off the shore of an immense continent, the four main islands of the former Empire of Japan remained, for a thousand years, sheltered by their natural borders and the proud traditions of their inhabitants. Then, the Japanese rediscovered the world, as their ships changed direction, tacking towards one another.

Judo, the Japanese national sport, is the very foundation of Japanese physical and mental education. When forced to yield to the use of force, the Japanese did not respond as one does in boxing. They used the *jiu-jitsu* principle ('taking one step back') to give the enemy the impression of having prevailed, while simultaneously making sure that his own strength backfired against him; so as to beat him on his own turf, in other words.

Commodore Perry's ultimatum dates back to 1853. In 1865, Japan signs a treaty with the Americans. Two years later, Meiji promulgates a decennial reorganisation plan. Within a few months, all potential energies are transformed into active ones, as the country changes face. Upon Meiji's passing in 1912, Japan had already exited the age of the hand fan and entered that of battleships.

Less than a century later, Hiroshima faces a new ultimatum. A new retreat, a new change of direction. The Japanese leave the forces of the Axis to join the Anglo-Saxon *big brother*. Expansion, in any shape or form, is henceforth forbidden. Except for one, that is — economic expansion. They espouse the latter with equal vigour and a matching will, launching the GNP's Olympiad. In 1968, Takeo Fukuda, the Japanese Minister of Finance and future Minister of Foreign Affairs, declares:

> Let us put up with the noise and the filth. In twenty years' time, we shall be the richest nation in the world.

In 1966, futurologist Herman Kahn stated:

> The twenty-first century shall be a Japanese one.

There is also a certain European diplomat who declared some time ago that 'modern Japan is no more than a mistranslation'. What he meant to say was that the copy was in no way a decal. And right he was. It is as if Japan had only consented to relinquish some of its customs in the hope of acquiring the necessary means to preserve others. Félicien Challaye had already stated the following:

> It only borrowed from Europe that which makes European states both strong and independent, undergoing Europeanisation so as to better remain Japanese.

The issue at hand is that of finding out how much wealth per square kilometre a country can handle without undergoing moral change. The sirens of the consumerist society may yet turn out to be the loudest; unless, of course, Japan has managed to grow a kind of cherry flower that can resist our era's pollution.

Whatever the case, it is all too clear that the Japanese mentality is no export product at all.

Le Japon, monstre ou modèle?,[208] an essay by Jean-François Delassus. Hachette, 318 pages.
Le Japon au rendez-vous de l'Occident,[209] an essay by Raymond Charles. Laffont, 338 pages.
The Japanese Miracle and Peril, an essay by Willard Price. William Heinemann, London, 341 pages.
Japon, troisième Grand,[210] an essay by Robert Guillain. Seuil, 368 pages.
Bushidō, a compendium published by Nitobe Inazō. Sannō-Kai editions (Via S. Biagio 38, 35100 Padova, Italy), 264 pages.

CONFUCIUS

DISPLAYING A THIN AND GREY silhouette, emaciated features and thick eyebrows, Chinese Premier Zhou Enlai received Zambian President Kaunda on 25th February, 1974. He made the most of the occasion and highlighted 'the great and far-reaching historical significance' of a new campaign whose purpose was to 'prevent the renewal of capitalism', as well as to 'prolong and develop the movement centred around the criticism of Lin Biao[211] and the rectification of the land's working style'.

'Lin Biao and Confucius are both reactionary figures seeking to turn the wheel of history in a backward fashion', he specified.

Shortly afterwards, all of China's enemies, namely Lin Biao's supporters, 'Chiang Kai-shek's[212] clique', American imperialism and the 'new Soviet tsars', were reproached for being 'Confucianist'.

208 TN: Japan: Monster or Model?

209 TN: When Japan Meets the West.

210 TN: Japan — The Third Great One.

211 TN: Lin Biao (5th December, 1907–13th September, 1971) was a marshal of the People's Republic of China who was pivotal in the Communist victory in the Chinese Civil War, especially in Northeast China. His death is a subject of great controversy and intense speculation.

212 TN: Chiang Kai-Shek (31st October, 1887–5th April, 1975) was a politician and military leader who served as the leader of the Republic of China between 1928 and 1975, first in mainland

Upon meeting Alain Peyrefitte in Beijing in 1972, however, writer Kuo Mo-jo had previously declared:

> Nowadays, it is Mao Zedong's line of thought which enunciates the basic principles of both reasoning and life. And yet we have also preserved the Confucian values of old, which we continue to honour, or, to be more precise, are now beginning to honour once again.

In early February 1974, *The People's Daily* gave the following explanation:

> Lin Biao's political line was a revisionist and counter-revolutionary one, belonging to the far-right spectrum and striving towards both restoration and regression. To use its own words, it consisted in moderation and a return to the rites. Embracing moderation and returning to the rites was, however, a programme proposed by Confucius for the reestablishment of slavery; and Lin Biao regarded its implementation as his life's work.

The fact that they chose to connect the name of a philosopher who had passed away some twenty-five centuries earlier with that of Mao Zedong's former successor, who died under mysterious circumstances in 1973, is very surprising indeed. It also compelled observers to re-delve into China's ancient history.

During the 6th century BC, the Chu empire, which had been founded around 600 years earlier (at the height of the Bronze Age) by tribes that had come from the west, seemed to be in the throes of agony. Its leaders had reigned for five centuries, enjoying an undivided sort of power. Little by little, however, the empire had come apart and rival principalities were now striving to tear each other to pieces. Institutions were thus in a state of decline.

A FEUDAL SOCIETY

The Indo-European element was perhaps not entirely absent from this empire's formation and development, for some Indo-European tribes seem to have emigrated eastwards from Central Asia (Turkistan, the Iranian highlands or the Pamir region). Taking into account the results of the excavations conducted in 1924 by a Swede named Anderson, researchers such as H. Schmidt and O. Kümmel postulated the existence of a link between the Indo-European culture and the emerging Chinese one. Analogous conclusions were drawn

China and then in exile in Taiwan.

by F. von Richthofen (1877) in the field of astronomical knowledge and in the linguistic domain by Koppelmann (1928, 1933) and Güntert (1930).

One particularly stressed the role played by the Hia or Ta Hia tribes, who O. Franke identified in 1926 as the Tocharian people, a people that had an agricultural lifestyle and a patriarchal type of social structure. These tribes, whose ceramics bore a striking resemblance to Indo-European linear pottery (*Bandkeramik*), clashed with the Miao indigenous tribes, whose familial structure was of the matriarchal kind, repelling them southwards.

6th-century Chinese society was of a feudal nature. The nobles, who were all freemen and affiliated with a certain clan, indulged in archery and war and frequently observed sacrificial rites. Alongside them, some 'bourgeois' families enjoyed hereditary emoluments. As for common people, they included all artisans, merchants and slaves.

It is in this turbulent era that Kǒng Fūzǐ, or simply Kǒng Zǐ, meaning 'Master Kong', lived. His name was later Latinised by missionaries to 'Confucius'.

Little is known about him, and even his name seems to be connected to myths that relate to his teachings. His date of birth may have been chosen for conventional reasons so as to fall 500 years after the birth of another Chinese philosopher, the Duke of Zhou. One has also perhaps deliberately decided to have him pass away at the age of seventy-two, since this number represents a significant reference point in the official and classificatory Chinese numbering system (additionally, Confucius is said to have had seventy-two disciples, a number that is also that of the brotherhoods). As for his work, it is widely known as *The Analects* (*Lun Yu*) and was compiled and penned by his disciples.

TO RE-CREATE ANCESTRAL AND TRADITIONAL VALUES

Confucius is alleged to have been born in 551 BC, in the state of Lu, Eastern China, into an ancient royal family of the Zhou dynasty. His father was a renowned army commandant. He is said to have had a brother, of whom nothing is known. Having received an extensive sort of education, he is thought to have then accepted his first official function (which may have been the position of grassland intendant or granary supervisor). At the age of twenty-two, however, following a decision to dedicate himself to his country's moral and social reform, he supposedly resigned from his post.

Having very rapidly become famous for his teachings, he was allegedly invited on several occasions to visit various imperial courts, where he is reported to have sometimes achieved genuine diplomatic success.

Around 500 BC, Confucius is believed to have accepted the post of prefect in the city of Chung-Tu. A year later, he would become the Minister of Justice, a supreme judge and perhaps even the acting Prime Minister in the state of Lu. He did, however, have some critics, who the Prince of Lu could not help lending an ear to; in 496 BC, Kǒng Zǐ handed in his notice and, together with his disciples, chose the path of exile, where he would remain for a period of twelve years.

At the end of this period, he returned to his native country, where he henceforth only concerned himself with the education of youths and the writing of classical books, before passing away in 479 BC.

Some authors, especially Hans F.K. Günther (*Die nordische Rasse bei den Indogermanen Asiens.*[213] J.F. Lehmanns, Munich, 1924), and Paul Neubert (*Indogermanentum im fernen China? Konfuzius und seine Lehre vom Edlen Menschen*[214]), have perceived Confucius as a descendant of one of the Indo-European invader families who contributed to the establishment of the first Chinese Kingdoms. Although this fact is obviously impossible to prove, it does acquire a certain plausibility when one notices the surprising similarity between the first Confucianist mindset and the most ancient European ethics.

The supreme being of Confucianism is the Sky (*Tiān*): 'The Sky, the designer of beings, treats the latter in accordance with their actions. It supports those who stand upright and strikes down those that bow'. The 'Sky's decree' (*Ming*) corresponds either to the Latin *fatum* or to *fortuna* — either to chance or to accident. The world order (*Dao*) is not a static one, but one of perpetual movement: 'Upon reaching its own end, time undergoes a transformation. By transforming itself, time flows, and by flowing, it lasts'. The very *meaning* of this universal becoming lies in producing life.

The purpose of a rite (*Li*) is to update and re-create ancestral values. Due to its connection to institutions, it has both *social* and *moral* value.

Confucius, however, was not a formalist. He writes:

---

213 TN: The Nordic Race Among the Indo-Europeans of Asia.

214 TN: Indo-Europeanism in Faraway China? Confucius and his doctrine of the Noble Man.

> With more naïve virtues than manners, what you are is a lout. With more manners than naïve virtues, what you are is a prig. For it is a balance of manners and virtues that makes one a man of quality.

Into the heart of man, the Sky has instilled a natural sense for things that is intimately tied to man's reason:

> The best means to preserve the spirit is for one to temper and control one's passions.

According to Master Kong, the basis of moral behaviour thus lies in one's seeking of the *golden mean*. It is this very equilibrium, this 'unvarying middle' that allows man to attain the prevalence of what is best and to establish sovereignty within himself; for those that are neither masters nor sovereigns of their own accord are not *subjects* but, instead, *objects*, meaning 'tools' (*k'i*). It is, likewise, this equilibrium that teaches man to take responsibility for his own actions:

> The archer shares a common aspect with the man of quality. When his arrow does not strike the centre of the target, it is within his own self that he seeks out the cause.

The Confucianist human model (*Sheng-jen*) is that of a man of *quality* rather than wisdom. His virtue (*Te*) corresponds to the Roman *virtus*, as well as to the virtù of the Renaissance. He displays courtesy, benevolence, self-mastery and loyalty and honours his commitments.

Confucius also contrasts the 'noble' man (*Junzi*) with the commoner (*Hsiao-jen*) — in this regard, aristocracy is given a moral definition. Mr Daniel Leslie[215] writes:

> There is a striking resemblance between the Chinese *Junzi* and the British *gentleman*. Both are of noble birth and must always engage in noble actions and social attitudes. Just as today the word "gentleman" no longer signifies a man that is born an aristocrat but rather one whose actions are noble and who is aware of the rules of politeness and property, so does the Chinese term "Junzi" depict a noble and cultivated man in *The Analects*.

Confucius' line of thought is thus a purely aristocratic one. Mr Leslie explains:

---

215 TN: Born in 1922, Donald Daniel Leslie is a sinologist.

In the context of the *Analects* (XII, 5), the phrase "within the four seas, all men are brothers" means that "all noble men are brethren".

THE MAN OF QUALITY

What matters to the superior man — the noble one, the gentleman, the man of quality — is, above all else, his *magnitudo animi*, his inner energy, his will:

> One can rob an army of its general, but never a man of his own will.

Indeed, energy is what determines a man's character and thus matters more than intelligence or strength:

> It is not a horse's strength which one appreciates, but its breed. (XIV, 35)

> The one that reigns through character is akin to the North Star. While he remains in place, all the other stars revolve around him. (II, 1)

The behaviour of any man of character is instantly recognisable:

> A noble man is proud, yet not arrogant. On his part, the common man is arrogant, but not proud. (XIII, 26)

> The noble man is calm and serene; the inferior man is ever agitated and worried. (VII, 36)

The noble man holds himself accountable:

> He suffers for not having the qualities that he lacks, and not as a result of other men's inability to recognise the ones that he does. … [He] never surrenders to any preconceptions. (IV, 10)

He surpasses others through his generosity and sense of responsibility:

> The noble man cannot be recognised on the basis of the smallest things; yet he is able to bear the greatest responsibilities, unlike the inferior man, who cannot bear the latter, yet is readily recognisable on account of the smallest things. (XV, 33)

> It is only a man of quality that can genuinely love and hate others. (IV, 3)

Morality is founded upon *jen*, a term which designates what a man of quality preserves in an unalterable state, regardless of the situation. Confucius defines it as the very essence of generosity (the *humanitas* of the Ancients), honour and sincerity (XVII, 6; in this respect, one thinks of the second book of the Bhagavad Gita, where Krishna speaks to Arhuna from within the inner core of his being, *purusha*, which, despite all the tragedies and outer erring ways, remains ever identical to itself).

> Should the man of quality abandon *jen*, how could he fulfil the requirements of that name? A man of quality does not, even for the space of a single meal, act contrary to virtue. In times of anger and irritation, and in the face of perils and tempests, he remains steadfast, never wavering. (IV, 5)

Another major Confucian virtue is *sincerity*. It is not, however, connected to the notion of an abstract sort of truth, as is the case in the West. As remarked by Marcel Granet, what it designates is rather 'the soul's complete adhesion to the accomplishment of conventional gestures through which the individual collaborates with universal order'. There is, additionally, no conflict between justice and charity. Master Kong was once asked, 'What is your view of returning good for evil?'; to which he replied:

> And how would you respond to a good deed, then? No, one must return justice for evil and good for good. (XIV, 36)

One must simultaneously remain faithful to the principles of nature (*zhong*) and see to it that these very same principles are benevolently applied to others (*shu*):

> Loyalty towards oneself and humaneness towards others — that is all. (IV, 15)

A pronounced conception of *duty* crowns this edifice:

> Tsze-lû said, "Does the superior man esteem valour most?" To which the Master responded, "The superior man holds duty to be of highest importance".

It is towards oneself that one has duties:

> What the man of quality demands, he demands of himself. What the common man demands only concerns others. (XV, 20)

These qualities bear no connection to any sort of renouncement. To Confucius, *jen* is not the trademark of a 'wise man' seeking to withdraw from the world, but that of the man of quality who plays a *creative* role. A man of quality is, first and foremost, a man of action. Master Kong describes him as being 'slow in his speech, quick in his action' (IV, 24), as someone who dreads the dishonour of having his words reach further than his actions (V, 4 and 24; XIV, 29) and 'dislikes the thought of leaving this world without having distinguished himself' (XV, 19).

> Duty as the very foundation of existence, elegance in one's actions, modesty in speech, loyalty in one's behaviour — verily, that is what makes a man superior. (XV, 17)

The Confucian thought keeps all jargon at bay. In it, we encounter the Chinese taste for parables, precise symbols, and specific examples. What Confucius cultivates is a sort of 'piety of vital transcendence', a 'religion of reality' (H. Mandel). Dismissing all dogmatic speculation, what he proposes is an ideal that is clearly part of this world. This is how he defines wisdom: 'To dedicate oneself to one's duties towards men and to honour both demons and gods while keeping one's distance from them'. When Tsze-lû asks him, 'Do I have the right to wonder about the nature of death and immortality?', he gives the following answer:

> When one does not even know life, how is one then to know death?

This morality is not deduced from any kind of revelation. The Chinese, incidentally, have never managed to believe in the existence of a unique, personal God. They find the notion of a deity that differs completely from man difficult to conceive of. In their eyes, man is, in his relation to the Sky, more of a partner and an *associate* than a mere *creature*.

Joseph Needham[216] writes:

> The Confucians were interested in human society and what the West termed the "natural law", meaning a rule of conduct in keeping with the real nature of man, to which the latter must thus conform. In Confucianism, ethical behaviour pertains to the very nature of the sacred, yet it is not divine nor bears any connection to divinity, since the presence of a creator God is completely unnecessary within this

[216] TN: Noel Joseph Terence Montgomery Needham (9th December, 1900–24th March, 1995) was a British biochemist, historian and sinologist known for his scientific research and writing on the history of Chinese science and technology.

> system. […] In it, the harmonious cooperation of all beings does not stem from the commandments of a superior authority (an authority that is external to the beings themselves) but from the fact that these beings are all part of a hierarchy of wholes that give shape to a cosmic and organic model and thus only abide by the (inner) commandments of their own respective natures. (*La science chinoise et l'Occident. Le grand titrage.*[217] Seuil, 1973)

RECTIFYING THE DENOMINATIONS

In the Chinese tradition, man is a microcosm within a macrocosm — each of his actions has repercussions upon the *entire* universe. This explains why society must strive to attain the *harmony* that the cosmos seems to display and why the establishment of orderly social relations (*Luen*) requires a 'rectification' of everyday language. Hence the following principle: 'To render denominations correct'.

What this doctrine of 'denominational rectification' implies is that all things must *mirror the name* that they bear. Indeed, names comprise a *specific* meaning that plays a normative role — it is because things are actually different that they bear different names. Men are, likewise, *different* from one another. They must therefore strive to carry out to the best of their abilities the duties implied by their own names and those of the 'categories' to which they belong. By behaving in such a manner, they *justify* those names, and it is only when the latter are 'justified' that the relations between men themselves, which thus find themselves clearly differentiated, can be regarded as corresponding to the universal harmony that acts as the world's immanent law, namely the Tao.

Mr Etiemble[218] explains:

> If a father acts like a father, and a son like a son, all is well; should the son, however, swap denominations with his father and behave in a fatherly manner, just as the son of princess *Nan-zi (Nan-tzu)* did with his own mother, the result is incest, disorder, and crime.

---

217 TN: Literally 'Chinese Science and the West. The Great Assaying', this publication is, it would seem, not a translation of any specific work by Needham, despite the fact that he has penned more than one book bearing the words 'Chinese Science' in its title. This French publication is actually a compendium that has been compiled using some of Needham's most influential writings.

218 TN: René Ernest Joseph Eugène Étiemble (26th January, 1909–7th January, 2002) was a French essayist, scholar, novelist, and promoter of Middle Eastern and Asian cultures.

The family is the basic cell of society: 'Principalities are the foundation of the Empire, families the foundation of principalities and individuals the foundation of families'. Marriage is the result of natural inclination, allowing to 'produce a descendance that remains in touch with the past'. Those who do not fulfil their familial duties, says the *Shu King*, are as criminal as any thief or rebel. The first of these duties is filial piety. It is exercised 'in accordance with the principle of reason' and requires one to espouse the cult of one's ancestors, the glorification of one's parents and the imitation of their virtues.

On the political level, 'to govern is to *rectify*', meaning to create a favourable atmosphere that would allow the people (*Min*) to 'follow the right path'.

Master Kong's fundamental idea is that the state is a natural form of communal life and that society, which is comprised of different and, therefore, unequal men, also constitutes a differentiated and hierarchised *organism*. This conception is part of a harmonious cosmic representation of the world.

The role of the *prince* is equally fundamental. To Confucius, the confidence which the people must have in their prince matters even more than the presence of food and the existence of an army (XII, 7):

> The virtue of a sovereign is akin to the wind, and that of little people to grass — the grass must bow to the passing wind. "The firmament revolves around the North Star, which remains fixed. Thus must the Empire revolve around the sovereign, driven by his influence". "What the heart is to the body, the prince must be to the people".

Yet it is not sheer despotism that we are referring to. So as to *justify* his own 'name', the prince must prove that he is endowed with more *jen* than his subjects. His authority is, above all else, exercised through example, and it is upon this example that the people's good or bad behaviour depends:

> To govern through punishment and decrees is to render the people evasive and devoid of any sense of shame. To rule through strength of character and found order upon ethics is to render people conscientious and to drive them upon the path of righteousness. (II, 3)

Wise men fulfil a critical function of their own. Whenever necessary, a wise man will call his prince to order, no matter the price:

> If you (the prince) did not covet things yourself, people would not surrender to theft.

Throughout Chinese history, many an educated person has declared himself 'ready to die in order to exercise the privilege of reminding the powerful that they must govern for the good of the lesser lords, the *Xiao Ren*' (Etiemble).

THE RIVAL BELIEFS OF MOHISM, TAOISM AND LEGALISM

As Master Kong's lay dying, his disciples suggested that sacrifices be celebrated in his honour; to which he proudly responded, 'Long has my prayer been said'.

Following his death, they mourned him for three whole years, as though he were their father. Next, they went on to create the very first 'disciples of disciples' schools, which were to produce countless generations of lettered men.

During the last few centuries that preceded the founding of the Chinese Empire per se, Confucius' doctrine only represented a school among many others, one that had to compete with, and even defend itself against, several rival beliefs.

First, Confucianism had to cross swords with Mohism. The latter school's founder, Mo Ti (also known as *Mo-tzu*, Master Mo), lived in the 5th century BC. The leader of a sort of warrior phalanstery, he was hostile to the feudal system and supported a purely utilitarian morality, rising up against the doctrine of virtues (considered 'discriminatory') and criticising the significance which Confucius attached to both fine arts and individual happiness.

Looking favourably upon the establishment of an egalitarian, pacifistic, yet highly militarised republic under the authority of a tyrant, what he preached was universal love (*kien ngai*) and equality in property repartition (*kien li*), a fact that has led many to regard him as a precursor of both socialism and Christian egalitarianism.

Unlike the Mohists, the Taoists reproached the Confucians for their excessive commitment to mundane affairs, proposing that one passively submit instead to nature's dialectic, in accordance with the 'every man for himself' formula.

Disuniting man's own environment so as to contrast the two terms that refer to it, namely *nature* and *society*, Taoism advocates a sort of spiritual nihilism, one that entails the dissolution of social ties and a joyous submission to a fate which man could never be in a position to influence. Man thus becomes pure nature — society is bad, and the notion of *Tao* ('the path of nature') replaces divinity. There is a certain universalistic, anti-cultural and anti-statist ideal connected to this belief, an ideal which demands that good be returned for evil, that the differences between men be abolished and that one *merges* into all that exists by depersonalising themselves.

This doctrine, which has often degenerated into superstitious practice, found its mystic and metaphysical expression in Lao Tzu's *Tao Te Ching* ('The Way and Virtue') and is sometimes reminiscent of a Rousseauian type of philosophy.

On its part, legalism appears to be rather a mixture of Machiavellian theses and the theories of the Prussian state. Just like Mohism, it aspires to replace familial morality and tradition with the laws of royalty and the feudal regime with a centralised system of virtually limitless power. In no way does it, however, draw inspiration from a concern to establish equality. Its principal representatives are Wei Yang Gongsun (Wei Yang)[219] and Yen Wen Tzu,[220] both of whom lived in the 4th century BC, as well as Han Fei Zi,[221] who was born around 280 BC and died in 233 BC.

219 TN: Shang Yang or Wei Yang Gongsun (c. 390 BC–338 BC) was a statesman and reformer of the State of Qin during the Warring States period of ancient China. His policies laid the administrative and political foundations that would enable Qin to conquer all of China, uniting the country for the first time and ushering in the Qin dynasty. He and his followers contributed to the *Book of Lord Shang*, a foundational work for the development of Chinese Legalism.

220 TN: According to legend, Wen Tzu was a follower of Lao Tzu who wrote additional sayings and proverbs in a second book beyond the *Tao Te Ching*. Although his identity has never been confirmed nor validated, he is considered to have played a pivotal role int the birth of legalism.

221 TN: Han Fei (c. 280 BC–233 BC), also known as Han Fei Zi, was a Chinese philosopher of the Warring States period. He is often regarded as the greatest representative of Chinese Legalism for his eponymous work the Han Feizi, a work which synthesised the methods of his predecessors.

MENCIUS AND QIN SHI HUANG

The *Analects* only mention the names of approximately twenty of Confucius' disciples. These names were subsequently engraved inside Chinese temples and arranged in an order that was decided on once and for all during the 12th century of our era. The four most important ones are Yan Hui, Confucius' favourite disciple, who died at the height of his youth; Zeng Shen, also known as Zengzi; Kong Ji, the Master's grandson; and Meng Ke or Mengzi, whose name was Latinised as Mencius.

Originally from Shandong (Zi prefecture), the philosopher and writer Mencius (372 BC–289 BC) applied himself most specifically to the renewal and completion of Master Kong's work. He insisted on the significance of political economy, proposing, in particular, a rather judicious system of both individual and collective tenure. He also stressed the Confucian belief in man's good nature, directing it towards Taoism to some extent and considering it to be the distinctive mark of our species compared to other living beings.

Another of Confucius' disciples, Xunzi (c. 300 BC–237 BC), attempted, by contrast, to reorganise Confucianism in its ancient form. Breaking with Mencius' 'naïve idealism', he asserted that man's nature was not a good one and that it 'requires either a master or a model before it can be rectified'. Man's humanity, he says, stems from an aptitude to 'make social distinctions'. It is therefore up to society itself to give human aspirations their *shape*, to channel them and eradicate all that is essentially evil in them. Unfortunately for Xunzi, he had the misfortune of educating two students, Han Fei Zi and Li Si, who would go on to distinguish themselves as legalist theoreticians. As a result of this, he was rejected by orthodox Confucians, who refused to acknowledge him as one of their own.

When the power of the Zhou dynasty collapsed, anarchy gradually set in throughout the immense Chinese continent. In the absence of any and all central authority, the small principalities waged merciless war upon one another. Such was the 'Warring States Period', which came to an end in 221 BC, when China's first emperor, Qin Shi Huang, imposed an absolute sort of authority upon the aristocracy and undertook to unify the country. Qin Shi Huang founded his capital in Xianyang, in the vicinity of today's Xian (Shaanxi). Shortly afterwards, he used the criticism that scholars had targeted him with as a pretext to take up arms against the Confucians, with the support of the 'legalists', whom he had turned into his personal advisors. In 213 BC, he proceeded to outlaw Confucius' works and burn the scholars' books (a fact that would later arouse Mao Zedong's admiration). He also unleashed his fury on people, arresting many of Master Kong's partisans. 460 of them would be buried alive.

A compilation of anecdotes, sayings and statements classified into twenty sections, the famous *Analects* ('Lun Yu') were among the books that ended up being destroyed. Later, however, they were reconstituted using two different versions recovered during the Han reign.

The other classic Confucian works are five in number: the *Yijing* or 'Book of Changes'; the *Shujing* or 'Book of Documents'; the *Shijing* or 'Book of Poetry'; the *Liji* or 'Book of Rites'; and the *Yue Jing* or 'Book of Music',[222] which is almost entirely lost to us. The oldest of these texts date back to around 1000 BC. Most were compiled and classified by Confucius himself.

The *Yijing*, which is well-known among esotericists, presents us with sixty-four hexagrams alongside some rather obscure comments. Dealing with the issue of the world's origin and nature, as well as with the manner in which a wise man is to adapt his behaviour to them, it has been the object of numerous interpretations. Thanks to an entire system of numerical correspondences and speculations in which the five elements (water, fire, wood, metal and earth) play a fundamental role, the *Shujing*, which comprises the history of the ancient Chinese emperors, proposes its own philosophical view of the universe. The *Shijing* and the *Liji* are respectively a collection of 300 poems and a compilation of rites divided into three separate parts.

THE EXAMINATION SYSTEM

Qin Shi Huang dies in 210 BC, following a reign that had spanned across an eleven-year period. A rather dreary figure, his successor only manages to remain in power for four years. In 206 BC, a common man, Liu Bang, organises a rebellion that puts an end to the authoritarian Qin dynasty and, by the same token, founds his own — the Han dynasty.

---

222 TN: The 'Book of Music' was a Confucian classic text lost by the time of the Han dynasty. It is sometimes referred to as the 'Sixth Classic' and is thought to have been crucial in the traditional interpretations of the Book of Songs/Poetry.

Under this dynasty, which would last for four centuries, the Confucians return in full force. Their doctrine even becomes the formal basis of the Chinese Empire, remaining so until the year of 1911.

In harmony with his own political tactic, it was Chinese Emperor Wu (140 BC–87 BC) who first chose to favour Confucianism over both Taoism and Buddhism (which had begun to seep into Chinese society). In 142 BC, he established a school where pupils were taught the Confucian precepts. It thus became customary to select future officials from among the ranks of the well-read. The rise of the mandarinate would go hand in hand with the development of the 'examination system'.

This system, which was not the sole prerogative of the aristocracy and practically granted the imperial bourgeoisie exclusive monopoly over state employment, soon acquired a tremendous sort of complexity. One thus invented fastidious questionnaires with the purpose of evaluating one's knowledge and personality. Every year, officials were assessed in accordance with the four traditional qualities and the twenty-seven conventional 'perfections'. As the centuries went by, the inevitable result was a stagnating system in which students would 'cram' their entire lives so as to memorise customary responses regarding not only philosophy and law, but also sacrifice, mathematics and writing skills. During that same period, various popular books proceeded to spread the image of the cruel, vain and incompetent mandarin among the people.

And yet, the Confucians recruited through examination were always subject to the duty of remonstrance, which they often carried out at the risk of their own lives. Etiemble writes:

> Let us add here that under the pretext of espousing a Confucian line of thought, a mind as free and agile as that of Wang Chong, China's own Voltaire or Lucien, proceeded to contradict the dogmas using a scepticism devoid of illusions, whereas Xu Shen, who authored the very first great Chinese dictionary, the *Shuowen*, thus preceding Bayle's philosophical and critical dictionary by more than 1,500 years, undertook to expound in his *Incompatibilities Between the Five Canons* all the incoherences that could already be detected in the texts that had become sacred to Confucianism, a Confucianism which, as he was able to demonstrate in a most perceptive manner, could never constitute one single homogeneous doctrine.

Already in the 5th century AD, Confucian morality had lost a great deal of its initial flexibility, with a number of rites surrendering to stagnation and becoming a set of old-fashioned ceremonies. Any respect for the established order only served to benefit imperial officials. The doctrine itself had become an eclectic sort of system comprising various elements that had been borrowed from other beliefs and popular superstitions.

Such syncretism should not come as a surprise, for the notion of 'school', in the exclusive sense of the word, is foreign to the Chinese mentality, which, by contrast, is almost always inclined towards embracing synthesis. One can thus, for instance, come across a single household abiding by customs that have been borrowed from several different religions, pursuant to the following principle formulated by Marcel Granet: 'Having a system of rites is necessary, and each rite can prove to be valuable'.

Furthermore, the equivocal character of certain formulae renders contradictory exegeses possible. Mr Daniel Leslie explains:

> Almost every single verse in traditional Chinese is subject to several different translations. There are many reasons for this, but the main one lies in the absence of grammar in ancient Chinese, including conjugation, tenses, plurals, etc. While this results in great stylistic simplicity, terseness, and beauty, it also leads to great difficulty when it comes to grasping the meaning, leaving a lot of room for contradictory interpretations.

At the start of the 10th century AD, China lapses once again into a fragmentation period, one that would last around fifty years. It is the period of the 'Five Dynasties' (907 AD–959 AD).

Unity is then re-established by the Song dynasty. Threatened by the Barbarians in the North, its members seek refuge in the South from 1127 AD onwards.

That is when neo-Confucianism surfaces. Its leading and founding figure is Zhu Xi (1130 AD–1200 AD), the father of the doctrine of norms or doctrine of reason.

A VAST EMPIRE FROM VENICE TO SEOUL

During the 11th century AD, Zhou Dunyi (1017–1073) had already attempted to demonstrate that the Buddhist notion of the infinite, or the 'unlimited' (*Wújí*), could be identified with the notion of the 'great pole' (*Taiji*) that the Confucians defined as an absolute in their system. It was a perilous undertaking, for it was tantamount to associating two very different doctrines — Buddhism, in which one is to *kill* one's desire so as to free oneself from the world; and Confucianism, where one must *temper* their desire in order to integrate into the world.

In other words, the purpose was to turn ancient Chinese naturalism, defined as a doctrine of adjustment to the world ('entry into the world'), into a philosophy compatible with the notion of illumination characterising Indian immanentism. And it is this very path that Zhu Xi chose to take.

Mr Etiemble writes:

> Just as Saint Thomas longed to reconcile Christian sensibility with Aristotelian thought, and Jewish messianism with Hellenic thought, Zhu Xi strived to reconcile a Buddhist absolute, the *Li*, with both Confucius' and Mencius' moral tradition.

In parallel to this, Zhu Xi replaced the great Confucian classics with thirteen official books and commentaries. The latter constituted henceforth the very substance of official competitions, with neo-Confucianism becoming the new orthodoxy.

It is under this renovated form that Master Kong's precepts were gradually disseminated across a major part of Asia. In Vietnam, following the second Chinese invasion (1405 AD–1427 AD), the studying of the books even became compulsory. Neo-Confucianism permeated Korea as well, especially during the reign of Sejong the Great, who, in 1401 AD, drove the bonzes out of his court and secularised part of the Buddhist church's possessions. Last but not least, neo-Confucianism seeped into Japan towards the end of the 15th century AD, developing there through the presence of several sects.

Beginning in the 13th century, China integrates into a vast global empire spreading from Venice to Seoul. The silk road is inaugurated under the *Pax Mongolica*. The yellow continent opens up to foreign influence, as Marco Polo marvels at everything that the Far East has to offer.

In France, a book on Master Kong is published in 1641. In his dialogues, Fénelon[223] pens a conversation between Socrates and Confucius.

---

223 TN: François de Salignac de la Mothe-Fénelon, more commonly known as François Fénelon (6th August, 1651–7th January, 1715), was a French Roman Catholic archbishop, theologian, poet and author.

During the 17th and 18th centuries, the Jesuits settle in China. The moral principles of the scholars are a source of surprise to them. Some venture as far as to claim that the Confucian Sky (*Tiān*) is analogous to the God of the Christians. After some lengthy debates (the famous 'Chinese Rites Controversy'), these propositions are condemned by Rome. The controversy leads to a temporary abolition of the Order of the Jesuits by the Pope himself, an abolition that would last approximately half a century.

Just like the Jesuits, Bayle, Leibniz, Voltaire, and the encyclopaedists declare themselves fascinated by Confucianism. They praise its practical character, tolerant spirit, benevolence and agnosticism, which they contrast with their own era's absolutism. Voltaire, whose *Age of Louis XIV* ends with a chapter on the Chinese Rites Controversy, writes two ironic and henceforth famous lines on Master Kong:

> He only spoke as a wise man, never as a prophet
> Yet everyone believed him, even in his own land.

After 1840, in the aftermath of the *Opium Wars*, the European pressure resulting from the great industrial and scientific revolution becomes extremely noticeable. Unable to respond to it, China proceeds to withdraw into itself.

At the dawn of the 20th century, the revolution of 1911 triggers the fall of the Manchu dynasty and the advent of the republic. The examination system is then abolished.

The socialist and liberal opinions, however, are different. Whereas the liberal philosopher Hu Shih attacks Confucianism with great virulence, Sun Yat-sen, the founder of the Chinese Republic, openly espouses its canonical principles. To the three powers it borrows from the West (the legislative, executive and judicial power), his Constitutional Project adds two more, with a corresponding Control Council and Examination Council. In 1915, Confucianism almost succeeds in reclaiming its position of state religion.

Certain communist intellectuals perceive Confucianism as a means to combat the Taoist ideal of non-action and contemplation, while others condemn Confucius' personal and 'petty bourgeois' morality, contrasting it with Lao Tzu's disinterested aspirations.

This is what Chen Duxiu, the future co-founder of the Chinese Communist Party, wrote in the highly influential *New Youth* magazine back in 1919:

> The task to be accomplished by the new generation is that of fighting against Confucianism, the ancient tradition of virtues and rites.

In the eyes of the Kuomintang, by contrast, Master Kong comes across as a precursor of liberal democracy. Having taken control of the Kuomintang in 1925, Chiang Kai-shek launches his New Life Movement (*Xīn Shēnghuó yùndòng*), which combines Confucianism with humanitarian socialism and comprises a few Christian ideas, as well as some formulas borrowed from Mo-Tzu.

MAOISM AND CONFUCIANISM

No sooner had he seized power in 1949 than Mao Zedong declared his intention to wage a relentless battle against Confucian principles. This is what he told Robert Payne:[224] 'I have hated Confucius since the age of eight'. He alluded to various personal memories — his mother was a Buddhist, his father a Confucian.

And yet, this is what he had previously proclaimed, in an interview conducted in 1936:

> The history of our great people has, for thousands of years, been characterised by national particularities... Today's China is a development of the historical one. We must turn ourselves into the heirs of all that is precious in our past, from Confucius to Sun Yat-sen.

In his book on *The People's Democratic Dictatorship* (1949), it was through his use of a Confucian term that he defined communism as the 'great harmony' (*Ta Tung*).

In 1956, he would also publish a poem entitled *Swimming*, which ends with the following words:

> It was by a stream that the Master said,
> "Thus do things flow away!"

And this is what one reads in Analects IX, 16:

> The Master, standing by a stream, said,

---

224 TN: Pierre Stephen Robert Payne (1911–1983) was an English-born author, known principally for works of biography and history focusing on prominent historical figures such as Leonardo, Hitler, Stalin, Marx, Lenin, Mao Zedong and Gandhi.

> "Everything flows like this, never ceasing, day or night!"

According to the Soviets, 'Mao Tse-tung, who had been strongly influenced by Confucianism in his youth, perceived Marxist theses through the deforming prism of Confucian thought. His philosophy stems from two sources: the traditional Confucian ideology, whose dominant elements are feudal ethics and chauvinism; and, additionally, a variety of bourgeois doctrines, whether Chinese or European' (M. Altaisky and V. Georgiev, *The Philosophical Views of Mao Tse-tung: A Critical Analysis*. Progress Publishers Moscow, 1971).

Former Chinese President Liu Shaoqi, who was eliminated during the Cultural Revolution, never attempted to conceal his admiration for Confucius. In his manual entitled *How to Be a Good Communist*, he even adopted one of Mencius's formulas. This is what he wrote:

> There are some who claim that the geniuses of the Revolution, namely Marx, Engels, Lenin and Stalin, cannot be equalled; but they can indeed, for Mencius has written that anyone can become Yao and Shun. (This is an allusion to the two sage-rulers of the golden legend.)

Writer Kuo Mo-Jo, the very archetype of the old and well-read Chinese man that has joined the communist regime, also belongs to those who have been inclined to interpret Marxism using Confucian terminology. In 1945, he presented Master Kong as the 'champion of little people's rights' (in 1966, however, during the Cultural Revolution, he would be compelled to embrace self-criticism).

In 1957, the campaign did seem to slacken. During a reception held in Beijing, Etiemble, the author who had greatly contributed to defending Confucius' thought against the distorting interpretations to which it was subjected, was surprised to see people make a toast in honour of the philosopher.

Mr Alain Peyrefitte, whose trip to China also took place in a period of calm, gained the impression of a return to Chinese eternal values. He writes:

> The golden mean is the answer. Although the developments of the Chinese revolution do often give an impression of excess, it is a middle path that ends up prevailing once the excesses have spontaneously discredited themselves. One thus finds oneself halfway between anarchist Leftism and conservative Rightism, between utopia and routine, and between challenging the world and renouncing one's global ambitions.

In China, the periods of struggle against Confucianism have, in fact, always coincided with periods of hard-line political attitudes that went hand in hand with an 'ultra-Leftist' attempt at a strong comeback. This is precisely what happened in 1974, when Maoist radicals labelled the Confucian undertaking 'a restoration of the ancient ruling class' (*Fu Pi*) and an attempt 'to get the former nobles that have been reduced to commoner status back on their feet' (*Chu Yimin*). The purpose was to prevent some former leaders of the Chinese Communist Party, 'purged' during the Cultural Revolution, from making a comeback to public life (the denunciation of Confucius was linked to the creation of a Shanghai newspaper controlled by the radicals, the *Hsüeh-Hsi Yü P'i-P'an*).

Furthermore, Mr Jean Daubier, who authored a book on the Cultural Revolution, asserts that 'Lin Biao's theory of the genius (i.e. the Chinese version of the *man of providence*); the doctrinal and moralising simplism which he advocated; the encouragement given to decentralisation; and the prominence of the military seemed to bestow upon the new regime many aspects of the previous one. The campaign against Confucius thus responded to the necessity to destroy the old cultural environment from which "Lin-Biaoism" had stemmed'.

Faced with his obligation to abolish natural hierarchies that experienced ceaseless rebirth, Mao Zedong could only mistrust a doctrine which, historically speaking, had served as the imperial regime's philosophical and moral basis. He could not allow the Chinese, who all share certain mental affinities, to unite under any other principles but those defined by the state itself. He equally mistrusted the old 'censorship' tradition exercised by generations of cultivated people towards the 'prince'. And last but not least, he was well aware of the fact that the creation of a 'new man' entirely devoted to the community required not only radical upheaval but also the Revolution's permanent reevaluation at the hands of the revolutionaries themselves, both within the institutions and within the Party.

Mr Etiemble writes:

> I deplore the fact that, of all the Chinese lines of thoughts, the only one that Mao Zedong intended to destroy was the one that had shaped the work-of-art embodied by the Chinese man of quality.

Confucius, an essay by Etiemble. Gallimard, 312 pages.

Confucius. Sa vie, son oeuvre, sa doctrine,[225] an essay by L. Eul sou Youn. Adrien Maisonneuve (11 rue Saint-Sulpice, 75006 Pris, France), 126 pages.

Confucius, an essay by Daniel Leslie. Seghers, 222 pages.

Confucius et l'humanisme chinois,[226] an essay by Pierre Do-dinh. Seuil, 188 pages.

Le confucianisme,[227] an essay by Albert Cavin. Garnier, 295 pages.

The Political Philosophy of Confucianism, an essay by L. Shihlien Hsü. Curzon Press (88 Gray's Inn Road, London WC1), 288 pages.

La religion des Chinois,[228] an essay by Marcel Granet. PUF, 177 pages.

Le taoïsme et les religions chinoises,[229] an essay by Henri Maspéro. Gallimard, 658 pages.

It has now been confirmed that the anti-Confucian campaign of 1973–74 (a campaign that was closely connected to the 'counter-current' movement initiated shortly before the Chinese Communist Party's 10th congress, as well as to other events such as the Huang Shai/Wang Ya-sho controversy and the denunciation of the 'Three Visits to the Fishers' Peak' regional opera) was launched by the Chinese Communist Party's ultra-Left, meaning by Mao's widow, Jiang Qing, and the members of the Shanghai group (Wang Hongwen, Zhang Chunqiao, Yao Wenyuwan). The campaign targeted Zhou Enlai and, by means of the latter, the former party executives that had been eliminated at the time of the Cultural Revolution and were beginning to be gradually rehabilitated. Mr Simon Leys[230] (*Images brisées.*[231] Laffont, 1976) has successfully demonstrated that Zhou was able to deflect the movement being directed against him by taking advantage of it and associating Lin Biao's name to Confucius'.

Mr Leys writes:

'How remarkable it is for one to notice that the movement of denunciation targeting Confucius was successively referred to using three different appellations: first "The Denunciation of Confucius" (pi Kung), then "The Denunciation of Confucius and Lin Biao" (pi Kung pi Lin), and finally "The Denunciation of Lin Biao and Confucius" (pi Lin pi Kung). The passage from one appellation to another reflects, in a most expressive manner, Zhou Enlai's victorious progression in his undertaking geared towards controlling, defusing and diverting the movement — the thunderbolt that was initially meant to strike him ultimately

225 TN: The Life, Work and Doctrine of Confucius.

226 TN: Confucius and Chinese Humanism.

227 TN: Confucianism.

228 TN: The Chinese Religion.

229 TN: Taoism and Chinese Religions.

230 TN: Pierre Ryckmans (28th September, 1935–11th August, 2014), who also went by the pen-name Simon Leys, was a Belgian-Australian author, essayist and literary critic, translator, art historian, sinologist, and university professor.

231 TN: Broken Images.

found itself entirely redirected towards the convenient lightning rod provided by Lin Biao. It was essentially during the month of February 1974 that this sleight of hand was accomplished'.

Regarding the relations between Maoism, Marxism and Confucianism, a good integrative study was conducted by Charles Wei-Hsun Fun and entitled 'Confucianism, Marxism-Leninism and Mao: A Critical Study' (in *Journal of Chinese Philosophy* volume 1, numbers 3–4, June–September 1974).

Europe is also home to a Society of Confucian Studies, whose headquarters are located in Geneva.

THE CHINESE MODEL

'EVERY PERSPECTIVE ON CHINA IS necessarily laden with questions, for our notion of the Chinese is bound to change as they themselves do'.

Such is the opinion of Alain Peyrefitte, the former French Information Minister, who was once the head of a French MP delegation to China.

Many French politicians had undertaken a 'trip to Beijing' before him — Mr Edgar Faure and François Mitterrand, Malraux and Mendès France, Bettencourt and Schumann, Couve de Murville, Chaban-Delmas and Georges Pompidou; yet none of them had brought back such a a large number of observations.

Today, there are two 'schools' that look upon China with interest or sympathy. The first is that of the 'pro-Chinese', who view Maoism as a possible means of regenerating the Marxist theory and as the prime example of the latter's more rigorous implementation. On the other hand, we have the 'realists', who, despite not approving of the regime established by Mao, consider it to be rather suited to the Chinese temperament. And what they believe above all is that, from a geopolitical perspective, one should be particularly wary not to disregard the 'Chinese fact', because this immense country, whose significance will ceaselessly be felt until the end of the current century, could end up indirectly serving our own interests.

The first ones created Franco-Chinese friendship associations before joining various Leftist groups. They are supported by several figures including Simone de Beauvoir (*La longue marche.*[232] Gallimard, 1957); Charles Bettelheim

[232] TN: The Long March.

and Hélène Marchisio (*La construction du socialisme en Chine.*[233] Maspéro, 1965 and 1969); and a number of journalists and authors.

Marxist essayist Maria-Antonietta Macciocchi (*Dalla Cina: dopo la rivoluzione culturale.*[234] Published in France by Seuil, 1971) considers Italian theoretician Antonio Gramsci to be the source of 'fundamental intuitions' that have allegedly come to fruition 'in the *praxis* of the Chinese Cultural Revolution'. Her husband, Alberto Jacoviello, who previously worked as an editor at *L'Unità* (the Italian Communist Party's organ), wrote the following in his *Chinese Hypothesis*:

> Today, China is the country that offers all revolutionary militants the most convincing evidence that it is indeed possible to create, within the path defined by the October Revolution, a society that is radically different and better than all other ones, meaning the very society which each and every revolutionary fights for.

And there is yet another conversion that has not escaped public attention — that of Reverend Cardonnel, a Dominican who, on 19th July, 1973, published in *Le Monde* an article entitled *Des millions de Chinois sans contrainte,*[235] in which he declares 'the very notion of individual freedom to be sick, gangrenous and vicious'.

These words have led some people to accuse him of neo-Nazism and earned him the following response from Alain-Gérard Slama[236] (in *Combat*, 24th July, 1973):

> This certitude that liberty is a luxury enjoyed by the affluent and that what counts above all is fraternity; this stupefaction upon his discovery of "a people whose members are clean, calm, non-vulgar and in control of their nervous reactions"; this witty distinguishing between freely accepted constraint and police constraint; this hatred for money; this worship of the working community and joy at the sight of women's chaste liberation — we have seen it all before. Indeed, this entire text lacks none of the aspects which, in pre-war Nuremberg, aroused the enthusiasm of enlightened Frenchmen.

---

233 TN: The Construction of Socialism in China.

234 TN: *Daily Life in Revolutionary China* is the book's official English title.

235 TN: Millions of Chinese People Without Constraint.

236 TN: Born on 25th February, 1942, Alain-Gérard Slama is a French essayist, journalist and historian.

The attitude of 'realistic' politicians differs completely. To them, it is *geopolitics* which, in matters of foreign policy, takes precedence over *ideology*.

The following explanation is offered by those belonging to the entourage of Bavarian Christian-Democrat leader Franz-Josef Strauss:

> During the days of the Cold War, everything was simple. We had the Communist Bloc (China and the USSR) on one side and, on the other, the Free World (Europe and the United States). Since then, however, we have witnessed a rupture in Sino-Soviet relations, Nixon's visit to Beijing, the Washington-Moscow reconciliation, and the death of Mao Zedong. A game that had previously involved two players is now being played by three. In an age of bloc politics and influence zones, it is geopolitics that reigns supreme.

And this is what the 'Movement for the Independence of Europe' (once presided by Mr Sanguinetti) has to say about it:

> The very same danger threatens both China and Europe, namely the twofold stranglehold of the great powers. Whether one wills it or not, we are faced with the factual convergence of Chinese and European interests.

THE DELUSIONS OF A POLITICAL 'DETENTE'

China is by no means Gaullist, yet it is pro-de Gaulle by choice. In Beijing, Kuo Mo-Jo surprised Alain Peyrefitte by proposing a toast:

> The ideas that General de Gaulle defended and embodied must not be allowed to die. I raise my glass in honour of General de Gaulle's immortal spirit.

In September 1970, in Colombey, the General had informed his niece, Marie-Thérèse de Corbie, of his intention to travel to Beijing, as he had received an invitation through Jacques Rueff[237] and author Han Suyin.[238] His passing would, however, prevent him from going there.

---

237 TN: Jacques Léon Rueff (23rd August, 1896–23rd April, 1978) was a French economist and advisor to the French government.

238 TN: Han Suyin was the pen name of Elizabeth Comber (12th September, 1917–2nd November, 2012), born Rosalie Matilda Kuanghu Chou. A Chinese-born Eurasian, she was a physician and a writer of English and French books on modern China, in addition to authoring both novels set in East and Southeast Asia and autobiographical memoirs that covered the span of modern China.

In this regard, Zhou Enlai declared:

> We would have given him a most warm welcome; but since destiny has decided otherwise, we are ready to welcome his successor.

Mr Georges Pompidou arrived in China on 10th September, 1973. His interlocutors immediately urged him to check the bloc politics implemented by the super-powers.

For several years now, Chinese leaders have been expressing their concern over the 'indifference' of European countries. They have reminded us that, in the space of less than four years, the USSR has increased its military forces from fifteen divisions to forty-eight and its fleet has been navigating across all of the world's seas. They thus implore Europe to unite, warning it against 'the delusions of a detente'.

When speaking to a group of Dutch MPs that had come to Beijing to meet him in August 1973, Zhou Enlai stated that 'the countries that consent to their own weakening can only bring misfortune upon themselves'.

There are some who longed to perceive the words of the former Chinese Premier as the 'first cymbal stroke of the Franco-Chinese opera'. Indeed, Zhou Enlai had retained a vivid memory of his stay in France during the 1920s:

> When I was in Paris, I felt as though I were attending an exhibition of all races. It was a place where all people, regardless of their race, were allowed to marry one another.

Mr Peyrefitte offers the following clarification:

> This admiration for interracial marriages is currently coming up against an official Chinese policy whose every effort is aimed at discouraging such unions.

'The Mao Zedong fact has a certain distressing aspect to it', remarked Mr Jacques Chaban-Delmas[239] when going to China, where he stayed from the 1st to the 15th of June, 1973. Upon his return, he observed that, in defence matters, 'the Chinese and French positions are so similar that one is almost allowed to equate them to each other: *yes* to the simultaneous and controlled

---

[239] TN: Jacques Chaban-Delmas (7th March, 1915–10th November, 2000) was a French Gaullist politician who served as Prime Minister under Georges Pompidou from 1969 to 1972.

destruction of bombs, their carriers and their means of fabrication; *no* to all conferences and agreements whose sole purpose is to ensure that two superpowers — whose positions are now converging as they continue to increase their own armament — retain mastery over the world and its peoples'.

As for Zhou Enlai, this is what he stated:

> Without its power of nuclear deterrence, France would be no more than Mongolia.

Mr Alain Peyrefitte, the fifty-two-year-old ENA[240] lecturer who previously acted as both a government minister and the secretary general of the UDR[241], has travelled across 6,000 kilometres of Chinese territory. He has had dozens of conversations and taken thousands of notes. The book that he has published is entitled *Quand la Chine s'éveillera... le monde tremblera!*',[242] a statement which was originally made by Napoleon. He writes:

> Chinese revolutionaries are neither angels nor demons. Let us strive to avoid the traps set by our tendency to think systematically.

MAO ZEDONG'S ARMY AND LINE OF THOUGHT

Since the end of the Cultural Revolution, the 'cult of personality' has been the most striking aspect that Westerners notice upon visiting Beijing. In a country where egalitarianism seems to have been taken to its most extreme limits, it is always a single personality that exercises absolute political and 'religious' power. Even after his death, Mao Zedong is encountered everywhere — in people's thoughts, words and actions, and especially on walls, across which countless portraits bloom. He is the spiritual father of all Chinese people, their patron saint. Mr Peyrefitte reminds us that 'Mao comes from the countryside, and it is the peasant spirit which, through him, is revived'.

In the Yan'an area, people visit the cave where Mao lived between 1937 and 1938, at the time of the Long March. 'Like a new Saint Martin, he shared his

---

240 TN: National School of Administration.

241 TN: The 'Union for the Defence of the Republic' (French: *Union pour la défense de la République*), which was renamed 'Union of Democrats for the Republic' (French: *Union des Démocrates pour la République*) after 1968, was a Gaullist political party whose existence spanned from 1968 to 1976.

242 TN: The World Shall Tremble... When China Awakens!

blanket with one of his guards. Having remained intact, half of the blanket can be seen there, in a display cabinet'. Elsewhere, one has preserved the iron bar that allowed him to cool his hand and alleviate his writer's cramp. These relics are exhibited amidst a prayerful atmosphere, under devout images accompanied by cautionary tales.

The man himself often refused to be the focus of such worship (in 1972, in fact, some excesses were attributed to Lin Biao). Mao was, however, also aware of the fact that the Chinese had adored their emperors for a period of 3000 years. American Edgar Snow[243] writes:

> During the first years of the Revolution, many were the peasants who, when marching on the occasion of the October anniversary, bowed down before Mao Zedong's tribune. One even had to place guards there to prevent them from doing so. It took people some time to comprehend that their president was neither an emperor nor a god.

In actual fact, 'the Chinese people are God and Mao their prophet. Chinese Marxism is a *people's religion*. Mao, the Moses of the Long March, is their inspired spokesman and priest, i.e. simultaneously their servant and their leader — being the leader of the people-god, and the latter's servant, he plays the role of a mediator', Mr Peyrefitte writes. He adds:

> Mao has become the symbol of the national bond. Through him, what the Chinese people adore is themselves. Thanks to his presence, China has found a national solution to its national issues, a solution that has sprouted out of the convergence of three elements — a unique people, extreme circumstances and an exceptional man.

[243] TN: Edgar Parks Snow (17th July, 1905–15th February, 1972) was an American journalist known for his books and articles on Communism in China and the Chinese Communist Revolution. He was the first western journalist to give a full account of the history of the Chinese Communist Party following the Long March and the first one to interview many of its leaders, including Mao Zedong. He is best known for his book, *Red Star Over China* (1937), an account of the Chinese Communist movement from its foundation until the late 1930s.

Mr Edgar Faure[244] once stated on television that Mao had replaced Marxism with 'massism'.

In Alberto Jacoviello's eyes, the 'cult' — if one can, indeed, speak of one — is not focused on Mao Zedong's person, but rather on his *thoughts*.

When one announced, in the aftermath of the tenth Congress of the Chinese Communist Party, that the 'anti-Party clique' of the 'bourgeois careerist, conniving double agent, counter-revolutionary renegade and traitor Lin Biao' had been eliminated, the news was greeted by the sound of people shouting 'Long live Mao Zedong's victorious thoughts'.

To Europeans, it may seem strange, even ridiculous, for one to speak of 'Mao Zedong's thoughts', especially when these thoughts are restricted to skimming through the 'Little Red Book' written by Lin Biao. Their impression would perhaps be a different one if, in order to grasp Mao's line of thought, they sought to situate it in the philosophical context of an eternal China. For it is indeed a *philosophy*, and not a collection of aphorisms, that we are dealing with here.

Kuo Mo-Jo says:

> A river is not a mere agglomerate of waterdrops; it is both movement and energy.

And there is yet another topic of astonishment: the country's militarisation, which appears to impact the whole of the population. Mr Edgar Snow writes:

> In China, soldiers are omnipresent. Most do not bear any arms, and their public behaviour is exemplary on all levels. Every foreigner is quick to realise that they are looked upon favourably by the population. Schools are filled with "little red soldiers", and there is not a single parent who does not aspire to have a son or a daughter capable of fulfilling the demanding conditions of military membership.

Writer Etiemble, who specialises in Chinese literature (*Connaissons-nous la Chine?*[245] Gallimard, 1964 and 1966), says:

> China is a militarised convent where kindergarten prepares children for their role of child soldiers.

---

[244] TN: Edgar Faure (18th August, 1908–30th March, 1988) was a French politician, essayist, historian, and memoirist.

[245] TN: Are We Truly Familiar with China?

And here is how Edgar Snow formulates things: 'China? A hell of virtues!'

China is, in fact, an enormous 'youth project' in which practical experience has overtaken abstract knowledge. A certain professor once said to Mr Alain Peyrefitte (who also acted as our Minister of National Education):

> Intellectual education is less important than its civic and physical counterpart. A pupil shall become a good worker, a good peasant, and a good cadre if he is, above all, a good citizen. And in order to be a good citizen, one must be a good soldier.

One must, however, refrain from speaking of *military* dictatorship; for although the army does remain the 'great school', it is the Party itself that 'commands the rifles'. According to Mao Zedong, 'what matter is the human factor, not the material one' (Maurras stated that 'politics comes first', to which de Gaulle added: 'The supply corps will follow').

A QUESTION OF ENERGY

This concern with ensuring man's precedence over technology has numerous implementations. It accounts for both the development policy which China has opted for since its breaking with the USSR and the failure of the 'Great Leap Forward'.

Mr Chaban-Delmas explains:

> It is not that Chinese leaders reject modernity; what they do refuse, however, is to allow it to grant foreigners the opportunity to exercise authority over their country.

As buyers, they always pay in cash. Rejecting any and all credit, they are prisoners of neither commitments nor debts: it is the future that they long to claim. They are well aware of the fact that national independence requires autarky (whether economic, financial or energetic) and are willing to pay the price for it by accepting lower living standards.

The very same principle is encountered in the military domain. When, in 1965, Lin Biao declared that 'it is Mao Zedong's line of thought that represents the best weapon, not planes, heavy artillery, tanks or the atomic bomb', in no way was his statement intended to be a joke. What he meant to say was that war was, first and foremost, a question of men and a question of *politics*; yet also a matter of *energy*—the countries that lack the latter are all 'toothless tigers', no matter how rich and powerful they may be.

Likewise, Chinese doctors believe that what must be considered is, *above all*, the patients, and not the illnesses, an attitude which coincides, in the general sense of things, with the following statement by Claude Bernard:[246] 'Microbes are nothing, the terrain everything'.

Mr Jacoviello asserts:

> In China, the patient is, above all else, a conscious subject that collaborates on health care.

In accordance with the Maoist principle which states that 'one divides into two', the Chinese physician makes use of the organism's healthy part to 'combat' the one stricken with illness and thus put an end to the functional imbalance affecting the organs or their appendages. He is wary not to substitute his own personality for the patient's and resorts to a great amount of psychotherapy.

Mr Alain Peyrefitte was highly impressed by the acupuncture-based surgeries that he witnessed, including the extraction of a four-kilo cyst, the ablation of ovaries, and trepanation. Once the surgical intervention had been carried out, those that had undergone surgery left in a most wing-footed manner, smiling and without ever having been rendered unconscious. In the spring of 1973, more than 700,000 surgeries of this kind were conducted.

The method itself dates back to the most ancient times: Chinese doctors contented themselves with re-reading a 2200-year-old Chinese treatise, the *Huangdi Neijing*, in the light of both Mao Zedong's thoughts and modern science (in this field, the revisionism implemented by Liu Shaoqi consisted in discrediting all ancestral practice and following exclusively in the footsteps of Western medicine).

In response to Professor Jean Bernard, who, just like a number of his colleagues, manifested scepticism, Mr Peyrefitte chose to place emphasis on the phenomenon of civilisation, instead of the actual medical act:

---

246 TN: Claude Bernard (12th July, 1813–10th February, 1878) was a French physiologist. Historian I. Bernard Cohen of Harvard University called Bernard 'one of the greatest of all men of science'.

What one should actually ponder is the following societal reality — the existence of an entire people whose members serve as lab rats in a historically and geographically unprecedented experiment and who bear it all very well indeed.

He adds:

Carried by the traditions of their own people's therapeutics and customs, these Chinese practitioners display a *will* to resolve every national health issue very rapidly; they are stimulated by "mass enthusiasm". What would European physicians, in a radically different context, be motivated by? [...] What this fact does is grant policies a confirmation of the very relativity of social phenomena. As Anouilh has said, men are equal but not the same. This is even truer for societies than for individuals. In both medicine and other domains, the Chinese advance on a different path to ours, existing in another time frame and accomplishing their revolutions along an orbit that is theirs alone.

This mixture of tradition and innovation finds its justification in Mao Zedong's (not very Marxist) watchword 'may the old serve the new'.

ORGANICISM

Twenty years ago, Mr Peyrefitte was fortunate enough to come across the twelve volumes of Lord Macartney's *Mission to China* at a bookseller's in Krakow: Lord Macartney had been the British Crown's very first ambassador to the country. Since then, Mr Peyrefitte has turned this journal into one of his favourite bedside books. He writes:

Reading Macartney is just like reading Tocqueville's[247] writings on the United Sates or Custine's[248] on Russia: it allows China's constants, the essence of its civilisation and its imperishable cultural mould to emerge. One thus realises that what one imputes to the regimes of Beijing, Washington and Moscow is actually due to the very reality of the Chinese, American and Russian *peoples*. Many political, economic and sociological analyses of contemporary China are prone to privileging

---

247 TN: Alexis Charles Henri Clérel, Viscount de Tocqueville (29th July, 1805–16th April, 1859) was a French diplomat, political scientist and historian. He is most famous for his works entitled *Democracy in America* (in two volumes, 1835 and 1840) and *The Old Regime and the Revolution* (1856).

248 TN: Astolphe-Louis-Léonor, Marquis de Custine (18th March, 1790–25th September, 1857) was a French aristocrat and author who is most famous for his travel writing, especially his account of the time he spent in Russia entitled *La Russie*.

> ideological factors and minimising ethnic determinisms. While acknowledging the role played by Marxist-Leninist texts in the intellectual shaping of Chinese leaders, what is desirable is for us to render unto Marx what is Marx's and unto China what is rightfully China's.

In *Le grand titrage*, a compilation of various conferences published in France in 1973, Professor Joseph Needham, who runs the *Science and Civilisation in China* series in London (of which four volumes, from a total of seven, have been published since 1954), presents us with an inventory of Chinese discoveries, whose number, significance and ancientness he highlights. He also demonstrates the very specificity of Chinese knowledge, labelling China's *philosophia perennis* as either materialism or organic naturalism. He points out:

> The Chinese way of thinking has never developed any mechanistic worldview, and it is, in fact, the organicist perspective, according to which each and every phenomenon is connected to all others following a hierarchical order, that has universally prevailed among Chinese authors.

This natural philosophy, which places great emphasis on experience, rejects any and all separation between the physical and the metaphysical — in the 12th century, Chinese philosopher Zhu Xi had already spoken of a 'spirituality that is inherent in matter'.

Chinese thought is not of an analytical but of a classifying nature. When taken literally, the Chinese term designating science, *kexue*, actually means 'classifying knowledge'.

Likewise, Chinese mathematical theory and practice have always been algebraic, not geometric. Euclidian geometry only took root in China upon the arrival of the Jesuits.

It is this lack of geometric perception and absence of an unequivocal conception of the relations of finality and causality that accounts for the fact that Chinese science was unable to keep pace with post-Renaissance European science.

Inversely, these very same characteristics allow us to better understand the Chinese aptitude to master the concepts of modern science, especially those of quantum physics: the interdependence of wholes, modelisation, general relativity, non-Newtonian dynamics, non-Cartesian kinematics, etc.

THE INCLUDED THIRD AND THE CONTRADICTION PRINCIPLE

The wave-particle antithesis comprised in the theory of waves fails to surprise those accustomed, since their very childhood, to taking into account the ebb and flow of the two fundamental natural principles. The use of ideograms is perfectly suited to the requirements of computer programming and facilitates symbolic reasoning. The notion of a basic identity of space and time corresponds to the *relativistic* truth which reveals to us that 'both the time gradually eroded by our clocks and the kilometric space inscribed upon our maps are but arbitrarily chosen coordinates among the phenomena of our cosmos, a cosmos to which we rather conventiently connect these facts' (as written by Mr Raymond Charles).

Mao Zedong's theories on the principle of *contradiction* are also in agreement with both the modern logic of antagonism and the ancient notions of *yin* and *yang*. In no way are they indebted to Aristotle or Descartes.

The mother superior of the Carmelites of Bernanos once said: 'It is not the monastic rule that keeps us, but we who keep it'. And upon hearing Mr Peyrefitte declare that the Chinese do not abide by the same logic as we do, a certain philosopher began to squirm with indignation and said: 'There is no such thing as Chinese and Western logic. All that there is is logic itself!'

What actually results from the absence of syntax in the Chinese language is that anyone who has been educated in classical culture finds himself juxtaposing various propositions without ever contrasting them nor ordering them using logical conjunctions. Descartes' 'I think, therefore I am' would thus be translated as 'I think, I am', or rather as 'I am *here*', since the verb 'be' has a specifically locative meaning in Chinese.

Mr Peyrefitte explains:

> Instead of resorting to Western binary thought, which distinguishes the positive from the negative, the licit from the illicit, and the true from the false, what the Chinese follow is a *ternary* line of thought, comprising a thesis, an antithesis and the result of the latter's opposition, which is not so much their synthesis as *the product of their attraction and repulsion*. [...] When in the presence of two contradictory propositions, is it necessary for one to be true and the other false, with a third option remaining excluded? Ever faithful to Chinese tradition, Mao challenges these fundamental laws. For contradiction lies at the heart of all living

> things and it is its very presence that keeps them alive. Mao replaces the logic of the excluded middle with the logic of the included third resulting from the fruitful *antagonism* of the first two words.

In 1957, Mao Zedong declared:

> To look upon one single aspect of things is to think in absolute terms, to envisage issues in a metaphysical fashion. In order to assess our work, exclusive approbation is as wrong as exclusive negation.

Instead of acting as a pitfall, contradiction thus becomes the very principle governing people's thoughts. Somewhere between two options, there is always a third path to take, and China is truly the Middle Empire.

With the singular only acquiring its significance in relation to what is general, the issue of freedom thus takes on a rather specific shape. Mr Alain Peyrefitte observes:

> Nowadays, there are simply too many testimonies regarding the infringements of individual liberties in China for anyone to doubt that the Popular Republic is founded on a powerful repressive apparatus ranging from plain monitored work or "re-education" to physical elimination, through all the subtleties of constraint, including open labour camps, concentration camps surrounded by barbed wire, prisons with or without cells, and capital punishment.

According to American experts, fifty to two hundred million Chinese people have allegedly been 'eliminated' since the start of the Revolution. In this regard, some interesting clarifications have been offered by Mr Simon Leys (in *Ombres chinoises*[249]. UGE/10–18, 1974; and *Images brisées*. Laffont, 1976). Mr Peyrefitte goes on to say, however, that the Chinese 'do not experience liberty deprivation the way Westerners do, because they have never genuinely exercised such freedoms. Indeed, liberty seems to them, just like Christianity and trade, a Western notion'.

249 TN: Chinese Shadows.

INDIVIDUAL FREEDOMS VERSUS NATIONAL LIBERTY

The philosophers of the School of Law, who were all Alexander's contemporaries, used to say that 'man is born bad and must, if at all possible, be persuaded to act correctly; should persuasion fail, he must then be compelled'.

In 1924, Sun Yat-sen, the 'Father of the Fatherland', made the following declaration:

> Ever since the notion of liberty found its way into China, only scientists have, by dint of continuous research, managed to comprehend it. If one were to speak of liberty to a countryman, to the man in the street, the latter would know nothing of it. Liberty only makes sense to those who have studied abroad. If this notion were applied to each and every person, we would revert to being nothing more than dispersed sand. Whereas the individual must sacrifice his freedoms, it is the nation that is to attain complete liberty.

Mr Alain Peyrefitte writes that the poet and philosopher Kuo Mo-jo 'represents the regime's cultural glory and is honoured as the greatest Chinese figure in the world of science, literature and art'. During the Cultural Revolution, however, he was accused of being a 'Mandarin'. Wearing a dunce cap and constantly targeted with jibe, he was forced to publicly embrace self-criticism and declare himself 'more foetid than manure'. 'He then emerged from the ordeal enjoying greater respect than ever before', adds Mr Peyrefitte.

Freedom of *action* or freedom of *creation*? That is the eternal question. In a country governed by group psychology where only the collective 'I' is ever cultivated, it was inevitable for 'individual rights' to come across as a dissolution factor.

Following in the footsteps of Marx, Mao Zedong repeats that 'to be free is to acknowledge necessity'.

On the religious level, the Chinese have Sinicised Buddhism, just as they have done with Marxism. They have, however, rejected Christianity. In the early 20th century, Christians represented a mere 0.4% of the entire continent's population; today, there are hardly any left at all.

Mr Peyrefitte explains:

> Within China's revolutionary logic, could the Catholic clergy, and even the faithful, ever be considered anything but agents acting at the behest of adverse powers? The orders that they follow disregard both China's national interests and the

> proletariat's revolutionary ones. They also have their own information network. And what do they live on, exactly? They are either given subsidies from abroad, which is an insult to the Chinese nation, or live off the alms given by the faithful, thus further impoverishing the already poor population. What they constitute is a state within the state, and this could never be tolerated.

CULTURAL SPECIFICITY

At the end of this journey, what takes shape before our eyes are the outlines of a *universe* which, although neither better nor worse than ours, is profoundly different from the latter. Deploring the 'conformism according to which any acknowledgement of the plurality of the human races is synonymous with one's approval of the cremation ovens', Mr Peyrefitte, a trained anthropologist, remarks:

> It is difficult not to believe in ethnic realities when one has seen how the Chinese live and studied their past.

He adds:

> The fact of imagining that all men are granted the same talents at birth and that all peoples are endowed with the same faculties can be classified as a mental disorder, the kind that was once known as "vesania". For men are indeed *different*, peoples *irreplaceable* and experiences *non-interchangeable*.

This leads him to formulate the following hypothesis:

> The Chinese are neither one hundred years ahead of us nor one hundred years behind. They do not live in the same time nor the same period as us, and do not advance upon the same path. The progress they make and the revolutions they conduct are strictly adapted to what they themselves are.

The Chinese model may well be a model, but not one for Europeans to abide by. Conversely, European systems are certainly worthless from the Chinese perspective. To evaluate a culture in accordance with the criteria of another is to expose oneself to accumulating misinterpretations.

'We, the Chinese, consider the civilisations of Europe and America to be barbaric', Sun Yat-sen once declared.

And in a display of witty humour, another Chinese native stated that 'to indulge in prophesying is a dangerous endeavour, especially when the prophecies concern the future'.

❧

Quand la Chine s'éveillera… le monde tremblera, an account by Alain Peyrefitte. Fayard, 475 pages.
In Cina due anni dopo,[250] an essay by Alberto Jacoviello. Seuil, 218 pages.
The Long Revolution, an essay be Edgar Snow. Stock, 320 pages.
La science chinoise et l'Occident. Le grand titrage, a compilation of texts by Joseph Needham. Seuil, 264 pages.

❧

As expected, Mao Zedong's death has not altered the reality of the Sino-Soviet antagonism at all. If anything, it even seems to have increased the threat with which the Kremlin has been burdening the Chinese nation and people. In *Le XXème siècle fédéraliste*[251] (number 4, 1976), Mr Thierry Maulnier remarks that 'this antagonism is more geopolitical than ideological in essence and cannot, therefore, be genuinely reduced through a mere change in political leadership'. He then adds that 'a reconciliation between the enemy brothers of Beijing and Moscow — the one-billion-people bloc — would put both world peace and the West in a state of immediate mortal jeopardy. Let us not forget this fact in our prayers — in the event that we do pray, of course'.

On 13th November, 1976, the Xinhua agency published the following text:

'After years of military expansion and war preparations, Soviet social-imperialism is tightening its grip on Western Europe. […] In connection to Western Europe, the Kremlin's strategy is clearly geared towards a surprise offensive and attack allowing it to take the initiative in the war. So as to ensure this strategy's success and achieve supremacy over the West, Soviet revisionists intensified their military expansion during the 1970s, while simultaneously speaking of "peace" at every turn. As part of their military preparations in Europe, they have placed an ever-increasing emphasis on the joint increase of their nuclear and conventional capacities in the developed regions that border on Western European countries.'

❧

Ammerland am Starnberger See, 18th October, 1975;
Vernouillet, 22nd February, 1977

250 TN: Although the title can be literally translated as 'Two Years Later, in China', the French translation seems to have rendered it as 'L'hypothèse chinoise', meaning 'The Chinese Hypothesis'.

251 TN: The Federalist Twentieth Century.

OTHER BOOKS PUBLISHED BY ARKTOS

Sri Dharma Pravartaka Acharya	*The Dharma Manifesto*
Joakim Andersen	*Rising from the Ruins: The Right of the 21st Century*
Winston C. Banks	*Excessive Immigration*
Alain de Benoist	*Beyond Human Rights* *Carl Schmitt Today* *The Indo-Europeans* *Manifesto for a European Renaissance* *On the Brink of the Abyss* *The Problem of Democracy* *Runes and the Origins of Writing* *View from the Right* (vol. 1–3)
Arthur Moeller van den Bruck	*Germany's Third Empire*
Matt Battaglioli	*The Consequences of Equality*
Kerry Bolton	*Revolution from Above* *Yockey: A Fascist Odyssey*
Isac Boman	*Money Power*
Ricardo Duchesne	*Faustian Man in a Multicultural Age*
Alexander Dugin	*Ethnos and Society* *Eurasian Mission* *The Fourth Political Theory* *Last War of the World-Island* *Putin vs Putin* *The Rise of the Fourth Political Theory*
Edward Dutton	*Race Differences in Ethnocentrism*
Mark Dyal	*Hated and Proud*
Koenraad Elst	*Return of the Swastika*
Julius Evola	*The Bow and the Club* *Fascism Viewed from the Right* *A Handbook for Right-Wing Youth* *Metaphysics of War* *The Myth of the Blood* *Notes on the Third Reich* *The Path of Cinnabar* *Recognitions* *A Traditionalist Confronts Fascism*
Guillaume Faye	*Archeofuturism* *Archeofuturism 2.0* *The Colonisation of Europe* *Convergence of Catastrophes*

OTHER BOOKS PUBLISHED BY ARKTOS

	A Global Coup *Sex and Deviance* *Understanding Islam* *Why We Fight*
Daniel S. Forrest	*Suprahumanism*
Andrew Fraser	*Dissident Dispatches* *The WASP Question*
Génération Identitaire	*We are Generation Identity*
Paul Gottfried	*War and Democracy*
Porus Homi Havewala	*The Saga of the Aryan Race*
Lars Holger Holm	*Hiding in Broad Daylight* *Homo Maximus* *Incidents of Travel in Latin America* *The Owls of Afrasiab*
Richard Houck	*Liberalism Unmasked*
A. J. Illingworth	*Political Justice*
Alexander Jacob	*De Naturae Natura*
Jason Reza Jorjani	*Prometheus and Atlas* *World State of Emergency*
Roderick Kaine	*Smart and SeXy*
Peter King	*Here and Now* *Keeping Things Close* *On Modern Manners*
Ludwig Klages	*The Biocentric Worldview* *Cosmogonic Reflections*
Pierre Krebs	*Fighting for the Essence*
Stephen Pax Leonard	*The Ideology of Failure* *Travels in Cultural Nihilism*
Pentti Linkola	*Can Life Prevail?*
H. P. Lovecraft	*The Conservative*
Norman Lowell	*Imperium Europa*
Charles Maurras	*The Future of the Intelligentsia & For a French Awakening*
Michael O'Meara	*Guillaume Faye and the Battle of Europe* *New Culture, New Right*
Brian Anse Patrick	*The NRA and the Media* *Rise of the Anti-Media*

OTHER BOOKS PUBLISHED BY ARKTOS

	The Ten Commandments of Propaganda *Zombology*
Tito Perdue	*The Bent Pyramid* *Morning Crafts* *Philip* *William's House* (vol. 1–4)
Raido	*A Handbook of Traditional Living*
Steven J. Rosen	*The Agni and the Ecstasy* *The Jedi in the Lotus*
Richard Rudgley	*Barbarians* *Essential Substances* *Wildest Dreams*
Ernst von Salomon	*It Cannot Be Stormed* *The Outlaws*
Sri Sri Ravi Shankar	*Celebrating Silence* *Know Your Child* *Management Mantras* *Patanjali Yoga Sutras* *Secrets of Relationships*
George T. Shaw (ed.)	*A Fair Hearing*
Oswald Spengler	*Man and Technics*
Richard Storey	*The Uniqueness of Western Law*
Tomislav Sunic	*Against Democracy and Equality* *Homo Americanus* *Postmortem Report* *Titans are in Town*
Hans-Jürgen Syberberg	*On the Fortunes and Misfortunes of Art in Post-War Germany*
Abir Taha	*Defining Terrorism* *The Epic of Arya* (2nd ed.) *Nietzsche's Coming God, or the Redemption of the Divine* *Verses of Light*
Bal Gangadhar Tilak	*The Arctic Home in the Vedas*
Dominique Venner	*For a Positive Critique* *The Shock of History*
Markus Willinger	*A Europe of Nations* *Generation Identity*
Alexander Wolfheze	*Alba Rosa*

Printed in Great Britain
by Amazon

40744193R00233